Meaningful Movement for Children
A Developmental Theme Approach to Physical Education

Hubert A. Hoffman   **Jane Young**   **Stephen E. Klesius**

University of South Florida
Tampa, Florida

ALLYN AND BACON, INC.

Boston   London   Sydney   Toronto

Library of Congress Cataloging in Publication Data

Hoffman, Hubert A.   1937-
  Meaningful movement for children.

  Bibliography: p.
  Includes index.
    1. Movement education.   2. Physical
education for children—Curricula.   I. Young,
Jane, 1931- joint author.   II. Klesius,
Stephen E., 1940- joint author.
III. Title

GV452.H63   372.8'6   80-12284
ISBN 0–205–06952–5

Series Editor: Hiram Howard

Printed in the United States of America

Contents

THREE

Bibliography   405

Indexes   413

Foreword

All the things encountered in the school—
space, people, activities and ideas—
are separate like eggs in a carton.

Things never are allowed to touch,
lest the shells be broken
and the contents mixed.

Lawrence F. Locke and Dolly Lambdin

If you don't break the eggs
You can't have an omelet!

Robespierre

If you are one of the many teachers, who like ourselves have yearned to create educational omelets from the school's array of attactive but isolated subject ingredients, *Meaningful Movement for Children: A Developmental Theme Approach to Physical Education* will be a happy discovery. No single book can break down the rigid walls of institutional structure that separate teachers, students, and subject matters, but here is a wonderfully subversive recipe that invites teachers to join forces in cracking a few subject matter shells. The resulting mixture of contents, when properly stirred and served, makes a tasty meal, the kind of substantial nutrition on which growing children can thrive.

Many of us have wished that as students move from history to physical education to arithmetic to music, they could experience some of the unity that exists within the human heritage. The synoptic sense that things are all of one piece is denied by the daily routine of dealing with learning tasks in isolated sets that provide little or no reference to each other. These discontinuities in experience are the source of statements like "I can spell, but I can't do math," "I like science, but I don't like English," and "Shop is useful, but history is a waste of time." These student beliefs often are less the result of good or poor teaching than the consequence of an egg carton curiculum; they are artifacts produced by encounters with fragmented bits of subject matter.

Many of us, too, have mourned conditions that produce learning while at the same time robbing that learning of its proper power—the power of transfer from the known to the unknown. This happens when what is learned in science class about the function and structure of the human body is disregarded

vii

entirely once inside the gymnasium or when the expression and understanding of human emotions explicated through literature are forgotten once the clock indicates that it is time for social studies. Problems like this have led teachers everywhere to seek better ways to integrate learning.

Meaningful Movement for Children takes us deeper into the omelet-making business than most previous attempts at curriculum integration involving physical education. This is not one of the now familiar attempts to encourage the use of active learning environments in the teaching of academic subject matter (such as the teaching of arithmetic or reading skills through movement activities). Nor is this a scrambled egg plate in which attempts are made to provide integration by concurrent introduction of a particular element into the work of various classes (study native Americans in history, write about them in English, make war bonnets in art and learn Indian dances in physical education). While these approaches do offer some contact between disparate subjects, they provide no substantial opportunity to help students come to grips with fundamental questions that go beyond superficial and often stereotypic concepts.

Meaningful Movement for Children provides a third alternative for bridging the discontinuities of school experience, one designed to overcome the limitations inherent in the other forms of subject matter integration. Classroom and gymnasium are linked as partners in the same educational enterprise. Whether it is the use and manipulation of practice to produce improvement in performance or the exploration of modes for the expression and understanding of human emotion, the essential questions forming the basis for learning are everywhere the same because the *same* students with the *same* needs sit at desks and run on playing fields.

Impediments to truly confluent learning experiences exist in more than just the architectural and social barriers of school structure. Such simple matters as finding time for teachers to talk about shared learning objectives and finding learning activities that lend themselves to an integrative curriculum constitute real problems. Even more difficult is the process of developing the instructional skills to ease the birth of powerful ideas that can cut across subject domains. All of these are barriers to the vision of integrated learning. *Meaningful Movement for Children* does not attempt to provide a solution for each of these problems. It does, however, provide a conceptually clear and realistic plan with which any teacher, or group of teachers, can begin the process of breaking barriers on their own.

The authors present a small set of learning themes around which it is possible to organize many of the learning activities in the school. The themes have been selected to reflect fundamental cognitive, affective, and motoric tasks which all students must master. Traditional subject areas in the curriculum, indeed all aspects of school life, are envisioned as contributing to the development of knowledge and skill in each thematic domain.

Because the authors are specialists in physical education, primary attention is given to organizing and presenting movement experiences in ways that will enhance learning in the six developmental themes selected for this curriculum. Detailed material on scope and sequence forms the framework for careful descriptions of specific movement activities that constitute the content of day-to-day lessons. In addition, supplemental examples are provided in a wide range of other subjects more suited to the classroom than the gymnasium. For these reasons both in-service and preservice elementary classroom teachers will find the text especially appropriate to their needs.

The chapters dealing with teaching methods are worth the attention of any teacher, tyro or vetran. The suggestions are at once sensitive to teacher values and student needs, to pedagogic theory and school reality, and to both the integrity of individual subject matters and broad curriculum goals. These nicely balanced concerns are the hard-won fruits from many decades of working experience by three master teachers.

Readers will find that the relation of movement activities to conceptual and affective learning objectives is natural and unstrained. The authors never seem to be reaching. The lesson plans, learning materials, and teaching strategies all seem practical and manageable by ordinary mortals.

There is not only an air of practicality in the vision offered here but also a special kind of credibility. Traditional rhetoric in education pictures curriculum design as proceeding from an examination of learning objectives to the selection of appropriate learning activities. Every teacher knows, however, that what happens in real schools rarely resembles this idealized model. The most common sequence of curriculum decisions turns the model on its head. First, activities are identified that are attractive in terms of traditional expectations, that appeal to both students and teachers, and that meet consideration of such constraints as time and resources. Second, with the first step accomplished, the choices of learning activities are rationalized as well as possible by appeal to concomitant learnings that might (or might not) accrue in the process.

The difference in these two sequences is subtle, but the educational consequences are immense and pervasive. It is one thing to determine that it is convenient to teach six weeks of basketball and subsequently to justify that decision as appropriate to educational objectives by asserting that students will be learning cooperation, leadership, courage, and good sportsmanship. It is quite another thing to define cooperation or courage in terms of explicit behaviors and then ask the question "Which learning tasks in the psychomotor domain might best help sixth grade students acquire such complex social skills?" In the latter case, basketball might or might not present itself as a reasonable learning activity.

To move persistently and honestly from objectives to learning activities requires more than just commitment to objectives that ordinarily exist only at the level of rhetoric. What is required is congruence between belief and behavior. The most fundamental presumption of this book is that teaching acts should, and can, flow consonantly from instructional intentions and thus from the teacher's own values.

The program of physical education proposed here emerges in a self-evident manner from persistent attention to the educational objectives selected by the authors. Finding activities to match objectives, rather than the reverse, however, is not an easy business. With this in mind, teachers will be pleased to find that the authors have not held themselves aloof from the difficult and sometimes perplexing task of putting theory into practice.

This is a practical book about a complex curricular problem that often is left at the level of abstraction or exhortation. More than a how-to-do-it manual, however, these pages obviously are a record of what did (and sometimes did not) work to accomplish the goals of the authors. No one familiar with the work of teaching will miss the authentic ring in this account.

May you be tempted to break a few eggs on your own. Bon Appetit!

Lawrence F. Locke

University of Massachusetts, Amherst, Massachusetts

Dolly Lambdin

St. Andrews School, Austin, Texas

Preface

The quality of elementary school physical education programs is of great concern to us. Together, we have had experience teaching elementary school physical education, and we have been involved in preservice and in-service professional preparation of regular elementary education, special education, and physical education teachers relative to elementary school physical education.

The motivation for writing this book grew from an awareness of the difficulty students and teachers have in integrating vast amounts of information to provide meaningful movement experiences. Knowledge of child growth and development, teaching methodology, and movement content are necessary for successful physical education teaching. This book not only contains the preceding information but it also includes topics such as listening, responding, discussing, values clarification, and disciplining. The strength and uniqueness of this book, however, are in the integrated manner in which this information is presented. The method of doing this is through a developmental theme approach.

A developmental theme describes a generic goal for elementary education and a specific goal for physical education. This approach provides integration of information and methods (why and how we teach) and content (the learning experiences used in physical education) in order to contribute toward the development of student behaviors that are desirable outcomes of an elementary school education. The developmental theme approach uses intended student behaviors, rather than specific physical activities, as the elements around which the physical education curriculum is planned, implemented, and evaluated. This conceptual structure incorporates numerous physical activity learning experiences in each developmental theme. The developmental theme approach is a meaningful and systematic way of organizing a comprehensive physical education program that is in harmony with the goals of childhood and the purposes of an elementary school education.

The first three chapters of the book, Part One, present a background, rationale, and detailed explanation of the developmental theme approach. Part Two, Chapters Four through Nine, are the developmental theme chapters. Each of these chapters presents information relative to children, teaching, and implementing that developmental theme. The section on implementing the developmental theme contains guides for planning and evaluation and sample physical education lessons. Chapter Ten is Part Three and is designed to help you become independent of this book. It contains information to help you avoid some common teaching errors and to help you extend the ideas presented in this book. Three aids for retrieving information are presented in this book. These are chapter previews, a general index, and an activity index.

This book was written by a process of joint authorship and was a personally and professionally meaningful experience. The developmental themes presented in this book were proposed by Stephen Klesius. They were refined, ordered, and elaborated as a result of many hours of discussion by the authors. The chapters were developed by each of us contributing ideas, drafting material, and reviewing and suggesting modifications for the work of the others. We view ourselves as having made equally important contributions to the development of the book. The names of the authors are listed in random order and will be rotated in subsequent editions.

The list of people to whom we wish to express our special gratitude is long. Marilyn Hoffman, Janell Klesius, and Lionel Young encouraged us with all the steadfastness that a spouse can provide. Jo Aaron typed the first lengthy drafts of the manuscript, and we deeply appreciate her efforts and dedication at a time when we needed so much help. Randall Williams, the artist, Melody Bailey and David Fricke, the photographers, have contributed their talent to present the message of this book more clearly and aesthetically.

We also thank Hillsborough County Schools and the Catholic Diocese of St. Petersburg for allowing us to photograph their students and teachers engaged in the teaching-learning process at Paul Mort and Progress Village Schools, and Morningstar School of Tampa, Florida, respectively.

Our editors at Allyn and Bacon deserve a special note of thanks. Frank Ruggirello encouraged us to follow our convictions about elementary school physical education in writing this book. Hiram Howard guided us through the process of getting the manuscript into production and ultimately into book form. Allen Workman was especially perceptive and helped us organize our complex manuscript into a manageable text.

And finally, we wish to extend our sincere appreciation to the many professionals who reviewed the manuscript. They provided critical and helpful suggestions for its improvement. A very special thank you is due Lawrence F. Locke and Dolly Lambdin. Their review of the manuscript was most helpful and encouraging, and motivated us during a crucial period in the publication process. We are most grateful to them for taking the time to write the foreword to this book.

The dialogue with our colleagues and students over the years and the lessons we learned from the children we have taught have contributed substantially to our thinking. To them, we sincerely say thank you.

ONE

chapter one

The Changing Image of Physical Education

ELEMENTARY SCHOOLS: PAST AND PRESENT

Think of an elementary school. What memories and feelings do you recall? How do you envision this school in terms of physical and human ingredients?

Your first image may be that of the exterior of the school. Do any of the pictures in Figure 1–1 come close to that image? These pictures camouflage the real heart of the school, namely, students and teachers working in settings where content, materials, teaching methods, and communications skills come together to achieve the goals of an elementary school education.

In the one-room schoolhouse, the teacher emphasized the three R's—reading, writing, and arithmetic—and was able to provide individual instruc-

One-room schoolhouse   Traditional school

Pod, or open-space design

FIGURE 1–1 Kinds of school buildings

tion by having older students teach younger children. In contrast with the one-room schoolhouse, the "modern," or "progressive" school had a broader curriculum, more students, teachers, and materials and used more educational methods than learning by rote memorization and drill. Today's schools still stress the three R's and the functions of a democratic society, while also teaching students how to think creatively and solve problems. Though you may still find a school using *McGuffey's Readers,* you'll find more using programmed reading workbooks, skill centers, and calculators. Today, placing children of different ages in the same room for instruction is called a nongraded or family grouping approach. Having one child teach another is termed "peer tutoring." Many schools have curriculum specialists and a media center with audiovisual systems, records, films, filmstrips, and educational television presentations. Teachers have had preservice and inservice education experiences designed to help them understand the behavior of children and identify areas of need. They have been taught how to utilize teaching methods, materials, management techniques, and evaluation instruments needed for a desired educational objective.

The fact that elementary school programs have changed does not mean that it is easier to be a teacher today or that teachers are more effective than they were in the past. Teachers have a more complex job today, because of the variety of *choices* they must make, the societal influences on the schools, and the high expectations placed on them to be accountable. Teachers are expected to adapt to and influence these new changes.

THE CHANGING VIEW OF
ELEMENTARY SCHOOL PHYSICAL EDUCATION

Changes in physical education programs have followed the trends that influenced the elementary school curriculum. A chronological presentation of photographs (Figure 1–2) illustrates some of these changes.

Again, the photographs reveal only surface differences between what physical education was or still is and what it can be.

Though physical education is unique in that human movement is the medium and focus of learning, many similarities exist between this subject and regular classroom subjects in terms of the instructional methods, management techniques, and interpersonal skills used. Succeeding chapters will present these similarities and show that physical education experiences can make a significant contribution to achieving major goals of elementary education.

FIGURE 1–2 Chronological sequence of physical education activities

---

BOX 1–1 On Boxes

This is a box. More boxes appear in this chapter and the other chapters in this book. A box is a means of setting off interesting and important information from the text. In a box you might find:

A poem
An assignment to complete
A listing of facts
A preview of material to be presented elsewhere in the text

It is important that you read each box since they help you to understand the meaning of movement in a child's development.

MISCONCEPTIONS ABOUT
ELEMENTARY SCHOOL PHYSICAL EDUCATION

A misconception is a falsehood that is widely believed. Physical education has its share of misconceptions.

Play Is Different from Learning
Data from both research and educational observations are eroding the credibility of this belief. In actuality, play is learning, and often learning is play. Because play seemingly is unproductive in terms of identifiable products or results, many adults consider it unimportant in the developmental process of children.

The process of play is essentially information-seeking behavior. Curiosity, spontaneity, creativity, and mastery characterize play, which is a voluntary activity. When children move over, around, toward, or beside objects or other people in play, they encounter new environments. Moffitt states that "through such sensory-motor activities, he [the child] learns much about the properties of matter and finds ways to adapt to a complex environment through experiences related to cause and effect."[1] Play is interaction within concrete, three-dimensional reality. Play, that is multisensory and movement-oriented activity, provides experiences that children use to give meaning to new, more complex, and abstract experiences. Thus play activities can be considered an initial stage in the development of intelligence. As children learn how to observe, compare, classify, sequence, and imagine, the processes of intelligence are being practiced.[2,3] In addition, play is an important aspect of a child's social development. The play between parent and child results in affective interactions (feelings, values, and attitudes) and helps a child develop an identity and feelings of self-worth. Play and games are used by various cultures to train children to accept challenges, to develop

FIGURE 1–3 Play learning center

perseverance, and to respect authority. Play is a medium for personal interaction and intrapersonal discovery.

Teachers and administrators today recognize the importance of play in child development, and they use games to motivate children to learn. Teachers have begun to use children's need to move as a modality for learning.

Play-learning centers are replacing playgrounds. Play is now considered part of the total learning experience rather than a diversion from academically respected experiences.

Children Need Physical Education to Release Energy and to Reduce Aggression

Many people believe that the longer a child sits, the more energy he or she stores up. At some point, this energy must be released either through physical activity in a physical education class or an outburst in the classroom, for example. Similarly, there is the misconception that physical activity diminishes aggression. It is generally believed that if children act out aggression in games they will be less likely to act aggressively toward others in later situations. When these statements are examined with respect to research findings, no substantial support can be found.

What is true and what is not true? Yes, children are energetic, active, moving beings. However, they do not store energy like an automobile battery. Most children enjoy being physically active, and being subjected to classroom confinement makes it appear that a child explodes with energy once allowed to move. It is also true that young children fatigue quickly because of their high rate of activity. However, after a rest, they quickly recuperate, and charge off again in some pattern of physical activity.

Whether or not these actions are aggressive encounters is another subject. Contrary to popular thought, physical action or watching competitive physical activities does not automatically diminish aggression. The cathartic theory, reduction of aggression through actions, has not been supported by research. Research tends to show that aggressive behavior is learned and often results from frustration in response to not reaching activity goals.[4] The energy-aggression release misconception is at a loss to explain how a group of children can return to a classroom shouting and scrambling after a soccer game, especially when one team felt they had been robbed of victory by a disputed goal scored in the closing seconds of the game. Imagine the energy this group would display after such an experience.

Martens[5] stated that physical activity does not reduce aggressive tendencies or serve as an outlet for aggression. Rather, it seems that aggressive behavior directed toward injuring others can be learned. Conversely, when children ". . . observe nonviolent behavior and are reinforced for nonviolent behavior, they are likely to continue to behave nonviolently."[6] The current scene in sports and physical education rarely presents this nonviolent model, making the task more difficult for teachers and coaches who want to help children control their emotions and to become responsible participants in play experiences.

BOX 1-2 Recess

Providing a break in any routine activity is desirable. The tradition of providing a break from studying is still practiced in many schools by allowing children to go outside and play. The practice of considering recess a physical education class is no longer acceptable. It is perfectly reasonable, however, for a school to provide both recess and a physical education class each day. It would be nonsense to say that nothing is learned during recess. Generally, though, whatever is learned may or may not be related to the instructional goals of a physical education program.

Ambrose Brazelton, a physical education teacher and educational consultant, expressed his views on recess in a poem entitled "What Phys. Ed. Ain't."[7]

>Recess is when two times each day
>The staff goes to smoke
>And the kids go to play.
>They slide, they swing, they
>Muddy their socks and
>Climb and jump and
>Even throw rocks.
>Boys tussle and wrestle,
>Chase girls 'til they faint.
>Recess is important, but
>Phys. Ed. it ain't.

Emotional control and responsible play are not developed merely as a result of being active. While it is true that physical activity can help by absorbing anxiety, activity can also have no effect, or it can generate tension, aggression, and violence.

Girls Develop Bulging Muscles from Physical Activity

This is only one of many misconceptions associated with physical activity for females. Research has shown that regular physical activity is beneficial and appropriate for females as well as males.

In regard to increases in muscle size, *hypertrophy,* the research evidence has demonstrated that females who engaged in a weight training program frequently increased their strength by at least 25 percent. The strength is not, however, associated with a noticeable increase in muscle tissue. The individual's muscle tone will increase, but the muscles do not bulge, possibly because of the effects of female hormones. In addition, females have more subcutaneous fatty tissue than do males, and this tissue layer helps to give females a more rounded or curving appearance than the angular or muscular body build of a male.[8]

Research findings regarding the effect of regular and vigorous physical activity for females indicates that there need be little difference between conditioning programs for girls and those for boys. Rather, differences in physical activity training programs and methods should be varied according to needs and desired results, not by the individual's gender. Physical activity is beneficial to girls in terms of body composition and appearance.[9]

Now that we have clarified some of the more common misconceptions about physical activity and its effects, you may want to begin a process of self-evaluation, providing evidence to modify or support your beliefs about physical activity. Physical education is indeed important and appropriate as a developmental/educational medium.

BOX 1–3   A Preview

What can a teacher do to help a sixth-grade girl decide how physically active she should be and in what types of activities to participate during menses? In Chapter 9 this situation will be dealt with. A main concept is stated, supporting facts are given, and experiential activities are presented. The purpose of this approach is to provide the teacher with information and activities that the female student can experience and draw upon in order to make an informed decision. This chapter is entitled, *Drawing Relationships: Comprehending the Significance of Movement in One's Lifestyle.* The implication of providing such information and experiential activities is obvious. But, how often is such a subject approached in school and how well are teachers prepared to effectively interact with female students to make this another significant learning experience instead of a problem?

John, a lonely child

A good class in physical education

Kids learning through discovery

Overweight children

Becky, a child struggling at her desk with a task

A happy child on the playground bars

Steve, a little leaguer

Karen, a belligerent child

FIGURE 1–4 All children need physical education

PHYSICAL EDUCATION: WHO NEEDS IT?

What do you think about the children in Figure 1–4? How is physical education going to help John make friends, Becky try harder in math, or Karen learn to control her aggressive behavior? Will the overweight child learn to reduce food intake and increase physical activity? Does recess take care of the need

FIGURE 1–5 Values are gained through experience

for physical activity for most elementary children? And how is physical education going to help any of them—including Steve—when they leave school for the day?

How about you? Are you a competent mover? Do you feel good about *doing* physical activity? Do you feel confident that you can make your body do what you want it to do? Or were you the child who was made the right fielder in baseball and usually batted last?[10] Was it a relief when you weren't the last to be chosen for a team?

How you answer these questions indicates the extent to which you value physical education. The value one places on physical education is determined by the positive and/or negative experiences one has had in physical education activities. As a teacher, you will discover that the developmental theme approach to physical education provides for meeting the needs of children. Since each child is developing physically, socially, intellectually, and emotionally, each will need physical education.

DEVELOPING MOVEMENT COMPETENCY

The literature on child development usually does not emphasize the achievement of movement competency in children. This is unfortunate. If teachers of young children understood the meaning of movement in children's lives, surely they would be willing to spend more time in this area of learning. Time alone, however, is not enough. Although free play and physical activity are very important in the daily lives of children, free play and physical activity are not synonymous with well-structured movement environments that help children develop necessary competencies, such as running, jumping, rolling, throwing, and catching.

In today's urbanized world, it is unlikely that the majority of children will develop movement competency to any high degree through free play alone. There is some evidence that children have always needed adult intervention in their play in order for it to develop any creative aspects.[11,12] Unless teachers believe and understand this, teaching physical education becomes the proverbial straw on the camel's back. Even though children have time to play before and after school, adult intervention through physical education classes can facilitate the development of movement competence.

Developing movement competency is only one aspect of child development. Movement is a meaningful way of learning and communicating for children. When teachers ignore this, they deny many children the opportunity for positive learning experiences. Children often are forced to use auditory and visual modes of learning too early, when learning through physical involvement (with concepts such as "roundness," "cooperation," and "momentum") can be a more successful and satisfying experience.

Despite the fact that we know more than our predecessors about how children learn and develop, we still lack specific information about the interrelationships between physical and intellectual development. However, the contributions of researchers in the field of perceptual-motor development have helped classroom teachers and physical educators to provide meaningful developmental and remedial experiences for children who have learning difficulties.

WHO SHOULD TEACH PHYSICAL EDUCATION?

Many classroom teachers have stated that they feel unable to teach physical education because of their own lack of competency in movement. Many of them believe it is necessary to demonstrate the task or activity, thus it seems that the specialist is the only person capable of teaching movement. It is true that the role of the physical education specialist is to emphasize some aspects of development that are different from those emphasized by the classroom teacher.

Physical education specialists have a vested interest in the child's motor development. The term "specialist" implies that the preparation of physical education teachers provides them with the knowledge and ability to assist children in developing specific movement behaviors, knowledge, and attitudes. But the specialist's pupil load usually is large and it takes time to learn individual needs. The observant classroom teacher, on the other hand, can determine such needs early in the school year or detect a change in someone's behavior as the school term progresses.

Classroom teachers can teach physical education and help children find joy in learning to move efficiently. The development of movement confidence and a love of activity are major attributes that help children to develop patterns of behavior that can lead to healthy lifestyles as adults. Developing these attributes and values is one of the primary tasks for the teacher of elementary school physical education, whether that teacher is a "specialist" or the classroom teacher.

BOX 1–4   Physical Education as a Basic Subject

For a variety of reasons, education authorities in France were disturbed about the heavy emphasis on academics in their elementary school curricula. Making children spend nearly all their time in academic pursuits, in the close confines of the classroom, seemed contrary to what was known about the growth and developmental needs of children.

As a result, in 1951 a longitudinal study was conducted. (The same research was later replicated in Belgium and in Japan.) In this study the amount of time students spent in physical activity was changed significantly. The children in the experimental classes spent up to one-third of their school day in well-planned physical education activities such as gymnastics, games, dance, and swimming.

Initially, parents of the children in the experimental classes were concerned that their children would fall behind academically. However, the opposite effect was found. Some of the results from the "one-third" time schools were that these students:

1. matured more quickly and were more independent
2. seemed less susceptible to stress
3. surpassed students in the control classes in academic performance

The researchers interpreted this last finding to mean that children in the one-third time schools were not ". . . more intelligent, but the *tools of intelligence* were much keener."[13]

WORKING TOGETHER

Physical education is an important part of the school curriculum. It is not merely "play," "letting off steam," or an activity that is divorced from the mainstream of learning experiences in elementary school. However, to achieve its rightful position as one of the basics, physical education must be seen in its relationship to the total curriculum. Classroom teachers and physical education specialists should work together; both have much to contribute that cannot be accomplished alone.

A professional relationship between the specialist and the classroom teacher can develop into a commitment of two teachers working together to correlate physical education activities with other learning experiences. The rewards for this effort can be found in the satisfaction of helping children develop their movement and learning abilities to their fullest extent.

ENDNOTES

1. Mary Moffitt, "Does Play Make a Difference?" *Journal of Health, Physical Education, and Recreation* 43 (June 1972): 45.
2. Ibid.
3. Jean Piaget, *Science of Education and Psychology of the Child* (New York: Orion Press, 1970), pp. 155–57.
4. Rainer Martens, *Social Psychology and Physical Activity* (New York: Harper and Row, 1975), pp. 118–122.
5. Ibid., p. 126.
6. Ibid.
7. Ambrose Brazelton, "What Phys Ed Ain't," *Teacher Educaring* (Long Branch, N.J.: Kimbo Educational Records, 1972).
8. Jack Wilmore, "Body Composition and Strength Development" *Journal of Health, Physical Education, and Recreation* 46 (January 1975): 38.
9. Ibid., p. 39.
10. H. A. Hoffman, "Right Fielder Bats Last," *The Physical Educator* 28 (May 1971): 94–95.
11. Margaret Mead, *Growing Up In New Guinea,* 4th ed. (New York: Dell Publishing Co., 1968), p. 19.
12. Susana Millar, *The Psychology of Play,* 2nd ed. (Baltimore, Md.: Penguin Books, 1971), p. 199.
13. D. A. Bailey, "The Growing Child and the Need for Physical Activity," *Child in Sport and Physical Activity,* ed. J. G. Albinson and G. M. Andrew (Baltimore, Md.: University Park Press, 1976), pp. 81–91.

chapter two

The Developmental Themes:
Behavioral Goals of Physical Education

GENERAL GOALS OF EDUCATION
GOALS OF PHYSICAL EDUCATION
THE DEVELOPMENTAL THEME APPROACH
THE DEVELOPMENTAL THEMES
THE DEVELOPMENTAL THEME CHAPTERS

GENERAL GOALS OF EDUCATION

From a historical perspective, the most widely known statement concerning the goals of education was the *Cardinal Principles of Secondary Education* prepared in 1918 by the Commission on the Reorganization of Secondary School Education. The preamble to this statement of broad goals was as follows:

> Education in a democracy, both within and without the school, should develop in each individual the knowledge, interests, ideals, habits, and powers whereby he will find his place and use that place to shape both himself and society toward ever nobler ends.[1]

It was felt that these principles, which were related to areas of daily living, should comprise the school program as follows:

1. Health
2. Command of fundamental processes
3. Worthy home-membership
4. Vocation
5. Civic education
6. Worthy use of leisure
7. Ethical character[2]

17

As a statement of educational goals, these principles helped to broaden the secondary school curriculum and had impact on the goals of the elementary school program.

Twenty years later, the Educational Policies Commission of the National Education Association advocated four general goals for education that were defined in reference to human responsibilities. The objectives were concerned with:

1. Self-realization relating to the development of the learner
2. Human relations concerning home, family, and community life
3. Economic efficiency pertaining to economic needs
4. Civic responsibility relating to civic and social duties[3]

The self-realization objective included references to health knowledge, health habits, and recreation.[4] These objectives, while expressed in other terms, can still be found within current elementary school curricula.

The Educational Policies Commission has influenced the goals of education in 1938, 1952, and 1961. The 1961 statement of purpose of education showed a shift from previous goal statements. In *The Central Purpose of American Education* it was stated: "The purpose which runs through and strengthens all other educational purposes—the common thread of education—is the development of the ability to think."[5] The development of intellectual ability became the central goal of American schools. It marked a shift away from goals stated in terms of social issues and simple accumulation of facts toward higher level cognitive, intellectual, scientific abilities.

In the late 1960s, a new direction was emerging for educational purposes that emphasized individual expression, self-control, and self-actualization. Dorothy Cohen, a proponent of this movement, stated that:

> Schools must make the effort to give children growing up in a society that worships the mechanical a full measure of childhood devoted to a visceral sense of being, to depth of feeling, to critical thinking, and to realistic coping . . . our children need skills, but they need even more the wisdom to use skills in ways that do not violate total human needs.[6]

In 1977 and 1978, many school systems were adopting a "back to the basics" curriculum orientation. As a result, Ammons found that . . . "particularly in the primary grades, reading and mathematics have achieved such importance that teachers have difficulty working science and social studies into the class schedule."[7] The back to basics movement stresses instruction in reading, language arts, and mathematics; and state assessment and minimal literacy testing programs have been developed and implemented. However, there is a debate whether the schools should only be concerned with literacy or with higher levels of competency and mastery as well. In addition, there is uncertainty as to what constitutes "the basics" of education. Frazier interpreted "the basics" as the areas of education which, when left under-developed, are the most damaging to children. These basic areas of education are as follows:

1. The fundamentals (reading, language, math, and science)
2. Getting a hold on the constructive arts
3. Managing the body and controlling the self.[8]

While the basics of education include "managing the body and controlling the self,"[9] the present focus of "back to the basics" is on literacy. However, this emphasis does *not* necessarily mean that there is a repression of the concern for the person in the process of "becoming." Literacy can be used to represent the bottom line or minimum level that a school system is responsible and accountable for achieving. As has always been true, the positive aspect of basic education is that the fundamental skills are the foundation for mastery learning in all school subjects and the development of a fully functioning person.

In general, statements of broad goals of education—whether related to social and civic responsibility, intellectual development, or the enhancement of human potential—have not been helpful to teachers in planning educational programs. When viewed in terms of the question, What do I teach tomorrow? these goal statements do not provide the answer. Broad goals may become meaningless, useless, and impossible to accomplish on a day-to-day level.

GOALS OF PHYSICAL EDUCATION

Statements of the broad goals and purposes of physical education have not been any more helpful to teachers than those related to general education. Halsey and Porter stated that "The purpose of physical education is to secure the best possible development of all children and youth, especially along the closely related lines of physical growth, motor skill, emotional maturity, and social adjustment."[10] As a result, development of fitness, healthy growth, possession of recreational skills, and desirable social patterns occur.

Siedentop stated that in the past fifty years the objectives of physical education have been identified as:

1. Organic development or physical development through movement
2. Neuromuscular development or development of movement skill and movement expression
3. Interpretative development, cognitive development, and communication through movement
4. Personal-social development or learning democratic behaviors through movement.[11]

Expression of the objectives of physical education in these terms has made curriculum development a hodgepodge of physical activities that have few or no common bonds and are frequently irrelevant to the personal needs of the student. According to Aldrich,[12] for a physical education curriculum to become meaningful, a comprehensive conceptual framework needs to be constructed and implemented.

An example of the result of the hodgepodge pattern of curriculum development of physical education is expressed below:

> It simply is inadequate for a child to experience "drop the handkerchief," "throw and go," and other cat and rat games in the primary grades; kickball and relays in grades four through six. . . . Probably none of these experiences assists the student with acquiring higher order objectives, and probably none of the experiences assists in preparing students for the future. Each day is an end in itself.[13]

What is needed is a conceptual framework with a "process orientation" for curriculum development. Corbin proposes a new wisdom of physical education which goes beyond performing movement tasks, achieving physical fitness, and acquiring motor skills. The essence of the new wisdom is to provide meaningful movement experiences so each individual can become a fully functioning person.[14]

In conventional wisdom, means (tools) and ends (goals) are blurred to the extent that in physical education programs it is often difficult to distinguish the means from the ends. Physical education programs that are in tune with the new integrated wisdom focus on problem solving, incorporate self-teaching, and use innovative movement experiences. The goals are high order objectives of valuing life, finding the meaning and joy of movement, understanding limitations, and achieving full potential.[15] This new view focuses on the totally integrated person rather than on developing discrete attributes. Instead of focusing solely on the physical activity or sport to be taught today, the goal should be helping students to discover themselves and find meaning in and through movement.[16]

The shortcomings of broad goal statements for physical education and an introduction to new methods have led some teachers to think of curriculum guides stated in terms of describing the physically educated person. Corbin described this person as follows:

> One who moves effectively within his environment. He possesses efficient movement skills, including a reasonable proficiency in a variety of dance, games, and sports and other physical activities. He possesses buoyant health and physical fitness. Retention of these qualities is insured by a knowledge of and a desirable attitude toward physical activity and related areas. A physically educated person with disability would use his body within his capabilities.[17]

The physically educated person has also been described in behavioral terms, as a person:

being able to select developmentally appropriate physical activities, participate voluntarily and regularly in these activities, and enjoy these activities as evidenced by positive verbalization patterns, and observable efforts to find opportunities to extend the repertoire of skill, increase the level of performance, or intensify the frequency of participation. This person is self-directing and self-actualizing.[18]

How can the purposes of elementary school physical education be stated in order to show that a significant and meaningful contribution can be made not only in terms of areas of child development unique to physical education, but also to the goals which appear throughout the entire elementary school curriculum? What can be done to operationalize a new approach for elementary school physical education? In a broader context, how does physical education relate to the basic goals of the elementary school curriculum in a way that promotes not just literacy, but the full functioning of each child?

THE DEVELOPMENTAL THEME APPROACH

While elementary school physical education programs partially have realized the goal of helping children to "learn to move and move to learn,"[19] the current framework for curriculum design is being judged as inadequate. The challengers are numerous. Aldrich[20] has stated that a conceptual approach to curriculum design and implementation is needed, while Corbin[21] called for new aspirations for physical education (in addition to developing physical abilities and skill) to include valuing, solving problems, and finding meaning in movement. Logsdon[22] expressed the belief that physical education must shift from an emphasis on products (specific skills, drills, stunts, games, and dances to be experienced, learned, and performed) to a product-process focus. As a result of this orientation:

. . . methods must be selected or developed on the basis of their capacity to stimulate the thought process and to involve the inner affective qualities of the learners as well as their potential for accommodating the development of motor-oriented end products.[23]

Physical education, especially as part of the elementary school curriculum, can not only help children to "learn to move and move to learn"[24] but can also become "more than movement, larger than sport, and greater than physical fitness."[25]

The preoccupation of physical educators with the delivery of products (services) ". . . based on tradition and trial-and-error techniques has precluded the need for a body of knowledge that is unified, codified, and abstract."[26] The hodgepodge, patchwork, folklore means of generating physical education curricula, especially at the elementary school level, must be re-examined. The Purpose-Process Curriculum Framework presented by Jewett and Mullan[27] provides one conceptual model. A developmental theme approach that emphasizes the instructional process as well as content is another example of a conceptual model for physical education curriculum development and implementation.

The basic tenets of the developmental theme approach to elementary school physical education presented in this book are:

1. To be meaningful, the study of movement must be integrated as part of a larger context—the process of development. Developmental themes describe generic goals for elementary education and specific goals for physical education. For example, the first developmental theme is Becoming Aware (generic goal): Learning about and Establishing Basic Movement Capabilities (physical education goal).
2. It is important to learn movement activities for their inherent value. However, the value of the learning experience is increased when the movement activities are learned in an environment that integrates movement content with knowledge about children and teaching as related to the total developmental process. In this way, physical education lessons are designed for physical, social, emotional, and intellectual development—a focus on the whole child.
3. Educational experiences can focus on movement activities that relate to developmental tasks and stages. The developmental theme approach is a systematic way of organizing movement activities that are integrated with other teaching activities to meet the needs of the student.
4. The developmental theme approach focuses attention on movement activities as part of the broad goals of the elementary school curriculum. In this context, physical education fulfills a greater role in the development of literacy and a fully functioning lifestyle.

THE DEVELOPMENTAL THEMES

The developmental theme approach provides for planning the curriculum around intended student behaviors instead of specific physical activities. Each of the six themes focuses on a specific kind of behavior that teachers seek to foster in students. The activities in each developmental theme are related to other curriculum areas so that teachers can plan coordinating and reinforcing experiences for their students. This approach assures that the development of the child remains the central focus of the curriculum. The six developmental themes are:

1. Becoming Aware: Learning about and Establishing Basic Movement Capabilities
2. Becoming Independent: Increasing Self-Reliance and Confidence in Moving
3. Accepting and Expressing Feelings and Ideas: Communicating through Movement
4. Accepting Responsibilities and Acting Cooperatively: Sharing the Movement Environment and Respecting and Interacting Productively with Others
5. Improving Quality of Response: Refining and Elaborating Movement Capabilities for a Purpose
6. Drawing Relationships: Comprehending the Significance of Movement in One's Lifestyle.

BOX 2–1   A Comparison of Goals

Take a few minutes to look at the lists of goals for school programs (pages 17, 18, and 19) and compare them to the developmental themes (page 23).

1. What does the developmental theme list have in common with the lists of goals?
2. Do you find it easier to perceive the use of one type of list as compared to another?

THE DEVELOPMENTAL THEME CHAPTERS

While each developmental theme focuses on a particular kind of behavior, there is a basic format for each of the theme chapters. Each developmental theme chapter includes the following:

1. The "why" of teaching. Information concerning growth and development of children with the meaning and application of this information to each developmental theme.
2. The methods or "how" of teaching. Generic instructional strategies within a curriculum framework: the individual learns through activity, discovery, and appropriate intervention.
3. The "what" of teaching. Suggestions for specific movement experiences with instructional and organizational guidelines.

4. How physical education can foster the goals and objectives of the total elementary school program. Relating and integrating movement experiences with other curriculum learning activities in a way that helps to give unity and totality to learning.

Following this design, there is no single chapter in this book on child growth and development; rather, the relevant information on child growth and development is presented with the appropriate developmental theme and is integrated with developmental-theme-referenced methods and learning activities.

If you need only the information on child growth or development, read the section called "About Children" in each of the developmental theme chapters. Or, if you would like to read only about teaching methods, read the "About Teaching" part of each developmental theme chapter. The third section of each developmental theme chapter, "Implementing the Developmental Theme," includes information on recommended movement experiences and sample lessons. Also, to help you find information quickly, two separate indices are presented, a comprehensive index and a movement experience index.

ENDNOTES

1. Commission on the Reorganization of Secondary Education, U.S. Office of Education, *Cardinal Principles of Secondary Education* (Washington, D.C.: Government Printing Office, 1918), Bulletin No. 35, p. 9.
2. Ibid., pp. 14–15.
3. Educational Policies Commission, *The Purposes of Education in American Democracy* (Washington, D.C.: National Education Association, 1938), p. 47.
4. Ibid., p. 50.
5. Educational Policies Commission, *The Central Purpose of American Education* (Washington, D.C.: National Education Association, 1961), p. 12.
6. Dorothy Cohen, *The Learning Child* (New York: Pantheon, 1972), pp. xvii–xviii.
7. Margaret Ammons, Kate R. Barrett, Marion R. Broer, Lolas E. Halverson, Bette J. Logsdon, Rosemary McGee, and Mary Ann Roberton, "Elementary Education—A Perspective," in *Physical Education for Children* (Philadelphia: Lea and Febiger, 1977), p. 3.
8. Alexander Frazier, *Adventuring, Mastering, Associating: New Strategies for Teaching Children* (Washington, D.C.: Association for Supervision and Curriculum Development, 1976), p. 72–82.

9. Ibid., p. 78.
10. Elizabeth Halsey and Lorena Porter, *Physical Education for Children* (New York: Holt, Rinehart and Winston, 1963), p. 9.
11. Daryl Siedentop, *Physical Education: Introductory Analysis,* 2nd ed. (Dubuque, Iowa: William C. Brown Co., 1976), p. 253.
12. Anita Aldrich, *Cooperative Development of Design for Long-Term Research Project Directed Toward the Identification of a Conceptual Framework for the Curriculum in Physical Education, Grades K–16* (Washington, D.C.: American Alliance for Health, Physical Education, and Recreation, 1976), pp. 1–2.
13. Dean A. Pease, "Physical Education: Accountability for the Future," in *Physical Education: A View Toward the Future,* ed. Raymond Welsh (St. Louis: C. V. Mosby Co., 1977), p. 147.
14. Charles B. Corbin, "A New Wisdom for Physical Education," in *Physical Education: A View Toward the Future,* ed. Raymond Welsh (St. Louis: C. V. Mosby Company, 1977), pp. 160–164.
15. Ibid., p. 161.
16. Ibid., p. 162.
17. ———, *Becoming Physically Educated in the Elementary School* (Philadelphia: Lea and Febiger, 1969), p. 9.
18. Stephen E. Klesius, "Physical Education in the '70's: Where Do You Stand?" *Journal of Health, Physical Education, and Recreation* 42 (February 1971): 47.
19. Sam Britten, Edrie Ferdun, Eleanor Metheny, Jerrold Russom, Paul Smith, and Joan Tillotson, *This Is Physical Education* (Washington, D.C.: The American Association for Health, Physical Education and Recreation, 1965), p. 3.
20. Aldrich, *Cooperative Development,* pp. 1–2.
21. Corbin, "A New Wisdom," p. 164.
22. Margaret Ammons, Kate R. Barrett, Marion R. Broer, Lolas E. Halverson, Bette J. Logsdon, Rosemary McGee, and Mary Ann Roberton, "Physical Education—A Design for Direction," in *Physical Education for Children* (Philadelphia: Lea and Febiger, 1977), p. 19.
23. Ibid.
24. Metheny, *This Is Physical Education,* p. 3.
25. Celeste Ulrich, "The Future Hour: An Educational View," in *Physical Education: A View Toward the Future,* ed. Raymond Welsh (St. Louis: C. V. Mosby Company, 1977), p. 138.
26. Hal A. Lawson, "From Futures Forecasting to Future Creation: A Planning Model for Physical Education and Sport," in *Physical Education: A View Toward the Future,* ed. Raymond Welsh (St. Louis: C. V. Mosby Company, 1977), p. 100.
27. Ann E. Jewett and Marie R. Mullan, *Curriculum Design: Purposes and Processes in Physical Education Teaching-Learning* (Washington, D.C.: American Alliance for Health, Physical Education and Recreation, 1977), p. 53.

chapter three

Using the Developmental Theme Approach

USING THE DEVELOPMENTAL THEME APPROACH

The developmental theme approach to teaching physical education will require a shift away from planning around movement activities (exercises, games, dance, gymnastics) toward a focus on desired student behaviors. The traditional activities are *not* replaced in the developmental themes, rather they are selected and combined with appropriate teaching methods to develop the desired behavior.

Teachers work in highly individualized ways and no attempt will be made in this chapter to get everyone started in the same manner. Some of you will want to "dive in" and get going using materials presented in this book. Others will want to be more cautious, preferring to adapt material to fit your ongoing program. While the developmental themes were designed to be used to implement a comprehensive elementary school physical education program, they are structured so that, if necessary, you may adapt selected parts to your current program.

Enabling Behaviors   Each developmental theme is a synthesis of objectives, methods, and activities and results in a practical and meaningful program guide. The developmental *themes* describe broad behavioral goals for children in physical education programs. To facilitate the attainment of these goals, each theme includes several *enabling behaviors.* An enabling behavior is a more immediately attainable competency than the behavioral goal indicated by the developmental theme. For example, in Chapter Five the developmental theme is Becoming Independent: Increasing Self-Reliance and Confidence in Moving. Such a goal can be achieved only as a result of many experiences over a long period of time. The enabling behaviors for the developmental theme, Becoming Independent, are:

   a. Following directions
   b. Making choices
   c. Developing safe behavior
   d. Developing courage

The attainment of these enabling behaviors aids the student in gaining self-reliance and confidence in moving. These behaviors are necessary for

TABLE 3–1 Developmental Themes and Enabling Behaviors

Theme	*Enabling Behaviors*
1. Becoming Aware: Learning about and Establishing Basic Movement Capabilities	a. Developing body image b. Developing movement potential c. Developing spatial awareness d. Developing manipulative abilities
2. Becoming Independent: Increasing Self-Reliance and Confidence in Moving	a. Following directions b. Making choices c. Developing safe behavior d. Developing courage
3. Accepting and Expressing Feelings and Ideas: Communicating through Movement	a. Expressing feelings b. Understanding and accepting feelings c. Increasing communicative abilities d. Creating ideas
4. Accepting Responsibilities and Acting Cooperatively: Sharing the Movement Environment and Respecting and Interacting Productively with Others	a. Developing concern for others and property b. Developing roles c. Exploring rules d. Developing cooperative and competitive behavior
5. Improving Quality of Response: Refining and Elaborating Movement Capabilities for a Purpose	a. Developing precision b. Increasing complexity of responses c. Challenging self beyond comfortable limits.
6. Drawing Relationships: Comprehending the Significance of Movement in One's Lifestyle	a. Developing healthful patterns of living b. Understanding environmental influences on movement c. Developing informed decision-making behavior.

independence: the broader curriculum goal. Table 3–1 lists all the developmental themes and the corresponding enabling behaviors.

Each of the thematic chapters (Chapters Four through Nine) contains a behavioral goal described by the developmental theme and the requisite enabling behaviors for more immediate competencies or objectives. The long-range goals of the developmental themes are attained by planning and teaching for the more immediate enabling behaviors. To assist teachers, a planning guide and teaching modules are presented for each enabling behavior in the developmental theme chapters.

Planning Guides Planning guides are presented in the thematic chapters for each enabling behavior. Teachers will find the guides useful in planning for instruction to implement the developmental theme approach. Each planning guide includes objectives for the enabling behavior and activity ideas for lessons (see Table 3–2).

TABLE 3–2 Planning Guide for Enabling Behavior: Developing Body Image

Developmental Theme: Becoming Aware

Enabling Behavior: Developing Body Image

Objectives	*Sample Movement Experience*
As a result of the learning experience over time, children will be able to:	
• identify different parts of the body.	• shake, touch different parts of the body • move different body-parts in response to a given task • name and locate body-parts with eyes closed
• identify the surfaces of the body. • demonstrate constancy of knowledge of body surfaces.	• name and locate different body surfaces • locate such surfaces from a variety of spatial orientations (facing the front of the room, lying down, etc.)
• demonstrate establishment of laterality.	• perform a variety of movements with first one side of the body, then the other
• demonstrate where different body-parts are in space as they move.	• lead with different body-parts with and without equipment • experience a variety of ways of traveling through space with different body-parts leading
• demonstrate understanding of the different size relationships that exist among different body-parts.	• measuring different body-parts and establish how much bigger or smaller some parts are to other parts.

Table 3–2 is an example of a planning guide; the guides can be used as an aid to long-range planning.

Modular Approach to Constructing Lessons Physical education lessons are presented in each of the developmental theme chapters and one lesson follows the planning guide for each enabling behavior. The lessons are composed of *teaching modules*. Table 3–3 presents the format and kind of information included in each teaching module. The modular approach to constructing lessons is used in this book as a tool in helping the teacher to adapt and construct lessons.

TABLE 3–3 Common Format for the Three Types of Modules

Enabling Behavior   *Type of Module: Introductory, Central, or Culminating*

Objectives

Objectives of the module are listed here.

Creating the Learning Environment

Class organization, methodology, equipment needed, activities are presented in this section.

Movement Experiences	*Related Experiences*
The actual lesson including teaching points and some rationale for the design of the lesson is presented here.	Activities that can take place in other curricular areas that reinforce or extend the physical education experience are suggested in this column.

In Table 3–3, three types of teaching modules are listed: *Introductory, Central,* and *Culminating*. Each lesson is constructed by combining an introductory, central, and culminating module and is not considered complete unless it includes all three types. The module designations indicate the general purposes of the modules.

Every lesson begins with an *introductory module*. Lessons in which new subject matter is being presented (Introductory Lessons) generally will have longer introductory modules than those lessons planned later in a series or progression. The length of time of the introductory module is a function of its purpose which may include one or more of the following:

To introduce a major concept (idea, purpose, activity)
To set the tone of the lesson
To provide a physiological warm-up for the activity of the central module
To allow an opportunity, when necessary, for vigorous activity at the beginning of the lesson.

The *central teaching module* follows the introductory module. Except at the beginning and end of a series of lessons, the central module is usually the longest lesson component. In these lessons (Acquisition Lessons) the

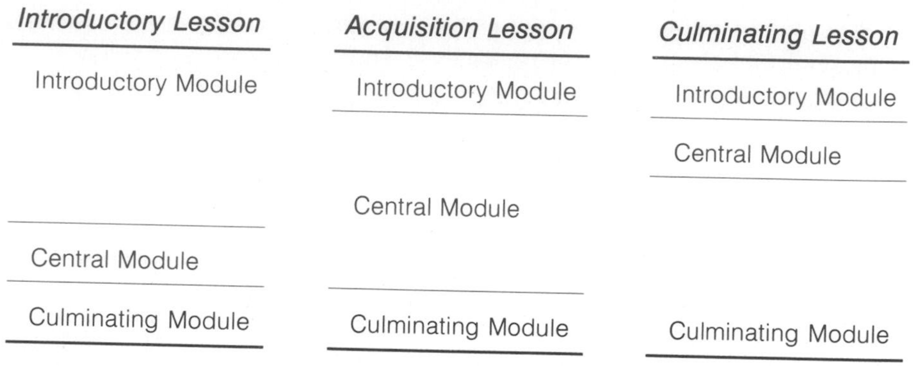

Introductory Lesson	*Acquisition Lesson*	*Culminating Lesson*
Introductory Module	Introductory Module	Introductory Module
		Central Module
	Central Module	
Central Module		
Culminating Module	Culminating Module	Culminating Module

FIGURE 3–1 Length of teaching modules reflecting purposes within a series of lessons

modules are designed to provide the primary opportunities for the learning of specific skills, knowledges, or values. They reflect the main purposes of the lesson.

Culminating teaching modules come at the end of every lesson and should be planned for a specific purpose. Examples are:

To review the day's lesson

To combine one or more previously practiced activities

To apply or extend what has been practiced in the central module

To prepare the class for the next lesson

To evaluate what has been learned.

Culminating modules would be longer in lessons at the end of a series of lessons (Culminating Lessons) than at the beginning. Figure 3–1 presents lessons that are planned for different placements within a series of lessons.

The modular approach to constructing lessons helps assure that the major purposes of a lesson receive appropriate emphasis.

Some teaching modules can be used in more than one lesson. For example, a single introductory module may be combined with different central modules and culminating modules to form a number of complete lessons. You will find the introductory modules are all designed for use with either primary or intermediate grade children. They are then combined with a central module and an appropriate culminating module to complete the lesson. In other instances, you will find that some modules provide options that modify the experiences for different age or interest groups. In these modules instructions are given for adapting the methodology or content for different age groups.

The teaching module approach to constructing lessons provides a flexible and instructionally sound system since it provides options that will help ensure that valid learning experiences will take place. To accommodate personal planning styles, four planning options are available to assist teachers in constructing lessons. These options are as follows:

1. Implement a sample lesson presented in a developmental theme chapter.
2. Construct a lesson by selecting one module from each of the three categories (*Introductory, Central,* and *Culminating*) where the option is presented.
3. Construct a lesson using one or two *teacher*-prepared modules: Introductory, Central, or Culminating in combination with other modules presented by the authors for that enabling behavior.
4. Construct a lesson where you create all three modules: Introductory, Central, and Culminating.

Teachers have different planning needs predicated upon their experience with the subject matter, available time, and style of preparation. Therefore, as you plan lessons for different enabling behaviors, the authors hope that you will use the teaching modules in ways that are personally meaningful and geared to your specific teaching circumstances.

Curriculum Guides Collectively, the six developmental themes outline a sequential and comprehensive elementary school physical education program. Figure 3–2 presents the developmental themes listed in order of relative appropriateness from

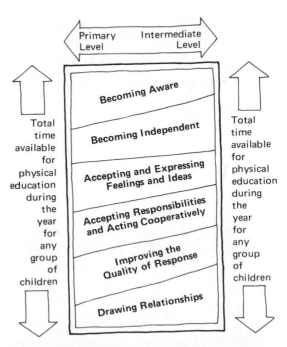

FIGURE 3–2 Relative appropriateness of themes to age

early childhood to middle childhood. The first developmental theme, Becoming Aware, would receive greater emphasis than Drawing Relationships, developmental theme six, in a program for very young children. The reverse would be true for older children.

If a teacher, planning for a specific group of children, wants to allocate an equal amount of time to each of the six developmental themes, then each theme should be scheduled for about 16 percent of the available time. No specific recommendations have been made regarding percentages of time to be allocated to each theme at a grade or age level. The relative importance of the themes to a particular age level, as shown in Figure 3–2, represent the judgment of the authors. You will need to make specific time allocation decisions when planning for your students.

It should be noted that in any given physical education class period, you may plan a lesson designed to work toward the goals of more than one developmental theme. For example, an intermediate grade class with students working individually on the development of specific skills (Improving Quality of Response) during the first part of a class, might then be followed by teacher-organized group activity where some social development (Accepting Responsibilities and Acting Cooperatively) can take place. In addition, the developmental themes are not designed in a hierarchical fashion

---

BOX 3–1   It's Your Turn to Plan

What age or level are your students? _____

In Figure 3–2 the authors presented the six developmental themes in order of relative appropriateness for younger children to older children. As you plan, it will be helpful if you make a chart to ensure that you provide a balanced program that gives adequate time to reach the goals of the developmental themes. Which developmental theme(s) should be emphasized (given the most instructional time) for your students? How much of the available instructional time will you plan to allocate to each developmental theme? When you complete the form in this box, you will have a basic plan for using the available time for physical education for your students.

Theme	Rank Order of Importance	% of Time Allocated
1. Becoming Aware		
2. Becoming Independent		
3. Accepting and Expressing Feelings and Ideas		
4. Accepting Responsibilities and Acting Cooperatively		
5. Improving Quality of Response		
6. Drawing Relationships		

where one must be mastered before going on to the next; rather, development can and should take place in all six themes at any age level. Only the relative emphasis and level of complexity of the thematic content will change.

THE THEMES IN DIFFERENT INSTRUCTIONAL ARRANGEMENTS

There are many patterns of organizing for instruction in elementary education today. Each pattern has its own advantages and each requires different utilization of the developmental themes. This discussion addresses itself to providing some answers to the question of who should teach physical education in the elementary school.

Classroom Teachers

Classroom teachers in elementary schools are responsible for teaching a variety of subjects. In most school systems today, classroom teachers still have responsibility for teaching all subjects, even when some assistance is provided by special teachers or consultants. Other instructional arrangements, such as team teaching, individually guided instruction, and open classrooms, have reduced the scope or range of planning that is necessary for each teacher.

One organizational arrangement for instruction is the self-contained classroom. Here, a single classroom teacher interacts each day with a relatively permanent group of children for the entire school year. Proponents of this arrangement state that the teacher has greater opportunity to know and understand the children. Also, the teacher is not required to observe fixed time schedules (typical of working with other teachers) and therefore can interrelate curriculum areas.

Opponents of the self-contained classroom, on the other hand, contend that no single teacher today can be competent in all subjects. They also argue that it might be better for a child to interact with more than one teacher each day. If you teach in a self-contained classroom, you will find that the developmental themes described in the following chapters can be incorporated into your program. You already are in an excellent position for providing interrelated learning experiences and the developmental themes might be most useful in providing a variety of concrete examples of lessons that cross the lines of subject matter.

If you are a classroom teacher in a team teaching or open classroom arrangement, there will still be ample opportunity for integrating learning experiences in all areas of the curriculum. In these arrangements, planning and teaching for the total group of students is a shared responsibility. Opportunities for regrouping students based on ability or interest and for teachers to have fewer subjects to plan are advantages of team situations. In a team situation, many opportunities for integrating learning exist. The developmental theme approach can be implemented in any of these teaching arrangements and is a particularly useful approach for classroom teachers.

Physical Education Specialists

When the assumption is made that subject matter expertise necessary for successful teaching in any area of the curriculum is beyond that usually found in most teachers, special assistance is provided. This assumption has been made in physical education, especially at the intermediate grade level. The use of elementary school physical education specialists has grown dramatically since the late 1950s and early 1960s. A variety of arrangements exist for providing assistance to classroom teachers in teaching physical education. Some school districts provide consultants, or resource teachers, who teach "demonstration" lessons, assist teachers in planning lessons, and help to initiate evaluation procedures. Other districts provide specialists who teach regularly scheduled physical education classes. In many instances, the specialist will teach the class two or three times per week and the classroom teacher will teach the class the remaining days. This instructional pattern has been used more frequently in the intermediate grades than in the primary grades but is becoming common at all grade levels. Some school districts provide specialists for teaching a daily physical education period for every child.

Unlike classroom teachers, the physical education specialist who shares the responsibility for the physical education program usually finds it difficult to relate these experiences to the rest of the school curriculum. The developmental themes described in the following chapters should help you deal with this problem.

Shared Teaching Responsibility

Classroom teachers and physical education specialists have many common teaching competencies as well as unique strengths. Working together, they can unify the learning experiences for children and accelerate learning far beyond that which can be accomplished separately. The developmental themes will assist classroom teachers and physical education specialists in communicating to each other what they are attempting to accomplish with their children.

No single way to organize for instruction is clearly better than any other. The developmental themes provide practical lessons to be used in a variety of instructional arrangements. Regardless of the instructional arrangement you choose to use the themes, it is the authors' belief that the physical education period will become an integral part of the elementary school curriculum, reinforcing other learning experiences and being supported by other curricular activities. This is the essence of the developmental theme approach.

TWO

chapter four

Becoming Aware

ABOUT CHILDREN

Teachers of young children recognize the potential of play in helping children learn. Moving in order to learn about things other than movement might properly be classified as something other than physical education. While the authors encourage the use of movement, play, or active games as a means for reaching other academic objectives, they equally encourage reading, computing, experimenting, and other instructional modes for attaining physical education objectives. Indeed, the developmental theme approach encourages the crossing of traditional subject matter lines.

Halverson has discussed learning to move and learning through movement and she suggested that, in practice, the two cannot be separated. She stated that "Emphasis on one need not exclude the other, but inadvertently, we could neglect, ignore, or completely forget one or the other in our work."[1] In this developmental theme, learning to move is the central thrust, and therefore contains the necessary information for helping children develop basic movement capabilities. The basic movements presented in this chapter are utilized in the subsequent chapters. In Chapter Eight, Improving Quality of Response, emphasis is placed on further developing these basic movements as game, sport, and other movement skills.

Motor Development

Motor development is a continuous process, beginning before birth and continuing through childhood into maturity. As a teacher, you need to be knowledgeable of the continuous nature of motor development in order to interpret your observations of children's movements. Being able to recognize certain developmental stages in throwing, for example, will assist you in providing an environment that is conducive to improving throwing performance. Halverson stated, "Study in motor development, as I see it, is the study of 1) the characteristics of behavior, 2) how these characteristics may change over time as a result of maturation and experience, and 3) how these characteristics may change under differing environmental situations."[2]

Much is known about the sequence of motor development in children. As early as the 1930s many studies described how, and approximately at what age, children could perform a variety of motor tasks. More recently, analysis of cinematographic studies have been helpful in describing what Halverson[3] called "process statements" of motor development. Process statements refer to the way in which a child accomplishes a movement task as opposed to simply viewing the results of a child's movement, or product statements. For example, noting that a child threw a ball twenty feet is a product statement. By itself, that statement tells you little about the developmental level of the child's throwing ability. A process statement, on the other hand, would describe the way in which the child threw the ball. The description of the form (an overhand throw, stepping forward with the foot on the same side of the body as the throwing arm) when compared to the sequence of throwing development would tell you more about the child's throwing development than just the product statement.

Wickstrom discussed the vast amount of literature describing motor development in young children. He stated, "The principles based upon the accumulated evidence indicate that the sequence of development is predictable and approximately the same for all children, but the rate at which specific changes take place varies from one child to another."[4] A working knowledge of developmental sequences will assist you in planning and conducting experiences for each of your students.

Body Awareness

The body movements of infants and very young children have been the subject of study by psychologists, child development specialists, and educators. The developmental sequence of infants' movements from birth through walking have been considered, along with other physical developments (such as eruption of teeth and ossification of bones), as indices of intelligence and maturation. More recently, these early movements have been studied by those concerned with a variety of interests in children who might be characterized as "slowly developing."[5] This concern with the early stages of child development has led to significant changes in the educational experiences provided for children. It has focused attention on the idea that moving and thinking are not mutually exclusive. Motor activities are now commonly used to enhance the perceptual abilities of children, and perceptual activities are used to assist in developing physical abilities. The emphasis on the "wholeness" of the child is exemplified by the concept of body awareness.

In discussing body awareness, Williams stated that ". . . it refers to the awareness, identification, and/or evaluation of the proportions, dimensions, positions, and movements of the individual's body and/or body parts."[6] Cratty presented a broader interpretation of the term "body-image," and he defined the term as: "the components of the self-concept having to do with physical performance and appearance, aspiration level as well as the children's perceptions of games they like to play."[7] What children choose to do is, in part, a function of how they view themselves, and how they view themselves is a result of what they have already accomplished.

Williams stated that it is only after the child comes to know his body that he can ultimately know his external space world. Table 4–1 is based on her work and describes the development of body awareness.[8] This development occurs in three segments (as shown in Table 4–1): the Sensory-Motor Component, the Conceptual Component, and the Feeling Component. Development is sequential within each component, but the components are relatively interdependent. There are many factors beyond the teacher's control that affect motor development of children. Teachers have no control over maturation rates, nutritional status, family conditions, and the quantity and quality of previous experiences. There is still much to be discovered about the development of body awareness. This is especially true in the Feeling Component. There is some evidence that the Feeling Component develops early and may persist even when real changes in performance occur.[9] The need for feedback when performance improves is suggested.

The following developmental sequences have been reduced to basic descriptions. Included in the discussion of developmental sequences are principles to follow for improving the motor development of children.

TABLE 4–1 Three Components of Body Awareness

Sensory-Motor Component

Activity of the body results in sensory feedback. Infant begins to know what is and what isn't part of his body.

Conscious reflection of the body results in more purposeful movement.

More reflective but nonverbal period leads to imitation of objects in his environment. Aware of body and spatial possibilities.

Early sensory-motor activity results in laterality and sensory dominance.

Behavioral Indicators

Sensory-motor feedback is important throughout life but particularly from 0–5 years.

Laterality—conscious, internal awareness of the two sides of the body. Child may not know names, right and left, but knows that each side occupies different position in space.

Sensory Dominance—preferential use of eyes, hands, feet.

Handedness—*preference* usually by age 4.
Ambivalence from age 5–8.
Dominance around 9 or 10.
Eyedness—age 5–9 ambivalent; 9–11 greater preference.

Footedness—preference usually by age 5. No ambivalent period.

Conceptual Component

Development of speech helps the child conceptualize. He can internalize the phenomena of body awareness.
Conceptual development is characterized by:

1. verbal identification of body-parts and their functions
2. spontaneous right/left discrimination of body dimensions
3. directionality.

Behavioral Indicators

Identification of body parts is facilitated by practice. By age 5 or 6 most children can identify major body-parts—failures infrequent after 8 or 9.

Right/left discrimination also concerned with top/bottom, front/back. Majority can discriminate by age 5½ or 6, and most by 8 or 9. Child usually masters top/bottom, front/back, and right/left, in that order.

Directionality—ability to identify spontaneously dimensions of external space. Usually not complete until around 9. Dependent upon conceptualization of spatial dimensions of own body.

Feeling Component

As body awareness develops, the child develops feelings about dimensions, appearance, and performance characteristics.

This is the beginning of the complex self-concept that is important in personality development.

Behavioral Indicators

As a result of many positive experiences, children express their feelings through their physical activity selection.

Walking, Running, and Leaping

Walking, running, and leaping are locomotor movements (moving from one place to another) that develop sequentially. Since children enter the formal education system already "knowing how" to walk and run, little attention is usually given to developing these basic motor patterns. Running, because it is used in many games and sports and is an "event" in the sport of track, receives instructional time in the physical education curriculum. This time is used most often for improving running performance in terms of speed and distance rather than for focusing on improving the basic pattern. Leaping is not observed as often as walking and running in the usual locomotor behavior of children. The leap is usually performed in response to specific situations or stimuli.

Walking   By the time children enter nursery school or kindergarten, they exhibit confidence in walking. In the mature walking pattern, one foot moves ahead of the other in the direction of the walk. The weight of the body shifts from one foot to the other. At one point in the walk, both feet are in contact with the ground; there is no point at which both feet leave the ground at the

FIGURE 4–1 Mature walking pattern

same time. The lead foot accepts the weight on the heel while the trailing foot pushes away with the toes. A walk may be done in any direction, forward, backward, or sideways. In the forward walk, there is a slight forward body lean, the head is held erect, and the arms move in opposition to the legs. The feet are usually pointed straight ahead.

The early walking pattern is characterized by a high degree of instability. A toddler carries his arms and hands high to help maintain balance, and the arms do not move in opposition to the legs. The stride is short and the sole of the foot makes contact with the floor with each step.

A young child demonstrates a more mature walking pattern. The foot now strikes the floor with the heel, the lead leg bends at the knee, and the arms are held more naturally at the sides in a relaxed position. Further development in walking reveals that the arms move in opposition to the legs and bend more at the elbow. As the situation demands, the walking form is modified. For example, a fast walk will cause the length of the stride to increase and the arm movement will be more forceful.

Running   Even before children's mature walking pattern develops, running begins. In running, as in walking, there is a shift of weight from one leg to the other in the direction of the run. Running can be performed forwards, backwards, or sideways. The basic difference in running and walking is that in running there is a period of nonsupport in which both feet are momentarily off the ground. The nonsupport phase ends when the leading foot takes the body weight as the ball, or forward portion of the foot, contacts the ground under the runner's body. In most cases, the weight should be taken on the ball of the foot. However, in slow running (jogging) the weight may be taken on the heel as in walking. Even in jogging, there is still a period of nonsupport of the body weight.

As children increase in age and have opportunities to run, their running patterns mature. Figure 4–2 shows the forward body lean, arm swing in opposition to the legs, a high knee lift in the leading leg, the period of nonsupport, and reestablishment of contact with the supporting surface on the ball of the foot. What would happen to the running form shown in Figure 4–2 if the runner were asked to decrease the speed of the run? What would you expect if the speed was increased? It is probable that the slower run would look like a less mature form of running.

Teachers can help children improve in running by encouraging children to:

- hold their head erect while running
- point their feet straight ahead
- land on the ball of their feet in moderate and fast running
- move their arms in opposition to their legs and more in a forward direction and less across the body
- increase their knee lift as speed increases.

FIGURE 4–2 Mature running pattern

Children need many opportunities to run. Running forward and in a straight direction precedes running backward, sideways, and in zig-zag patterns. As children gain confidence in running, they will be able to accept the challenges of running in relationship to other children and equipment, and to keep their bodies under control while changing the speed and direction of the run.

Leaping   The leap is an elongated running step. As the running step increases in height and distance, the period of nonsupport increases. Chil-

FIGURE 4–3 A leap has a long period of nonsupport

dren leap naturally when running over some obstacles or when trying to get to a selected spot, such as a base, with one less step.

Continuous running, interspersed with single leaps, provides a long period of nonsupport which permits children to move other body parts and to make shapes during the leap.

Jumping and Hopping

Jumping and hopping are closely related motor patterns. Like the run and leap, each of these motor patterns has a period of nonsupport of the body weight. Jumping normally precedes hopping, but children will usually demonstrate immature forms of both before the mature pattern of either is developed. As with other motor patterns, maturation alone does not lead to the development of mature forms of jumping and hopping. As children increase in strength, increased performance, in terms of height or distance of jumps and hops, may be observed, but there may be no improvement in the form of the motor patterns.

Jumping   A jump is a locomotor movement in which the body is projected up and/or in any direction from one or both feet followed by a landing on both feet. In jumping, the projection of the body into the period of nonsupport is much more vigorous than in running. There are special requirements for some jumps when used in sports, games, or when a jump is used as a measure of motor performance. For example, in the sport of track and field, the high jump requires the performer to take off from one foot, while in rope jumping a two-foot take-off is often seen.

Experiences which stimulate children to jump higher and/or farther, combined with maturation, will lead to the development of mature jumping form.

Two forms of jumping are shown in Figure 4–4. These jumps may be stimulated by the need to reach some high object or to get over obstacles. Evidence of a more mature jumping pattern is characterized by an increase in the preliminary crouch, increased arm extension, first away from and then in the direction of the jump, and greater body extension at take-off. All landings from jumps should be "soft." Bending, or "giving" with the force of the landing, should take place in the ankles, knees, and hips in order to land softly. Children with a less well-developed jumping pattern usually take off from one foot even when asked to jump using a two-foot take-off.

Hopping   A hop is a movement pattern in which the body is projected into a period of nonsupport from one foot, followed by a landing on the same foot. Hopping on the preferred foot will precede hopping on the nonpreferred foot. A hop may be done in any direction and can emphasize height or distance. The leg which is not used in the hop is usually bent at the knee. In order to hop more vigorously the performer will increase the initial crouch, arm swing, and body lean, and extension at the point of the take-off. Hopping in more

High

Far

FIGURE 4–4 Two basic forms of jumping

controlled situations, requiring accuracy and control, usually will result in the arms being used more for balance than to create momentum.

Skipping, Sliding, and Galloping

Skipping, sliding, and galloping are locomotor movement patterns that are more complex and develop later than those discussed up to this point. The walk, run, leap, jump, and hop are rhythmically "even" movements. The skip, slide, and gallop are rhythmically uneven movements. They are combinations of two other basic movements, and they are rhythmically uneven because a different length of time is used in each of the two parts of the pattern.

FIGURE 4–5 Skipping

Skipping   Skipping is a walking step followed by a hop on the same foot. The rhythmic pattern of more time used in the hop than the step characterizes mature skipping form. Figure 4–5 illustrates skipping.

Some children will be able to do a step-hop, but not in the rhythmical pattern for it to qualify as a skip. Others will be able to skip, but only on the preferred foot. The mature skipping pattern is a continuous sequence of a skip on one foot followed by a skip on the other foot. In Figure 4–5 a skip on the left foot is completed and one on the right foot is beginning. Preschool and primary grade children exhibit wide variances in skipping ability and need many experiences before becoming proficient. Another frequently observed pattern in the development of the mature skipping pattern is a skip on the preferred foot, running on the nonpreferred foot, and then a skip on the preferred foot again.

Skipping is viewed as a happy and free movement. As children gain confidence, they are able to increase speed and height in their skipping. However, when challenged beyond their ability, the skipping pattern is likely to deteriorate into a less mature pattern of skipping involving more running and less hopping.

Sliding   A slide is a two-part, uneven rhythmical movement that combines a walking step and a running step performed in a lateral or sideways direction. More time is spent on the second part of the movement, the run, than on the walking step in the first part. In the slide, the same foot always leads the movement. The extended period of nonsupport in the run part of the slide, which follows the quick walking step, gives the slide its characteristic rhythm.

Galloping   A gallop is a slide performed in either a forward or backward direction. Galloping is frequently observed in preschool children not long after running has developed. Usually a child will gallop with the preferred foot leading before galloping with the nonpreferred foot in the lead. Children who have not developed hopping will have difficulty in skipping, and their attempts will often result in galloping.

Throwing

Throwing is a movement pattern of the arm and hand used to propel an object through space. There are variations of the throwing pattern, such as underhand and sidearm, and special throws such as the two-hand chest pass in basketball. The most common throw, however, is the one-arm overarm throw, and, in our society, may be considered one of the most important motor patterns related to sports and games.

The development of accuracy, distance, and velocity in throwing has been studied with children and adults, using a variety of ball types and sizes. Variations in experimental methods and variables make specific performances difficult to compare. Generally, throwing improves in terms of both accuracy and distance from year to year or grade to grade throughout the

FIGURE 4–6 First-stage throwing

preschool and elementary school years. While the development of throwing performance and form are often parallel, the developmental pattern of throwing form has been the object of relatively few studies.

Wild[10] used film analysis to identify four stages of development in the throwing of children aged two through seven. Her stages of development are useful as criteria for measuring the maturity of throwing patterns in children. She indicated that after age six, learning rather than maturation greatly influenced the throwing pattern of children.[11]

Figure 4–6 shows the first stage of throwing development. This pattern is usually observed in children two to three years of age. This form does not permit the child to generate a great amount of force. The feet remain stationary and the arm has limited range. This pattern favors accuracy rather than speed and is observed in adults throwing darts.

The second stage of throwing, as reported by Wild, permits greater force. The throwing hand is brought further back and there is some backward-forward rotation of the trunk. This pattern is observed in many preschool children.

Figure 4–7 presents the third throwing stage. This stage includes a step forward on the foot on the same side as the throwing arm as the throw is made. This permits greater force to be imparted to the object thrown. Many children, and even some adults, exhibit stage three throwing form. This pattern might be expected when the throwing task does not require a very forceful throw. However, when the throw requires maximum effort, and stage three form is consistently shown, you may conclude that the thrower has not developed the mature throwing pattern.

The mature, or fourth stage, is illustrated in Figure 4–8. The rotation of the trunk is greater as the throwing arm is brought back, and the step forward is on the foot opposite the throwing arm. This mature pattern can be observed

FIGURE 4–7 Third-stage throwing

FIGURE 4–8 Mature, or fourth-stage, throwing

in many primary grade children and some younger children who seem to have had much practice.

While development of the mature throwing pattern emerges in many children "naturally," its course of development is frequently delayed in others. Practice and instruction can assist this development. To stimulate throwing development it is important to know that:

1. Large balls require two-handed throws by young children
2. Small balls that can be securely held in one hand facilitate overarm throwing
3. The appropriate ball size for throwing may be different from the appropriate ball size for catching.

Throwing form is often a function of the task. Greater effort in terms of speed or distance usually stimulates more mature form. It should be noted, however, that under the stress of attempting to perform at a maximum level, regression in form may occur.

Catching

The basic motor pattern of catching is concerned with the use of the hands to bring a moving object under control. Since catching is dependent upon visual tracking, most children will develop proficient throwing patterns earlier than mature catching patterns.

Catching a rolling ball is usually the first pattern mastered by young children. Often, the catch is actually a trap of the ball between the child's hand(s) and the floor. This is as one would expect, since a rolling ball is traveling only in one plane, which makes it easier to track. Most children show improvement in catching throughout the preschool and elementary school years.

FIGURE 4–9 Young catching pattern

Figure 4–9 shows a preschool child catching a large ball. The hands contact the ball just before, or at the same time, the ball is trapped against the body. For this level of catching, a large ball is appropriate.

When children have not had much catching experience, or when they are afraid of being hit by the ball, they will often turn their heads away from the ball when trying to catch it. This is especially true when a small or hard ball is used, or when the ball is thrown too fast (see Figure 4–10).

A mature catching pattern is shown in Figure 4–11. The arms are extended to meet the ball. At contact with the fingers, the arms "give" to absorb the force of the throw. What might happen if the arms were kept extended?

Most teachers recognize that a fast-moving ball is difficult to catch. A ball moving too slowly is also difficult to catch. Balls should be thrown at a

FIGURE 4–10 Young catching pattern

FIGURE 4–11 Mature catching pattern

moderate speed so that they travel in a fairly straight trajectory. Other points to remember when teaching catching are:

- In the early stages of development it is easier to move to either side than to move forward or backward
- Effective catching requires that the fingers contact the ball rather than the palms
- Using large balls for too long with young children hinders development of catching.

Many of the activities presented in physical education textbooks have been suggested for developing throwing and catching simultaneously. Due to the different developmental patterns of throwing and catching, such activities are frustrating to children and tend to be counterproductive. It is suggested that while an activity may require throwing and catching, only one pattern or the other should be clearly emphasized.

BOX 4–1   How Would You Make a Ball?

If you were manufacturing a ball for catching experiences for young children, what properties would it have? How would you "introduce" the ball to the children so that they could learn about its characteristics? Remember, while a small ball would be appropriate for overarm throwing, a large ball should be used for initial catching experiences. Children should have a chance to handle and feel a ball *before* it is thrown to them. A soft ball will give them the courage to attempt a catch of a ball tossed to them.

Kicking

Kicking develops slower in American children than other motor patterns because it is not used as much in the play and games in our culture. Kicking is a basic striking pattern that uses the foot to impart force to an object, usually some kind of ball. There are two basic kicks: the punt, where a ball is kicked after being dropped from the hands and before it hits the ground, and the place kick, where the ball is resting on or moving along the ground when kicked.

Children are ready to kick when they can balance on one foot. Mature kicking has been observed in some preschool children.

Kicking progresses from the immature form, where little force can be generated, to the mature form, where great force can be imparted. In Figure 4–12, the kicking leg is relatively straight, the arms are not used in opposition to the leg, and the rest of the body does not seem to be used at all. This pattern of movement is ineffective in generating force.

A mature kicking pattern is shown in Figure 4–13. In this pattern, the leg is brought backward and bent at the knee in preparation for the kick. The other features, which allow great force to be generated, are that the body leans backward, the arms are used for balance, and there is a continuation of the movement after contact is made.

Children should learn how to kick with the instep rather than with the toes so as to prevent injury to the toe and to provide a larger kicking surface for better control in kicking. A relatively soft ball is appropriate for early kicking experiences. While playing many kicking games, children walk or run to a stationary or moving ball in order to produce greater kicking force. The placement alongside the ball of the support, or nonkicking, leg is important in order to produce a good place kick. When the ball is moving, this placement is more difficult to accomplish with precision.

FIGURE 4–12 Early kicking pattern

FIGURE 4–13 Mature kicking pattern

FIGURE 4–14 Effective punting form

A common error in punting a ball is throwing it up, rather than dropping it, out in front. Figure 4–14 shows an effective punting form. As in place kicking, the maximum force is generated by bending the knee in preparation for the kick, leaning slightly backward, and using the arms in opposition to the legs.

As in most motor patterns, the mature form may not always be used to accomplish a motor task. For a kick where maximum force is not required, a less mature pattern may be used even when the performer has developed a mature pattern. Children need many opportunities to develop mature kicking patterns and to learn to vary their kicking pattern in response to a specific situation.

Striking

Striking is a motor pattern used to impart force to an object with either a body part or an implement. Children can show improvement in striking throughout the preschool and elementary years provided that they have many opportunities for practice. Often even good form will not produce a successful result because the child still must make many perceptual judgments in order to contact the object, especially if the object is moving.

The striking pattern is developed into specific skills in such activities as baseball, tennis, badminton, and golf. Each skill has its own specific techniques and each requires different equipment. However, the fundamental striking pattern develops in a uniform manner.

The first striking pattern observed in children is similar to the one-arm overhand throw. In Figure 4–15, the child is facing the object to be struck and is holding the implement in one hand. This permits the child to see the object easily and does not require difficult body rotation.

FIGURE 4–15 Early striking pattern—similar to throwing

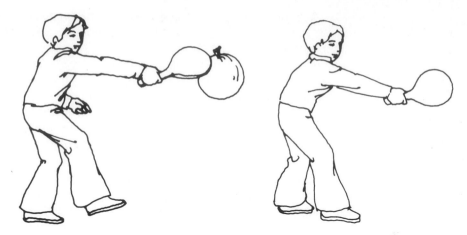

FIGURE 4–16 Side-arm striking

A two-handed vertical striking pattern will follow the one-handed pattern shown in Figure 4–15. This pattern is stimulated by an implement which requires the child to use both hands in order to control it and to impart greater force. The pattern of facing the object to be struck is even observed in adults who have not had extensive striking experiences. There is a natural progression of striking observed in children from the overhand to the sidearm pattern. This progression can be stimulated by use of manageable equipment in terms of length and weight, and by control of the object to be struck. For example, striking with the hands, then with lightweight, short paddles, should precede striking with long rackets or bats. To aid this development, large and/or lightweight balls can be suspended by a cord or placed on a cone prior to being thrown or pitched to children.

Figure 4–16 presents a sidearm striking pattern. This pattern is seen with children using paddles or rackets that are held in one hand. This pattern permits greater force to be generated by allowing for body rotation and a shift in body weight from the back foot to the forward foot at the time the object is contacted. Specific striking skills will have techniques designed to use the characteristics of the equipment to the best advantage and for the purpose of the game.

Maturation and Experience

The previous section described the developmental sequence of basic motor patterns. Knowing these characteristics will assist you in evaluating the motor development of children. For example, Wickstrom[12] discusses a four-year-old child and a fifteen-year-old high school student who were using the same throwing patterns. The pattern of stepping forward with the leg on the same side of the body as the throwing arm is recognized as an immature form of throwing. For the four-year-old, this pattern would not be viewed as atypical, but for the fifteen-year-old, it would represent a definite deficiency in motor development.

Whether or not motor development is uniquely determined by maturation or experience is not clear. Most of the developmental studies describe what appears "naturally," and not what could be expected with different experiences. The concept of critical learning periods (the idea that there is an optimal time for a child to learn a specific skill) has tended to influence teachers to delay teaching until some motor pattern appears spontaneously. It is suggested that children are capable of using motor patterns long before they are asked to try them, and that skill development is started too late more often than too early. Assume that the fifteen-year-old student, previously described as exhibiting an immature throwing pattern, was a normally developing person. It would be generally accepted today, that if this student had had more experience in throwing at a younger age, he would have developed the mature pattern. Skillful teaching provides developmentally appropriate experiences that will facilitate the motor development of children. The recognition that children mature at different rates and that children bring diverse experiences with them requires teaching methods that are sensitive to these facts.

ABOUT TEACHING

Learning In Figure 4–17,[13] did Tiger succeed as a teacher? He stated that he taught Stripe how to whistle, but Stripe just didn't learn. What is learning? What can teachers do to facilitate student learning? Learning has been defined as:

> Relatively permanent changes in behavior that cannot be accounted for by maturation, injury, or psychological alterations of the organism, but which result from experience. . . .[14]

> . . . learning occurs only when there is a new experience—a stimulus, a challenge, or a problem, leading to change in the individual's perception of himself or the world . . . and a change in one's perceptions is a change in meaning.[15]

Learning is, at the least, a change in behavior. An observable change in performance level, either qualitatively or quantitatively, provides evidence that learning has occurred.

Watson provided information about learning that can be applied to teaching physical education. Children are likely to learn when the following conditions are present:

> Behaviors which are rewarded (reinforced) are more likely to recur.

> Reward (reinforcement), to be most effective in learning, must follow almost immediately after the desired behavior and be clearly connected with that behavior in the mind of the learner.

> Threat and punishment have variable and uncertain effects upon learning; they may make the punished response more likely or

FIGURE 4–17 What is learning? © *King Features Syndicate, Inc., 1974*

less likely to recur; they may set up avoidance tendencies which prevent further learning.

Readiness for any learning is a complex product of interaction among such factors as a) sufficient physiological and psychological maturity, b) sense of the importance of the new learning for the learner in his world, c) mastery of prerequisites providing a fair chance of success, and d) freedom from discouragement (expectation of failure) or threat (sense of danger).

The type of reward (reinforcement) which has the greatest transfer value of other life situations is the kind one gives oneself—the sense of satisfaction in achieving purposes.

The most effective effort is put forth by children when they attempt tasks which fall in the "range of challenge"—not too easy and not too hard—where success seems quite possible but not certain.

Children are more apt to throw themselves wholeheartedly into any project if they themselves have participated in the selection and planning of the enterprise.

Pupils think when they encounter an obstacle, difficulty, puzzle, or challenge in a course of action that interests them. The process of thinking involves designing and testing plausible solutions for the problem as understood by the thinker.

What is learned is most likely to be available for use if it is learned in a situation much like that in which it is to be used and if it is immediately preceding the time when it is needed. Learning in childhood, then forgetting, and then relearning when need arises is not an efficient procedure.

No two people make the same response to any school situation. Differences of heredity, physical maturity, intelligence, motor skills, health; experiences with parents, siblings, playmates; consequent attitudes, motives, drives, tastes, fears; all these and more enter into production of each individual's unique reaction. People vary in their minds and personalities as much as they vary in their appearance.

Children are less likely to learn when:

> Reaction to excessive direction by the teacher is likely to be a) apathetic conformity, b) defiance, c) scapegoating, or d) escape from the whole affair.

> Many pupils experience so much criticism, failure, and discouragement in school that their self-confidence, level of aspiration, and sense of worth are damaged.

> When children (or adults) experience too much frustration, their behavior ceases to be integrated, purposeful, and rational.[16]

These points provide information that teachers should know and apply to the development of lessons and teaching modules. Further study of the psychology of learning will be needed before a teacher can understand fully the teaching-learning process.

Teaching Methods

According to Cohen, children should not only be helped to acquire skills, but also (and more importantly) they should be helped to acquire the wisdom to use those skills with understanding and with humane intentions. Therefore, acquiring subject matter is not enough. The goal of learning,

> then, is to produce human, or humane, beings, whole beings, not automatons, or intellects, but thinking, feeling, living—or acting—persons, persons who can love, feel deeply, expand their inner selves, create, and continue the process of self-education.[17]

Mosston calls this person the *independent person.* The independent person has ". . . the ability to make choices among convictions . . . the courage to be different and to accept the difference . . . the ability to interact with others so that they, too, remain independent."[18] To achieve this goal, teachers will have to do more than present subject matter and arrange the learning environment. Mosston is firmly convinced that teaching methods are the link between subject matter and learning.[19] The teacher's behavior (consciously directed actions), such as knowing when to tell an answer and when not to; when to decide for students and when to let them find out for themselves; and when to develop common abilities and when to facilitate individuality and creativity, is a crucial element in the development of the independent person.

How *can* different methods of teaching be categorized? What are the salient features which allow discrimination among ways of teaching? Mosston stated that two factors can be used, the degree to which instruction is individualized, and the degree to which the learner is cognitively involved.[20]

The concept of individualization of instruction is a familiar idea in education. The concept of cognitive involvement of the learner is less well known. Cognitive involvement can be as low as cognitive passivity (following simple directions, rote memorization, or the recall of unrelated facts). On the other hand, problem solving and inquiry with the intent to discover or verify information is an example of higher order cognitive involvement. The learner must think in order to make judgments, comparisons, and associations required in the testing of an idea. These intellectual operations are stimulated by a need to find a solution once the learner becomes interested in or curious about the task. This need to find an answer is called cognitive dissonance. Cognitive dissonance is intellectual disharmony that calls for some action on the part of the learner. The dissonance is produced by the individual's need to discover a solution to a problem that has personal meaning to the learner.[21]

What is the difference in the teaching methods that result in only low level cognitive involvement as compared to higher level cognitive involvement? When students acquire information, they mainly are concerned with content. *Content* teaching methods are based on the premise that telling equals teaching. Content teaching involves an agent (parent, teacher, coach, machine) who gives information and solutions to the student. The goal is for the student to be able to retain and retrieve on cue, these data. The cue may be a direct question, command, or problem requiring that the memorized content be used to arrive at a standard solution. The student and teacher are evaluated on how well and how often the learner is able to perform these functions. The steps in the *content method* of teaching are as follows:

• Information output by the agent from the storehouse of knowledge	• The learner receives the information	• The learner is asked or told to recall the information	• The agent rewards the output of the desired information	• The learner feels good because the information given pleased someone else and resulted in an external reward.[22]

BOX 4–2 Riddles

Riddles are very popular with children. Have you ever wondered why? What is the appeal of a riddle?

A riddle: What part of your body is like a tropical island?*

A riddle is a question. If the question is interesting to you, you begin to wonder about it and feel that you have to find the answer. This tension to find the answer is evidence of cognitive dissonance. To resolve this dissonance you actively seek the solution to the question.

*The answer: Your hand because it has a palm.

If teaching is *solely* directed to content learning, the risk is increased that the educational experience:

Does not prepare a child to be "free," that is, to cope effectively, resourcefully, and flexibly with the demands of his changing world

. . . Dampens the child's intrinsic interest in learning and coping, and substitutes external motivation and control of his behavior with the results that:

    a. There is a high degree of boredom with the formal educational process

    b. There is a high degree of risk that problems and "subjects" selected for study, and the work materials chosen, will not be relevant to the students

. . . Fosters a tendency to avoid uncertainty and ambiguity and concomitantly to view the world as fixed

. . . Leads to a dependency relationship between training agent and trainee: where the child or student comes to perceive the parent or teacher as omnipotent

. . . Fails to develop an internal sense of causation in the child (I am master of my own destiny).[23]

What can be done to avoid these problems? What methods of teaching can be used that will increase the chances that a student will explore the environment, inquire and discover solutions to relevant problems, be flexible and adaptive in responding to changing conditions, and be capable of making value judgments? The alternative is to incorporate *process learning* into one's pattern of teaching. Process learning is teaching students how to think . . . how to seek and process information.[24] The focus of process learning is not only on how much new information is learned but also on how the information is used in either conventional or innovative responses to problems. Innovative or creative responses can occur in any situation that has answers previously unknown to the learner. The process styles of teaching produce cognitive dissonance, invoking inquiry behavior on the part of the student. In process style teaching, learning proceeds in steps as follows:

• A problem either self-identified or presented by another exists	• A degree of cognitive dissonance is felt by the learner	• The learner initiates a process of inquiry	• Action to discover one or more solutions to the problem is undertaken	• A workable solution is discovered	• Cognitive dissonance is resolved and the learner feels satisfied[25]

Through continued use of process oriented teaching, several benefits other than content learning can occur. These benefits, according to Schroder, Karlins, and Phares are the development of:

1. Intrinsic motivation for learning—when learning is guided by internal (intrinsic) rewards rather than external (extrinsic) rewards, the process of information seeking and problem solving becomes joyful and self-fulfilling

2. Adaptability and innovativeness—thinking creatively, diversely, and critically can generate both numerous and efficient solutions to problems which enable the individual to better control, rather than be controlled by, the environment

3. A self-considered value system—when values are arrived at by self-determination, from a personal and relatively free perspective, they are held with greater esteem and are easier to modify when new relevant information is processed.[26]

When the aspects of learning theories useful in teaching (see page 58) are reviewed, comparing the content style of teaching to the process style of teaching, some new insights can be drawn. Some of the points presented in the list *cannot* be followed by the content style of teaching. For example, "Pupils think when they encounter an obstacle, difficulty, puzzle, or challenge in a course of action that interests them. The process of thinking involves designing and testing plausible solutions for the problem as understood by the thinker."[27] This cannot occur in content teaching when the learner is told what to do, when to do it, how many times to do it, and when to stop. Using the process style of teaching, certain points in the list can be avoided, such as "Reaction to excessive direction by the teacher is likely to be a) apathetic conformity, b) defiance, c) scapegoating, or d) escape from the whole affair."[28]

The specific *know how* concerning methods of teaching will come later in this section. What is important at this point is that you are aware of the general advantages and disadvantages of content and process teaching methods.

Using Different Teaching Methods

A movement task is a statement that indicates to students what, how, where, and when to do something. As previously stated, the content and process approaches differ in terms of the opportunities students are given to be involved in the what, how, where, and when of learning. Teachers constantly must be making decisions as to which teaching method will facilitate the learning of different movement tasks. The degree of the student's cognitive involvement has profound impact on the contribution of a learning experience on his or her development.

Three specific ways of stating a movement task will be explained. (These ways are not the only methods that exist for stating a movement experience.) Each explanation will include:

a. an example consistent with this method of teaching
b. a description of the teacher and student roles
c. an analysis of the developmental contribution of the teaching style

    d. a note presenting additional information, and
    e. a reaction question.

Read each description and compare portions of one presentation of a teaching method to another. Try stating a movement task using the same content (such as jumping for distance or throwing a ball at a target) but using each of the three methods of stating a movement task. When you have completed this, you should be more aware of the differences among the styles of stating a movement task. Furthermore, you should feel more comfortable when beginning to implement different styles of stating a movement task to achieve the objectives of a lesson.

Stating a Movement Task: A Content Approach

Example: "Watch me jump." The teacher demonstrates the exact way the students are to jump. "When I say jump, jump the same way I did and jump as high as you can. Jump!" Teacher watches students jump and then repeats the command "Jump!"

Teacher-student roles:

The Teacher Decides	*The Students Decide*
What: vertical jump	whether or not to jump
How: as demonstrated	
Where: a specific movement area location	
When: the student will perform the movement task on command	

Developmental Contribution: The psychomotor contribution could vary from high, if the command "Jump" is repeated very quickly, to a moderately low contribution if the command is repeated slowly. In this example, the opportunities to jump are limited because the students are only allowed to jump

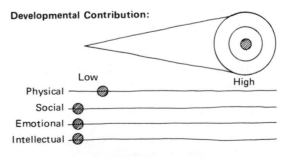

FIGURE 4–18

BOX 4–3   Teaching and Learning

Which of the following learning experiences do you think can make the greatest contribution to becoming aware?

Pre-experience learnings:

"Earlier today we talked about big things and little things. We learned how to decide what we could call big and what we could call little. To do that, we compared the two items. The next thing we did was to use this method to identify and label objects as big or little, and bigger or littler."

Movement Experience A	*Movement Experience B*
Can you move your arm in big circles? Hold your right arm straight out to your side. Now move your arm around in a big circular pathway. Make big circles.	Move your arm in the shape of a circle. Call your circle a little circle. Now, move the same body-part in a bigger circle shape. Each time you move your arm, make your circle bigger. How big can you make your circle?

Which of these two learning experiences did you identify as making the greatest contribution to the student's becoming aware of how the arm can be moved and the concept of big? Was it Experience *A* or Experience *B*? If you would like to, you can defer your response until the end of this section.

when told to do so. In addition, the frequency of the jump commands could be too fast for some students and too slow for others, or the height too high for some students and not high enough for developing skill or physical fitness for others.

The affective (feelings) contributions of the movement experience are almost nil. Social interaction is limited to listening. Emotional involvement is also limited. Furthermore, a potential negative influence exists because the student's autonomy is short-circuited as the student has not been involved in the how, where, and when of the movement task decisions.

Cognitive involvement consists of knowing what "high" means and being alert enough to move on command. What the student discovers about self and movement potential is drastically limited by the content approach to stating a movement task.

Note: This style of teaching was called the Command style by Mosston. The Command style of teaching is one of five content styles of teaching which Mosston analyzed.[29]

Questions: Why would you use the Command style of stating a movement task? What would you hope to achieve in regard to student development?

Stating a Movement Task: Two Process Approaches

Guided Discovery Example: "Today you will practice jumping. When I say go, find out how high you can jump, without bending your legs to push off for your jump. Remember to land softly. Go." Time is allowed for the students to jump several times. "This time find out how high you can jump when you bend your legs to jump." Allow several trials and then stop the students. "Could you jump higher when your legs were straight or bent?" Have students demonstrate or state their answer. Summarize this part of the experience by asking, "How far should you bend your legs to jump as high as you can? Should you bend your legs a little and jump? Who thinks they need to bend them all the way to jump as high as you can?" Encourage the students to try different jumping positions and then ask the following question: "Who can tell or show how much you should bend your legs to jump as high as you can?" Summarization and culminating jumping experience and remarks should be made before the lesson is ended.

Teacher-student roles:

	The Teacher Decides		*The Students Decide*
What:	vertical jump	How:	different angles of leg flexion, bend at the knees
How:	without bending the legs and bending the legs to different positions		
		Where:	in a movement space of their own choosing
Where:	a general movement area	When:	at their own pace
When:	students respond after instructions are given		

Developmental Contribution: Psychomotor contributions are controlled by the students working at their own pace. The amount of time for jumping is limited by the amount of time taken for discussions and the readiness of the student to jump frequently.

Cognitive and affective contributions are increased, as compared to the previous example, because the students are expected to think, feel, wonder, and discover. The students must share movement space and discussion time. The child's knowledge of movement potential and capability is increased. The child's knowledge of what actions cause her to be able to

Developmental Contribution:

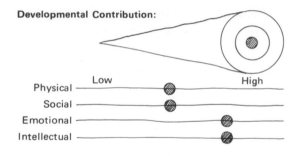

	Low		High
Physical			
Social			
Emotional			
Intellectual			

FIGURE 4–19

jump high makes it easier to transfer this concept to other movement situations and tasks. As a result, the student has begun to discover much about self and how to move.

Note: This process-style of teaching is called Guided Discovery by Mosston. The teacher guides the student by means of a series of discovery experiences. The teacher designs a learning sequence that progresses from the known to the unknown, and simple to complex responses. By never directly telling the answer to a movement task, the teacher guides the students to a movement problem solution. In the Guided Discovery style, if the student fails to succeed after making valid attempts, it is the teacher's responsibility to redesign the movement task sequence to assure achievement in later attempts by the student.[30]

Questions: Why would you use the Guided Discovery style of stating a movement task? What would you hope to achieve in regard to student development?

Problem Solving   Example: Starting from a stationary position, find at least three ways to get different body parts as far away from the ground as you can without using any body support.

Teacher-Student roles:

The Teacher Decides		*The Students Decide*	
What:	vertical jump	How:	to jump getting
How:	while varying body		different body parts
	positions		as far from the ground
Where:	within the defined		as possible
	movement area	Where:	in any space I want
When:	students respond	When:	as I think of or see
	after instructions are		new patterns to try
	given		

Developmental Contribution:

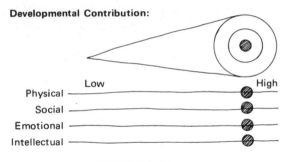

FIGURE 4–20

Developmental Contribution: Physical involvement might be initially de-layed. However, once movement activity is initiated, the action can be rapid and varied to test solutions to problems. Thus, the psychomotor contribution range is wide.

Affective development can occur as a result of independent or group action to solve a problem. Cooperation, self-reliance, concern, and self-confidence are a few of the specific characteristics that can be fostered.

Cognitive outcomes are numerous. The student can apply the steps of the critical-creative thinking process. Creative, impractical, and/or efficient responses can be thought out. By varying the task, the teacher can direct students to find the best way to get their feet or waist as far from the ground as possible.

With the process orientation of this style of stating a movement task, the developmental categories (psychomotor, affective, and cognitive) become only convenient labels. In reality, the unity of these attributes of the moving being become more closely interwoven and inseparable. The individual becomes free to pursue the solution of a problem at a level of difficulty and pace of his own choosing. Furthermore, the individual is free to find, express, and redefine himself as a moving being.

Note: This type of process oriented movement task is called Problem Solving by Mosston. The teacher becomes a facilitator as students explore alternatives and discover that usually more than one appropriate solution exists to a problem.[31] "Whereas in Guided Discovery, the dependency of the student's expected responses upon the teacher's clues is the essence of the style, in Problem Solving, the student is expected to seek out the answer or answers completely on his own."[32]

Question: Why would you use the Problem Solving style of stating a move-ment task? What would you achieve in regard to student development?

The *exclusive* use of the content approach to teaching should be avoided. A guide to choosing a method of teaching and stating a movement

---

BOX 4–4 Comparing Teaching Styles

On page 60 it was stated that two factors could be used to discriminate among styles of teaching. These factors were the degree of cognitive involvement and individualization of instruction.

On the chart presented below, mark an X to show the degree to which each teaching style contributes to achieving these factors.

Style of Teaching	Cognitive Involvement	Individualization of Instruction
Command	Low ———— High	Low ———— High
Guided Discovery	Low ———— High	Low ———— High
Problem Solving	Low ———— High	Low ———— High

If you need help in responding with confidence and certainty reread pages 64 to 69.

---

task is to use the method that makes the greatest contribution to achieving the immediate developmental theme goal(s) and ultimately the general goal(s) of an elementary school education.

If the students have always been exposed to the content approach to teaching, that is probably how the teacher should begin providing instruction. However, eventually, both content and process styles of teaching should be used during a lesson as the situation requires. To state that a teacher should never use a given style would be erroneous. What should guide the selection of a teaching style is its contribution toward meeting educational goals.

Control Phrases A common feature of stating a movement experience in any style of teaching is a phrase that indicates to the student when they may respond. A control phrase has two purposes: to serve as an attention cue to students to get ready to listen carefully, and to control the initiation of action until the instructions have been given.

> Examples of control phrases are:
> On the (starting) signal . . .
> When I say "go" . . .
> When you hear (see) the starting signal . . .
> Wait until I say "off you go" before you . . .

Other control phrases may have special effectiveness in your local situation and geographic area.

BOX 4–5   The Pause That . . .

What would happen if you were stating the following movement tasks to a class and you paused to take a deep breath before finishing the instructions?

1. "Go get a ball (long pause) and use body-parts that bend to move the ball through your own space."
2. "When I say go, get a ball (long pause) and use body-parts that bend to move the ball through your own space."

Which pause might cause students to be more difficult to manage? The pause in task 1 or 2?

Control phrases are not needed when the teacher is stating a movement experience to students who are already moving. Students are able to listen while moving. Some movement experience statements are designed to give additional cues to clarify the original task or to encourage more varied and/ or difficult responses. Stopping student learning activity for this type of communication would be inappropriate. Furthermore, if the teacher observes that most of the class needs new information, encouragement, or cannot hear the instructions, then the activity can be stopped so the teacher can repeat the instructions or give new information.

After control phrases have been used for a time, the students will move on a starting signal, such as a beat on a drum or the words "off you go," without a preceding control phrase. Even then, a control phrase may need to be given for the first movement experience in a lesson or when the students are excited and anxious to begin moving.

Class Organizational Arrangements

Classes can be organized in many different patterns. Some patterns save time, and emphasis should be on uniformity and conformity. Other organizational arrangements emphasize individual decision making and development of a sense of self-awareness as a moving being.

The traditional organizational patterns in physical education are the line and circle. Line and circle formations are shown in Figure 4–21.

A different arrangement, which does not use either lines or circles, is the scattered pattern. This pattern requires the students to find their own movement space within a defined area. See Figure 4–22. The directions given to students to form a scattered pattern, for example, could be "When I say 'Go!' find your own space where you can reach out in all directions around you and not touch anyone." Another procedure is to place small equipment (e.g., hoops, bean bags, fleece balls) to be used initially in a lesson in a line, circle, or scattered pattern within the movement area. The students are told "On the drum beat, go quickly to a piece of equipment where no one else is

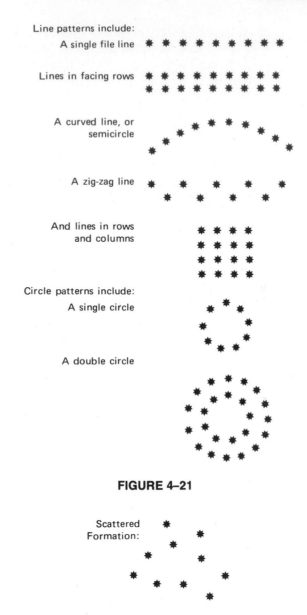

Line patterns include:

A single file line

Lines in facing rows

A curved line, or semicircle

A zig-zag line

And lines in rows and columns

Circle patterns include:

A single circle

A double circle

FIGURE 4–21

Scattered Formation:

FIGURE 4–22

and, in your own space, practice tossing and catching." Either everyone in the class can go at one time or the students can be sent in smaller numbers to find a piece of equipment.

Another aid to organizing students in lines or circles is to paint these patterns, in different sizes, on the hard surface area or gym floor. However, this procedure lacks flexibility in regard to spacing intervals between students. Another reference point that can be used to help students to line up is to use a wall, baseball backstop, or a rope stretched out on the ground.

During a lesson, the need may arise to change an organizational pattern from a line to a circle. One way to do this is to have the students face in the direction of the line leader and then follow the leader. The leader moves in a circular path so that the front of the line catches the end of the line.

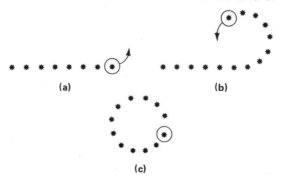

FIGURE 4–23

This method may also be used to move from a circle to a line. In this case, the leader moves so that the group doubles back to form a line or the leader moves past the last person in the circle. In the other method, the leader continues the movement of the group until the last person in line has reached the desired stopping point (see Figure 4–24).

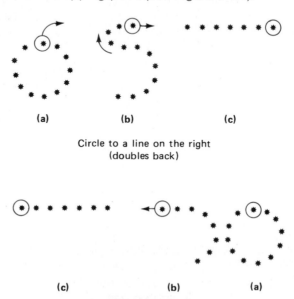

FIGURE 4–24

If children know what a circle or line is, and the teacher believes that the children will be able to follow instructions at that particular moment, then the teacher can state, *"Form a circle* (line)." This is the preferred approach to having children get into a formation. However, circumstances and conditions may prohibit this method from working (or it may just be quicker to move as a group from one formation to another).

Being able to control the movement of the children is not enough. Other procedures for organizing students for instruction must be considered:

1. Face the students away from or at an angle to the sun so they are not looking into the sun.
2. Face the students into or at an angle to the wind so the teacher's voice, when standing in front of the students, is carried toward them by the wind.
3. Keep equipment to be used later in the lesson out of sight, either in a bag, equipment cart, or another area in order to avoid distracting the students.
4. Choose an activity area that minimizes distractions.
5. Observable boundary markers for a movement space are easier for students to respond to than abstract instructions. A space marked off by plastic containers, flags, cones, or painted lines is easier for students to adhere to than instructions, "Don't go too far away." or "Stay in line with that tree."
6. The teacher should circulate among the students to provide individual teaching points, ask and respond to questions, give praise or intervene in a potentially hazardous situation.
7. When speaking to the whole class, the teacher should be in a position which allows him/her to see all the children, regardless of the formation used, and allows for observation of the actions of each student.

The teaching style and organizational pattern for instruction should be chosen for its contribution toward meeting the objectives of the lesson. Lines and circles are required in many group game activities. The scattered formation is advantageous when students are to work independently or in groups to solve or practice a movement task.

IMPLEMENTING THE DEVELOPMENTAL THEME

Developing Body Awareness   The learning experiences in this developmental theme (Becoming Aware) focus on the self as a moving being. What are the parts called that make up the body? What feats can the body perform by moving some body-parts independently? Or together? Or moving the body as a whole—along the ground, in the air, in relation to other objects and people in the environment? Learning the names of different parts of the body and internalizing the knowledge of where those parts are, where they can move, and what they can do, either alone or in conjunction with other parts, are some of the primary learning experiences for Becoming Aware. Other experiences have to do with the concept of size. It is important for children to have concrete evidence of how big or small certain parts of the body are as well as the physical changes in their body that have taken place during the school year. Contributing to the development of body-image is the ability to identify the different surfaces of the body. Children need to be able to identify these surfaces in different orientations: facing or not facing the teacher, and lying prone or supine. In this way, teachers can determine the constancy of the concepts "my front," "my back," which are not synonymous with *facing* an object or person.

Learning "what I can do with my body" provides the foundation for all future movement. In these sample lessons, children are encouraged to explore the range of movement options open to them and to gain proficiency in basic motor activity necessary for body control.

About Movement

Learning about movement and learning to move are interdependent. If children are to gain a global view of movement, they need to understand the commonalities existing in all movement. Becoming Aware includes an analysis of some of the universals of movement. Much of the methodology in this and the other developmental themes emphasizes the theoretical framework and practices of Rudolph Laban,[33] Joan Russell,[34] and Margaret H'Doubler.[35]

Rudolph Laban, an Austrian, developed his philosophy of movement and disseminated his methods of analyzing and recording movement in the middle of the twentieth century. The impact of his work has been felt not only in dance, which he taught, but also in the functional aspects of physical education. Many of the teaching modules in this book reflect his methodology and movement analysis. Laban identified Time, Weight, Space, and Flow as "motion factors." He perceived each factor as a continuum along which children range, gradually increasing their movement capabilities and subsequent control. For example, young children move with quick, strong actions and only gradually learn to move in a slower, sustained manner with lighter effort. In the United States, Weight as used by Laban has been replaced by the use of the term Force.

The Space factor in movement is all the space that the child can reach from a fixed position (Personal Space) and the space that surrounds the child beyond his reach (General Space). When children first begin to use space, they tend to use mostly straight movement. Laban suggested that children need to be able to use space in an imaginative way before they can be expected to respond to an imposed design, such as a given pathway for movement.

The Flow of movement is a motion factor that Laban believed is critical to the development of personal harmony. "If a child has flow, he is in perfect harmony with all the motion factors and is mentally and physically, happily adjusted to life."[36]

Of all the interpretations of Laban's work, it is the authors' opinion that Joan Russell has made an excellent contribution by rendering Laban's analysis in terms of children's understanding. Russell's book *Creative Dance in the Primary School* is helpful for teachers who want to teach more creative dance to children. Russell provides the analytic framework for helping children develop movement potential, and she identified appropriate movement experiences for children under the following major headings:

Body Awareness—movement of the body in and through space, or "what" the child can do

Effort—working with, and gradually gaining control over, the motion factors, Time, Space, Force, Flow—"how" children can move

Space—"where" the child can go in space, moving at high, medium, and low levels in all directions in space

Relationship—working with others, such as the teacher, or as a partner, or a member of a group—learning about the concept of *Relationship* includes the interactions among the different parts of the body as it moves.

This simplified analysis forms the basic material for designing children's movement experiences.

In addition to learning about movement, children need to learn to move safely in their environment. Being able to judge distances correctly, and learning how to control their movements are crucial components of controlled movements.

Manipulative Skill   Another aspect of learning about one's movement capabilities is manipulating a variety of objects in many ways. All ball games that children play in and out of school employ one or more of the skills practiced in this developmental theme. Children lacking these abilities are often not chosen by peers to play these games; they cannot play games with any degree of competency.

Becoming aware is an infinite process. The potential range of human abilities is vast. As the newly acquired or refined movement behaviors are combined with previous learnings, a wellspring of increasing possibilities and options becomes available to the developing human being. Consequently, the activities in this theme should not be thought of as being suitable only for primary grade children; nor should it be thought that once these activities are performed, they can be set aside. The same tasks can be given in consecutive years and still provide new learning experiences because of the changing variables of the child, such as increased weight and height (especially in the trunk and limb proportions) together with the increase in levels of strength and skill.

DEVELOPING BODY IMAGE

Planning Guide

Objectives	*Experiences*
As a result of the learning experiences over time, children will:	
1. identify different parts of the body and its surfaces	• locating and naming different body-parts; move different body-parts in response to a given movement task; locate surfaces of the body while maintaining a variety of positions
2. demonstrate establishment of laterality	• perform a variety of movements with both sides of the body
3. demonstrate ability to control different body-parts in space	• lead with different body-parts; experience a variety of ways of traveling through space with and without equipment
4. demonstrate understanding of the different size relationships that exist among different body-parts.	• measuring a variety of body-parts and drawing conclusions about the similarities and differences.

For evaluating students' progress in development of body-image, see page 81.

Teaching Modules

Introductory Module

Objectives

As a result of the learning experiences over time, children will demonstrate understanding of:

1. the configuration of their bodies
2. the differences in proportion of the various parts of the body.

Materials

A large piece of drawing paper for each child, chalk/crayons.

Learning Experiences	*Related Experiences*
1. Give each child drawing materials and instruct them to draw a picture of themselves. Tell them to use as much paper as they need to do this.	• Sculpting in plasticine, homemade play dough, creating "busts" of myself and others.

Learning Experiences

Make sure that they have enough time to accomplish this task to their satisfaction.

Related Experiences

- Finger painting and making patterns with hands in different positions: balled fist; open palm; knuckles, etc.
- Looking at others' painting and placing body-part name labels on corresponding parts.

Central Module

Objectives

As a result of the learning experiences over time, children will be able to:

1. describe the size relationships that exist between certain parts of their bodies
2. express those relationships in mathematical terms according to their level of understanding.

Materials

String, or jump rope for each child. Ropes with plastic cylinders are very suitable for this activity since the cylinders can be counted; rulers and yardsticks.

Learning Experiences

1. Each child measures the length of his/her own foot, then makes comparisons with other body-parts to see how many measure the same as the foot. (Length can be compared with width in this task.)
2. Discuss the result of this task. Most will have discovered that foot length corresponds to forearm length or ankle circumference.
3. Find out which body-parts have the same measurement as each other, or even twice the measurement. Check measurements with ruler. (Emphasize working alone.) Some possible comparisons:
   - circumference of head = length from thumb to shoulder
   - waist is twice neck circumference.
4. Test their own comparisons with others. Use the three closest people to check your results against theirs.

Related Experiences

- Make a list of everything in the room that is as long as your neck is round.
- Measure your hand and see how many hands long the bulletin board is.

- Find out how people in other cultures measure when no rulers or fixed measuring instruments are available.

- Make a pattern using two shapes, one of which is twice the size of the other.
- Construct a bar graph showing the various leg lengths of the children in the room.

FIGURE 4–25 Measuring and checking own comparisons with others

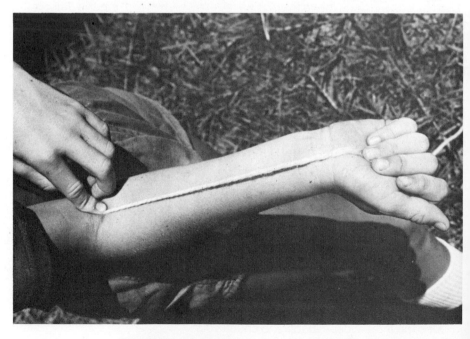

FIGURE 4–26 Measuring length of forearm

Culminating Module

Objectives

As a result of the learning experiences over time, children will be able to:

1. name and locate a variety of body-parts
2. locate a variety of body-parts correctly without looking
3. find ways of using specific body-parts in the development of a game
4. demonstrate cooperative ability to work as a group to make up and keep a game going.

Materials

A playground ball for every four children for Option B.
NOTE: Both options can be used in this module, however, Option B is more appropriate for intermediate grade students than Option A.

Option A

Learning Experiences

1. In their own space, have the children make a variety of body-parts touch other body-parts: knees to nose, forehead taps knee, one ear brushes foot, etc. Try to vary words for "touch."

Related Experiences

• Play "Pin the Tail on the Donkey."
• Make a list of all the movements the body can do: wiggle, creep, run, hop, dive, etc.

FIGURE 4–27 Nose near to knee

Learning Experiences	*Related Experiences*

Learning Experiences

2. Have children make up movements to do with each body-part. (Emphasize isolated movement before moving with two body-parts at the same time.)
3. Modify song that begins, "If you're happy and you know it": clap your hands, tap your wrist, wiggle your nose, touch your toes, wave your thumbs. Encourage children to add movement ideas that all can respond to.
4. Repeat song with eyes closed. This is a more difficult task since the children must rely on their own kinesthetic sense. They can't copy others!
   - Begin this task with the children sitting down because this removes the problem of balance.
   - Many of the children will know the major parts of the body by the time they get to school. However, smaller or less noticeable parts such as shoulders, wrists, ankles, shin, and eyebrow may not be as familiar.

Related Experiences

- Dance the Hokey-Pokey.
- Make a list of how many parts of the body we have two of.
- Write a story about a land where everyone had *three* parts where we have two.
- Describe some of the advantages and disadvantages the people had.
- Finger paint with eyes closed.
- Encourage the creation of patterns or designs before moving on to outlines of subjects.

Option B

If Option A is not used, review the names and locations of different small body-parts (wrists, ankles, fingers).

Learning Experiences

1. In groups of four, make up a game so that everyone touches the ball. Allow a few minutes for initial organization.
2. Continue with the task, but make sure that the ball and all four people are moving all the time. This is to prevent static play.
3. Change the game so that only small body-parts are used to keep the ball moving.

Related Experiences

- Begin to assemble a list of games that are played all over the world.
- Identify those sports in which a good sense of body image is important: diving, gymnastics, etc.
- Discussions about the universality of play.
- Finding out about other cultures and the kinds of games they play(ed).
- Make up a game using sticks and pebbles that can be played on a hike or on a trip.

Teaching Points

Begin most tasks with the statement: "When I say GO! . . ." This clarifies the instructions and controls when the children start working on the task.

Convene the ball-carriers and give them the initial instructions for the game. They are more likely to pay strict attention to the instructions when there are fewer of them. Most children will find this activity quite absorbing if the teacher develops some expertise in guiding and increasing the challenges in meaningful ways.

FIGURE 4–28 Everyone must touch the ball

Summary

Enabling Behavior: Developing Body Image

This enabling behavior deals with the *self.* Some of the behaviors that indicate children are gaining a realistic self-image are when they can:

1. Draw themselves with increasing accuracy. In self-portraits, the obvious body-parts are present, but not necessarily in proportion.
2. Name and locate the parts of the body, such as abdomen, ankles, knees, hips, and shoulders.
3. Move one side of the body in isolation from the opposite side.
4. Move both sides of the body simultaneously, as well as in opposition.
5. Easily move parts of the body in isolation from other parts, or in conjunction with those parts.
6. Orient themselves quickly if asked to "face the clock," or stand with their backs to the desks.
7. Demonstrate constancy of the body-image, for example, correctly identifying the "top" of the head when they are lying on the floor.
8. Move to use specific body-parts in complex movement tasks, such as a game.

DEVELOPING MOVEMENT POTENTIAL

Planning Guide

Objectives	*Experiences*
As a result of the learning experiences over time, children will be able to:	
1. demonstrate a variety of locomotor movements that can be performed with control	• moving in a variety of ways at different levels, speeds, and in different directions with control
2. demonstrate understanding that the body can form three basic shapes: straight, curved, and twisted, and that all body shapes consist of one or a combination of these shapes	• balancing on different body-parts to make a variety of body shapes; making shapes in the air; making sequences that show a variety of body shapes
3. demonstrate ability to control their bodies in static and dynamic balance situations	• balance on a variety of body-parts; maintain balance while moving on one or more body-parts with and without equipment
4. demonstrate control of movement at slow speeds and make smooth transitions from one movement to another	• perform sequences with a variety of speeds; move slowly on different body-parts; use flow in moving from one position to another
5. explain why strength is the underlying component of fluid movement	• performing everyday movements at very slow speeds; experience strength requirements of slow motion
6. construct sequences of movement of varying complexity	• linking two or more movements to make a sequence that can be repeated several times
7. demonstrate understanding of the Time, Force, Space, and Flow concepts as they apply to movement.	• apply the qualities of movement in daily tasks; emphasize different movement qualities in sequences of movement.

For evaluating students' progress in developing movement potential, see page 88.

Teaching Modules

Introductory Module

Objectives

As a result of the learning experiences over time, children should be able to:

1. travel in a variety of ways at different speeds
2. control their movements and make smooth transitions from one movement to another
3. explain the importance of strength in movement fluency.

Materials

Two pictures denoting "fast" and "slow."

Learning Experiences

1. "When you hear the signal, show me how you can move about inside the boundaries using your hands and feet. Watch out for others!"
2. "Now, find two other body-parts to travel on." (This task can be repeated several times to obtain variety in responses.)
3. Gather the children around and show them the pictures of fast and slow movement. Ask them to tell you how the pictures are different. The answer you are seeking is one indicating the difference in speed.
4. "Now as you continue to move, try to change the speed of your movements—making some *very fast,* and some *very slow.*"

    As they move, use general reinforcing comments or questions: "Are you really moving fast?" "I like the way Mike is moving very slowly!" Young children find it very difficult to change speed radically.
5. "This time, think about the slow movements. As you travel, show me how smoothly you can change from one slow movement to another."
6. Conduct a brief discussion about how one gains smoothness in movement. Many adults and children do not understand that strength is a prerequisite for grace in movement. "Tell me some words that describe how you felt when you were moving slowly." If there is no word given to indicate "strength" or "control" try to elicit one by having the children shake one foot very rapidly, and then make a slow circle in the air with the same foot as they are sitting down. Ask which movement took the most strength.
7. "As you move this time, think about what we've talked about and show me what you've learned by the way you travel."

Part of the purpose of the preceding discussion was to improve the quality of the movement described.

Related Experiences

- In *My Discovery Book,* the students begin to list all the movements they can do.[1]

- Write a poem about someone or something that you like to watch moving.
- Conduct a discussion about what accounts for speed (force, mass relationship).
- What causes the Concorde to fly faster than sound?
- Why can some people run faster than others?
- Finger Paint using:
    - a series of fast and slow movements
    - smooth and jerky movement
- Make a collage of things that move very fast.
- Construct a mural that shows a change from slow movements at one end to fast movements at the other.
- Make a list of all the animals that use speed to save themselves from their enemies.
- Make another list of those animals that use stillness to save themselves from predators.
- Write a report about a device that helps us move in a different way:
    - sliding
    - flying
    - gliding
    - floating
    - spinning

[1]The idea of a Discovery Book can be introduced at the beginning of the school year. The children should be encouraged to record in it those things they discover about themselves and their abilities. They can illustrate the book with drawings or write poems about how they feel.

Central Module

Objectives

As a result of the learning experiences over time, children should demonstrate understanding of:

1. the three basic shapes that the body can make: stretched, curled, and twisted
2. how any shape that the body makes is one or a combination of these.

Materials

A drum, or similar signal.

Learning Experiences	*Related Experiences*

Learning Experiences

1. "When I say GO, show me how you can move lightly on your feet inside the boundaries, then stop with this sound (signal). GO!" Repeat this task several times so that they get used to moving and stopping. Reminding children to move lightly should prevent wild running around.
2. "This time, when you stop, make a statue that stays very still." (This is a progression because the children have an additional task to attend to.)
3. At this point, identify a child showing a stretched shape. "Look at the shape Joe is

Related Experiences

- Make a statue in clay or plasticine.
- Make a list of things that stretch.
- Sort pictures of twisted, straight, and curved things.
- Make a design of tall shapes.
- Find pictures of people making stretched shapes in magazines and paste them on construction paper to make a montage.

FIGURE 4–29

FIGURE 4–30

Learning Experiences

making. What words would describe this shape?" (straight, big, stretched, long) "Show me how you can make a stretched shape that is different from Joe's."

4. Repeat the moving and stopping task, this time emphasizing the use of stretched shapes.

   If children are to achieve a high level of performance, it is important that they practice and implement the teaching points that are made.

5. Introduce the other two basic shapes by asking the children to show a shape that is opposite to the stretched shape (curved, twisted). Having identified each basic shape, repeat the task of moving and stopping, but show a different shape each time.

6. Bring the children together to discuss how any shape that the body makes is one or a combination of these three basic shapes. Comparing a wide, stretched shape with a small, curved shape can help children see instantly how the body can assume a wide variety of shapes. This discussion can lead

Related Experiences

• Make up a story about a boy or girl who is a "Magic Mover." Describe some of the magic movements he/she can make that are different from those of ordinary people.

• Draw a picture of yourself doing this activity.
• Collect ten things that have different shapes and make a display.
• Find different plants and flowers that have straight, twisted, or curled shapes.

FIGURE 4–31 Comparing different shapes made while moving quickly

FIGURE 4–32 Comparing different shapes made while moving slowly

Learning Experiences

children to an understanding of how activities such as diving, gymnastics, and figure-skating can be viewed as "moving art." Ask one child to perform a forward roll while another one performs a cartwheel. Have the children compare the two different shapes.

Culminating Module

Objectives

As a result of the learning experiences over time, the children will be able to:

1. create combined shapes that emphasize specific features, such as symmetry/asymmetry, curved, twisted, stretched
2. make shapes by balancing on different body-parts
3. use stretch ropes to make different group shapes with a partner.

Materials

One small stretch rope for each child. These can be made from linked rubber bands or elastic.

Learning Experiences

1. "In this part of the lesson you will be working on ideas of making shapes with the stretch ropes as well as with your body. Find a way to make a triangle with your rope using different body-parts . . . see if you can find two more ways to make the triangle."

   Variety in experiences does not always entail novelty. It is more important to extend the activities in a thorough manner, rather than always changing all the features in the task.

2. "This time, work with your partner to make identical shapes with your ropes. Begin when you have an idea." Allow a few minutes for the children to begin thinking. If some seem at a loss for an idea, try to stimulate responses by asking what kinds

Related Experiences

- Make a montage of different triangles: isosceles, equilateral, scalene.
- In pairs, using the stretch rope, one person make a triangle and the other one measure the area of it.
- Make a collage of objects that are triangular in shape.
- Make a Super-8 movie of students' sequences showing contrasting shapes.
- Make a "cine-book" of geometrical shapes that appear to move as you flip through the pages quickly.
- Hold a discussion of what "selection" involves:
    - comparing and contrasting
    - identifying desirable features
    - living with decisions
- Hold a discussion about "how we remember things."

Learning Experiences

of shapes are there to make rather than making a direct suggestion.

3. "This time, see how many different shapes you can make, using your body and the rope together. Try to make three different shapes. If you have a good idea to share with the class, practice it and then tell me when you are ready to show it to everybody." After presenting this problem, move among the children to reinforce ideas, or redirect those who are not on task.

4. "We've seen a number of different ideas that people have worked on. Select three or four ideas that you like best and see how you can use them to develop a sequence of shapes with yourselves and your jump ropes. Remember, you must be able to repeat your sequence over and over again." Young children will find this task difficult. Have them select only two or three movements to repeat.

5. It is often at this point that the children can become bored with the task. Perfection of performance is not an inherently appealing goal for children. They need practical help in valuing competent work. You can assist with this problem by conducting a brief discussion about the demonstrations. Depending on the time this module takes, the activity can be extended in many ways:
   a. adding a change of speed, so that part of the sequence is in slow motion
   b. combine with two other children to make a sequence with fours
   c. vary the challenge to include different relationships: side by side, facing, in opposition, mirroring.

Each of the suggestions could form the central concept of another module or set of modules.

Related Experiences

• Play games that emphasize remembering where things are.

• Paint a silhouette from shadows thrown by partners and their ropes.
• Write a paragraph describing your feelings about this movement activity.
• Perform your sequence of shapes with the ropes to music.

FIGURE 4–33 Developing a sequence by using a jump rope

Summary

Enabling Behavior: Developing Movement Potential

This enabling behavior lays the groundwork for improvement in movement competency. Children are developing movement potential in a positive manner when they demonstrate improvement in:

1. Increasing control over their movement. They can change speed with ease and they can move with deliberate slowness.
2. Making curved, stretched, or twisted body-shapes in balancing positions or in movement. More experienced children can make symmetrical and asymmetrical shapes in place or while moving.
3. Recognizing the three basic shapes in movement, such as stretched shape in a cartwheel or the curved shape in the backward roll.
4. Maintaining balance positions on a variety of supports as a result of increasing levels of strength and coordination.
5. Linking two or more body actions that they can repeat accurately.
6. Responding accurately to challenges that emphasize concepts of Time, Force, Space, and Flow.

DEVELOPING SPATIAL AWARENESS

Planning Guide

Objectives	*Experiences*
As a result of the learning experiences over time, children will be able to:	
1. demonstrate understanding of the difference between personal space and general space	• explore the limits of personal space; explore the possibilities of movement in personal space—curling, stretching, twisting, making independent shapes with different body-parts; moving in different directions in general space on a variety of body-parts—backwards, sideways, forwards, up and down
2. demonstrate ability to move at a variety of levels	• change from one level to another while moving
3. demonstrate understanding that they create different floor and air patterns as they move	• traveling in different floor patterns; making specific air patterns with different body-parts; constructing sequences of movement using a variety of floor and air patterns
4. identify the spatial relationships that exist between different body-parts, or themselves and other people or objects.	• moving so that different body-parts are assuming a variety of relationships to each other—beside, in front and behind, near and far; working with other people to achieve a

Experiences

variety of relationships such as circling around, back-to-back, over and under, meeting and parting; as a member of a group (inclusion), being rejected from a group (exclusion), as an individual within a group (as opposed to being a contributing member).

For evaluating your students' progress in developing spatial awareness, see page 93.

Teaching Modules

Introductory Module

Objectives

As a result of the learning experiences over time, children will:

1. be able to move in many directions
2. demonstrate understanding that forwards, backwards, sideways, up and down, and varying combinations of these constitute "directions" in movement.

"Direction," in movement has a number of interpretations, depending upon the theoretical framework used. The theoretical framework of Rudolph Laban is used in this book and Direction refers to movement in which the body is the referent: forwards, backwards, sideways (both ways), up, down, and combinations of these.

Materials

A signal for Start and Stop.

Learning Experiences	*Related Experiences*

1. "When you hear this starting signal, find a way to travel in a forward direction. Remember, you don't have to travel always on the feet. Find as many ways of moving forward as you can." It is important for children to learn that "direction" remains a constant. "Forward" is still "forward," whether one is moving on the feet, or hands and feet, so long as the reference point for "forward" is the front of the body.	• Discuss situations in which "direction" has different meanings:
	    –geographical contexts
	    –moving to a new city and finding one's directions
	    –following directions
	 • Make observations about the directions that specific animals move in:
	    –porpoise
	    –flies

Learning Experiences

2. "Now, let's see who can think and act quickly. Every time you hear this change signal, I'm going to call out a direction, and you must show me how you can move in that direction—and keep moving that way until I call another direction. Let's practice one time. Everyone start moving forward slowly and be ready for the signal to change . . . (**) SIDEWAYS!" (Check to see that everyone is moving sideways.)

    Young children can become confused about the direction of movement initially. Older children need less time spent on such relatively simple tasks, and can move on to other, more complex modules in spatial awareness.

3. "I liked the way you seemed to think before you moved! This time, I'm going to call out directions one after another. Let's see who can keep up with me."

4. "Very well done. You kept up with me well. Now, show me that you can move in many directions without my saying their names. Every time you hear the signal, change the direction you are moving in. It must be different each time." This task makes the children responsible for the decision to choose the direction in which they will move. They need to show very clear changes of direction.

Related Experiences

    –seagulls
    –seahorse
    –chimp
    –others

- Identify those animals that can move sideways.
- Compare the degree of versatility of movement between different animals.
- Observe the direction of the movement of rebounding balls of various sizes and consistencies. What statements can you make about:
    –what determines the flight path of the rebound?
    –whether a ball has a "front" and "back"
    –how you make the ball come back to you.

FIGURE 4–34 Changing speed and direction while moving

Central Module

Objectives

As a result of the learning experiences over time, children will:

1. demonstrate understanding of the terms "low" and "high"
2. be able to assume different shapes at both these levels.

Materials

Signal for Start and Stop.

Learning Experiences	*Related Experiences*

Learning Experiences

1. "You have been moving in many directions, now let's think just about up and down. Show me some different ways that you can move up and down." Children need to learn that up is not always synonymous with high and down with low. It is possible to move parts of the body up and down at many levels.

    Encourage the children to move in extremes—projecting the whole body in an upward direction, and bringing all parts of the body down as far as possible.
2. "Some of you are moving up very well. Are you working on moving *all* the body-parts in a down direction?"

    If the children are performing only jumping movements, remind them that they can move at a slower pace; structure a task to elicit this response. When you sense that the children have tried several possible solutions, stop the activity.
3. "This time we are going to think about *where* we are in space as we move. Everyone show me a way to move your whole body downward in slow motion. Keep moving until you can't go any further." Give the children time to start, and then continue talking as they move: "Where are you in space now?"

    (You may get several answers: "down" "near the ground." If no one uses a term indicating "low," ask them for other words to describe where they are.)
4. "If you are at a low level now, at what other levels can you move? Show me!"

Related Experiences

*   Make a list of all the words that begin with up or down.
*   In two's, take turns measuring your partner's reach from a fixed point.
*   Make a graph showing the different class members' "reaches."
*   Discussion about why only certain things can move upward:
    –smoke
    –flame
    –a balloon
    –helicopters
*   Watch a seasonal game (football, baseball, tennis, etc.) and count the number of times a given player changes direction in the game movement. This is a helpful task for answering the questions of older children about the necessity for this kind of activity.
*   Discussions about why gravity "pulls" us downward.
*   Write a story about what would happen on "The Day Gravity Stopped."
*   Make a montage of:
    –things that move up and down
    –things that move only at a low level
    –things that move *best* at a high level
*   What animals are specifically adapted to living at high (low) levels?
*   Are there any animals that can survive well at both levels?

Learning Experiences

5. "In your own space, show me how you can make a shape at a low level and then one at a high level. Some of you might be able to find shapes that you can make at both levels." Spend a few minutes on this and reinforce those who appear to be working at the task, even though their performance may not be remarkable. It is important to reward on-task behavior as well as focusing on the accomplishment level of the performance.

FIGURE 4–35 Changing levels while moving

Culminating Module

Objectives

As a result of the learning experiences over time, children will be able to:

1. identify "space words"
2. create sequences that demonstrate clarity of movement.

Materials

One colored streamer for each student. Music for accompaniment (optional).

Learning Experiences

1. "We were working on making shapes at different levels. When I say GO!, I'd like each of you to pick up a streamer and find ways of moving so that the streamer floats far away from you."
2. "Some of you are just waving the streamer about. Think of moving the streamer really far away from you at different levels. Change the space words you are showing. For example, can you show the space word behind? or beside? or above? What other space words can you think of to show in your movement? Try it again." Give the children a few moments to improve the quality of their responses. If this does indeed occur, you should make some appropriate comment before you go on to the next task. For example, "I could really see some different space words being used that time."

Related Experiences

- Identify when space words (near, far, beside, behind) are adjectives and when they are adverbs.
- Make a list of as many prepositions as you can. How many of these can be used as *space* words?
- Draw a picture of how all the streamers looked as they were moving.
- Make a design using the idea of streamers to show a variety of spatial relationships.
- Make a poem about your streamer and how it felt when you were dancing with it.

Learning Experiences

3. List some space words and space phrases on the board (or a large sheet of poster board). Elicit as many as possible from the children: inside of, circling around, back-to-back, side-by-side, etc.

4. "I'm going to give you a few moments now for you to work together and see how you can make up a short dance with your streamers that shows one space word or space phrase." By focusing on only one space word, initially, teachers are encouraging clarity of responses.

FIGURE 4–36 Working on a sequence emphasizing facing

FIGURE 4–37 Working on a sequence emphasizing facing

Summary

Enabling Behavior: Developing Spatial Awareness

Well-developed spatial awareness is essential for us to move easily in our environment. Children are improving in spatial awareness when:

1. There are fewer accidental collisions with desks or other children.
2. They can *move through space* without colliding with each other, even though they may be traveling in different directions.
3. They are able to change levels quickly as they move.
4. They can deliberately change the spatial relationships of different body-parts through movement.
5. They can work with an object or a partner in a variety of spatial relationships such as beside, around, or back-to-back.
6. They can work with a partner, or small group in increasingly complex spatial relationships, such as mingling, in unison, or in opposition.

DEVELOPING MANIPULATIVE ABILITIES

Planning Guide

Objectives	*Experiences*

As a result of the learning experiences over time, children will:

1. be able to propel a variety of objects with different body-parts

2. be able to demonstrate increasing accuracy and form in propelling objects
3. be able to absorb the force of objects rolled or tossed to them

4. apply throwing, striking, and catching skills in a game.

• rolling, tossing, throwing, and striking a variety of objects, such as playground balls, bean bags, fleeceballs, and newspaper balls; manipulating hoops and jump ropes
• throwing balls at various speeds and heights at selected targets
• catch and trap balls or bean bags with different body-parts; receive bean bags on different body-parts; receive a rolling hoop using hands
• play games that require different propulsion forms such as volleying, striking, rolling, throwing, and catching; create games that focus on a particular skill.

For evaluating your students' progress in developing manipulative skills, see page 100.

Teaching Modules

Introductory Module

Objectives

As a result of these learning experiences over time, the children:

1. will learn to make newspaper balls of varying sizes
2. will gain experience in hitting the ball in different ways.

Materials

Two double sheets of newspaper for each child. A four-foot length of masking tape for each child or several pieces of tape of shorter lengths, pre-cut and attached to the back of the child's chair to save time. Permanent colored felt-tip pens or crayons.

Learning Experiences	*Related Experiences*

1. "Everyone take their newspaper and wad it up into a ball. Make it as tight as you can. Now begin to wrap it round with the tape. Keep working to make your ball a firm round shape." Older children will have no problem with this, but very young children may. Simply making the balls is a form of manipulative activity, and the decorating of the finished product provides challenges of drawing or writing on an uneven surface.
2. "When you have finished your ball, decorate it so that you will be able to tell it from all the others."
3. "When you are satisfied with your design, see how you can keep the ball in the air near you. Don't let the ball get away from you!" If this activity becomes a bit wild, remind the children to keep the ball *near* them. Remind them about the kind of force they need to use.

- Other projects involving modeling with newspaper:
  - –hand tearing of newspaper to make different shapes.
  - –folding and cutting or tearing of paper into doilies or dolls, other designs.
  - –papier maché work.
  - –models formed from paper and tape.
- Making designs from letters of own name or initials.
- Draw/paint your design on paper and put them on the bulletin board to see who can guess the names.
- Measuring the perimeters of different balls and comparing them.
- Make a graph showing comparisons of all the perimeters.
- Compute the diameter, radius, and area of a cross section of the ball.

Central Module

Objectives

As a result of the learning experiences over time, children will be able to:

1. keep a ball airborne by hitting/striking it with different body-parts
2. use two parts of the body alternately to keep the ball airborne
3. demonstrate understanding of the relationship between the flight of the ball and the point of contact.

Materials

One newspaper ball for each child. Boundaries.

Learning Experiences	*Related Experiences*

1. "When I say GO, show me how you can keep the ball in the air so that it stays *near* you." Although this module focuses on striking the ball with different body-parts, it

- Discussions about why the newspaper ball "flies" more slowly than a golf ball. (Drop a golf ball and a newspaper ball from the same height and see which hits the ground first.)

Learning Experiences

can be adapted for kicking or throwing. The tasks can also be repeated using only the feet or an implement.

2. "If you find it easy, try to make the ball go to the same place in the air every time. Go!" Reinforce those children who are controlling the *force* and/or direction of their hits.

3. "I saw some of you were using body-parts to hit the ball. Can you name some that you were using (arm, shoulder, hand, etc.)? Let's *all* try to hit the ball using as many different parts of the body as you can to hit the ball."

4. "How many people found more than three body-parts to hit the ball with? Now, choose two body-parts and hit the ball in the air, first with one part, and then with the other. Ready? Go!" Two body-parts can be two hands, or one hand and one arm, *any* two body-parts. As the difficulty of the task increases, the performance may be lowered temporarily. As children gain control in the new situation, their performance will improve.

5. When the children have worked with this task for two or three minutes, stop the activity and make sure that they can all hear your next discussion: "I'd like you to see what happens when you hit the ball at different points. Try hitting it on the side, on top, underneath. Go!" After a few minutes, stop the activity and ask for their results. When possible, allow the major points to be made by the children. However, it is your responsibility to see that there is clarity about the results. If the ball is struck on *top,* then it will go downwards—if on the side, it will go to the opposite side.

6. "Now, if you want the ball to go *straight up* in the air where will be the best place to hit it?" (directly underneath the ball at the center point) "Now, practice hitting the ball in that way using the two body-parts you chose."

Related Experiences

- Make a montage of all the sports you have seen where the player strikes the ball. Conduct a discussion about striking action. What does it mean? Is kicking striking? What about hockey? Tennis?
- Draw a picture of yourself hitting the ball to show how many body-parts you used.
- Make up a song that you can hit the ball in time to.
- Make a list of all the different body-parts you could use to hit a ball.
- List jobs where it is important to hit objects at the right point:
  - –carpenters nailing wood
  - –the kicker in football
  - –a diamond cutter.
- Make a collage of pictures of hands working with objects:
  - –baking
  - –sewing
  - –hitting a ball
  - –carrying
  - –writing.
- Make a list in My Discovery Book of "All the Things I Can Do with a Ball."

Culminating Module

Objectives

As a result of the learning experiences over time, children will be able to:

1. control the ball by applying varying degrees of force in tossing the ball
2. increase the degree of control over the ball while dribbling with either hand
3. manipulate a variety of objects, such as bean bags, balls of various sizes, and frisbees.

Materials

A variety of objects such as balls, bean bags, frisbees.

Learning Experiences

The activities in this module can be adapted to accommodate different age groups and a variety of skill levels. Teachers should select the option that best suits the students' needs. Regardless of which option the teacher selects, there should be a summarizing discussion relative to the concepts, ideas, and facts learned in the lesson.

Option #1

Either choose *one* of the activities suggested and work on it for five to ten minutes or allow the students to select an activity to practice from those offered in this option.

a. Toss the ball high, emphasizing high, straight flight paths. Catch after one bounce.

FIGURE 4–38 Striking the ball with different body parts

Learning Experiences

b. Alternate extremely forceful, high tossing with light, soft ball-tossing that keeps it within personal space.
c. Choose a large area (wall, fence, or other target) and experiment, throwing with different degrees of force. (Throwing hard, using a full range of motion is necessary if skill development is to occur.)
d. Repeat Step c and see how you can be consistent in your *application* for force.
e. Extend Step d by aiming at a target.

Related Experiences

• Watch any ball sport contest on television and count the number of times the ball hits the target.
  –Basketball
  –Soccer
  –Baseball
  –Football

FIGURE 4–39 Striking the ball with different body parts

FIGURE 4–40 Bouncing the ball while balancing on different body parts

Option #2

a. Find a way to bounce your ball while balancing on different body-parts.
b. Change body-parts as you bounce the ball using your hand.
c. Make the ball bounce very hard (and high) and then softly (and low). Alternate these two kinds of bouncing. By changing the movement factors (Time, Force, Space, Flow) in the task, the child learns to deal with and control these factors.
d. Travel while you bounce the ball. Try using different locomotor movements, then combine the locomotor and nonlocomotor movements.

Option #3

a. Find different ways to catch the _____ (object) using one hand, two hands, etc. (Remember to "give" with force of the _____.) Children who are having difficulty in developing manipulative skill should *not* work with catching in the same lesson as throwing. Teachers should select a catching activity and develop a central module around this activity.
b. Throw the _____ high in the air and see what actions you can do before the _____ touches the ground (clap hands; turn around; roll; perform a cartwheel).
c. Repeat Step b and see how you can perform the action and then catch the _____.
d. Find a way to throw (or bounce) the _____ to make it return to you.

FIGURE 4–41 Catching the ball after a light bounce

Summary

Enabling Behavior: Developing Manipulative Abilities

This enabling behavior underlies major movement competencies needed in ball games. Children are improving in manipulative skill when they can:

1. Accurately roll a ball over longer distances.
2. Throw balls or bean bags with increasing speed and accuracy over longer distances.
3. Catch balls or bean bags of various sizes and consistencies that are rolled, thrown, or bounced to them.
4. Successfully strike a ball at a target, or over an obstacle, or in a designated pattern with a variety of body-parts from different supports.
5. Successfully manipulate jump ropes or hoops for their own or another's movement task.
6. Use rolling, throwing, striking, and catching skills in games of increasing complexity.

ENDNOTES

1. Lolas E. Halverson, "The Young Child—The Significance of Motor Development," in *The Significance of the Young Child's Motor Development,* ed. Georgianna Engstrom (Washington, D.C.: National Association for the Education of Young Children, 1971), p. 18.
2. Ibid.
3. Ibid., p. 20.
4. Ralph L. Wickstrom, *Fundamental Motor Patterns,* 2nd ed. (Philadelphia: Lea and Febiger, 1977), p. 6.
5. Harriet G. Williams, "Perceptual-Motor Development in Children—Information and Processing Capacities of the Young Child," in *Proceedings, Region East Perceptual-Motor Conference,* eds. L. E. Bowers and S. E. Klesius, mimeographed (Washington, D.C.: American Alliance for Health, Physical Education, and Recreation), p. 4.
6. ————, "Body Awareness Characteristics in Perceptual-Motor Development," in *A Textbook of Motor Development,* ed. Charles B. Corbin (Dubuque, Iowa: William C. Brown, 1973), p. 140.
7. Bryant J. Cratty and Sister Margaret Mary Martin, *Perceptual-Motor Efficiency in Children* (Philadelphia: Lea and Febiger, 1969), p. 156.

8. Williams, "Body Awareness," pp. 140–48.

9. Cratty and Martin, *Perceptual-Motor Efficiency in Children,* pp. 159–60.

10. Monica R. Wild, "The Behavior Pattern of Throwing and Some Observations Concerning Its Course of Development," *The Research Quarterly* 9 (October 1938): 20–24.

11. Ibid., 24.

12. Wickstrom, *Fundamental Motor Patterns,* p. 11.

13. Bud Blake, *Tiger* (New York: King Features Syndicate Division, The Hearst Corporation).

14. James M. Sawrey and Charles W. Telford, *Educational Psychology* (Boston: Allyn and Bacon, 1964), p. 92.

15. C. H. Patterson, *Humanistic Education* (Englewood Cliffs, N.J.: Prentice-Hall, 1973), p. 94.

16. Goodwin Watson, *What Psychology Can We Trust* (New York: Bureau of Publications, Teachers College, Columbia University, 1961), pp. 2–14.

17. Dorothy Cohen, *The Learning Child* (New York: Pantheon House, 1972), pp. xvii–xviii.

18. Muska Mosston, *Teaching Physical Education* (Columbus, Ohio: Charles E. Merrill, 1966), p. xiii.

19. Ibid.

20. Ibid., p. 8.

21. Ibid., pp. 143–149.

22. Harold M. Schroder, Marvin Karlins, Jacqueline O. Phares, *Education for Freedom* (New York: Wiley, 1973), pp. 9–12.

23. Ibid., p. 17.

24. Ibid., pp. 25–27.

25. Mosston, *Teaching Physical Education,* pp. 143–49.

26. Schroder, Karlins, Phares, *Education for Freedom,* pp. 44–50.

27. Watson, *What Psychology Can We Trust,* p. 15.

28. Ibid., p. 5.

29. Mosston, *Teaching Physical Education,* pp. 19–30.

30. Ibid., pp. 143–49.

31. Ibid., pp. 183–88.

32. Ibid., p. 183.

33. Rudolph Laban, *Modern Educational Dance,* 2nd ed. Revised by Lisa Ullman (London, Macdonald & Evans, Ltd., 1963), pp. 22–23.

34. Joan Russell, *Creative Dance in The Primary School* (London: Macdonald & Evans, Ltd., 1965), pp. 33–38.

35. Margaret H'Doubler, *Dance a Creative Art* (Madison, Wis.: University of Wisconsin Press, 1968).

36. Laban, *Modern Educational Dance,* p. 23.

chapter five

Becoming Independent

ABOUT CHILDREN

The process of becoming independent is life-long and complex. In almost any society, it is doubtful that anyone can become a completely independent person, but for the most part people prefer to decide what they will do rather than have their behavior controlled by others. The process of becoming independent involves the development of physical skills, knowledge, and a value system that affects one's lifestyle.

The goal of this developmental theme is to assist each child in becoming more independent. The scope of this theme extends from almost complete dependence at birth to almost complete independence as a mature adult. The process is never complete, as increased knowledge and changing skill levels (improving or deteriorating) constantly modify one's behavior. A comparison of dependent and independent behavior will illustrate the nature of the process.

Observe infants climbing on furniture. They are exploring their environment and discovering what they can do. Unfortunately, they cannot always predict the consequences of their actions, and often they fall or climb to a point where they need assistance to get down. Repeated falls can lead not only to discovery of what they can do, but also to injury and reluctance to try additional physical feats. Frequently, adults or older children intervene and restrict the choices available to the children. "Don't climb on the furniture!" or "No! No!" are instructions designed to keep children safe.

Contrast the behavior of infants with that of adults who have achieved a high degree of independence. They have developed a repertoire of movement skills that permits them to be safe in their daily movement tasks and recreational pursuits. They know how to project the consequences of their movements and avoid dangerous environments whenever possible. They are still stimulated by physical challenges and will attempt movement tasks with a degree of confidence that is built upon past successes. Their positive feelings of self-esteem give them the courage to resist potential danger, even when there is social pressure to perform some movement task beyond their known or assumed abilities. When faced with decisions, independent persons can examine the known alternatives and make a choice. If none of the choices meet their needs, they can create new ones. They feel they are in control of their movement behavior.

Developing Independent Behavior

Just as no two personalities are identical, no two people are exactly alike in their degree of independence. This is to be expected in view of the fact that developing independent behavior is the result of the interaction of many aspects of a person's life. One's physical and intellectual development, family and social interactions, and cultural pressures all combine in unique ways. However unique this development may be, most people follow similar generalized developmental patterns as they move toward independence.

As in most kinds of development, successful completion of one stage assists in the development of the next. For example, as children develop a degree of physical independence (walking, riding a tricycle), they might still have a need for emotional dependence (knowing a parent is close by). They will now strive for emotional independence, while continuing to develop physical skill for even greater overall independence. This is the nature of development; successful completion of one stage assists in the development of the next. All of this development is modified by individuals' inherited abilities and interactions with their environment. Teachers can do little about innate abilities, but as significant adults in the lives of children, they can greatly influence development through skillful intervention using appropriate methods and activities.

Emotional Development

The development of emotional behavior does not seem to progress in as orderly a sequence as does physical and intellectual behavior. Havighurst[1] has described developmental tasks of children, Erikson[2] has described healthy personality development, and Gordon[3] described the development of the concept of self. All agree that the developing child is struggling for emotional independence.

Even from birth, infants seek to control their environments. Examples of the developmental tasks of infancy and early childhood described by Havighurst are: learning to walk, learning to take solid foods, learning to talk, and learning to control the elimination of body wastes.[4] Each assists the young child in exercising greater control of his environment and in becoming more independent.

Erikson stated that infants will learn that their needs for food, and for being comforted will be met by people they recognize. Also, they discover that they can control some objects in their environment in a predictable way. He called this developing a "sense of trust."[5]

Having developed some sense of trust (of both people and things), infants will spend the next year or two asserting themselves. Much of their behavior is a response to their growing physical ability. Parents have been aware of this stage when they recognize the need to "child-proof" their homes. Erikson described this stage as developing a "sense of autonomy."[6] The improving physical development of children contributes to their developing control of self and environment.

Increasing numbers of children are being introduced to formalized learning environments, such as day care centers, nursery schools, and kindergartens, between the ages of three and six years. Erikson described this period as the time when the "sense of initiative"[7] is developing. It is also a time for intruding into other people's space and venturing into the unknown. According to Erikson, children know what they can do and are now seeking to discover what they can become. Often, children will imitate the behavior of adults and other children around them, especially the ones they want to be like. In the process of discovering Who Am I?, children will imitate a variety of behaviors, including aggressiveness.

This early childhood period is a critical time in children's development of independence. Havighurst[8] and Erikson[9] identified this as the time when children's conscience is developing. Probably more than at any other time, children need help in learning what behavior is acceptable rather than the continuing admonishments "Don't do that!" and "No!"

As children enter the primary grades (grades 1–3), Erikson stated that the next stage of personality development begins. This is the development of a "sense of accomplishment."[10] At this time, fantasy activity (such as pretending to be animals and spacemen) begins to diminish, and children seek to engage in real tasks (counting, measuring, planning) that can be worked on through completion. Havighurst identified this as a developmental task for middle childhood called "achieving personal independence."[11] Children's increased motor control and knowledge stimulate them to gain greater independence. Gordon[12] agreed that children need to struggle for independence at this stage, and parents and teachers need to learn to cope with this behavior in nonpunitive ways.

With the onset of adolescence, another period of personality development begins. Erikson identified this as developing a "sense of identity."[13] Children seek to clarify who they are and what their roles in society will be. Today, some children are reaching adolescence prior to leaving the elementary school.

Accidents are a major cause of death and injury to young children. Early in their development, children are told how to behave safely, and the environment is designed to remove potential hazards. Later, improved motor development assists children in avoiding collisions and falls. This same motor development also causes children to get into dangerous situations. Thus, education regarding safe behavior becomes important in assisting children to develop the ability to project consequences of their behavior. The inability to project consequences results in dangerous behavior. As children begin to move away from the immediate security of their homes, they must develop an awareness of safety and become more responsible for their own behavior.

ABOUT TEACHING

The ways a teacher communicates with students and the climate for learning are crucial in aiding students to become independent. The information in this section has relevance not only to Becoming Independent, but it also builds on the material presented in the previous chapter and lays the foundation for the information about teaching and learning that is given in subsequent chapters.

Information Processing

Imagine a class of children moving through the area the teacher defined as their movement space. The children are moving in different directions and at various speeds. Some are walking, others are running, and a few are hopping or scooting along on the floor on their hands and toes. No one bumped into anyone else and everyone stopped when the teacher used a pitch pipe to sound a long low note.

What were these children doing? They were *processing information.* The teacher presented a movement task and the children had to do more than just listen. They had to receive the information, termed *input;* make sense out of this information, *interpret the input;* and make an expressive response, termed *output.* This series of steps is called *information processing* or the *perceptual-motor process.* Figure 5–1 provides a diagram of the information processing model.

The eyes, ears, nose, tongue, skin, tendons, and muscles have sensory receptors which when stimulated send nerve impulses to the brain. Perception is the decoding of these impulses and giving meaning to sensory input. It is the sensory input (see Phase 1 in Figure 5–1) that provides the "raw material" to which meaning is assigned and decisions are based. Present sensory impulses and memories of past experience are synthesized at a higher brain level. Because the past experience of two individuals are not the same, the interpretation of the same sensory input by these individuals may be different (see Phase 2 in Figure 5–1). The difference in perceptions partially accounts for differences in the responses of the two individuals.

The output phase can occur as an expressive verbal and/or motor response (see Phase 3 in Figure 5–1). Observable human behavior requires movement, which is produced by the action of the muscular system. Speaking requires muscles to force air from the lungs and to shape the lips, tongue, and mouth to make sounds. Muscles pull a pencil across a page to make symbols. A smile is the result of muscular action that lifts the corners of the mouth. The large muscles of the legs propel an individual as the body thrusts upward in a dance step or a jump to block a basketball shot.

As a person acts, on the basis of his perceptions, things change. New stimuli arise and new experiences are encountered when one moves from one position to another. The feedback loop, the fourth part of the perceptual-motor process, is an information flow that can be used to modify and refine the information processing and movement ability. This phase (see Phase 4 in Figure 5–1) most graphically demonstrates the dynamic nature of the information processing model. For example, as you reach out to pick up a

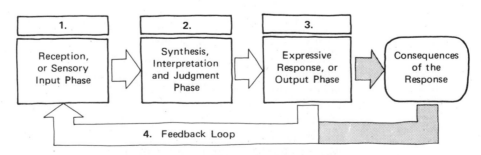

FIGURE 5–1 Information processing model

glass of water, the distance between the glass and your hand decreases, and you slow and slightly change the direction of your movement. These changes in a voluntary and purposeful response are the result of new information and judgments based on the feedback of sensory input. The process of reception of sensation, interpretation, motor response, and feedback is basic to controlled movement and precise expression.

Communicating with the Learner

One reason that teachers interact with students is to facilitate the acquisition of information, attitudes, or skills. Teachers communicate with students prior to and after the students' instructional experience. This section focuses on ways teachers can communicate with the learner in order to provide instructions and give information prior to student movement attempts.

When learning a movement skill, students begin to know what to do by seeing, hearing about, or by being moved through the pattern of the movement. These three input modes are how teachers give instructions about tasks to be learned, and these input modes may all be used in the course of one lesson. Teachers shift from one input mode to another in order to facilitate the progress of the learner. Effective teachers use different input modes for giving information to learners at different points in the learning process.

In order to understand how to make the decision of which input mode to use or what combinations are needed in a lesson, the teacher must know certain information. Being aware of the limitations of a method of input and the function that method can play in child development allows the teacher to begin to make considered choices.

Demonstrations

Demonstrations are most useful in helping students come to know the purpose, speed, and pattern of movement of an unfamiliar motor task. To effectively accomplish these goals, a demonstration should show the movement performed within the broad limits of proper form and at the speed at which the task will actually be performed. This means that a demonstration can be performed either by an able student or the teacher, and/or by means of a film or television presentation.

Demonstrations provide learners with information about what they are expected to do and the way the movements go together. However, demonstrations may serve to restrict creativity in situations where varied or unique responses are desired. Children are quick to learn that what the teacher does is what the teacher usually wants. This is especially true if the teacher positively evaluates or praises the movement response demonstrated, or even a response that is similar to the one demonstrated.

Demonstrations are valuable as a means of having students, individually or in a group, show their movement response. Often students find it easier to show the teacher what they have learned or the movement sequence they have developed by demonstrating rather than by verbal explanation. Demonstrations can be used initially to give information, to refocus effort, or to share responses to a movement task.

A demonstration may be performed by a teacher or student. Demonstrations by a member of the class provide a model that the other students can identify with. In addition to a live demonstration, teachers can use demonstrations presented by filmstrips or television.

Verbalization

Speaking to the learner, verbalizing, is probably the most frequently used and misused instructional method. Verbalization can range along a continuum from direct to indirect statements. At the *direct* end of the continuum, students are given little or no choice about the task and how to respond to it. Consequently, students have few opportunities to make decisions and demonstrate independent behavior. On the other hand, statements that are more toward the *indirect* end of the continuum provide frequent opportunities for making choices and acting independently.

Direct statements are efficient in terms of the time required to have students respond. Indirect statements increase the degree of cognitive involvement and individualization of instruction for students. For these reasons, indirect statements are most effective in promoting independent behavior.

Movement is difficult to describe verbally, especially the sequence and flow of movement. Even if the teacher uses words accurately and completely to describe a movement, there can still be a lack of attention or misinterpretation by the listener. The use of unfamiliar words can cause the listener to respond in ways that could be labeled erroneously as a discipline problem by the teacher.

In Box 5–1, verbalization is used to call attention to a demonstration ("Look at me!"). In addition, a verbal label or word was used in association with the action it represented. The students saw the movement and heard the name for the movement. Another effective use of verbalization is illustrated by the statements that can be given following a demonstration. If the students were unsuccessful showing different ways to "swuzzle" their arms, the teacher could give one or more of the following statements:

Have you tried swuzzling your arm at different speeds?
What are different directions you can swuzzle your arm?
Remember the levels in space, what help does this give you to find different ways to swuzzle your arm?

These statements should be used only after the students have been given an opportunity to respond but were unable to solve the problem. The use of the indirect form of input makes the statements suggestions rather than commands; students can either use the information or choose to ignore it. When teachers give suggestions, they should remember that it is the students who make the decision as to how best to use that information.

BOX 5–1   How Would You Respond?

A teacher states to a class in which you are a student "Show me different ways to make your arm swuzzle." What do you do? How do you respond?

How would you respond to the same question if the teacher said, "Look, I am making my arm swuzzle as it goes up."

"Now, show me different ways to make your arm swuzzle!!" How would you respond to this instruction?

Hint: To think of different ways to swuzzle your arm recall the headings used in the analysis of movement presented on page 75.

Manual Guidance

Physically moving a person's arm through the path of motion of an overhand throw is an example of manual guidance. Manual guidance can be accomplished by moving a relaxed body-part through a movement or by having the learner supply the muscular force, with the teacher directing or steering the body-part through the path of movement. Either type of manual guidance is usually used to assist the learner when other methods have not been beneficial. Manual guidance, therefore, is used by a teacher working with a student on a one-to-one basis, and it is intended to provide only limited information.

The traditional teaching procedure for giving initial instructional input is to explain the task, demonstrate the task, and make additional verbal comments, in that order. In addition to the traditional form of providing instruction, teachers may:

1. use an indirect statement to verbalize a movement task and refrain from giving a demonstration
2. demonstrate without verbally giving information, except to direct the students' attention to particular parts of what is being shown.

The way in which the teacher communicates with the learner should depend on the goals of the instructional encounter. The appropriate choice of information input can enhance the attainment of lesson and developmental theme goals.

Instructional Signals

Signals may be used to communicate information. A signal can be a verbal statement, a sound from an instrument, or a gesture. Often teachers will use a variety of signals in one lesson. A whistle, pitch pipe, flag, drum, cymbals, tambourine, or hand gestures can be used to communicate information for students to go, stop, freeze, or come back to the teacher. Instrumental signals are very useful when the students are scattered over a large space. The instrument should make a sound that is easy and pleasant to hear. Instruments such as a tambourine or drum are more versatile than a whistle because of the different sounds that can be produced.

Hand signals have the disadvantage of having to be given within the sight of each student. This would mean a slow reaction to the signal because often students have their backs to the teacher, and the students would receive their cue to stop or come back to the teacher from the movements of the students around them. However, the fact that hand signals are silent signals is an advantage because they can be used without presenting a distraction to other groups engaged in activities near by.

TABLE 5–1 Basic Instructional Signals

Information to Be Communicated	Type of Signal		
	Verbal	*Instrument*	*Gesture*
		Whistle	*Drum*	
go	say "go"	one short blast	one beat on the drumface	move one or both hands from the level of the head to the side
stop	say "stop"	two short blasts	two beats on the drumface	one hand held motionless overhead
freeze	say "freeze"	one long blast	many fast beats on the drumface	both hands held motionless overhead
come to the teacher	say "come here"	three short blasts	three beats on the drumface	repeatedly move one hand from the level of the waist toward the head

Students need to be given introductory and review practice sessions in order to learn and remember the meaning of instructional signals. The consistent use of one pattern of sound (see Table 5–1) for essential signals promotes the ease with which children respond to those signals. Four basic signals are needed. Signals must be established to communicate when to go, stop, freeze, and come to the teacher. Freeze means to stop and hold the position you were in when you heard the sound, whereas stop means complete the movement you have already initiated, but don't start any new movements.

The four signals should be taught during one lesson. However, all basic signals should be learned by the children and reviewed during the first weeks of class. Teachers need these signals to control the pace of movement and initially to safeguard the well-being of their students. As their students become more independent and responsible for their own actions, the basic signal patterns can be modified. Signals help students to work away from the teacher, who can still communicate information and maintain a degree of control over the students' actions.

Creating a Humanistic Climate for Learning

The mere presentation of information does not equal learning.[14] The extent of learning, as well as the attitudes associated with what was learned, are affected by the conditions that make up the learning environment. What are the conditions that enhance the teaching-learning process? How can a learning atmosphere be created to make learning not only more efficient but also more humanistic?

The learning environment can be divided into two broad categories— the human and the nonhuman. The human portion of the environment includes self and other persons encountered. This section will focus on the human element of the learning environment.

Three specific procedures can be used to promote a humanistic learning environment: providing an affirmative learning atmosphere, listening actively, and using appreciative praise. By means of these techniques, teachers can establish a class climate that is conducive to learning and becoming, and especially the development of independence.

Affirmative Learning Atmosphere

An affirmative learning atmosphere helps to develop self-reliant and confident behavior. Patterson identified empathetic understanding, respect, and genuineness as being basic to constructive personal relationships, whether in psychotherapy, counseling, or teaching.[15] Empathy is defined as knowing something from another's point of view. Respect means acceptance of another individual as a person of worth, as he is; "a warmth and liking for another as a person with all his faults, deficiencies, or undesirable or unacceptable behavior."[16] This nonpossessive warmth and nonevaluative acceptance allows the teacher to relate to a person without approving or excusing that person's behavior. When empathetic understanding and respect are achieved, then both student and teacher are free to be genuine. Genuineness is authentic expression of feelings, open reasons for behavior, and honest, as compared to contrived, relationships.

Listening

Teachers need to learn to listen and teach students how to listen. Listening is a vital part of the process of interpersonal communications. Listening is not just receiving the verbal statements that other people are sending, but being able to comprehend the meaning of these statements as well. In order to fully comprehend what a person is saying, a message, the listener has to receive and identify all the parts of the message. These parts are the words a person uses, the imbedded feelings, and the associated physical gestures. To help people become better listeners, Gordon[17] advocates the use of what is termed active listening.

Active listening is close listening. The active listener attempts to use both the words and feelings expressed by the speaker to comprehend the verbal message. The listener then paraphrases, rather than directly quotes, what he understood the speaker to have said. The paraphrasing should be the listener's personal perception of what the speaker said, and it should reflect the feelings content of the verbal message. The following messages are accompanied by paraphrased replies to provide an example of the active listening technique.[18]

Student's Verbal Message	*Teacher's Paraphrased Message*
• "I can't wait 'til we go outside for physical education class today."	• "You are really excited about physical education and anxious for the lesson to begin."
• "Jimmy hit me and I am going to get him. I'll clobber him. You wait and see."	• "You are angry and hurt that you were hit."
• "I don't like dance. It's for sissies. I want to play ball."	• "You like playing ball better than dancing and you think only sissies dance."

Paraphrasing is only part of the active listening approach. Paraphrasing shows that you care about what the person said and it communicates what you heard the person say. Gordon stated that the person who received the message:

> . . . *does not* send a message of his own—such as an evaluation, opinion, advice, logic, analysis, or question. He feeds back *only what he feels the sender's message meant*—nothing more, nothing less.[19]

After the active listener has fed what he understood back to the speaker, the speaker will usually verify if the listener received the intended message. The listener provides the opportunity for this by remaining silent for a few seconds after paraphrasing a message. Once a message is verified or corrected, the listener may become the speaker. Through active listening, a person can better understand the verbal messages others send. In turn, the rewording of the ideas and feelings expressed by the speaker can play an important part in interpersonal communications and personal development of students.[20]

BOX 5–2 What Would You Say?

A student comes to you, the teacher, and says "I want to try a jump from the high box instead of the low box." How can you say "Yes, I know you can do that" in a way that builds the child's confidence in his ability to make proper judgments?

What would you say? _____

_____

Did you say:

> "If you want to."
> "You decide about that."
> "If that is really what you like."
> "It is entirely your choice."
> "Whatever you decide is fine with me."

Dr. Ginnott called these statements freedom phrases because they foster the child's independence. If the teacher thought the student should not try that activity, a different statement would have been warranted. However, in this case a reply which expresses confidence and allows the student to be self-reliant is appropriate.[21]

Compare what you said with the "freedom phrases." Did you use a statement that freed the student to make a decision or did your response leave you, the teacher, in control as the decision maker?

Responding

When one responds to another person's statement, the communications process can be opened or closed, and thus the interpersonal communications atmosphere of trust, acceptance, and warmth can be enhanced or diminished. Nonaccepting responses are especially damaging. A nonaccepting response shows that the person or what the person said was not regarded by the listener as significant or important. Gordon has identified twelve categories of responses that have a destructive effect on communications. These typical nonaccepting responses are:

1. *Ordering, Directing, Commanding*—Telling the child to do something, giving him an order or a command: "Now, you go back up there and play with Ginny and Joyce."
2. *Warning, Admonishing, Threatening*—Telling the child what consequences will occur if he does something: "One more statement like that and you'll leave the room."
3. *Exhorting, Moralizing, Preaching*—Telling the child what he *should* not or *ought* not to do: "You shouldn't act like that."
4. *Advising, giving solutions or suggestions*—Telling the child how to solve a problem, giving her advice or suggestions; providing answers or solutions for her: "Go make friends with some other girls."
5. *Lecturing, Teaching, Giving Logical Arguments*—Trying to influence the child with facts, counterarguments, logic, information, or your own opinions: "Children must learn how to get along with each other."
6. *Judging, Criticizing, Disagreeing, Blaming*—Making a negative judgment or evaluation of the child: "That's an immature point of view."
7. *Praising, Agreeing*—Offering a positive evaluation or judgment, agreeing: "I think you're right."
8. *Name-calling, Ridiculing, Shaming*—Making the child feel foolish, putting the child into a category, shaming him: "You're acting like a wild animal."
9. *Interpreting, Analyzing, Diagnosing*—Telling the child what his motives are or analyzing why he is doing or saying something; communicating that you have him figured out or have him diagnosed: "You feel that way because you're not doing well in school."
10. *Reassuring, Sympathizing, Consoling, Supporting*—Trying to make the child feel better, talking him out of his feelings, trying to make his feelings go away, denying the strength of his feelings: "You usually get along with other kids very well."
11. *Probing, Questioning, Interrogating*—Trying to find reasons, motives, causes; searching for more information to help you solve the problem: "Why do you suppose you hate school?"
12. *Withdrawing, Distracting, Humoring, Diverting*—Trying to get the child away from the problem; withdrawing from the problem yourself; distracting the child, kidding him out of it, pushing the problem aside: "Just forget about it."[22]

Basically, a nonaccepting response gives a solution, puts the person down, denies the person's feelings and ideas, or shows the listener to be phony or unconcerned. One technique for avoiding nonaccepting replies when communicating with others is to say your answer to yourself silently first. Then identify how you would have felt and reacted if the statement had been made to you. If the effect was constructive, say it, but if the reply has a destructive effect, then think of something better to say.

Praising

Some people may have been surprised that one of the typical destructive responses identified by Gordon[23] was praising and agreeing. How the teacher gives praise can influence a student's feelings of self-respect, self-confidence, and self-esteem. Praise that evaluates or judges a person or the person's efforts can be damaging to the affirmative atmosphere for learning. Instead of increasing motivation, developing openness, or enhancing independence, evaluative praise may have the opposite effect. An example of evaluative praise in the case of a group of students who just did something the teacher liked would be: "You sweet angels, you are so good. Keep up the good work." If the children have acted inappropriately prior to this instance, such praise can bring about feelings of guilt, shame, or embarrassment. Furthermore, it was the teacher who decided that this act was good, as if the students weren't capable of being good or recognizing that they were acting in an acceptable and responsible manner.[24]

BOX 5-3   Recognizing Types of Praise

Two types of praise were explained in this section. The point was made that appreciative praise was more effective in acknowledging student accomplishments than evaluative (judgmental) praise.

To increase your ability in using appreciative praise the following guides are presented:

Do not	*Do*
• evaluate the person or the person's character	• tell the person what you appreciated
• attach adjectives to the person's character	• praise specific acts or aspects of an event
• always praise a person in public.	• describe what you saw including recognizing the students' feelings about the act or thing
	• occasionally give written praise.[26]

Read and label each example as appreciative praise (A) or evaluative praise (E)

1. "I liked that movement sequence. It was very good." _____
2. "I could feel the rhythm of that sequence. The movements flowed together." _____
3. "You looked like you enjoyed that movement series. It was fun watching you move." _____

(Answers: 1. E, 2. A, 3. A)

Praise that expresses the teacher's feelings, reports what happened, or shows appreciation is productive. An example of appreciative praise is as follows: "I like it when everyone is waiting quietly. I can start the lesson right away. I really enjoy teaching when I can do that." Appreciative praise reports how the teacher feels and/or describes specifically what was done. The students are then able to infer that the teacher was pleased, evaluate their own behavior, and draw positive conclusions about themselves.[25]

Teachers should continue to use praise. For some teachers, this change will require greater concentration in order to give appreciative praise rather than evaluative praise. The specific or supportive information given in appreciative praise helps the student to learn, recognize feelings, and to come to value self-judgments of their capabilities. When students feel respected and listened to, their feelings of security are enhanced. The individuals then have the foundation for becoming independent, confident, and self-reliant.

IMPLEMENTING THE DEVELOPMENTAL THEME

Following Directions and Making Choices

It may seem paradoxical to say that one should learn to follow directions as a step toward becoming independent; yet it is an important step. Following directions constitutes the earliest form of decision making that students perform when they begin any kind of formalized instruction. The decision to follow or not to follow directions is sometimes the only form of decision making that some students experience throughout most of their school lives. It is important for children to practice making decisions. Through the experience of choosing and acting on their choices, children come to understand the concept of the consequences of actions.[27]

Making choices between viable alternatives is another important aspect of developing independence. The choices should require some real involvement on the part of the children. A follow-up discussion could focus on how the choice was made, and especially how appropriate the choice was. (Chapter Nine deals further with making choices.)

Frequently, decisions are made by the teacher for the children ahead of time in an effort to expedite the learning activity. An example of this is to offer the same sized balls, same colored streamers, or same length jump ropes to the class. There may be situations where this is necessary to prevent squabbling and other unproductive behavior; however, this practice hinders the development of decision-making behavior and, in the long run, may mean more problems for the students and more work for the teacher. The use of problem-solving helps to create a learning climate in which children make real decisions about their choices of equipment and activity. This method requires that children assume responsibility for their actions, which are a result of the decisions they make. Only by gradually assuming increasing responsibility for their actions will children ever learn to project consequences.

It takes physical and psychological courage to be independent. It has long been postulated that some tumbling and gymnastic activities, such as vaulting, help to develop courage. However, there is little research evidence to support this contention. It is possible that these generalizations have been made after the fact, i.e., the children who performed the vaulting activities more readily were those who were judged to be courageous. There is a very real possibility that these children were able to use the apparatus more effectively because they were more courageous to begin with.

Strength seems to be one factor that is a constant when considering how confident children are about engaging in new movement situations and how confident they feel about themselves. Therefore, it seems logical that providing activities that lead to the development of strength, particularly in relation to supporting one's own body weight, should help in developing a general feeling of "I can . . ." which is related to becoming independent.

Interdependence of Courage and Safety Awareness

Because of its seemingly high-risk nature, vaulting types of activities often have been difficult to cope with for the classroom teacher. Traditionally, it was assumed that for teachers to be in control of the situation, they had to know exactly what the child was going to do on the apparatus. Deviation from the teacher-set activity on the monkey bars, climbing ladder, or vaulting box was discouraged—and sometimes punished.

The use of the problem-solving method in tumbling and gymnastics activities can help to preclude many of the presupposed difficulties. It has been the experience of teachers who have employed a problem-solving method in tumbling and gymnastics that children tend to do those feats they feel capable of doing. In an affirmative learning atmosphere, children are freer to choose *not* to do an activity that they may feel uncertain about performing successfully. In such a class, teachers reinforce sound judgment as well as good performance. Gradually, through self-paced practice, children learn their limitations and capabilities. Over time, the teacher also becomes familiar with the children's capabilities and becomes more skillful in giving encouragement and appreciative praise at appropriate times. This is especially important for the timid child.

Developing courage and safe behavior are interdependent. Children need practice in managing those situations that provide an element of risk, thereby developing movement behaviors that either preclude an accident or reduce its seriousness. *Courage* is gained from knowing how much you can trust yourself, as opposed to trusting luck, which is recklessness. Courageous acts are not reckless acts.

The Teacher's Role

The experiences presented in the teaching modules provide progressively more difficult challenges for children. By overcoming the challenges, children can develop the self-confidence in which courage is rooted. This development can occur if children are allowed to test the various facets of their motor capabilities under safe conditions.

Teachers do not need to be constantly directing the children's work in an effort to prevent boredom. The nature of the activity is usually an incentive to continue working. For example, swinging is more exciting than just holding on; swinging with one hand is even more exhilarating; and swinging upside down can be a goal that one sets for oneself. Teacher intervention in the form of setting tasks that help children discover what they can do is a crucial factor in helping children gain self-confidence.

Children need reinforcement for exhibiting self-discipline, rather than relying on the teacher to determine what is safe and not safe. Positive approaches that focus on what the child can do will be more profitable in the long run for both students and teachers than constantly reminding everyone to "be careful!"

FOLLOWING DIRECTIONS

Planning Guide

Objectives

As a result of the learning experiences over time, children will:

1. be able to start and stop with a sound signal
2. start and stop with a movement sign from the teacher or a partner

3. be able to follow simple diagrammed instructions for working at a series of learning stations or centers
4. work with a partner in a productive manner.

Experiences

- attending and responding to a variety of signals; starting and stopping on a signal
- working with a partner, responding to a variety of body-signs; devising ways of giving signs
- working at learning stations of increasing difficulty; taking initiative for moving to a station that is available
- making up sequences that focus on leading and following; matching partner's movements; mirroring partner's movements.

The sample lesson presented for this enabling behavior can be used for both primary and intermediate grade children. The difference will be in the complexity of the expected responses to the tasks.

For evaluating your students' progress in this enabling behavior, see page 124.

Teaching Modules

Introductory Module

Objectives

As a result of the learning experiences over time, children should be able to demonstrate that they:

1. can follow a hand signal for changing direction
2. can follow a sign signal.

Learning Experiences

Have the children gathered round you in the activity area.

1. "This is the signal that we are going to start with today. Raise your hand the *instant* you hear it." Practice signal (**). There should be a distinct difference between the signal to start, and the signal to stop:

   Start—2 drum beats
   Stop—1 drum beat

2. "Now, everyone shake both hands in the air, and stop the instant you hear *this* signal."

   Practice stop signal.

Related Experiences

• Conduct a discussion about the variety of traffic signals and what they mean.

FIGURE 5–2 Learning to respond to signals

Learning Experiences

Related Experiences

3. "This time you are going to move any-where inside the boundaries, starting with this signal (**), and stopping on this signal (***).
Are you ready?" Signal (**).
Practice this several times.

4. "Sit down where you are now. Some of you are letting the drum (or tambourine) catch you! See if you can make your starts and stops as quickly as when you were just us-ing your hands. You should start moving the *instant* you hear the signal, and stop the *instant* you hear the stop signal. Let's try it again." Provide specific, positive re-inforcement for those children who dem-onstrate precise responses.
   This activity can also provide the oppor-tunity to detect mild hearing problems. If a child consistently fails to respond to the "stop" signal, it might indicate some hear-ing loss.

5. Bring the children together in a group. "Which is the more difficult signal to hear?" (The stop signal because there is more noise interference. It is harder to pick up cues from others.)

6. "Now, we are going to change the signal. I'm going to use my hand. Whichever way I point, that's the direction you will travel in." Briefly go over the possible directions: right, left, up, down, forward, backward. "Now, find a working space where you can see my hand." This will limit the children's activity somewhat because they must be able to see the teacher.

7. "I like the way that you really followed my hand and made quick directional changes." Show an arrow sign to the chil-dren. "See if you can respond as quickly to this arrow when I move it." Point the ar-row in different directions, increasing the speed as the children become more proficient.

- Write a story about a town that had no traffic lights. Tell how they solved the problem.

- Discuss the importance of hearing. What must it be like to live in a world without sound?
- Hold a discussion about people whom the children know to be deaf. What are some of the problems that they have?
- Conduct a discussion about what are some other sound signals we respond to in life?
    - police/firetruck/ambulance sirens
    - tornado warnings
    - different school bells.
- Discuss other sound signals that tell us something:
    - ice cream truck
    - door bells.
- Discussion about traffic signs and what they mean.

- Make a collage of different signs.
- Discussion and listing of *signaling words* that get people's attention:
    SALE!!
    REDUCTIONS!
    FREE!
and how they are used.

Central Module

Objectives

As a result of the learning experiences over time, children should be able to demonstrate that they:

1. can attend to sounds of varying duration
2. can respond autonomously to sounds of different duration
3. can respond to a change in signals by varying their movement.

Materials

1. Cymbal, gong, or triangle to make sustained sounds.
   Sustained—sound which continues for some time after the instrument is struck or played.
2. Tambourine or shaker-type instrument to make vibratory sounds.
   Vibratory—sounds of very short duration that follow in rapid succession.

Learning Experiences

1. Have the children close enough to you to permit good eye contact. They should also be able to hear the instrument clearly. Use the cymbal first. "Listen to this sound (*****). Can you move one hand until the sound stops?" Play the cymbal again. "Now, see if you can move both hands to the sound."
2. "This time see how you can move your whole body to the sound. Keep moving until the sound stops for you." Reinforce movement that is slow and sustained.
3. "Can you really think about the sound you are hearing?" So long as you hear any sound at all, keep moving, even if some other people have stopped already."

   Children need practice in acting autonomously. It has been the writer's experience that in this task the children will often take their cues from other children, rather than rely on their own judgment.

Related Experiences

- Finger painting in response to different sounds (triangle, maracas, tambourine, and drum). Start and stop with each sound.
- Listen to and describe different sound patterns and sound sequences.
- Discussions about which sounds can save lives:
  - telephones
  - car horns
  - train whistles
  - train crossing bells.

Learning Experiences	*Related Experiences*

4. "I am going to change instruments now. Listen to the sound that the tambourine makes. Show me how you can move to this sound, but stay in your own space. Don't forget to start and stop with the sound." Repeat the sound at short intervals.

- Create a poem about how the tambourine was first invented.

5. Discuss how the tambourine sounds differ from those of the cymbal. The children should then be encouraged to seek descriptive words for each sound. This discussion is then related to how the *movement* follows the sound, not vice-versa. It would be helpful here for the class to observe a student who performs well in response to this task. Conduct a brief discussion about what contributed to the demonstrator's good performance: precision of response, and involvement of total body in movement.

- List words that describe sustained and vibratory sounds.
- Draw a picture of how they looked moving to the cymbal sound.
- Make a design of long, curving lines and short, zig-zag lines.
- What are some of the ways in which a cartoonist indicates movement? Bring in some examples from newspapers.
- Discussions about which sounds are irritating:
    - chain saws
    - air hammers
    - fingernail on the blackboard
- Discussion about volume of sounds:
    - car radios
    - classroom chatter
    - amplified music
- What are some of the results of high volume?
    - irritability
    - impaired hearing

6. "Now, see how you can show, by your movement, which sound you hear. Sometimes I will play the cymbal, sometimes the tambourine." Continue to reinforce:
    - precision of response
    - involvement of total body in movement
    - extreme contrast in movement and facial expressions.

7. "I am going to play only the tambourine this time. See how you can make your vibratory movements take you to the door, ready to go back to the classroom. Think about what you have to do to help everyone perform this task safely." If this activity is performed too boisterously, have the children repeat it satisfactorily.

Culminating Module

Objectives

As a result of the learning experiences over time, children will demonstrate that they:

1. can verbalize the major points of the previous two modules
2. can apply the concepts of the modules to other situations.

Learning Experiences

1. Conduct a brief discussion about the activities in previous modules.
2. Continue discussion regarding when this behavior might be important: in unfamiliar surroundings, e.g., swimming at a strange beach, walking on an unfamiliar path, rock-climbing.

    This discussion takes the children beyond the present situation. It allows them to hypothesize about ways to apply the concepts to other situations.

Related Experiences

• Make up a play about a city where no one followed directions. Tell how the city council resolved the problem.

Summary

Enabling Behavior: Following Directions

Some of the indications that students are improving in following directions are when they:

1. Recognize beginning and ending signals that have been established.
2. Attend to verbal directions that do not have to be repeated several times.
3. Can follow directions given indirectly by the teacher, such as audiotaped or written instructions.
4. Can begin tasks immediately upon hearing the directions.
5. Recognize various forms of directions, such as hand signals, arrows, or pictures drawn on a board or projected by an overhead projector.
6. Demonstrate willingness to take directions from a fellow student who has been assigned this responsibility.

MAKING CHOICES

Planning Guide

Objectives

As a result of the learning experiences over time, children will be able to:

1. decide between two alternatives

2. decide between a number of alternatives

Experiences

• making choices between two types of equipment; choosing between two different activities

• choosing suitable equipment for a task; choosing between several activities

Objectives	*Experiences*
3. operate within the limits of the conse-quences of their decisions	• staying involved with a task once chosen; exploring the possibilities that the equip-ment affords for moving over, under, around
4. create new ideas by combining or select-ing activity choices	• combining choices to expand the range of alternatives available
5. demonstrate understanding that avoiding a decision is simply another form of deci-sion making.	• discussions on obstructive behavior focus-ing on resolution of problems of difficult choices.

For evaluating your students' progress in making choices, see page 129.

Teaching Modules

Introductory Module

Objectives

As a result of the learning experiences over time, children should demonstrate that they:

1. can decide between two alternatives that are offered
2. can cope with the consequences of that decision.

Materials

Sufficient hoops and jump ropes for one per child.

Learning Experiences	*Related Experiences*
Instructions for this activity are given in the classroom. The children then take their se-lected equipment to the activity area to begin self-practice.	

1. "When I say 'Go,' each one of you will se-lect either a jump rope or a hoop on your way out to the activity area. When you get there, you may practice anything you like with your equipment so long as you stay in your own working space. Think about some activities you can do with your equip-ment before you decide. There is enough equipment for everyone to choose which they like." Give the children about a minute to think, and then say "GO!"	• Discuss which behaviors "choosing" in-volves:
	    –knowing purpose of activity
	    –establishing criteria
	    –hypothesizing about outcomes of dif-ferent alternatives
	• Write an explanation of how you would spend $10, and why you chose to spend it that way.
	• Write a story about a time when you made a wrong decision.

FIGURE 5–3 Self-selected activity with a rope

Learning Experiences

The availability of the equipment provides the children with a real choice, as opposed to a "forced" choice, caused by having only a limited amount of equipment of each type. Once the choice is made, however, it is important to stay with one's decision.

Children find it difficult to resist rushing to be the first to choose. Reinforce desired behavior quickly by such comments as: "I like the way Randy is waiting for his turn quietly," or "Kathy remembered that she doesn't have to push because there is enough equipment for her to choose which she likes."

Related Experiences

- List the kinds of decisions that are made constantly in certain types of jobs: doctor, pilot, judge, etc.
- What do they have to consider when making decisions?

Central Module

Objectives

As a result of the learning experiences over time, children will demonstrate that they:

1. can remain in a working space
2. can stay involved and within the limits of the task
3. can adapt the task to their selected equipment.

Materials

Signal for Start and Stop.

Two large signs: one with "Over" the other with "In and Out" written on it.

| *Learning Experiences* | *Related Experiences* |

Learning Experiences

The Introductory Module is structured so that the children will be active immediately after they arrive in the activity area. Permit this self-practice to continue for about three to four minutes, then stop the activity with the Stop signal.

1. "Everyone hold their hoop or jump rope still . . . Many of you found a lot of interesting things to do with your equipment."
2. Hold up both signs. "What are the words on these signs? . . . Choose *one* of the directions and work with that using your hoop or jump rope." Reinforce preciseness of response. "In and Out" is not the same as "Through"; "Over" does not imply "Under" also. Allow time at this point for the children to demonstrate their ideas. Have all those who selected "In and Out" to perform, regardless of which piece of equipment they chose. Do the same for "Over."

Related Experiences

- List some everyday things we have to make decisions about:
  - −what kinds of food we eat
  - −menu selections
  - −what type of shoes to wear
  - −which TV program to watch.
- How do people make decisions about the previous items?

FIGURE 5–4 Into and out of equipment

Learning Experiences

3. "This time see how you can work on your movement idea and at the same time use a different body-part to take your weight. If you were just using your feet last time, see what other part of the body can support your weight as you move." Reinforce the children who are attempting to take weight on their arms, or are assuming an inverted position.

Related Experiences

- Discussions about crucial decisions one makes in terms of movement in daily life.
  - –when crossing the road
  - –riding a bicycle
  - –playing on a playground

Culminating Module

Objectives

As a result of the learning experiences over time, children should demonstrate that they can:

1. stay involved with a task
2. create new alternatives from those offered
3. vary their own learning environment.

Materials

Hoops and jump ropes previously selected by the children.
Signal for Start and Stop.

Learning Experiences

1. "See how quickly you can find a partner who has a different colored shirt or dress from yours." Reinforce those children who select partners quickly.
2. "When you hear the signal, see how you and your partner can arrange your equipment so that you can continue to work in the direction you chose. This means that if you chose "Over," you must find as many ways as you can to go over the equipment, but you will have your partner's equipment to work with as well as your own. Keep working until you hear the stop signal." This task is structured so that the children may choose a partner who is working with either piece of equipment, or direction.

Related Experiences

- Make a montage of similar items that have different colors: flowers, clothing articles, cosmetic items, people, etc.
- Discuss how one chooses a friend.
- Discussions about what is a *real* decision:
  - –how does a squirrel "decide" where to hide his store of food?
  - –why do birds "choose" to fly south in winter?
  - –how do the giant turtles "decide" to swim to an island they have never seen to lay their eggs?
- Write a poem about the kind of pet you choose and why you would choose it.
- Discussions about how people make different kinds of choices:

Learning Experiences

Encourage the exploring of many ways to move over or in and out of the equipment. Move among the groups for this activity, giving reinforcement or teaching points where necessary. Allow sufficient time for meaningful exploration before stopping the activity.

3. "You have been finding many different ways of moving over or in and out of your equipment. Now, choose two of those movements and see how you can keep moving by repeating those two movements over and over again. If you and your partner come up with a good idea, you may show it to the rest of the class. Work out your sequence so that you both keep moving all the time. There should be no waiting around!"

The final activity should be a brief discussion about the number and kind of decisions that the children have made during the lesson. By helping the children to summarize their decision making, the teacher avoids assuming that the children recognize this for themselves.

Related Experiences

  −style of house
  −where to live
  −furniture
- Choose one geometric shape from a selection offered and make a design using that shape.
- Choose two geometric shapes and make a repeating design.

Summary

Enabling Behavior: Making Choices

This enabling behavior is basic to more complex decision-making behavior. Children are improving in their ability to make viable choices when they:

1. Demonstrate an understanding that all decisions have consequences.
2. Recognize when *they have* made a decision, as opposed to having something imposed on them.
3. Are able to stay with a decision once they have made it, rather than continuously doubting the appropriateness of the decision and wanting to change it.

DEVELOPING SAFE BEHAVIOR

Planning Guide

Objectives   *Experiences*

As a result of the learning experiences over time, children will be able to:

1. maneuver in a crowded environment with control and awareness of others

   • moving in scatter formation; changing directions quickly and with control; varying the speed of movement

2. absorb the force of their own momentum by receiving their body weight with control

   • landing on feet from on- and off-balanced positions; landing softly on feet with resilience after a jump, or flight from a height; rolling after landing on feet from on- and off-balanced positions

3. absorb the force of an object such as a ball or frisbee

   • catch and trap a variety of balls from various heights and positions; catch a frisbee in flight or rolling

4. propel a variety of objects with control
5. make sound judgments about the safety of proposed activities.

   • throwing, tossing, and rolling objects at a variety of targets; experience a wide variety of movement tasks on various equipment; emphasize choosing safely for self and not allowing others to select activities that are not safe.

For evaluating students' progress in developing safe behavior, see page 133.

Teaching Modules

Introductory Module

Objectives

As a result of the learning experiences over time, the children will be able to demonstrate that they:

1. know the major concepts to be worked on in the lesson
2. know where the boundaries are for the activity
3. understand the formation to be used.

Learning Experiences   *Related Experiences*

"We're going to our activity in a few minutes. There are some important things for you to think about: What helps a car move in and out of a busy traffic lane? (Possible answers: steering wheel; steering mechanism.) How do humans 'steer' (change direction)? We are

• How is changing direction used in some games?
• What games do we need it in?
• In which games is it *most* important?
• What else helps us to avoid collisions? (general movement control; changing speeds)

Learning Experiences

going to be working on changing direction. When you get outside, look around at where the boundaries are and then find a space of your own to begin the activity in."

Either review activities from the Introductory Module of Developing Spatial Awareness or devise a similar short experience on changing directions.

Central Module

Objectives

As a result of the learning experiences over time, the children will be able to:

1. identify stretched and curled shapes
2. roll in a variety of ways from different positions.

Materials

A signal. A jump rope for each child.

Learning Experiences

1. "Curl up into a small shape and practice rolling in any direction you like. When you hear the gong, change the direction of your rolling." Emphasize smooth transfer of weight as the children roll. Reinforce tightly curled shapes with body-parts tucked in. Signal about six or seven direction changes.
2. "Now, make a stretched shape on your hands and feet. When you hear the signal, collapse quickly into a curled shape.

Related Experiences

- Identifying things that roll.
- Identifying things that are "adjacent" (like body-parts in a roll).
- Make a design where contrasting colors are adjacent to each other.
- Identifying geometric shapes that have wide bases.
- Why do objects roll? What causes rolling? What is momentum?
- Finding out what unequal weight distribution has to do with rolling.

FIGURE 5–5 Learning to roll with equipment

62

Learning Experiences

3. "This time you're going to make a different stretched shape each time. Think about collapsing quickly and making a good curled shape."
4. "Now, you're going to roll once each time you curl. So, you'll be stretching, curling, rolling, and finding a new stretched position. Hold the stretch until you hear the signal."
5. "Now, make a low, curled shape on your feet. Find out how you can roll from this position."
6. "Let's think about putting all that together, now. Can you make a tall, stretched shape, then collapse and roll?" (Falling involves a rapid change of position for the center of gravity. This task provides practice in managing that.)
7. "Now, see how many different stretched shapes you can make as you do this activity. Remember to collapse and roll after each stretched shape." If the children are managing themselves well, you might want to remove the signal now. Emphasize landing on the feet before curling and rolling.
8. "Everyone take a jump rope and find a working space of your own. Put it on the ground in a long shape. Practice making stretched shapes over it, then curl and roll."

Related Experiences

- What parts of the body weigh most?
- What does this do to our rolling movement?
- Make a design of round shapes.
- Make a design of stretched and curled shapes.
- Write a story about a land where rolling was the way everyone moved.

Culminating Module

Objectives

As a result of the learning experiences over time, children will be able to:

1. make rapid adjustments in spatial relationships
2. curl and roll from different stretched shapes.

Learning Experiences

1. "Work with the person nearest you. You will be partners. Take turns doing the stretch, curl, and roll over each other's rope, as well as your own. Both of you should be working all the time."

Related Experiences

- Draw a picture of how you think you and your partner looked while you were doing this activity.
- Make a design of long, curled shapes made of string. Glue them to some colored construction paper.

Learning Experiences	*Related Experiences*
2. "Now, we're going to make the task a little more difficult. See how you can travel from one rope to another. Every time you come to a new rope, make a different stretched shape before you curl and roll. Travel to the empty ropes so that there is no waiting to work."	• Write a paragraph on what the differences would be in the movements if you did this activity on the moon.

3. Summarize the central threads of the modules:

    a. landing safely on feet

    b. curling up before rolling

    c. rolling can help to make you safe.

Summarizing helps to effect closure in a lesson.

Summary

Enabling Behavior: Developing Safe Behavior

Children are making progress in developing a sense of responsibility in their behavior when they:

1. Can manage themselves in a dispersed or crowded formation without colliding with other students or objects in the environment.
2. Can make quick changes of direction.
3. Can roll in many directions from balanced positions, and while moving.
4. Quickly react as they move.
5. Properly land on their feet after jumping from a height.
6. Are able to refuse "dares."
7. Demonstrate responsibility in urging others to undertake an activity.

DEVELOPING COURAGE

Planning Guide

Objectives	*Experiences*
As a result of the learning experiences over time, children will be able to:	
1. support their own body weight in a variety of positions	• taking weight on different body-parts, taking weight on hands in an inverted position; supporting self on equipment in different positions

Objectives	*Experiences*
2. control their movement while in the air	• moving on and off equipment such as boxes, bars, balance beams and ropes; making shapes in the air after leaving equipment
3. test themselves in different situations	• identifying tasks to accomplish
4. discriminate between acts of courage and acts of recklessness.	• evaluate the safety of intended tasks; identify current tasks that are possible and equipment that is within a safe range; discussions on what constitutes *courage* and what are the criteria for judging an act to be courageous.

For evaluating student's progress in developing courage, see page 140.

Teaching Modules

Introductory Module

Objectives

As a result of the learning experiences over time, children will be able to:

1. take off into air from one or two feet
2. maintain balance while in flight
3. land with control from symmetric position in the air.

Materials

Signal and jump ropes.

Learning Experiences	*Related Experiences*
1. "Moving in general space, without bumping into anyone, see how you can run lightly and take a little jump in the air when you hear the signal." Give them many repetitions emphasizing light, careful running, and springy, flexible landings. Jumping in response to the signal sets the "tone" of the class. It prevents wild behavior since the children are not allowed to run too far before jumping (a factor in unruly behavior).	• Conduct activities that reinforce concept of "balance" and "off-balance" (symmetry and asymmetry) 　　—ink-blot design created by folding paper in half after ink or paint has been put on it 　　—draw a picture of the class making stretched shapes.
2. "This time, when you take off into the air, think how your feet help you. Try taking off from one foot, and then from two feet."	• Depending on age group, discuss the idea of gravitational pull on a falling body—on different body-parts in flight.

Learning Experiences

Develop this progression by:

   a. removing the signal for jumping and having children decide when to do this;

   b. have them focus on what happens to their landings when they take off from one or two feet. (It need not make any difference. They can still land on one or two feet no matter how they take off).

3. "As you take off into the air this time, see how you can make large, stretched shapes. Continue to land softly and spring up again to start moving and jumping again." Reinforce good stretched shapes. Children can observe an exemplary movement sequence and identify *why* the shape has quality—no angles, fingers and toes stretched, head up, not poking forward or rolling back.

4. "Take a jump rope and make any kind of shape with it you like. Practice making stretched shapes in the air over your jump rope. Make sure you have enough room to run and jump over the rope."

   The introduction of the jump rope adds some interest to the repetition of the task. The task essentially remains the same, but the new equipment can add further challenge.

5. "Make a circle with your rope. This time take off from one side of the rope and land on the other side after making your stretched shape."

Related Experiences

• Health science activities can be related to how the legs and feet work to absorb the body weight. Bones and large-muscle groups can be identified.

• Using magazine pictures, identify those pictures that show a stretched shape.

• Make a picture of things that balance in the air: birds, planes, divers, gymnasts, skydivers, etc.

• Join all your ideas together and construct a mural for the bulletin board about "airborne things and people."

Central Module

Objectives

As a result of the learning experiences over time, children will be able to:

1. dismount from a piece of equipment in a variety of ways, with control
2. land safely on the feet after jumping from a height
3. land safely on the feet and follow with a forward or back shoulder roll.

Materials

Equipment for jumping off, such as vaulting boxes or balance beams.

The more experienced the children are (and this is not always correlated with grade level), the greater the challenges needed. An 18-inch high box is very suitable for many first and second grade children, but third and fourth grade children will need boxes or tables that are two feet to three-and-a-half feet high.

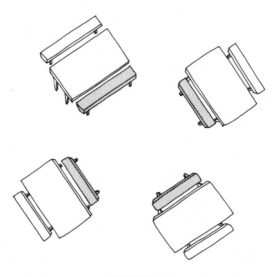

FIGURE 5–6

Learning Experiences

Divide the children into groups before this activity begins. Give each a group letter or word (intermediate grade groups could be identified by using synonyms for *courage, boldness, bravery,* etc.), and have the same word at one of the stations so they know where they are to go. Groups could be maintained for a few days to save time in subsequent lessons.

"When I say 'Go,' move to your station and find ways of getting on and off the equipment safely. Keep everyone moving so there is no waiting in line. Go!"

Until children are accustomed to working in this manner, they will tend to line up behind the equipment simply to get on and get off

Related Experiences

• Make a list of synonyms for *courage* and *courageous.*
• Find at least two books in the library that deal with courage.
• Make a list of courageous people for your class to study:
    –write a biography of one of them
    –make a collage of pictures you can find of some courageous people.
• Find out all you can about a special sports personality who has been labeled "courageous." Explain why she/he was called courageous.
• If you had the chance to be like a courageous person, who would that be? Write about why you chose that person.

Learning Experiences

quickly, returning to the end of the line to wait again. The following tasks are designed to eliminate this behavior and help them use their time productively.

a. "This time experiment with ways of getting on and off the box using your hands. Make sure your feet always touch the mat first when you land." Provide appreciative praise on this task before moving on to other groups: "Jim, I was happy to see that you got your feet high that time. Notice how Donna used her hands to get on the box, but used a high jump to get off."

Related Experiences

- Read a story about a courageous animal. Draw some illustrations for the story.
- Hold a discussion about why some acts are called courageous by some and not by others (the Viet Nam draft "objectors" for example).
- Describe the most courageous thing you've ever done.
- Draw a picture of yourself performing a courageous act.
- For intermediate grades, investigate high-risk sports, such as sky diving, bob sledding, mountain climbing, ski jumping.

FIGURE 5–7 Arriving on equipment safely

FIGURE 5–8 Leaving equipment safely

Learning Experiences

b. When the children are challenging themselves in finding novel ways to get on and off the box, pursue the second part of the problem—rushing to get in line again: "Now, see how you can work so that you use the space all around the equipment and not *just* the box. For example, what could you do after you land from the box? Could you do two movements on the mat? Or one across and two on the floor (or the ground) before you return to the box?"

Children need to learn to "work, and not wait." If this expectation is consistently held to, it results in children working productively alone or in groups. This is a learned behavior that takes a little time to develop.

The first three tasks in this module lay the groundwork for further, more challenging experiences. The following suggestions are examples of ways to vary tasks designed to develop courage, and should be selected to meet the needs of your particular students. The suggested variations are examples of ways to modify *any* movement task. One way to become accustomed to using problem solving in movement education is to give one of the examples to the whole class and then pursue that task to its limits. There are probably many ways to answer the problem set in Direction (a). It is more important for children to explore a task in depth than to rush from one response

Related Experiences

· What kinds of people do these sports? Are they alike in some ways? Different in some ways?

· Make a list of things that make us scared.
· How do we learn to be scared of things?
· Read a book about a courageous boy or girl and then draw some illustrations for it.
· Find out about "Old Yeller" and why he was a courageous dog.
· Make up a story about an animal that saved a family's life.

FIGURE 5–9 Finding a safe way to swing upside down

Learning Experiences

to another *new task.* The task can be varied by focusing on:

Direction:

a. find a way to get on/get off your equipment sideways
b. arrive on the equipment from one direction and take off in another.

Relationship:

a. find a way to go over the equipment using one or two hands.
b. find a way to get on the equipment with all body-parts close together, and take off with body-parts far apart.

Body-Shape:

a. find a way to make a twisted shape as you move over the equipment.
b. show a balanced, curled shape on your equipment.
c. make a wide, stretched (narrow, twisted, curled) shape in the air before you land.

Speed:

a. find a way to show a change of speed as you move on and off your equipment.
b. make your approach fast and change to a slow speed as you dismount from the equipment.

For Intermediate Grade Students: All of the previous variations of the tasks can be used with other equipment, such as hanging ropes, steel bars, cargo nets, window ladders, and inclined beams.

FIGURE 5–10 Traveling sideways on equipment

Culminating Module

Objectives

As a result of the learning experiences over time, children will:

1. identify acts that demand personal courage
2. demonstrate understanding of the relationship that exists between the activities in the central module and the development of courageous behavior
3. set goals for self in accomplishing acts that require a degree of personal courage.

Learning Experiences

The content of the discussion in this culminating module will depend on the activities in the central module. The *nature* of the discussion, however, will not necessarily change.

1. "You were all working with the equipment, getting on and off in different ways. What were some of your feelings as you got on and off the equipment?" Reinforce responses that get to inner feelings relative to *movement* more than remarks about "it was fun" or "Daryl kept getting in front." Some responses you might anticipate are:
   - It was scary sometimes.
   - I felt like I was flying.
   - It was fun seeing everything upside down.
2. Discuss personal courage by a starter question, such as "Did anyone try something they were scared about?" Try to bring out the following points:
   - what is scary for one person may be easy for another person
   - it's hard to admit you *are* scared.
   It takes time for children to develop the idea of a "supportive" community in which people are not ridiculed. Finding out that many people are often afraid, but not necessarily about the same thing, helps children to become more a part of a group, and develop a sense of empathy and sensitivity to the personal needs of others.
3. Conclude the discussion by having everyone identify a "personal courage goal," that they will work toward over a period of time.

Related Experiences

- Write or tell, a story about a time when you were scared and everything turned out all right.
- Investigate the lives of some medical pioneers. Why did their beliefs and achievements require courage? (They were often ridiculed, since much of what they advocated ran contrary to popular opinion.)
- Draw a picture of how the whole class looked doing the activity.
- Write a poem about being scared for no reason.
- Write or tape a mystery story.
- Make a collage of brave people.
- Compare two or three people identified as heroes or heroines. Find out if they are alike or different in any ways.
- Watch the film *Leo Beverman* and conduct a discussion about the courage required to live under such conditions.
- Another film that is suitable for this discussion is *Tom Thumb in King Arthur's Court.*

Summary

Enabling Behavior: Developing Courage

Children are becoming more courageous when they:

1. Choose equipment and movement activities that are appropriate for their ability level, yet safe and still provide a challenge.
2. Demonstrate willingness to try new or unfamiliar activities.
3. Demonstrate greater confidence in being in an inverted position.
4. Can state the difference between courage and recklessness.

5. Can list sound reasons for judging whether a person is courageous.
6. Set reasonable goals for themselves.
7. Can explain that learning to be courageous involves a certain amount of fear.
8. Can explain the meaning of "risk" in positive and negative terms.

ENDNOTES

1. Robert Havighurst, *Developmental Tasks and Education* (New York: David McKay, 1972).
2. Helen Witmer and Ruth Kotinsky, eds., *Personality in the Making* (New York: Harper and Brothers, 1952). This reference constitutes the final version of the *Fact-Finding Report to the Midcentury White House Conference on Children and Youth.* Erik H. Erikson's contributions to the conference are cited in this reference.
3. Ira Gordon, *Human Development From Birth Through Adolescence* (New York: Harper & Row, 1969).
4. Havighurst, *Developmental Tasks and Education,* pp. 9–12.
5. Witmer and Kotinsky, *Personality in the Making,* pp. 8–11.
6. Ibid., pp. 11–15.
7. Ibid., pp. 15–17.
8. Havighurst, *Developmental Tasks and Education,* pp. 16–17.
9. Witmer and Kotinsky, *Personality in the Making,* pp. 15–17.
10. Ibid., pp. 17–19.
11. Havighurst, *Developmental Tasks and Education,* p. 31.
12. Gordon, *Human Development From Birth Through Adolescence,* p. 120.
13. Witmer and Kotinsky, *Personality in the Making,* pp. 19–22.
14. Carl Rogers, *Freedom To Learn* (Columbus, Ohio: Charles E. Merrill, 1969), pp. 177–78.
15. C. H. Patterson, *Humanistic Education* (Englewood Cliffs, N.J.: Prentice-Hall, 1973), pp. 70–72.
16. Ibid., p. 71.
17. Thomas Gordon, *P.E.T. Parent Effectiveness Training* (New York: David McKay Company, Inc., 1972), pp. 49–61. Reprinted by permission.
18. Ibid., p. 53.
19. Ibid.
20. Ibid., pp. 53, 57–58.
21. Haim G. Ginott, *Between Parent and Child* (New York: Macmillan, 1965), pp. 89–90.
22. Gordon, *P.E.T.,* pp. 41–44.
23. Ibid., p. 43.
24. Haim G. Ginott, *Teacher and Child* (New York: Macmillan, 1972), pp. 125–35.
25. Ibid., pp. 135–37.
26. Ginott, *Teacher and Child,* pp. 125–37 and Gordon, *P.E.T.,* pp. 324–25.
27. Ginott, *Between Parent and Child,* p. 75.

chapter six

Accepting and Expressing Feelings and Ideas

ABOUT CHILDREN

Most movement forms (sports, games, gymnastics) have a goal orientation. This is to say that the movements result in some kind of scoring (such as counting the number of runs, strokes, goals, or points) or in bettering some performance scored in terms of time or distance. In most sports and games,

143

the form, style, or aesthetic appearance of the movement is secondary to the outcome of the performance. Stated another way, it's not how good you look while performing, it's whether or not you get the job done.

In activities such as diving and gymnastics the scoring is based on the judges' perceptions of the participants' form, as compared to a predetermined "model" performance. The goal is to achieve perfect form in order to score as many points as possible. Usually, the desired form is a combination of aesthetic and functional qualities. In this chapter, the movement forms of dance and creative rhythmic movement are identified as non-goal-directed movement. The aesthetic qualities of movement will be emphasized.

Participation in physical activities is a personal experience, and participants frequently express what their reasons are for engaging in such activities. Physical fitness, competition, relief of tension, and an opportunity to be aggressive in a socially accepted manner are often mentioned as reasons for participation. There can be no doubt in the mind of the performer or the observer that in almost all movement forms, the participants express their feelings. Usually, the expression is spontaneous and not necessarily meant to communicate to someone else, although it frequently does. Dance and creative rhythmic movement focus on expressing feelings and ideas and communicating through movement. Thus, while any movement form may provide opportunities for a participant to perform aesthetic movements and to express one's feelings, only dance and creative rhythmic movement have these as primary purposes. This developmental theme focuses on the use of human movement in expressing and communicating feelings and ideas.

Why Children Need Dance Experiences

The question might be asked, "Why should we have programs in dance when children already use nonverbal techniques to communicate?" It is true that the early communication skills of infants are nonverbal, but as language skills develop, the use of nonverbal communication is reduced. Throughout life, movement continues to be an effective means of communication. Frequently, some movement or gesture expresses a feeling or idea as no other language can. The aesthetic quality and precision movements of the dancer or mime represent the highest level of expressing and communicating feelings and ideas through movement.

Dimondstein defined dance for children in elementary school as the ". . . interpretation of a child's ideas, feelings, and sensory impressions expressed symbolically in movement forms through the unique use of his body."[1] Dimondstein answered the question Why a dance program?:

> Thus, the importance of a program in dance for children is to help them develop a kinesthetic awareness of their ability to use their bodies expressively. *Kinesthetic awareness* refers not only to a child's bodily reactions or muscle memory, but to a conscious perception of his body's ability to "feel" movement. Because dance is an art form and is not simply physical activity, the per-

ception must be aesthetic. This awareness is made perceptible through his senses and involves him in the total process of perceiving, feeling, and expressing.[2]

And Winters, in speaking of the value of creative rhythmic movements, said:

His reward is simple self-satisfaction and pleasure through the awareness he develops of his own movement and those of others, and being able to direct his movement in order to express and communicate his feelings and ideas in a nonverbal way.[3]

While it is true that all people express feelings and ideas nonverbally, often the level of communication is quite low. The well-designed and conducted dance program does not leave development of aesthetic and expressive movement to chance. The dance program develops not only the necessary physical skills, but also an awareness of one's own and others' feelings. Our society requires awareness and sensitivity to others.

Expressing Feelings

Movement is one means of expressing feelings. Yardley[4] indicated that movement is the first means of expression for children and even after they develop a speaking vocabulary, their body movements remain as a way to express their feelings. She also stated that movements may more adequately express emotions than words. Often the expression of one's feelings through body movements is neither creative nor conscious, but is spontaneous and reflects one's personal feelings.

Winters[5] identified the difference between expressing and communicating. She indicated that expressiveness implies that something of the individual is revealed through personal and intuitive exploration of the means at hand. This does not say that others will be able to properly interpret the movement or that the individual would necessarily move in the same way under similar conditions. Winters also provided a list pertaining to a child's expression of feelings and ideas through movement. She wrote that children will:

- express only what has impressed them
- express themselves on the physical, psychological, emotional, and social level of children, not adults
- usually express themselves nonverbally more readily than do adults
- express themselves through movement more spontaneously than do adults
- have had less time to learn universal gestures and symbols of movement expression, and therefore express themselves in a more spontaneous way, free from constraint
- not have a large enough verbal vocabulary at their immediate command to be able to adequately express themselves verbally.[6]

As mentioned earlier, dance activities are valuable in providing a conducive environment for helping children understand feelings and ideas. These activities are equally valuable in creating an awareness of how one expresses feelings and ideas through movement.

Understanding and Accepting Feelings and Ideas

The development of the understanding of feelings, one's own and those of others, is a slow process. The informal play of children in which they pretend is an important part of the process. Breckenridge and Vincent indicated that "Make-believe and other imaginative activities occupy a considerable part of the mental life of nearly all children from 3 or 4 to 10 or 12 years of age."[7] This is the time when children learn from the reactions of others to their "play." Frequently, they copy adult behavior and experience a wide range of emotions.

Elementary school-age children are aware of their own imaginations. It has been stated that:

> As children enter the primary school period, they can begin to control imagination for useful purposes, such as storytelling and painting, on the one hand, or sympathy and understanding on the other. Sympathy, as based upon the capacity to imagine how other people feel in given situations, develops from four years through the elementary school years.[8]

This period, then, presents an opportune time for dance activities to be used in helping children understand and accept feelings and ideas; both their own and those of others. Use of creative dance and rhythmic activities, as well as folk and ethnic dance forms, provide the environment and stimulus to understand feelings and ideas. Dimondstein stated that the value of dance as an art is ". . . in helping children achieve an awareness of the importance of organizing their emotions and of communicating them. . . ."[9]

Increasing Communicative Abilities

As was discussed earlier, a description of the expressive act was written by Winters. Her statement describes the act of communicating.

> Communication implies that a point has been reached at which children can call upon their experience and order it; through their growing awareness and expertise they will show their power of selection and memory. At this point, not only do the children know what their intent is, but the observers will also be able to recognize elements in the child's movements which are common to all, and which will permit them to share the idea, image, or the feeling that the child is expressing.[10]

Thus, while people express themselves in many ways, frequently their movements are intuitive and not consciously designed to communicate an intended message to anyone else. The communicative act implies that what one expresses will be understood, or at least has the potential to be understood by others. Children can learn to communicate feelings and ideas by practicing movements that are understood by others. Practice in giving impressions of feelings is helpful in learning to understand feelings and in learning how feelings and movements are related. Alice Yardley spoke to this point when she stated:

> Children need to explore consciously their feelings of strength and lightness, of suddenness and sustainment, of variations in direction, and of all the qualities which make up human activity. They need to become aware of the partnership between emotion and movement, and of how patterns of movement can develop into dance. They need to learn through their bodies the vocabulary of movement, and to explore its possibilities as a means of communication.[11]

Children need to develop a wide repertoire of movements that can be used for expressing and communicating feelings and ideas—a movement vocabulary. Often the movements that children use can be a stimulus for development of their verbal and written vocabulary. The opposite is also true. In addition, children can learn how specific movements influence their feelings, and how their feelings influence their movements. As children develop their movement vocabulary, they will increase their ability to communicate feelings and ideas through movement.

Creating Ideas After they have begun to understand feelings and ideas, and they have built a movement vocabulary, children can begin to develop sequences of movement, or dances. Children require practice in replicating movements in order to develop their movement memory. The ability to replicate movements in sequence is valuable in movement forms other than dance and should be developed early. Torrance and Myers pointed out that "At times, children lack confidence to learn creatively because the things that they are expected to do require skills that they have not achieved . . ."[12] The emphasis on becoming aware and developing basic movement capabilities, discussed in Chapter Four, provides a foundation upon which creative ideas can be expressed and communicated through movement.

The ability to think creatively increases steadily from the first to the third grade, diminishes during the third and fourth grades, and is regained and expanded in the fifth and sixth grades.[13] The creative thinking of primary grade children and their freedom from peer judgments provides a situation that teachers have found delightful in terms of children's responses to creative challenges. In addition, young children have difficulty in responding to situations requiring everyone to "keep in time" and to be in a precise place at a precise time. Creative dance experiences provide an ideal setting for helping children create ideas and communicate them through movement. These experiences provide an opportunity for the creative expression of children, and they provide the environment for further development of movement vocabulary and memory.

ABOUT TEACHING

Discussions   Many opportunities exist within the school day for students to listen and respond. Other than the "show and tell" (or, as teachers say in private, "bring and brag") period, children don't have many opportunities to discuss feelings and ideas. Discussions are important developmental experiences because children can express themselves, gain an understanding of other children's feelings and ideas, learn that there is more than one side to an issue, and identify alternative ways of solving a problem.

The circle discussion group is one procedure, and this relatively uncomplicated approach is advocated by a number of authorities.[14] The basic rules for a circle discussion are:

1. the speaker can talk without fear of being ridiculed
2. everyone else in the circle listens to the speaker and may be asked to summarize what the speaker stated
3. everyone who wants to talk will have a turn, but a person can "pass" rather than speak.[15]

Discussions work best when the teacher poses questions that require divergent or evaluative thinking. The skill of questioning has two facets: the planned questions and the spontaneous questions. The planned questions are thought out in advance so the essential points will be discussed and the time available for the discussion will be used wisely. Planned questions are either "take-off" or focusing questions. Take-off and focusing questions call for divergent responses (e.g., What are the different feelings that a person might experience during a long-distance run?) or evaluative responses (In your opinion what are the beautiful movements during a team game such as soccer?). Spontaneous questions arise during the discussion and are used to have students make value judgments or to clarify a previous statement.[16] Examples of thought-provoking questions are:

1. Can you say more about that?
2. What would happen if _____?
3. Who has another (different) idea?
4. What do you think we should try (do) now?[17]
5. How did you feel when that happened?
6. Did you consider any alternatives (other ways of doing that)?
7. Where would that idea lead; what would be its consequences?
8. Is that a personal preference or do you think most people should believe that?
9. Do you have any reasons for saying (or doing) that?
10. How do you know it's right?[18]

These *stock* phrases and questions should be reviewed periodically, and it will become easier to spontaneously state a thought-provoking question during discussions.

Another skill needed by teachers when conducting a discussion is the use of silence. During a discussion, the teacher needs to be able to wait up to thirty seconds while making eye contact with students in the discussion group. If one of the students does not talk within this time, the teacher should clarify the question being discussed, verbally encourage someone to speak, or state a new question to be discussed. However, silence usually gets the discussion going again because the students feel tense as a result of the period of silence. The tension is relieved when someone says something.[19]

BOX 6–1   Thirty Seconds

Thirty seconds is a long time when no one in a discussion group is talking. Do you have a feel for how long thirty seconds is?

Using a wrist watch or clock, time several thirty-second intervals. Next, when the second hand is at the 12 o'clock position, close your eyes and open them when you think thirty seconds has passed. Try this several times until you develop this sense of time.

How accurate were you on your initial attempt? _____ seconds
How accurate were you after practice? _____ seconds

Try this skill during a discussion. If necessary, sit where you can see, without being conspicuous, a wall or desk clock that has a second hand to help you remain silent for thirty seconds.

Many teachers have difficulty keeping a discussion from getting sidetracked by irrelevant talk. This is a critical moment in the development of a discussion. The teacher must be able to refocus discussion in order to reduce the frustration of wasting time, and must channel energy toward the main question. The teacher must sense when the discussion needs to be refocused and tactfully assert the necessary leadership without causing the speaker to permanently withdraw from the discussion. The following are useful ways to refocus a discussion:

1. ignore the comments that get away from the point and push on
2. point out, either to the class or to an individual, that the focus has been lost, and bring the class back to it
3. ask for clarification, i.e., how a comment relates to the focus
4. ask the student to postpone his comment until a later time in the discussion, if the comment is one that will be relevant later
5. paraphrase a rambling response or one that is only partly relevant; this clarifies and refocuses at the same time
6. accept the comment, or at least the feeling of the student involved, and add to it in such a way that you bring discussion back to the point[20]

7. name the disruptive behavior without threatening the student ("Greg, you are making unpleasant noises.")
8. tell a disruptive student, "Return to your desk and stay there until you are ready to follow the circle discussion rules. When you return to the circle, it will tell us you are ready to follow the rules."[21]

These strategies must be practiced. An effective practice technique is to choose two or three different statements and use one of them when the need arises during a discussion. Tape record a discussion to check the effectiveness and appropriate timing of strategies for dealing with irrelevant talk or disruptive behavior.

Chase, in *The Other Side of the Report Card,* offers suggestions for teachers beginning to use circle discussion. Some of these are:

1. Give it a try for a couple of weeks.
2. Start with easy topics, such as "Tell me something that makes you feel good" (personal opinion or preference technique) or "If I had the power to make something happen, I would," or "I wish . . . ?" (incomplete sentence technique).
3. Begin the first session of each week with the question "Do you remember what we did last session (week)?" End each session with a summarization, either by the teacher or by the students.
4. Use the student's names when addressing them, and encourage the students to use names. Also use names when summarizing.
5. Don't start the initial discussion question with the phrase "Today's topic is . . . ."
6. Avoid questions that cause students to answer defensively. "Why" replies by the teacher do this and should not be used. When challenging a student's response, use an open-ended question. ("Do you think it would be better to do X or to do Y?")
7. The teacher should not sit in the same place in the circle each discussion session. The teacher should especially avoid sitting near positions that reflect authority (e.g., at or near his desk, in front of the chalkboard).
8. Develop an atmosphere for the discussion where students feel that they are listened to and that their expressions are accepted. Acceptance indicates "I heard you," that "You are entitled to your opinion or feelings," and "My acceptance does not mean that I endorse or agree with what you said."[22]

Long lists of things to do and not to do, such as the one just given, are often difficult to implement fully. If a person can gain direct experience under controlled conditions or observe a teacher working with students in a circle discussion, the meaning of the Do's and Don'ts become more vivid. The following description is a hypothetical situation and is presented to illustrate how a circle discussion would progress.

Mr. Jones was already seated in one of the chairs in the *circle,* reviewing a list of discussion questions. One by one the students found a chair and sat

FIGURE 6–1 Using a cartoon as a discussion stimulator. @ 1976 United Features Syndicate, Inc.

down. When the ten children who were not scheduled to the afternoon's learning or listening centers were seated, a paper was passed around the circle. Each child looked carefully at the pictures and read the words in the *Nancy* cartoon.

The teacher asked the first question: "What did you think of when you were reading the cartoon? What did it make you think about? Who wants to start off? OK, Doug will be the first speaker. . . . Remember that anyone can 'pass' if they don't want to speak yet."

After most students had spoken, including some who initially had passed, the next question was stated. "Nancy used the word 'gorgeous' to describe how she thought she looked. What word or words would you use to describe the way your body looks?" Later, the following directions and question was given. "Let's brainstorm to come up with answers to this question. What are the different things people could do to help them feel better about how they look?"

After the expression of ideas slowed down and a large number of possibilities had been given by the students, the teacher asked for a show of hands of the students who wanted to summarize the discussion. Several students volunteered and he also encouraged Joe to take part in helping to recall what was said in today's discussion. Jane said that a lot of people thought the cartoon was funny or that Nancy was happy. However, one person said that she hoped Nancy didn't eat a candy bar as it might make her fat. It was also remembered that the remark was made that sometime we don't like what we see when we look in a mirror.

Next, the summarizers stated many of the words the students used to tell how they felt about their bodies. Words like:

> thin
> happy
> pretty
> strong
> ugly teeth
> fat

Joe said that it sounded to him as if some people were unhappy about some things, but happy with some other things about how they looked.

Secretly, the teacher wondered if too many suggestions had been given by the students for ways to improve the way a person looks than the summarizers could have been expected to remember. However, he was pleasantly surprised when, among the responses recalled by the students, the following statements produced a lot of head nodding and smiles within the circle group:

- go to a doctor to get glasses or braces to straighten your teeth
- do exercises
- dress neatly and try to smile a lot
- eat fruit, nuts, or other health food rather than candy and junk foods
- nobody is perfect, so find something you like about the way you look and think about that.

BOX 6-2 Evaluating a Discussion

As the teacher who conducted the discussion about the *Nancy* cartoon, what notes would you have made concerning the effectiveness of the discussion in helping children to accept and express feelings and ideas?

A. What was accomplished? Who expressed feelings and/or ideas that were significant to an individual in the group or to everyone in the group?
B. What discussion skills did *you* use effectively? Which discussion skills do *you* need to improve?
C. What would be some questions *you* would plan for the next circle discussion concerning this topic?

After the students returned to their desks for their next lesson, the teacher made some notes about the discussion and listed some ideas for other magic circle discussions.

Disciplining How does a teacher handle discipline in a way that does not have a destructive effect on the child's self-concept and the class atmosphere for creativity and learning? To the teacher, discipline should mean to train or develop moral character, not just to warn and punish students who exhibit inappropriate behavior. The development of responsible behavior occurs through a process involving disciplinary encounters and modeling.

Admonishing

What is the most productive way for a teacher to tell a student that he or she is doing something that is inappropriate? The teacher could say:

> "You should not sit on a volleyball."
> "I like to see people working with a volleyball. Volleyballs are not made for sitting on."

Two important differences exist in these examples. The first point is that one message only tells what not to do, while the other tells both what is acceptable and unacceptable behavior. Another difference is the use of the pronouns you and I. You-messages come across as an evaluation of the student. An I-message is a statement of fact and communicates feelings as well as facts.[23] Gordon stated that: "The 'I-message' is much less apt to provoke resistance and rebellion. To communicate to a child honestly the effect of his behavior on *you,* is far less threatening than to suggest that there is something bad about *him* because he engaged in that behavior."[24]

What should a teacher do if the student ignores an I-message? The first thing to do is to use the child's name and repeat your original I-message. When a student replies to your I-message, use active listening. I-messages tend to open up communications, as both parties are stating their ideas and are taking a risk by divulging their feelings. By using I-messages, teachers can admonish a student without feeling guilty, in that their intervention is instructive and can serve to enhance the child's self-concept.[25]

Using Reality Therapy

Feelings and discipline are closely related. Sometimes the way students express their feelings results in behavior that violates a class rule. Following a disciplinary encounter with a teacher, a student will experience feelings ranging from relief to guilt and decreased to increased estimation of self-worth. The approach a teacher uses to deal with a student who behaves inappropriately has a direct influence on the student's self-concept. If the major goal of education is to help an individual become an independent, self-

BOX 6–3 A Traditional Approach to Discipline

How do you think a student would react to each of the following teacher actions?

Teacher	Student's Reaction
1. Makes the rules for the class	1. _____
2. Catches the rule breaker	2. _____
3. Tells the rule breaker what he did wrong	3. _____
4. Lectures the rule breaker; tells why the student shouldn't have disrupted the class	4. _____
5. Administers punishment or refers the student to another person for punishment	5. _____
6. Warns the rule breaker that he is expected to follow the rules in the future and if this doesn't happen there will be more trouble	6. _____
	Overall—
	_____

What is accomplished by a teacher using this approach?

- Does it help a child develop self-responsibility and self-discipline?
- Does it contribute toward the student's independence?
- Does it enhance the child's feeling about himself or herself?

confident and competent person, then the manner by which teachers and students interact, especially in a disciplinary encounter, is one of the key contributors toward achieving this goal.

The approach proposed as the method of handling disciplinary encounters is the Reality Therapy Approach developed by William Glasser.[26] Reality therapy, unlike the traditional approach dealing with inappropriate student behavior, does not place the teacher in the position of being a *policeman, judge,* and *jailer.* Instead, the reality therapy approach clearly conveys the message to students through the teacher's verbal and nonverbal actions that you are responsible for your own behavior. The reality therapy approach is concerned with what the child did rather than why the child acted in an unacceptable manner. Likewise, this approach is concerned with the here and now rather than the student's past record and reputation as a trouble-maker. These points are important, in that a teacher can more easily understand what a student did and react to present events without scolding the student and listing all the student's past failings. Verbalization of this type usually serves to alienate the student and creates feelings of hostility.[27]

Maintaining consistency in using the traditional disciplinary approach is extremely difficult because the teacher must faithfully play so many different roles. What happens to a rule breaker when the teacher feels very cheerful? When the rule breaker is a student who usually doesn't break any rules? What if the disruptive student is one of the teacher's favorite students, or a kid who is dirty and smelly? In addition, most teachers don't enjoy their role as disciplinarian, and they feel guilty when they have to "throw the book" at a student who acts inappropriately. Frequently, the result is inconsistency on the part of the teacher. There is also a tendency to overlook inappropriate behavior when the teacher is not directly involved in the situation. Consequently, students adopt an attitude of "Take a chance that I won't get caught and if I do, maybe I can talk my way out of it."

On the other hand, when a teacher uses the reality therapy approach to disciplinary encounters, it is much easier to be consistent. An important difference is that the teacher shows commitment and concern by ensuring that the student has a plan for acting appropriately.

The steps in the reality therapy approach are as follows:

Step	*Teacher Verbalization*
1. Involve the students by at least giving them a voice in rule making.	"We are going to discuss the rules we need to make for our class."
2. When a student breaks a rule, have the student identify what she did.	"What were you doing?" or "What happened?" or "What's going on here?"
3. Have the student evaluate her behavior by making a value judgment about how the behavior helped her, the class, or the school. In addition, have the student verbalize the negative consequences of her behavior.	"How did that help you?" (your class)? or "Is what you are doing helping you?" "What happened as a result of what you did?" or "What good did you get out of that behavior?"
4. Have the student make a plan of action to behave differently the next time.	"What could you do differently?" or "What could you do to follow that rule?"
5. Have the student make a commitment to follow the plan or decide which one of several plans is the best to follow.	"What is your plan?" or "Which plan are you going to use?"

6. Help the student follow the plan. Support behavior attempting to follow the plan. Accept no excuses for not following the plan, rather redirect the student by starting over at Step Four or even Step Two, if needed.

"I see you are using the plan."
"What happened to your plan?"
"When are you going to start using your plan?"

7. Allow the student to experience the consequences of inappropriate behavior, behavior not following the plan. This may mean a trip to the principal's office, a time out, denial of starting to work on something before successfully completing the first task. Above all, have the student complete each step of the reality therapy approach questions.[28]

"What would have happened if you had followed your plan?" or "What were you doing?"
"What did you tell me you were going to do?"

It is important that the teacher recognizes and acknowledges even limited progress when students act responsibly. The teacher should not expect miracles, and above all should not give up when immediate success is not attained. It is important to estimate the student's progress during the first week the behavior change plan is being implemented. This progress check will aid in determining the student's commitment to the plan. It also shows the teacher's continuing concern in the student as a person of worth. When positive behavioral changes are identified as a result of the progress check, both the teacher and students are motivated to follow through with the plan.

The reality therapy approach uses a nondirective method of verbal interaction with students. The teacher asks questions that make the student think and face the responsibility of her behavior. The teacher helps the student to think through, clarify, and plan a course of action that will lead to success. The teacher does not tell the student what to do and how to do it. The teacher does not set the punishment for the students, but allows them, when feasible, to experience the consequence of inappropriate behavior. Moreover, reality therapy is a positive approach to helping students develop responsibility for their behavior.

Modeling

Modeling is the use of an individual's behavior as an example for others to emulate. Teachers are models for behavior, whether they are acting with this purpose in mind or not. Children are models for other children to imitate. Modeling can be used by teachers to promote student self-discipline by recognizing individuals who are acting in an appropriate way.

The "Do what I say, not what I do" approach is reverse modeling. Instead of building credibility and genuineness, the result is that the teacher's effectiveness is diminished. However, when a teacher is a positive model, the teacher's credibility and genuineness is reinforced. When incongruity exists between teacher verbalizations and actual behavior, the students will be confused as to the intended meaning of the communications and will tend to believe the physical behavior as the true message.[29]

The term "targeting" is used to describe the delivery of appropriate verbal or nonverbal information to the children who need it. Errors in targeting exist when one, or a combination, of the following situations occur:

- A student receives a positive interaction for a behavior that should not be supported.
- A teacher targets an imitator of a good behavior without having first targeted the initiator of the good behavior.
- A negative interaction is directed to the wrong child, that is, a student who was not actually engaged in the inappropriate behavior.
- An onlooker, rather than an initiator, is targeted for negative interaction.
- A less serious misbehavior is targeted, while a more serious misbehavior occurs without interaction.[30]

Teachers who eliminate targeting errors are positive models. They demonstrate concern, a sense of fairness, and the use of good judgment. When students identify with a model, in this case the teacher, it is more likely that they will pattern their behavior in that way.

As models, teachers should express their feelings. I-messages are the teachers' delivery system for conveying feelings. When it comes to behavior, however, teachers must decide what to do, based on the consequences of their actions and not solely on their emotional state. It is natural and appropriate for teachers to have feelings and to express their feelings.[31] When it comes to interactions with students, teachers must respond judiciously according to a predetermined objective and with a full sense of awareness of the probable consequence of their actions.

Fostering Creative Behavior

Listening attentively, responding honestly and warmly, using appreciative praise, sending I-messages, and using the reality therapy approach are specific ways to encourage expression and creative behavior. Constructive interpersonal communication techniques and the self-concept-enhancing practices of humanistic psychology are key ingredients to developing an affirmative atmosphere for creative behavior.

The development of creative thinking cannot be left to chance. It has to be incubated, nurtured, and encouraged. Teachers can be powerful agents in helping students to express ideas and feelings in personal and unique ways. The following check points describe positive practices teachers should use to foster creative behavior. These points are expressed in the form of questions to enable teachers to evaluate the contribution of their instructional approaches and atmosphere for enhancing creative expression by students. These questions are:

1. Do I recognize and acknowledge potentialities? Am I constantly looking for and fostering these signs of creativity?
   - intense absorption in listening, absorbing, doing
   - intense animation and physical involvement
   - challenging ideas of authorities
   - checking many sources of information
   - taking a close look at things
   - eagerly telling others about one's discoveries
   - continuing a creative activity after the scheduled time for quitting
   - showing relationships among apparently unrelated ideas
   - following through on ideas set in motion
   - manifesting curiosity, wanting to know, digging deeper
   - guessing or predicting outcomes and then testing them
   - honestly and intently searching for the truth
   - resisting distractions
   - losing awareness of time
   - penetrating observations and questions
   - seeking alternatives and exploring new possibilities.
2. Am I respectful of questions and ideas?
3. Do I ask provocative questions (not just for reproduction of information given)?
4. Do I recognize and value originality (or do I discredit an unfamiliar idea)?
5. Do I try to develop elaboration ability in my students? Too often creative ideas are dropped simply for lack of opportunity to elaborate them.
6. Do I give my students the opportunity for unevaluated practice and experimentation?[32]

One of the responsibilities of a teacher is to help students to feel free to explore, discover, and express their feelings and ideas. Skills, such as those previously described, are important competencies that a teacher should acquire. Even with these skills, teachers will find that it will take time and a variety of learning experiences to develop a child's self-confidence, sense of trust, and openness.

IMPLEMENTING THE DEVELOPMENTAL THEME

Movement as a Means of Expression

For primary grade children, movement is often a more immediate and effective mode of expression than language. Even as they grow older, children's repertoires of expressive modes should extend beyond words to using their bodies as instruments for conscious expression and communication. Combining movement with art, music, or both in a variety of ways can help children to increase the number of ways of expressing their feelings and to further the development of aesthetic awareness. (This is why so many of the activities in the teaching modules in this chapter emphasize expressive movement as opposed to more functional movement activities.) Also, the opportunity for moving, for the sheer joy of moving, probably exists more in dance than in any other aspect of the physical education curriculum.

Dance and related expressive movement activities usually receive little emphasis in elementary schools. It is the area in which many classroom teachers and physical education specialists need practical help, because many feel uncomfortable in teaching dance.

Many of the learning experiences in the teaching modules allow for the children to work alone initially. This is important because *expressing* feelings does not necessarily require interaction with another. *Communication,* however, requires someone to communicate with, whether it be a general audience, a partner, or a group.

It is also important for children to learn the difference between denying or *repressing* their strong feelings (like anger) and *suppressing* inappropriate or overly aggressive behavior. They need to learn that feeling angry is OK, but punching someone is not OK.

Apprehensions about Dancing

Verbal discussions play an important part in helping children express how they feel about different activities. Many children have a stereotyped view of dance, believing that it is supposed to be "pretty," performed only on the feet, or for girls only. Consequently, they are apprehensive about dancing. Discussions that take place during, or after dance activities can help children to recognize these misconceptions where they exist.

Controlling Feelings

Included in the teaching modules are learning experiences that provide for relating how children feel about their own performances, identifying what makes them feel angry or happy. Through these experiences, children can discover the role of the *self* in feelings—"I make me angry"—which contributes to their emotional development. These, and similar tasks suggested in the teaching modules, are not one time tasks, but are essential for emotional well-being, and they should be worked at over time for most effective results. Children can learn that if they think different thoughts, they *can* change their moods and feelings. Such an ability results in greater control over one's emotional life.

EXPRESSING FEELINGS

Planning Guide

Objectives	*Experiences*
As a result of the learning experiences over time, children will be able to:	
1. show how they feel through movement	• reacting to a variety of stimuli to express feelings—happy, sad, lonely, joyful; pictures that evoke emotional responses that can be interpreted through moving
2. identify movement as one of many means of expressing feelings	• isolating expression to different parts of the body through movement; identifying appropriate movements for expressing strength, weakness, tiredness; acting out or dancing stories or poems of their own or others' composition; combining drawing with movement
3. find acceptable ways of expressing or demonstrating strong or negative feelings.	• using powerful words such as "angry" and "loving" for devising movement sequences; using movement to make negative statements, such as "no!"

For evaluating students' progress in their ability to express feelings, see page 166.

Teaching Modules

Introductory Module

Objectives

As a result of the learning experiences over time, children will be able to:

1. demonstrate their feelings through movement
2. use acceptable ways of expressing strong feelings and negative feelings.

Materials

A variety of "word cards." A word list. Selected rhythm instruments: drums, tambourines, cymbals, triangles. (The children can make their own instruments from a variety of common materials.)

Learning Experiences

Group the children near you for the introduction to this activity.

1. "Imagine you are in a television show that has just lost the sound. You have to let the viewers know how you feel without talking! The only way they can tell what's happening is by the way that you move. Moving anywhere safely in the activity area, show me how you would move if something really great had happened. Start as soon as you are ready."

Related Experiences

- Look at some silent films to observe how actors exaggerate movement and facial expressions to express different feelings.
- Make lists of synonyms for expressive words:
  happy
  sad
  angry
  disappointed
  joyful

FIGURE 6–2 "Feeling good!"

Learning Experiences

Related Experiences

2. "Now, I'm going to call out some different words. Show me how you move differently to all these words":

   strong
   sad (dejected)
   sleepy
   joyful

Give the children time to respond to each word. Allow at least fifteen seconds for them to move according to the word before you change it. This is one way to extend the children's vocabulary. Emphasize exaggeration of movement, and encourage children to both travel and stay in one place for variety. A list of suggested words follows:

happy	nervous
sad	depressed
content	perky
miserable	strong
furious	serene
afraid	smooth
relaxed	thin
tense	jerky
superior	proud

- Select groups of words as a stimulus for drawings.
- Cut pictures from magazines to illustrate some of the words the class has worked with in the movement experience.
- Conduct a discussion on "the happiest thing that happened to me this week." and/or "the thing(s) I am most worried about right now."
- Discuss the differences between words. For example is "dejected" the same as "sad"?

Central Module

Objectives

As a result of the learning experiences over time, children will:

1. be able to express the meaning of selected words through movements
2. increase their vocabulary of movement words relating to familiar elements in their lifestyles.

Materials

Pictures showing different kinds of leaves in motion and the various ways water can move. A word list on the bulletin board that can be added to as children work with new words.

Learning Experiences

1. The transition from the introductory module can be made if the teacher uses some imagery, such as "Show me how you would move if you were an ice cream cone left out in the hot sun." Emphasize slow "melting," and use any comments that will assist the children in focusing on the task. "It's the middle of the day and the sun is *so* hot!" "You are thawing and losing your beautiful shape!"

    Imagery can be very useful if teachers emphasize the movement qualities of the image. There is a difference in *moving* lightly, like a cloud, or quickly, like a gust of wind, and "being" the cloud or the wind. The first task allows for variety in movement, whereas the second task tends to limit the movement.

Related Experiences

- Make a series of clay shapes that show an increase in height.
- Examine the scientific concepts underlying "melting."
- Tell a story about how an ice cream cone feels when it is melting.
- List synonyms for any of the words used in the movement class.
- Draw pictures of the shapes you made in space as you moved.
- Write a poem or a song about a leaf that doesn't want to leave the tree.
- Make a collage of leaves of different colors.
- Write a poem about the fall.
- Let the children tell stories on tape that can be replayed for other children in the class.
- Make up a "rain" song that can be danced.
- Hold a discussion about the different forms that water takes.
- Draw pictures of different situations in which water plays a major part: sailing, water-skiing, plants growing, steam generators, etc.

FIGURE 6–3 "Melting"

Learning Experiences

2. Talk about different words that mean "melt." (All the words used in this activity should be put on the word list in the classroom after the lesson.)
3. Show the picture of the leaves and ask the children to identify some of the movements that the leaves are doing. Explore other movements of leaves: shake, swirl, fall, settle, spin, spiral, float, etc. "Let's think about how leaves float in the wind. Show me how you can move like the leaf floats. . . ." Encourage feelings of *suspension* and "whole" movement.
4. "Make up a sequence (dance) that shows the leaf shriveling, then being shaken off the tree, and blown away. Start when you are ready."
5. The same module format can be used over and over with different word groups. Some examples of different stimuli are:

   birds—fly, dive, perch, flutter, float, soar
   rain—plops, streams, dances
   water—falls, trickles, drips, dashes, ebbs, flows

   Teachers need to be alert to helping children refine their movement sequences. For example, the movement of a bird "perching" is different from a leaf "settling."

Culminating Module

Objectives

As a result of the experiences over time, children will:

   1. be able to devise movement sequences based on word stimuli
   2. recognize "doing" words as being verbs.

Materials

Three shoe boxes with openings in the tops big enough for a child's hand to be inserted. Flash cards for verbs and words denoting other directions.

Learning Experiences

1. "We have been working with moving to different words and making up dances about how things move. Now, we're going to pick cards out of these boxes and see what kind of a dance you can make up using them."

    Children often have misconceptions about what constitutes dance. They often believe that dance is a feminine activity performed to music and uses only the feet. To involve the children more, you could have them pick out the words from the boxes. To begin, select one word from each box. The following sequence is an example of the procedure you might follow:

2. "Mark has picked his word from the verb box and it says *'Skip.'* Mary can choose a word from the 'how' box and it says *'Lightly.'* Now it is Diane's turn to pick from the 'shape' box, and her word is *'Spiky.'* So! Your dance is going to show skipping movements, that you do lightly, and you must end your dance in a spiky shape. Everyone find a place to begin. . . ."

    Although the elements of the dance are imposed, the children still have many decisions to make about *where* they will skip, and how they will approach their final shapes. Children do not necessarily move in creative ways naturally. They often have to be helped to see the possibilities available to them.

Related Experiences

- Hold discussions about what the children know about dance:
    - what dance performances they have seen on television
    - what people learn who go to dance classes
    - how well they think they can dance.
- Make a bulletin board display about famous dancers—men and women.
- Make a list of verbs that can be used in the verb box.
- Draw up lists of words suitable for the "how" and "shape" boxes.
- Encourage highly descriptive words.
- Draw a picture of yourself doing the dance (sequence) you liked best.
- Make a short poem about how you felt when you were performing your dance.
- Write a poem using the words for your dance.
- Find some music you would like to dance to. After you have made up your dance, tell what words would describe your dance.
- Hold a discussion about why humans can dance, but other animals do not seem to do this naturally.

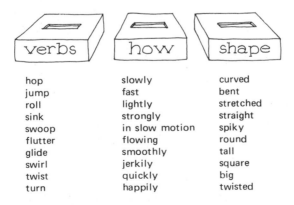

verbs	how	shape
hop	slowly	curved
jump	fast	bent
roll	lightly	stretched
sink	strongly	straight
swoop	in slow motion	spiky
flutter	flowing	round
glide	smoothly	tall
swirl	jerkily	square
twist	quickly	big
turn	happily	twisted

FIGURE 6–4 Suggested words

Summary

Enabling Behavior: Expressing Feelings

The underlying emphasis in this enabling behavior is helping children become comfortable in using movement as a means of expression. They are improving in this when they:

1. Demonstrate increasing involvement with tasks. They are so absorbed that they temporarily forget their inhibitions.
2. Respond to words with variety of movement. "Happy" evokes more than just one stereotyped response such as skipping "happily."
3. Involve the whole body in moving to express feelings. There is often a tendency initially to use just the limbs, or the extremities in movement.
4. Express satisfaction in movement experiences that focus on dance or dance-drama activities.

UNDERSTANDING AND ACCEPTING FEELINGS

Planning Guide

Objectives	*Experiences*
As a result of the learning experiences over time, children will:	
1. demonstrate active listening skills	• follow a partner's verbal and nonverbal instructions
2. show reduced apprehension about having strong feelings, such as anger	• hold movement "conversations" with a partner that center on the idea of some conflicts; identifying through movement things that make me feel angry
3. be able to resolve hypothetical conflict situations through movement.	• making up group dances that focus on the theme of conflict resolution.

For evaluating students' progress in this enabling behavior, see page 169.

Teaching Modules

Introductory Module

Objectives

As a result of the learning experiences over time, children will be able to describe their feelings verbally and precisely.

Learning Experiences

Related Experiences

Ideally, this particular discussion should take place in a "teachable moment." An example of such a moment might be when the class has suffered some disappointment, or a member of the class has related an incident that produced a strong positive or negative response.

"Think for a minute, and then we're going to go round our circle finishing the phrase, 'I'm happy when . . .' " There are many such beginning phrases to help children state their feelings:

I feel better when . . .

I don't like it when . . .

I know it's dumb, but . . .

It makes me angry when . . .

At an appropriate point, the teacher picks up on a child's statement to lead the class into a deeper discussion on the issue. For example:

"I don't like it when our coach yells at us in our baseball game."

Teacher: "Tell us about that, Donald," or "Who else feels that way and would like to tell us about it?"

- Draw a picture to make your friend feel happy. Think about some things that make your friend feel good.
- Make a design of colors that make you think of different feelings.
- What colors do you think of when you think: angry, love, warm?

Central Module

Objectives

As a result of the learning experiences over time, children will:

1. be able to devise movement sequences that express emotions
2. be able to express emotion using different body-parts
3. be able to devise a short dance based on two different emotions.

Materials

A variety of rhythm instruments, one for each child. A signal that is different from the sound of the rhythm instruments.

Learning Experiences

1. If there has been some time lapse since the Introductory Module, teachers can briefly review it to set the atmosphere for this module. "Now, choose an instrument and find a space. Then make your instrument make some 'happy' sounds."

   It is important to give children their first task before selecting their equipment. Preferably, the task should be an exploratory one, because it is natural for children to want to play with the equipment immediately.

2. "You found many different sounds to make with your instruments, now show how you can move to those happy sounds. Start as soon as you are ready." Children need encouragement to really explore a task. Moving too quickly from one task to another results in perfunctory kinds of movement.

3. "That time, most of you used your whole body to show happy movements. This time, can you show how happy you are by just moving your feet?" Expand this task by focusing on other parts of the body—hands, head, knees—for short periods of time.

4. "Now, see how you can make up a short dance that starts out with just one part of the body being happy, and then bit by bit your whole body ends up doing a happy dance. Start as soon as you are ready."

   Because teaching dance is not easy for many teachers, there is a tendency to say "good" to any response that resembles the hoped-for outcome. Specific comments about the movement are usually more helpful:

   "I can't tell which body part is really starting your dance, Terry."

   "Can you find two more movements to put in the middle of your dance?"

   "Could you show a change of level in your dance, John?" etc.

5. "Practice your dance until you feel it is good enough to show someone else. Make sure your ending position shows happiness, too!"

Related Experiences

- Children can make their own rhythm instruments from a variety of everyday materials.
- Draw a picture of yourself doing your "happy" dance.
- Sing the song "My Favorite Things" from *The Sound of Music.*
- Make a list of your favorite things.
- Write (or tape) a story about a city where no one knew how to be happy until one day . . .
- Make a collage of happy pictures, sad pictures, or angry pictures.
- Use the collage to conduct discussions about what makes people sad, angry, and how we can help sad people to feel better.
- Draw a picture of happy hands.
- Make up a poem based on happy words.
- Practice thinking happy thoughts, or sad thoughts, in conjunction with discussions about how we are all responsible for our own feelings. ("*I* make me angry, therefore, *I* can make me happy.")
- In two's, make up a play that starts out sad and ends up happy.
- Draw to a selection of music that reflects different moods.

FIGURE 6–5 Making happy sounds with an instrument

Culminating Module

Objectives

As a result of the learning experiences over time, children will:

1. be able to devise short dances that show a change of emotions
2. be able to work cooperatively with a partner.

Materials

A rhythm instrument for each child. A signal that is different from the sound of the rhythm instruments.

Learning Experiences

"Find a partner who has a rhythm instrument that makes a different sound from yours." This may take a few moments to accomplish. As soon as everyone is partnered, continue the instructions. "You did so well making up dances on your own, you can make up a dance together now. In your new dance, you must start out feeling *not happy* and end up feeling *very happy.*

"What are some feelings that are different from happy?" (Possible answers: sad, lonely, frightened, angry.) This short discussion will help children to see the range of possibilities other than just "unhappy."

"Your instruments should help your dance by making different sounds at the beginning and end of the dance."

Related Experiences

- A series of pictures that show different everyday situations provides a take-off point for discussions about feelings.
- Watch an audio-visual presentation that focuses on people's feelings in different circumstances.
- Find poems that have emotions as a central theme.

Summary

Enabling Behavior: Understanding and Accepting Feelings

The activities in this enabling behavior emphasize children's creative movement responses to sounds they create with their voices or instruments. They are improving in this enabling behavior when:

1. They seek several different movement responses to the same sound.
2. They can deliberately isolate one part of the body to emphasize expressive movement.
3. Their sequences demonstrate obvious cohesiveness in that they have definite beginnings and endings.

4. Older or more experienced children can respond to another person's movement.
5. Intermediate students can demonstrate increasingly complex responses when working in pairs or groups. They are sensitive to what is going on in the task.
6. All students can identify thoughts and ideas that stimulate sequences or dances.

INCREASING COMMUNICATIVE ABILITIES

Planning Guide

| *Objectives* | *Experiences* |

As a result of the learning experiences over time, children will:

1. gain experience in communicating feelings nonverbally

2. be able to use and integrate a variety of modes for communicating feelings and ideas

3. demonstrate ability to act out stories and poems created by others and/or self.

- perform movements for others who have to guess what feeling is being portrayed; miming actions
- dancing and drawing one's dance; drawing to sound and interpreting drawing through dance
- respond in movement to selected words; combine words for using in a movement sequence; select poems or songs for interpretation through movement.

For evaluating your students' progress in increasing their communicative abilities, see page 174.

Teaching Modules

Introductory Module

Objectives

As a result of the learning experiences over time, children will:

1. increase the clarity of their movement
2. gain competence in miming activity.

Mime is often confused with "Pantomime." Mime is the detailed performance of movement behavior observed in oneself or in others. Pantomime is a more generalized imitation of actions, things, animals, or people.

| *Learning Experiences* | *Related Experiences* |

Learning Experiences

Primary grade teachers may want to introduce the activity by their own demonstrations which the children can guess.

1. Select a child who enjoys performing for others. "Tom, come up here and help me for a few moments."

    The first example (whatever is chosen) should be common enough that all children do it as part of their everyday lives. Mimics have to be very familiar with the activity they mime. "Everyone watch Tom, and decide what he is pretending to do." (Cleaning his teeth)

2. "What else do we do when we clean our teeth?" (Get out the toothbrush and toothpaste; put the toothpaste on the brush, etc.) "Go through all the actions of cleaning your teeth, right from the beginning to the end."

    This differentiates true mime from the pantomiming actions that Tom probably performed (just imitating the brushing action). "Who would like to come to the front and mime some actions for us to guess?" You can do one of several things at this point:

1. allow the performer to pick her/his own action
2. provide suggestions written on slips of paper
3. have the children in pairs, one partner performing for the other.

Related Experiences

- Mime some actions of games or sports. This is a good way to introduce dance.
- Look at famous art works and their reprints. What are some of the problems in reproducing works of art?
- Look at movies of the famous mime artist, Marcel Marceau.
- Read about Marceau and how he develops an act.
- (Sixth grade) Hold a discussion about the concept of "cloning." How does this concept differ from that of the "assembly line" method of manufacturing?

Central Module

Objectives

As a result of the learning experiences over time, children will:

1. be able to use words as a stimulus for creating movement experiences
2. work with a partner or small group in developing expressive movement sequences.

Materials

A list of words or word cards for children to react to/task cards with words. (See the list at the end of this module.)

Learning Experiences

1. Organize the children so that they are in pairs (primary level) or small groups (intermediate level). "Everyone close their eyes and think about the word *Boil.* Open your eyes and, in your own space, show me some movements that show what the word means to you."
2. "Now, I'm giving each group/pair a word of their own. The group/pair must work out a sequence that contains the movements of the word. Your sequence must have a beginning and end position, and you should practice it until you feel it is good enough to show to someone else." The task is much more complex because the children have to work out a coordinated sequence.

    You can organize the word-giving in several ways:

    a. tell every group the same word.
    b. give out words on small cards, a different one to each group.
    c. provide four or five words and allow groups to select the one they would like to work with.

The first method is very suitable for children who are inexperienced in this work, or where it is the teacher's first attempt at working in this mode. This experience is easier to monitor and to provide help for students than the second method (b).

Related Experiences

- Add to the list of words that can be used for this task.
- Use the same word you were given for your sequence and draw a *design* that shows the movements in the word. (Note: emphasize abstract designs rather than literal interpretations of it.)
- Write a descriptive paragraph about someone performing a vigorous activity: sprinting, playing football, a cycle race, kayaking, wrestling, etc.
- Make up a poem about your word(s).
- Extend this experience to using phrases that are familiar:
    –feeling free
    –going to the fair
    –all's well that ends well

FIGURE 6–6 Working out a group sequence

Some Appropriate Words for This Module

*fireworks	ice cream
explosion	*snow man
volcano	*popsicle
earthquake	*wind
waves	*circus
whirlpool	machines
waterfall	percolate
geyser	storm
fine	bubble
fizzy	merry-go-round
*fun	*popcorn

*Suitable for primary grades.

Culminating Module

Objectives

As a result of the learning experiences over time, children will:

1. demonstrate knowledge of how to increase the effectiveness of performance by refining and increasing the variety of movement
2. be able to add sounds to their sequences to highlight certain parts.

Materials

A variety of rhythm instruments, one for each group.

Learning Experiences

1. "Now, we are going to see how we can make our sequences more interesting. Think about the movement part of your sequence. Have you really got all the movements of your word in there? Remember when I used *Boil*? Rick's movement told me he was really *boiling*—popping up like the bubbles in a pan of boiling water! If you had worked on the word *boil,* what else could your movement have shown? Talk to your partner for a few minutes and see if you have really used all the movements in your words."

Related Experiences

- Use the same words as a basis for the design to be scratched on super 8mm exposed film.
- Find poems or stories that would make good movement sequences.
- Make costumes or props that would help your sequence.
- Make up a poem you can say *while* you are doing your sequence.
- Make up a play in which people can only talk by using movement.
- Find some music that can be used as background for your sequence.

Learning Experiences	*Related Experiences*

Learning Experiences

The following teaching points are applicable to almost any work in expressive movement. The focus on even one or two of these points will almost immediately improve the performance.

a. Nearly all the suggested words imply a change of speed (even ice cream can melt slowly at first, and then become fast).
b. The movement employed can vary in level.
c. As they interpret the word, children need not work in unison, but develop different, complementing movements.
d. Rising movements can be lead by different body-parts.
e. Are the children making full use of twisting? This is a simple way of introducing an interesting pattern.

2. "Those of you who wish, can add sounds to your sequence, either sounds you can make yourself, or with a rhythm instrument. Only use it if it will *help* your sequence."

Related Experiences

• Make a sequence of appropriate word interpretations and film it.
• Possible sequences:

1. volcano
   explosion
   earthquake
2. wind
   storm
   waves
3. machines
   bubble
   explosion

Summary

Enabling Behavior: Increasing Communicative Abilities

This enabling behavior is an extension of the previous two enabling behaviors. Students are increasing the clarity of their movement responses when they:

1. Can act out everyday activities with attention to detail.
2. Demonstrate understanding of the difference between *mime* and *pantomime*.
3. Need less help from the teacher to get started on tasks requiring creative responses.
4. Develop their movement responses beyond the "first answer." In other words, they stay involved with the task, seeking more complex responses and/or refining their first responses.

CREATING IDEAS

Planning Guide

Objectives	*Experiences*
As a result of the learning experiences over time, children will:	
1. demonstrate divergent responses in movement	• find many ways to travel on different body-parts; travel in different directions; given a movement task (skipping), incorporate it into a sequence
2. perceive the value of trying new ideas	• make up games; devise tasks for a partner or group
3. demonstrate an understanding of their own ability to create ideas.	• devise and modify simple dance sequences; given a piece of equipment (or prop, such as a streamer or scarf), devise a short dance study to explore the attributes of the equipment.

For evaluating your students' progress in creating ideas, see page 180.

Teaching Modules

Introductory Module

Objectives

As a result of the learning experiences over time, children will:

1. be able to copy a rhythmical pattern made by hand clapping
2. be able to respond by moving to a rhythmical pattern.

Many young children have a problem in "keeping with the music." The experiences in these modules are designed to enhance primary children's rhythmical awareness.

Materials

Three short rhythmic patterns the teacher can clap.

Learning Experiences

Rhythmical patterns that are clapped, clicked, or sounded out with sticks are easier to identify than musical rhythmic patterns.

1. "Listen to this pattern I'm going to clap." (Pattern #1) Repeat the pattern at least three times.
   "Now, see how you can clap it with me. . . ." Continue this until the children appear to have mastered the pattern.
2. "How about this one?" (Pattern #2) Again, repeat the pattern until the children have grasped it.
3. "Now, see how you can move, while you clap to the pattern. Try to make your movements happen at the same time as the claps in the pattern." Many children will pick up the rhythmic pattern by watching others at first and synchronizing their responses to those of the model(s).

Primary

Pattern #1: / __ __ / __ __ / VVVV / ____ /
Pattern #2: / ____ / __ __ / ____ / __ __ /

Intermediate

Pattern #1: / VVVV / __ __ / ____ / __ __ /
Pattern #2: / __VV / __ VV / __ __ / __ VV /
/   / = measure, V = accent

Related Experiences

- Hold a discussion on "where we can find rhythm": in nature, in pictures, in music, in ourselves, etc.
- Make a cloth design that shows rhythm through the repeated use of a pattern.
- Listen to music and determine the rhythmic patterns. (Music for this experience should have a variety of rhythmic patterns in the same composition.) Make up a chant to go with your movement sequence.

FIGURE 6–7 Clapping a rhythmic sequence

Central Module

Objectives

As a result of the learning experiences over time, children will:

1. be able to create rhythmic patterns of their own
2. be able to mark the rhythm by using a variety of body movements
3. will be able to work productively with a partner to seek many solutions to the same problem.

Materials

A signal that can be heard above clapping sounds.

Learning Experiences

1. "Keeping to the same rhythmic pattern (as in the Introductory Module), find two more ways of moving to it. Try to emphasize a strong movement on the first beat!" Observation of each other helps to set a model for beginning dance behavior. Children rarely see other children or beginning adults dance, and, therefore, have no model of what is accepted "beginning" movement in dance. However, watching is not always seeing. Children need help in observing movement details.

2. A short discussion on how much movement variety there was, even though the basic pattern was the same, can focus the group on specific aspects of the task.

    "When I say GO! find a partner (small group for intermediate groups) and make up your own rhythmic pattern. Then see how many different ways you can find to move to the same pattern. Go!"

    Teachers of very young primary children may prefer to continue this task with the children working alone. Teachers of intermediate grade children should encourage:

    a. brainstorming for movement ideas; everyone should contribute an idea.
    b. finding three or four responses and working them into a group sequence.

Related Experiences

- Draw sequences demonstrating children responding to rhythmic patterns.
- Hold a discussion on "being creative."
    - Who thinks they are creative?
    - What do creative people do?
    - Name some famous creative people and write about them.
- Provide a very ordinary article (example: a large box from the supermarket). List 20 ways in which it could be used.
- Make a design using a single shape that produces variety through color, size, position and angle.
- Make a list of "50 things to do with a nail.
- Hold a discussion on people who have found new ways to use common elements:
    - inventors of the Pet Rock.
    - the umbrella stroller
- Brainstorming should be discussed and practiced in class.
- Examine the commercials of a certain product that make a claim for a "new improved" product.
- How is it improved? Does the improvement make it new? Why do advertisers talk so much about the "new" models/products?

Learning Experiences

c. use of elements of movement—different body-shapes, change of level, change of direction and/or pathways. Provide an opportunity for the partners or groups to demonstrate their product to another group.

Culminating Module

Objectives

As a result of the experiences over time, children will:

1. become accustomed to using phrases, poems, or stories as a stimulus for dance sequences
2. be able to move to the rhythm of words and phrases
3. be able to interpret stories and poems emphasizing the movement aspect rather than the literal aspect.

Materials

Phrases, nursery rhymes, poems (including those the children have written), and stories suitable for the age level of the class.

Learning Experiences

1. Have the children seated in a group with you. "So far, we have made the rhythmical patterns by clapping only. Listen and see if you can hear the rhythm in what I say:

    Primary (lively)

    "Jack be nimble

    Jack be *quick*

Related Experiences

· Write short verses or phrases that can be used for this module.
· Practice some choral speaking and make up a chant that can be used as a background for a movement sequence. The chant should emphasize an unusual or uneven rhythm.
· Learn some of the "chain-gang songs" or work songs.
· Find instances of songs or chants being used to speed up work output.
· Make up a work song for the class to sing while tidying the room before leaving at the end of the day.

Learning Experiences

Jack jump over
 ⌄ ⌄ ⌄

the candlestick!"
  ⌄   ⌄

Intermediate (flowing)

"H*ear* the wind
   ⌄   ⌄

blow-ow-ow"

"Say it with me."

This task is more complex than listening to a clapped rhythm. It is a preparation for listening to more sophisticated musical rhythmic patterns.

2. "Experiment with some movements that will go to that rhythm. Say the words as you move." (Intermediate children should use the phrase three times.) Encourage exploration at this point. The idea is to find a number of ways to respond to the task.
3. Allow enough time for the children to explore the possibilities of the phrase. "Now, with your partner (or in your groups), make up a short dance sequence that not only shows the rhythm, but also tells us something about the words." (You may have to define "nimble" at this point.) "We should be able to see 'Jack Be Nimble' (or the 'blowing of the wind') in your sequence."

Related Experiences

• Find stories in the Reading Series used that can be a basis for designing dance or movement sequences.
• Use a single rhythm instrument to highlight one part of the rhythmic sequence.

FIGURE 6–8 "Nimble Jack!"

Summary

Enabling Behavior: Creating Ideas

The modules in the sample lesson for this enabling behavior focus on finding more than one idea in a movement task. When children improve in creating ideas they:

1. Include more than one concept in their movement sequences. For example, in "Jack Be Nimble," the children could generate a whole "scene" sequence that revolves around the central character of Jack.
2. Go beyond the obvious in interpreting poems, phrases, or songs, instead of merely portraying the characters or the actions of the poem. They look for deeper meanings, or are able to respond in more abstract ways.

ENDNOTES

1. Geraldine Dimondstein, *Children Dance in the Classroom* (New York: Macmillan, 1971), p. 3.
2. Ibid., p. 5.
3. Shirley J. Winters, *Creative Rhythmic Movement for Children of Elementary School Age* (Dubuque, Iowa: William C. Brown, 1975), p. 99.
4. Alice Yardley, *Senses and Sensitivity* (New York: Citation Press, 1973), pp. 83–84.
5. Winters, *Creative Rhythmic Movement,* p. 91.
6. Ibid.
7. Marian Breckenridge and Lee Vincent, *Child Development* (Philadelphia: W. B. Saunders, 1965), p. 301.
8. Ibid., p. 302.
9. Dimondstein, *Children Dance in the Classroom,* p. 6.
10. Winters, *Creative Rhythmic Movement,* pp. 92–93.

11. Yardley, *Senses and Sensitivity,* p. 90.
12. Paul Torrance and R. E. Myers, *Creative Learning and Teaching* (New York: Dodd, Mead, 1970), p. 41.
13. Breckenridge and Vincent, *Child Development,* p. 308.
14. Leif Fearn and Robert E. McCabe, *Magic Circle, Supplementary Idea Guide,* ed. by Geraldine Ball (La Mesa, Calif.: Human Development Training Institute, 1975); and Larry Chase, *The Other Side of the Report Card* (Pacific Palisades, Calif.: Goodyear, 1975).
15. Chase, *The Other Side of the Report Card,* p. 15.
16. Harry V. Scott, "Conducting Classroom Discussions: Some Useful Competencies," *Kappa Delta Pi Record* 10 (April, 1974): 102.
17. Lydia Gerhart, *Moving and Knowing* (Englewood Cliffs, N.J.: Prentice-Hall, 1973), p. 178.
18. Louis E. Raths, Merrill Harmin, and Sidney B. Simon, *Values and Teaching* (Columbus, Ohio: Charles E. Merrill, 1966), pp. 57–62.
19. Scott, "Conducting Classroom Discussions," p. 103.
20. Ibid.
21. Chase, *The Other Side of the Report Card,* pp. 23–24.
22. Ibid., pp. 14–19.
23. Thomas Gordon, *P.E.T. Parent Effectiveness Training* (New York: Peter H. Wyden, 1970), pp. 117–20.
24. Ibid., p. 118.
25. Ibid., pp. 135–36.
26. William Glasser, *Schools Without Failure* (New York: Harper & Row, 1969).
27. Ibid., pp. 19–20.
28. Exerpted from the film *The Reality Therapy Approach* by permission of Media Five Film Distributors, Hollywood, Calif. 90068
29. Jacob S. Kounin, *Discipline and Group Management in Classrooms* (New York: Holt, Rinehart and Winston, 1970), pp. 80–81.
30. Daryl Siedentop, *Developing Teaching Skills in Physical Education* (Boston: Houghton Mifflin, 1976), pp. 95–96. Reprinted by permission.
31. Gordon, *P.E.T.,* pp. 115–17.
32. Bonnie Cherp Gillion, *Basic Movement Education for Children* (Reading, Mass.: Addison-Wesley, 1970), p. 27. Reprinted with permission.

chapter seven

Accepting Responsibilities and Acting Cooperatively

ABOUT CHILDREN

To many people, sports and games are synonymous with physical education. Perhaps this is because sports receives a great deal of attention in the news media, and the public has opportunities to observe students participating in sports activities. Sports and games have not always been part of the elementary school physical education curriculum; when they were introduced, it was for their contribution to the social development of the child. Soon, sports and games became the dominant movement form in physical education programs. Based on the recommendation of authorities in the field, as much as 50 percent of the physical education curriculum was allocated to games.

In the 1960s and 1970s, games were criticized by two groups of people. One group was concerned about the physical fitness of students and charged that a curriculum dominated by games was inadequate in developing physiological efficiency. They were particularly critical of games, such as softball, where students were not required to be very active most of the time. A second group was concerned about the development of movement patterns and skills. They expressed concern that specific skills were being developed prior to the development of basic movement patterns. This group also pointed out that frequently in games, too much time is spent waiting for turns or in breaks in the action of the game; and not enough time is spent in developmental activity. While both groups expressed legitimate concerns about some games, they failed to recognize that the primary purpose for including games and sports in the elementary school curriculum is the development of social skills.

It should be recognized that physical fitness and skill development can result from participation in sports and games, and this is important. However, skills and fitness can be developed in other ways as well, often more effectively and efficiently. This chapter will present information on the role of games, sports, and other group activities in the social development of children.

Socialization   The socialization process is the means whereby people learn to function effectively in their society. Not only is the process life-long, but it is very complex. Schools have attempted to assist in the socialization process, in that they have attempted to teach the values of the community through their curricula and instructional practices. For example, as late as the 1960s, our American culture did not rank vigorous physical activity and competition very high in the accepted behavior patterns of women. Schools generally reflected these values in their curricula, but by the mid-1970s, it had become more common to see high school and collegiate female athletic teams, even in activities such as soccer and rugby. Likewise, our culture has come to recognize the value of dance as a movement form, for men as well as women.

From the beginning, children learn what is socially acceptable behavior and what behavior is viewed as inappropriate. What is socially acceptable in one situation is not necessarily acceptable in another. Most children will follow a similar pattern in the development of social behavior, particularly as it relates to functioning in group situations.

Development of Group Social Behavior

The following discussion is based on Breckenridge and Vincent's work on the development of group social behavior in preschool and school age children.[1] The vocabulary of young children stresses *me* and *mine,* rather than *we* and *ours.* Even when children may be together in the same room, most of their play prior to age two will be solitary. There is no cooperative behavior, and children seem unaffected by others in the environment. Solitary play is characteristic of infancy and early childhood, but may persist when children have had limited opportunities for group play and social development.

Parallel play follows solitary play. As children grow older, they start to be affected by the presence of others, even though they do not "play with" or cooperate for the purpose of achieving some common goal. Usually, children at this level enjoy playing in the company of other children, and they tend to stimulate each other by sharing ideas. They also tend to play longer than when they are by themselves.

A more mature child can be a very positive social force in a group of young children by sharing ideas and toys. The mature child is a model for more complex play patterns, while a less mature child who takes playthings from other children will diminish the social quality of the play environment. "Parallel" play is common behavior in nursery school and kindergarten age children.

From as early as three years of age, to about age eight or ten, children engage in group play. At this time, children play together, sharing ideas and toys, yet each still maintains a degree of autonomy in the activity. They group together more on the merits of the activities than on friendships established with other children, e.g., playing "school" or "store." Frequently, children will shift from group to group. Some leadership behavior may be observed at this stage, but it too will emerge from different children at different times.

Toward the end of the early childhood years (around eight years of age) children can participate in more structured group activity. Group projects and games, where each child plays a role in helping the group achieve a goal, are important at this time in the social development of children. Relay races (see page 395) can be useful in helping children learn the interdependence of group members in achieving a common objective. Team activities where children "play positions" and frequently have long waiting periods between direct involvement in the activity are not recommended at this level. Differentiated roles, complex rules, and team competition become more developmentally appropriate as children move into the "gang" stage.

Children reach the gang stage at the upper elementary school level. This is the time when peer groups become important to children, and the group itself is often more important than the group's activities. At the same time, however, individual friendships are important to children at this age. Both groups and individual friendships tend to be same sex relationships. Children learn leadership and followership roles within these groups. Team games are generally accepted as appropriate activities for this level, and often the success of the team is regarded as more important than individual accomplishment.

Social Development and the Use of Games

Many activities in physical education require social or interpersonal transactions. Educators have used group activities to develop positive social behavior in children, and many people believe that games and sports provide an opportunity for children to learn cultural roles. The value of athletic programs in teaching athletes not only the sport but also how to play the "game of life" has been proposed frequently. Loy and Ingham, in writing about games and social development stated

> On the one hand, by providing a source of personal pleasure, games serve to express the needs of the people who choose to play them. On the other hand, games serve as models of cultural activities. Games are an important subset of a larger class of expressive models, including art, dance, drama, folktales, and music.[2]

BOX 7-1   Games as an Instructional Strategy

Contemporary educators recognize games as an effective structure for learning. The view that learning is a quiet, serious, and very formal process is waning. Howard G. Ball, in an article entitled "What's in a Game?"[3] observed that games:

- are enjoyed by people of all ages.
- are fun. They motivate, encourage, and excite players.
- usually model a real process or situation.
- in an educative process are used in relation to other learning activities.
- usually require thinking and planning.
- should encourage social interaction and influence attitudes.
- are usually both instructive and entertaining.
- should be selected like other media for instructional purposes.
- should be selected and used to meet specific educational objectives.

Classroom teachers and physical education specialists today recognize that games are useful in the development of social behavior as well as in the acquisition of knowledge and skill in almost all curriculum areas.

While games and other group activities have the potential for positive social development in children, the potential also exists for negative outcomes. For example, in the game of Red Light, Green Light, the emphasis is on practicing starting and stopping skills in running. The usual rules for this game allow children to move towards the finish line when the leader (usually a student) is not looking. This permits the winner to be a person who can sneak (move the most when the leader is not looking) rather than the person

---

BOX 7–2   Rules for Red Light, Green Light

Red Light, Green Light

```
X  |          |
X  |          |
X  |          |
X  |      0          The leader stands with her back to
X  |      leader     the group. She calls out "red light,
X  |          |      red light, red light" and at some ran-
X  |          |      dom point, "green light." Children
X  |          |      can move only on "green light."
Start     Finish
```

When "red light" is called again, the leader turns to see who stops immediately. Children who don't stop immediately or who fall while trying to stop must return to the starting line. When the leader again turns her back to the group saying "red light," children may "sneak up" towards the finish line. If the leader turns and sees anyone moving, that child must also return to the starting line. The first child to the finish line becomes the new leader and the game is repeated.

---

who has the best body control in starting and stopping while running. Thus, the wrong behavior is rewarded.

The idea that participation in games and other group activities does not always result in positive social development is reason to re-examine the curriculum. Martens has stated that

> Participation in physical activities—including games, play, and sport—provides the opportunity for considerable social interaction under a wide range of situations. Certainly, positive social learning may occur from such participation, but negative social behavior may also be acquired.[4]

Morris, in his book *How to Change the Games Children Play,*[5] contended that too often people believe that the outcomes of games are automatic; that they will occur simply by playing the game. His framework for analyzing games identifies six categories that the teacher can control and/or modify in order to insure that specific objectives will be met. Included is the category named "purpose." This component permits teachers and children to redesign games. Included in the "purpose" category are not only skills, knowledges, and attitudes, but social behaviors, such as "develop competitive spirit" and "to promote cooperative behavior." Morris' framework for analyzing games reminds teachers that attention to all game components can be useful in attaining specific objectives, including developing social behaviors.

Writing on the topic of games and social development, Loy and Ingham stated that in order to achieve educational outcomes, specific planning is necessary:

> It is suggested that if physical educators seriously wish to pursue educational objectives (especially those related to social development) through physical activity, then they must attempt to operationalize their particular educational aims and explicitly, by design, develop and conduct innovative games and sports which are likely to aid the student in attaining these specific goals.[6]

There can be no doubt that games provide the opportunity for the social development of children. Whether this development is positive or negative is usually not inherent in the game itself. The same game that provides the opportunity for the development of positive social behavior can also assist in the development of negative social behavior. Adult leadership and modification of games can determine the quality of the social behavior resulting from participation in games.

Developing Concern for Others and Property

In almost any group of children that one would observe in a preschool group or elementary school classroom, there exists a wide range of social behavior. Some children seem willing always to share their possessions and others do not. Some children always appear polite and courteous to adults and other children, and others do not. Some children are careful as they use toys and equipment and others seem destructive. Some children seem to have many friends and others are almost always alone. No attempt will be made here to explain how the social behavior described could have developed in each child. However, it is generally accepted that home and peer group influence have shaped the behavior of children in very significant ways prior to their entering school. Nonetheless, schools still appear to be one of the major influences on the behavior of children.

The egocentric nature of children in the early childhood years causes tension when children are in groups. When there is limited equipment or opportunity for active participation, there is likely to be more tension and frequently conflict. Most conflict can be avoided by creating an environment where the children are active. Also, for development of skills and knowledge, maximum participation by children is essential for maximum learning. There are times, however, when children must take turns and share equipment. For example, limited participation may be necessary at times to insure safety or for evaluation purposes.

Children need to learn to share the movement environment and to interact productively with others. Teachers need to help children learn these behaviors. The reasons for classroom procedures and care of equipment should be discussed and, whenever possible, children should participate in establishing many basic group routines.

In Chapter Six, ideas for helping children understand feelings were presented. Teachers should use such techniques as the "magic circle" and role playing to help children develop behavior that shows concern for others and for property. Teachers should evaluate with children not only skills and knowledges, but also social behavior. Children can begin to answer questions, such as:

How do I feel when I make a mistake?

How do I like people to correct my errors?

Would I like someone to help me learn a new skill?

What happens when I don't take care of my things?

How do I feel when I don't get a turn to do something?

Do others feel the same way as I do?

It is common in groups of children to observe mild and sometimes more violent fighting. Arguments and fights occur over use of equipment (*I want that*), space (I was here *first*), and sharing (it's *my* turn). As previously mentioned, teachers should be able to structure the environment so that most conflicts are avoided, and whenever children exhibit positive social behavior it should be acknowledged. Reinforcing positive behavior will result in that behavior being displayed more frequently. Of course, frustrations in children will lead to negative behavior at times. In these situations, teachers should provide positive alternative behaviors as solutions to the problems, rather than simply reprimanding the inappropriate behavior.

Developing Roles

According to Martens, "Status is a position in the social structure, and a role is the expected behavior of a person occupying a particular status."[7] Parents often express surprise at reports of their child's behavior in school as described by teachers. Adults demonstrate roles as they move from status to status as members of various groups. The behavior of a person as a tennis player may be quite different from the behavior of the same person as the "boss" at work, a member of the board of directors of a civic group, or as a student in a class. Children learn early that for each status they occupy, there are expected roles. Children demonstrate their understanding of roles in much of their play, e.g., playing doctor, store, and school. Much of the learning of roles results from interactions within the family, peer groups, and school. It is obvious that children model the behavior of important adults and peers, and those roles that are reinforced are the ones that become part of the behavior patterns of the child.

Children are expected to learn many roles. Within the school day there exist many opportunities for children to develop positive leadership and followership behavior. Children can be given responsibility for varying tasks in group activities such as baking, plays, special projects, and group and team games. One needs to experience the status of being a team captain, coach,

> ### BOX 7–3   On Being an Umpire
>
> It has been a common school practice for the teacher to be the chief mediator when children have arguments in games. Frequently, arguments are avoided by having the teacher be the umpire. When this happens, it is usually because the teacher believes that the students can't handle the situation. This practice is expedient, but it denies children the opportunity of having "umpire status" and of developing the appropriate behavior.
>
> Perhaps children would learn to appreciate the task of an umpire if they could have this experience (under the guidance of adult leadership). This would mean learning the skills of umpiring or officiating prior to assuming the role. As with other skills, learning should begin with simple tasks and progress to more complex ones.
>
> The practice of having adults, or children who cannot play due to illness or injury officiate children's games is highly questionable. It denies an important learning activity for all students.

or umpire in order to learn that role. It is important for children to develop empathy for people in varying roles. Play is a primary way for this to occur. Schools should provide the opportunity for children to experience many roles in a supportive atmosphere.

Being a member of a team is a common role that children need to learn, and the concept that the success of a team is dependent upon the behavior of all team members needs to be developed. Relays (see page 395) have the potential to help children understand the concept of a "team." In traditional forms of relays, each child performs the same role but the outcome is dependent upon the collective effort of the group. As children mature, team games, where each player has a different role, are appropriate.

Exploring Rules   As has been stressed throughout this chapter, games and other group activities are important in the socialization of children. One common feature of all games and groups is the existence of rules. While children are frequently required to learn rules for specific activities and situations, teachers often do nothing to help them understand the nature and basis for rules. Exploring the rules that affect their lives can lead to this understanding. Morris[8] has concluded from the work of others that there are three stages of development in understanding rules. Prior to the age of seven, children view rules as absolute. From ages seven through nine, rules need not be absolute, and from age ten and older, rules are relative.

One reason young children view rules as being absolute is that they are learned from and enforced by people they view as having absolute authority such as parents and other adults. When rules are broken at home, at school and in other social settings, children are usually punished. At times, children learn to follow rules so completely and without questioning, they sometimes will exercise poor judgment. For example, many children are taught never to talk to strangers. Parents may reinforce this behavior and a child may learn the rule very well. However, if such a child becomes lost in a public place, it is possible that the child will obey the rule "never to talk to strangers." This would prevent any well-meaning adult from helping the lost child find his parents.

Thus, children should be helped to understand rules as early as possible. They need to learn that rules:

- are made by people and can be changed by people
- are designed to balance individual desires and group needs
- often are used to help prevent accidents and/or injuries
- can help individuals achieve their own goals
- provide for fair competition in games.

As children come to understand that rules are made by people, they will also learn that there are reasons for those rules. Many people view rules as restrictive. For example, driving on the right side of the road restricts anyone from driving wherever one pleases. At first, this rule does appear to be restrictive. In fact, if there was only one driver, it would be. Yet, most drivers know that without such a rule, no one would safely be able to reach any destination. In sports and games, rules are not absolute. As conditions change, so do the rules. Children should have opportunities to participate in setting and changing the rules of their games. They need to learn who makes rules and that some rules can be changed.

It has been observed that even some adults believe that "official" rules for some popular games should always be used. These people have forgotten that rules are made to serve the players and not to make players slaves to the rules. While it is important that all participants know the rules before playing the game, modifying the rules to meet the needs of the particular situation is not only acceptable, it is evidence that the players can control their own affairs. "Local" or "neighborhood" rules are those that apply to a particular situation and are common in many sports and games.

Children also need to learn about the "spirit of the rules." Rules are designed to keep competition fair, but some people use the rules to take advantage of others. Clearly, this behavior violates the spirit of rules which are generally designed to keep competition fair. Unfortunately, children see and hear examples of how some coach or player took advantage of a rule to achieve a victory. This behavior is often characterized as "smart" or clever. The professional sport ethic of winning at any cost is contrary to the concept of sportsmanship.

Under competent adult leadership, sports and games can help children understand the spirit of the rules and the concept of sportsmanship. (The concept of sportsmanship will be explored further in the next section.) Children can learn that rules do not always apply in the same way when conditions are different. The player's value system of what is fair and right will guide the interpretation and application of rules in different situations.

Developing Cooperative and Competitive Behavior

Competition is a social process in which a person strives against some force (people, time, record, etc.) to reach some specific goal. It is basically an individual process, although people do refer to group competition. Even when groups are competing against each other, it is possible to observe various degrees of competitive behavior demonstrated by members of the teams. Cooperation, too, is a process requiring interaction among two or more people. And as in group competition, different degrees of cooperative behavior can be observed among the participants.

In many group or team games, an individual may be required to be both cooperative and competitive. Competition and cooperation should not be considered to be on opposite ends of a continuum of behavior; each is a social process used by people to attain some goal.

Singer[9] listed five situations that can be classified as competition for an individual experience in terms of performance:

1. against an established standard for a norm group
2. against a self-specified standard
3. alone in opposition to another person
4. as a member of a group in opposition to other members of your own group
5. as a member of a group in opposition to another group.

Competition is a commonly used motivational device. Coleman[10] stated that an important factor of competition is the recognition and respect the superior performer receives from other children. However, there are other views of the importance of competition to the learning process. Campbell[11] stated:

> We have created, through competition, a system based on mistrust. In school, the assumption is that no one learns without threats of grades, failure, being less than first; i.e., that these extrinsic factors are prime motivators for learning.

Martens has reviewed much of the research on competition and its effect on motor performance, and stated:

> Although the generalizations are rather tenuous, evidence suggests that competitive situations facilitate performance on muscular endurance and strength tasks, as well as on well-learned and simple skills. Competitive situations appear to impair performance, however, on complex tasks or on tasks not well learned.[12]

While the above generalizations may be useful, the reader is reminded that human behavior is very complex and any generalization may not hold true for a particular individual. Thus, competition will not have the same effect on all individuals. In fact, an individual who benefits from competition in one situation may not benefit in another situation. For example, the child who performs better in running in a competitive situation may perform worse in spelling in a similar competitive situation.

Cooperation has also been shown to improve performance. In an article in *Psychology Today,*[13] Elliot Aronson and others reported on their experience in the Austin, Texas, schools. Aronson reported that high racial tension existed in integrated schools, the self-esteem of minority children was declining, and, generally, minority children were not learning in classrooms where competition was commonly used to motivate children. A system termed the "jigsaw puzzle method" was instituted. In this cooperative system, small groups of children were given information from a story to learn; yet, no single group had all the information needed to understand the story. The children had to learn their parts and meet with children from the other groups in order to get all the information and understand the story. The children soon learned that they were dependent on each other. The author concluded that the children in the cooperative groups improved their self-concepts and their grades. Aronson stated:

> The important thing is that the kids were happier, felt better about themselves, and liked their classmates more as a result of cooperative groups, and that these good feelings did not interfere with learning and performance.[14]

Even though cooperation has been shown to be effective in promoting learning, it is safe to assume that today competition is still prevalent in the American culture, and this competitive spirit is reflected in school practices throughout the land. Competition is not evil, in and of itself; rather it is the way in which it is used that can sometimes be harmful. What frequently happens in competitive situations is that:

> As individuals try to excel each other, to win, to beat each other, they tend to evaluate the goal as the most important value, and as they compete for these kinds of ends, they tend to undervalue the worth of human beings.[15]

Furthermore, even for the "winners," competition may create such a strong need for achievement and recognition that they act unethically (cheat or lie), and then they experience feelings that undercut their feelings of self-worth (guilt or embarrassment). Competition can create a class atmosphere that inhibits learning and personal development. Competition as a process for motivating children is being questioned increasingly by many teachers and adults. This is particularly true in many sports activities designed for

BOX 7–4   "On Being Number One"[16]

I am observing in a new open-space elementary school staffed by very young and attractive people I am supposed to help become open class-room teachers. Positioned to the rear of one pod, I can observe two math teachers simultaneously. One is using a game of tic-tac-toe with addition and subtraction problems instead of X's and O's. It is boys versus girls, third grade. A small boy comes forward for 7 +2 and guesses at 8. The boys groan; the girls cheer; the teacher looks pained. The "motivation" is high. There is good attention and "involvement." It's a good lesson—by normal standards. It seems that the girls frequently win. The chagrined boy returns to his seat and while his efficient teacher continues through *her lesson,* which she imagines is arithmetic, the real lesson is demonstrated in front of me as the little boy punches the little girl next to him as hard as he can, saying "I hate you, I hate you, I hate you." In the adjacent bay the other teacher is using flash cards in the same manner. Children are guessing answers, "2 . . . 4 . . . 8. . . ." One boy always wins and the others hate him.

young children. As a result, the effect of competition on children has become the topic of many studies.

Rarick[17] has reviewed policies, extent of participation, and the effects of participation in competitive sports programs for children. Basically, educators and the medical profession have taken conservative views and these have been expressed in policy statements which discourage intense competition for children below the ninth grade. The data which have been collected to date, however, are not clear enough to give direction to the way competitive sports can positively affect the total growth and development of the child.

Much of the concern expressed over competition for children focuses on the effects of *intense* competition on the physical and psychological well being of children. In most instances, intense competition is stimulated in formal situations (usually under the direction of adults). Coaches who push children to win at any cost should recognize that:

- while physical activity generally stimulates growth—pushing children to fatigue and trauma may be harmful to physical growth
- children are more susceptible to injury under conditions of fatigue and psychological stress
- competition in sports causes emotional stress that is normally not harmful, but children should not be made to feel *guilty* when they have lost a contest
- damage to the skeletal system can occur in many kinds of activity, and undue risks should not be taken in contact sports and activities that place stress on the joints. Use of protective equipment as a weapon can cause serious injury to both parties.

Both proponents and antagonists can find support in the professional literature for their positions on competition for children. In the final analysis, much of the controversy is philosophical. One group argues that life is competitive and winning is all important. The other side argues that man is more cooperative than competitive. Each position has some merit, and what is best for children probably lies somewhere in between the extreme positions. Sports and games are fun for children. They provide experiences that are important for personal and social development.

Adults can maximize the potential of games and sports in helping children learn how to win. Perhaps children can learn that winning does not always mean beating someone else, but it means achieving a degree of personal excellence. Many activities can be structured to emphasize cooperation and participation, while maintaining their potential for physical development and social growth. There is nothing inherently positive or negative in games, sports, and other group activities. The quality of these experiences are influenced by the participants, the structure of the activities, and to a great degree by the adult leadership.

ABOUT TEACHING

Groups and Group Membership Humans are social and gregarious by nature and like, if not need, to form groups. Penland and Fine give an additional reason why people group together.

> In a group, a person becomes aware of capabilities and capacities that are only potential as long as he remains an individual by himself. The group is more than an aggregate of individuals, for in a group each individual is more than he is in isolation.[18]

In groups, one can express feelings and ideas; influence actions and responses; and enjoy brotherhood and accomplishments. These feelings can be shared, and the members can support and recognize each other's efforts.

A group can be formed to undertake a variety of learning activities such as discussing an issue, solving a problem, completing a task, or providing for fun and enjoyment. Individual feelings and talents are pooled within the group, enabling the members to realize benefits that would have otherwise been unavailable to them. The cost of group membership, in part, is that the children forming the group must develop rules governing behavior, provide leadership, and approve or censure the conduct of group members.

Establishing Rules

Groups need rules in order to limit disruptive or nonproductive behavior, initiate and terminate a meeting, and to indicate what is expected of group members. Group structure can be comforting or discomforting. In the simplest terms, it is a case of

> group goals versus member needs—it is the quality and sensitivity of the balance between the two that leaves group members with a negative memory or provides them with a sense of personal and social growth, a truly meaningful experience.[19]

The processes of rule making, rule modification, and acceptance of rules are a critical part of the developmental value of establishing and working in groups. Some rules are made in a formal manner (i.e., all members of the group are entitled to vote in the decision-making process). However, many unspoken rules evolve (i.e., we must stick up for each other and help our fellow group members). It is important that students understand the rules and/or codes of behavior for the groups to which they belong. In order to function effectively and with personal satisfaction, a group member must learn and, within limits, follow the rules of the group. It is the teachers' responsibility to communicate the rules of the school and class and to help children learn the rules and codes of their groups.

Circle discussions should be held to involve students in making rules. In order to do this, the teacher must remind students of the rules for a discussion (see page 148). The teacher may even establish a procedure where rules are proposed in one discussion, and in a later discussion decisions are made concerning which rules need to be adopted as the code of behavior.

In rule-making discussions the teacher should:

1. develop and maintain an intraclass atmosphere that encourages and supports participation
2. help the students to word the rules in positive terms and in appropriate vocabulary and grammar
3. help the students to develop broad rules that will apply to many different situations, rather than develop numerous specific rules
4. inform students that future class discussions will be held to review the rules and to modify the rules as changes become necessary
5. have the students make a poster or mural of the rules, or have individual copies of the rules for the students to keep and share with their parents.

The teacher should remind the students of rules at times other than when someone has failed to follow a rule. Furthermore, the teacher should keep a record of the times when the rules were discussed and announced to the students. This record serves as a check that the teacher has reminded the students of the rules and helps to determine when a rule should be reannounced as a reminder to the class.[20]

Group Leadership

Research has been unable to identify any consistent set of characteristics, qualities, or personality patterns which separate a leader from a nonleader. Moreover, the concept of leadership and the expectations of a leader has been slowly changing as our society changes. Often in defining leadership the easiest approach is to describe what the effective leader does.[21] What are the functions of a leader?

Today, a leader is viewed as "a group member who differed from his fellow group members only in the quantity of the acts of influence he contributed, but not in any quality."[22] A leader is not just a director, but a facilitator.

Basically, there are three functions that any person, whether a teacher or student, must serve when acting as a group leader. These functions are related to the specific needs of the task, group, and individuals who make up the group. These needs are interactive and are presented by Adair as interlocking circles to illustrate this point. Table 7–1 presents specific acts that are grouped under each type of leadership function.

TABLE 7–1   Functions of a Group Leader[23]

Task Functions

- Describing the task
- Planning
- Determining resources
- Attending to evaluation of the plan
- Facilitating modifications of the plan

**TASK
NEEDS**

GROUP NEEDS

Group Functions

- Setting standards
- Maintaining discipline
- Developing team spirit
- Encouraging, motivating, and giving a sense of purpose and identity
- Recognizing and using sub-leaders
- Ensuring communications
- Instructing the group

INDIVIDUAL NEEDS

Individual Functions

- Attending to personal problems
- Recognizing and accommodating to individual abilities
- Praising, awarding status
- Instructing a person

No leader should expect or be expected to provide for all the needs that arise as tasks, groups, or the individual group members change. A leader must be able to direct the efforts of others and to delegate authority, set a serious tone for the work atmosphere, know when to help others relax and laugh, say "no" when an incorrect procedure is proposed, and say "thank you, I value what you did." The single greatest challenge a leader faces is creating the appropriate decision-making framework for the group. Figure 7–1 shows a decision-making continuum that is based on whether decision making is leader or group centered.[24]

The following considerations are revealed by a close examination of the decision-making continuum:

1. A situational approach to decision making is preferred to a fixed or rigid approach. For example, when a crisis arises, the leader must determine whether or not the time available allows for shared decision making and whether or not the group has the necessary information or resources to come to a quick but considered decision.

2. When the degree of decision making shifts toward greater group involvement, commitment to the course of action usually increases in direct proportions. However, does every decision need to be unanimously supported by the group members, or should each person have the opportunity to vote their preference?

3. Some tasks are more or less routine matters and the leader can use policy and the precedence of past group action under similar conditions to guide decision making. However, what can be done to help assure correct interpretation of a task, policies, and conditions surrounding a task by the leader? (The answer to these decision-making questions seems to be rooted in the strength of the mutual understanding and shared concern between the leader and the group members.[25] Providing appropriate leadership is a dynamic and delicate endeavor.)

LEADER				LEADER
Makes decision	Makes decision	Makes tentative decision	Defines problem	Accepts decision
Accepts decision	Asks questions to clarify decision	Gives suggestions and influences decision	Involved in making the decision	Makes decision
GROUP				GROUP

FIGURE 7–1 A continuum of leadership decision-making styles

Evaluating Group Effectiveness

Success of a group can be defined in a number of ways. In school groups, the personal growth factor is as important (if not ultimately more important) than the group's accomplishment. Goal or task accomplishment can be termed "product achievement." Winning the game, completing a task, or showing an appropriate response are examples of product achievements; but in the area of personal growth development, successes are not so obvious as with product achievement. The teacher must observe students working in a group, looking for specific behaviors, such as:

- which children work together, who attracts a wide circle of co-workers, and who always seems on the fringe of the group?
- which children get right to work, either trying to figure how the group should work or how to complete the task, and who wastes time and is off-task?
- who provides leadership and shows that they can follow directions without misusing power or being uncommitted and apathetic?
- which children use resources and take time to think before they determine alternative or final responses?
- who is confident and enjoys working in a group, and who is fearful and anxious when working in a group?
- which children are sensitive to how others feel, think, and act, and who uses people to meet personal needs?
- who makes steady contributions and who lags back, working hard only when the task is about to be completed, or takes credit for what others have done?

These are not all of the important areas of personal growth to which a teacher should be attuned. Positive responses to group membership by students should be recognized, and when negative behaviors are identified, the teacher needs to develop group or individual experiences that foster desirable behavior. The importance of groups is that they can be an effective medium for the development of interpersonal competencies.

Competition and Cooperation

Three Ways of Working with Competition

To compete means to invite another person or group to a challenge where some reward goes to the superior performer. People can compete with themselves, as they would against other people, when they set a standard of performance or have a past record to exceed. People like to compete, to be able to control their environment, and to gain a sense of mastery. When people compete, they can be involved in either a competitive or a cooperative-competitive situation. The first way of working with competition proposed is that the terms "competitive situation" and "cooperative-competitive situation" be used to differentiate the behaviors needed to participate and succeed. Competition can exist without cooperative behavior, as when two people try to see who can throw a ball the farthest. Purely competitive events are usually individual in nature.

When people work together in a competitive situation, they must cooperate in order to perform the tasks involved in the event: e.g., a tug-of-war contest, a relay race, or a game of basketball. Cooperative-competitive situations are traditionally team or group oriented. Teachers should use the terms "competitive event" and "cooperative-competitive event" to serve as a cue to appropriate participant behavior. The use of the label cooperative-competitive focuses attention on the role and importance of cooperation in competition.

The second proposal is for teachers to use the terms "compete" or "competitor" when stating goals and objectives for the students (i.e., to teach children how to compete and to assist a student to become a competitor). By doing this, the teacher focuses on the process element of competition, not on the product (being the winner or loser). The emphasis is on learning how to compete, and on understanding the role of a competitor.

When a person is a competitor, she is usually judged to be a winner or loser, providing that one score is superior to the other. The traditional procedure at all levels of sports, particularly professional sports, is to ultimately have one winner (with everyone else ending up as a loser). From among all the professional football, baseball, or other teams, there is only one champion at the end of the season. The remainder are "losers." The alternative is the "non-sum zero" concept of competition. This concept can be applied to either a competitive or a cooperative-competitive situation. The non-sum zero concept is based on the premise that effort should be recognized and rewarded. Winning within this frame of reference is expressed as a function of effort, as well as performance level as the measure of degree of success.[26] Total success would be judged in terms of effort *and* performance on par with or above one's ability level, regardless of whether that competitor had the best results. For example, partial success would be accorded an individual when less effort is put forth than he/she is capable of giving or performs at a level lower than would be normally expected even though the opponent was out-played and the contest was won. Thus, in losing a contest one can still be termed a winner and in winning there may be substandard performance according to the non-sum zero approach. This approach redefines losing to indicate only the quantitative outcome of a game. Thus, losing a game and being a loser are not synonymous.

The non-sum zero approach is implemented when a person or group sets a goal (i.e., to make only two errors and make 10 hits in a game of kickball), or uses a handicap system (points are added to the performance score before the winner of the contest is announced), or when a point spread prediction is maintained (i.e., to keep your score at least within six points of the opponent's score). When the outcome of a contest is decided on the basis of a system such as those described above, interest is increased be-

BOX 7–5 What Would You Tell Them?

One problem that can arise with the non-sum zero approach involves the team (team A) that before the game wasn't picked as the winner, but which almost wins the contest (for example, lost a volleyball game by two points). What should the teacher for team A say? (Choose one of the following statements.)

    a. congratulate the members of team A because they played better than expected.
    b. voice disapproval that if it hadn't been for a few mistakes that they could have scored higher than their opponents
    c. both of the above, probably statement b) before statement a).

This situation is indeed a dilemma. The team performed extremely well, probably far above what was expected, so they are winners. However, only a few mistakes kept them from also out-performing their opponent. The act of performing better than expected means that the previous expectation might have been too low. Furthermore, the teacher has the responsibility to point out, in one way or another, the opportunities which the team had but failed to take advantage of or the mistakes which were made and what should have been done.

The correct response for the teacher is response (c). Do you agree?

cause the differences between teams in terms of ability to perform is factored out. The interest can be expressed as increased motivation for the underdog team, which now has a real chance of winning, as well as for the superior team because the degree of challenge has been increased.

The third alternative is based on the fact that competition can be on a direct or indirect basis. Direct competition occurs when the competitors are in close proximity and perform at the same time (as in the 50-yard dash). Indirect competition, on the other hand, is when the opponents perform at different times (as in the softball throw for distance).

Direct competition can be either head to head, or it can be parallel. Head-to-head competition exists when the participants have the opportunity to hinder the other player's attempts to perform, and the contest is decided in terms of which competitor excelled. Examples of head-to-head competition are tug-of-war, tag, and soccer. The parallel form of direct competition does not allow one competitor to interfere with the other's performance. Either they are taking turns to perform, as in shooting baskets in a game of horse, or the performance goes on side by side, as in running a race.

The proposal is to use indirect competition before the direct forms of competition, and to use parallel competition before head-to-head contests. The idea is that the stress involved even in the indirect or parallel forms of competition and cooperative-competition is strong, and for the novice, the effects of the direct form may be overwhelming. Once students have gained experience and have a background of success, they should be better able to cope with more difficult competitive or cooperative-competitive situations.

Rules for Using Competition

An understanding of the basic rules that should be used to guide the development and conduct of a competitive or cooperative-competitive event are important in securing the educational value of these experiences. Competition and cooperative-competition must be valid educational experiences, in terms of both academic and interpersonal development. The following guidelines should be carefully studied as aids in planning and conducting competitive and cooperative-competitive endeavors.

1. Competition should be held on a voluntary basis.
2. Children should be allowed to specify the areas of competition.
3. The teacher should evaluate the competitive situation to determine if it will be detrimental to any student's development.
4. The goals of and rewards for competition should be reasonable, realistic, and changeable, rather than a temptation to unethical and unfair tactics.
5. Competition should be held under reasonable controls to insure the physical safety and psychological well being of the participants.
6. Competition should not be the motivation for achieving basic needs.
7. Unfair, unethical, and dangerous practices should not be allowed, and the participants should be able to depend on a self-initiated process, the teacher, or another authority figure to provide protection.
8. Children should be provided a reasonable chance to achieve success in every competitive situation.
9. Competition should not be held with all contestants always being compared to the highest level of success.
10. Competition should proceed on the participant's schedule of readiness, not in terms of a calendar date.
11. Children are people and should be free from the undue stress and tension of competition, and they should be made to understand that a person doesn't have to finish first to be a "winner."[27]

Raths summed up by stating:

> . . . competition isn't all bad. We can have fun and games that are competitive and at the same time not vicious and not dangerous to ongoing friendly relations among all the competitors. We can help children anticipate the possibilities of losing and how they

would feel if and when they lose. We can talk about winning and losing and the conditions which make competition reasonably fair. We can, in the process, help our children see that the process needs to be vigorously controlled in terms of trust and security.[28]

Play in games and sports is important to realizing educational objectives. Games and sports generate student interest and provide opportunities to excel. Conversely, games and sports can be misused and misguided. The teachers' attitudes and behaviors are important in helping children realize the potential contribution in games and sports to facilitate students learning about themselves.

Developing Cooperative Behavior

Children don't learn how to cooperate by chance. They need to observe others in cooperative-competitive and cooperative situations. They need to participate in discussions to discover ways in which people cooperate in everyday life and sports. Discussions should focus on cooperative acts that occur in school and how everyone involved in the cooperative process feels and is affected. Experiments can be conducted to contrast effectiveness of action, and how personal feelings are influenced when people cooperate as compared to when they are self-centered and unwilling to help others.

The following learning experiences are designed to enable children to learn the value of cooperation and to show the ways in which people can cooperate. The activities can provide children with behavior models, with experiences to discuss, and with relatively straightforward experiences in cooperating.

Balancing an Object   In this experience, two students work together to share the responsibility of keeping an object in balance. The task can be to carry an object from one place to another, or to keep it in balance while going over, under, through, or around obstacles. For example, balancing a tennis ball on an eight-inch wide by two-inch long board.

The challenge of the task can be increased by having the students work against the clock to see how far they can travel in a set time, or by using an object with a smaller base of support, or one with a higher center of gravity.

Setting Up a Playing Area   Giving students responsibility has many potentials for developing cooperative behavior and for fostering feelings of confidence and independence. At first, the teacher should provide a list of equipment and a diagram of the playing area. One group of students could be given the responsibility to set up the playing area for the entire class, or the class could be divided into groups, with each setting up its own movement area for a game or learning center.

Conducting a Five-Event Relay Race   For a five-event relay race, each of the five students in a group practices all of the five different tasks in the relay. The relay should involve five different ways of moving. After practicing each task, the students discuss and decide who will perform each task in the relay. The next step is for each group member to do his/her event in the relay according to the predetermined order. Each performer can be timed, and a total time for the group can be recorded. The individuals can repeat the relay to attempt to improve their performance records as individuals and as a group.

Developing Original Games   Original games can be developed by the teacher, students working individually, students in small groups, or students and their teacher together. The teacher has the responsibility to directly or indirectly help children to develop safe games that provide opportunities for

---

BOX 7–6   How Original Games Work

Marie Riley has worked with elementary school children in grades one through six to develop original games. She found that in original games children generally seem to:

1. choose cooperative situations where improvement of skill is the goal and where the partner is used to contribute toward that goal
2. develop games that use two or more balls
3. choose small groups (four or less students) of similar ability level participants; however, when differences in ability level exist, the games are developed to allow variations in skill
4. make rules, but not in every case, and they are willing to alter the rules as needed to make the game a success
5. not be concerned about naming the game and, if asked to do so, will usually incorporate a description of the action as the title
6. be individual or self-centered and, when younger children are involved, are of the parallel play type
7. ignore score keeping and announcing winners except when asked to and then they frequently keep score by subtraction (errors count against the player and are deducted from a given number of points)
8. work toward making the game serve the interests and needs of the participants.[30]

Did Riley's findings support or refute your ideas of what children would do when they have the chance to change or develop a game?

Do you think children's expectation of what is fun is always the same as the teacher's?

active, meaningful, and satisfying participation by all players. The teacher must also make sure the original games become a part of the sequence of experiences that contribute to realizing instructional objectives. Original games are not played primarily to develop specific motor skills, but to provide a valid experience in an activity that is interesting, demands problem-solving and cooperative behavior, gives insight into the demands and forms of games, and shows how people can plan and play together.[29]

Cooperating in the Classroom   There are many opportunities for cooperation in the classroom. Some of these are learning centers, peer tutoring, and club activities. The acts of sharing, being dependent on others, and providing a specialized talent are the process portion of classroom cooperation situations that are often overlooked in order to achieve the content objectives of the activity.

One method of learning cooperation which was discussed earlier in this chapter is the "jigsaw puzzle" process.[31] In this method, children work in groups of four to six students and must cooperate to complete a task. This method could be used in a physical education lesson in which each child acts out a movement. When all the actions are put together, an idea, feeling, or event is recognizable, as is in the game "charades." Another method is to have each member of a small group develop a movement, teach it to the others in the group; then the group develops a movement sequence composed of each member's movement.

Another cooperative teaching technique is *chain teaching.* In this technique, the teacher or one student who has the skills to teach a simple activity teaches one student what to do. This student in turn teaches another student, with the process being repeated until everyone has learned the task. The last person could be given the responsibility of teaching the task to the person who started the chain.

Classroom governance and maintenance activities are excellent opportunities for developing a sense of group identity and cooperative behavior. Cleaning activities, textbook and workbook shelving, or class leadership committees are situations in which children must cooperate to achieve a goal for the mutual benefit of the class.

These examples of cooperative learning experiences are presented to provide situations where children must work closely together to achieve a goal. The accomplishment of the goal is secondary to what the children must do to find and refine cooperative and responsible behavior skills.

Developing Sportsman-ship   The concept of sportsmanship is complex. According to Ingham and Loy, there are at least eight player roles that can be viewed as *un*sportsmanlike. These are the:

1. *compulsive game-player*—who is addicted to sport and considers it more important than life and human well being

2. *put on*—who verbally underplays his/her ability to con the opponent into not playing their best
3. *psyche-out artist*—who outplays the opponent as a result of what is said and done off the playing area as much as by how well he plays the game
4. *rule modifier*—who changes the sport by changing the rules to gain an advantage
5. *flagrant rule-breaker*—who bullies and openly plays the way he/she wants to without respect for the rules or the opponent
6. *"blaah" player*—who does not care about the game, never really becomes involved, and is a negative influence on the mood of the experience
7. *the cheater*—who disguises an inability to perform by manipulating the rules, thus taking advantage of the opponents
8. *the bad sport*—who acts unethically to willfully and deliberately interfere with the opponent's attempts to perform.[32]

Each of these types of unsportsmanlike behavior can be recognized in all levels of play, from school playgrounds to stadiums around the world. Although each of the first seven types of behavior is viewed as unsportsmanlike, the most despicable violations are related to the deliberate acts of interference.[33]

It might be expected that with experience in games and sports, sportsmanlike behavior would be enhanced. This is not the case, according to Singer.[35]

> . . . the sparse data reveals that poor sportsmanship and values, as usually interpreted by our society, are associated with sports participation. Athletes have been demonstrated to score lower on a values test than nonathletes. Athletes who are subsidized have demonstrated poorest sportsmanship attitudes. A few studies in which various athletic groups are compared reveal that football players have generally indicated that they would win at any cost.

Singer, however, is quick to point out that the intense competition of high level athletics may place more value on the outcome of the game than how the game is played.[36] More importantly, with regard to elementary school age children, a less intense and critical situation in terms of winning, combined with sensitive and responsible instruction, are more likely to produce acts of sportsmanship and ethical conduct in games and sports.

It has also been found that, as the level of competition and experiences increases, the participants may develop different perceptions of what constitutes good sportsmanship. Thus, one behavior at the beginner's level would be termed unsportsmanlike, but it would not be considered unsportsmanlike at a higher level of play. A code of ethics for participants may be viewed differently by the players, as compared to the coach's or teacher's expectations. While research isn't available for elementary-age school children, one study[37] suggested that ideas of what constitutes ethical conduct

BOX 7–7 Participants' Code of Ethics

Read each of the statements listed below. The statements were developed from an athletic association's code of ethics for players.[34] They are listed in a random order and not as published by the association. Mark a 1 by the four statements you believe are the most important in terms of ethical behavior and good sportsmanship.

_____a. The player should exhibit dignity in manner and dress when representing one's school, both on and off the court or playing field.

_____b. The player should strive for the highest degree of excellence.

_____c. The player should accept victory or defeat without undue emotion.

_____d. The player should treat all players, officials, and coaches with respect and courtesy.

_____e. The player should refrain from partaking of alcoholic beverages and drugs unless prescribed by a physician for medical purposes while representing one's school.

_____f. The player should willfully abide by the spirit of the rules as well as the letter of the rules throughout all games and practices.

_____g. The player should keep personal disagreements away from practices and contests.

_____h. The player should seek to know and understand one's teammates.

Find someone who has also completed this task. Compare your rankings and discuss your areas of agreement and disagreement. Identify types of ethical codes you believe are most important. Think about and discuss what concepts you and your partner have listed as being important to following a code of ethical behavior for sport and game participants. How could you modify this task to provide a take-off point for helping your students to develop their own code of ethics?

may vary not only among levels of competition but also between male and female participants. The implication of this study for teaching is that it is important for teachers and students to engage in a dialogue to express their views of what constitutes good sportsmanship and ethical conduct in game and sport. Through mutual understanding, the players might be better able to work out their operational definitions of sportsmanlike and unsportsmanlike behavior.

Situational questions are useful in having students take a stand, to express their beliefs, and examine the values upon which their opinion is based. An example of a situation question is as follows: The score in a game of basketball during a physical education period is 14 to 18 in favor of the team that was favored to win. The game is almost over, the teacher has the whistle in his hand and is looking at his wrist watch. The team that is ahead has the ball. Their best dribbler has the ball. She and her teammates know that if they spread out, pass the ball safely, and dribble the ball, the other team will never be able to score enough baskets to beat them in the short time remaining. How do you rate this action?

_____   _____   _____

good sportsmanship   *unsure*   *poor sportsmanship*

After making a choice, a small group of students should compare and discuss their responses. Early questions could focus on your opinion concerning a situation evaluation of immediate and long range consequences of a sportsmanlike or unsportsmanlike act. At a later point in the discussion, the students could identify situations in which it took courage to be a good sport. The result is that students can begin to develop a code of ethics for their own play and begin to value fair play more than just winning.

IMPLEMENTING THE DEVELOPMENTAL THEME

In a world where people find themselves living, working, and playing in more and more crowded conditions, it becomes increasingly urgent that children develop abilities and attributes that will help them to function in a socially demanding environment. Acting cooperatively, taking responsibility, making decisions with confidence, and learning to enjoy working with others are some of the attributes that will be even more necessary in our society twenty or thirty years hence. Physical education provides an opportune environment for teachers to help their students acquire these attributes.

Developing Concern

Learning to share, to respect others' points of view, and to care about others takes time. Some behavioral changes will be easy to bring about, such as demonstrating care in handling equipment. Some other changes, however, may not be as evident to the teacher, even though they exist.

Developing concern for others is a behavior that is promoted verbally in the classroom. However, designing experiences that actually result in the development of such behavior is much more difficult.

The teaching modules in this chapter include some of these experiences, such as sharing equipment and taking responsibility for safety.

Leading and Following

Experiencing leadership is crucial to the development of leadership qualities. Assuming responsibility for more than oneself begins in working with a partner. Partner work is important for primary grade children and those upper elementary students who are slower in developing leadership qualities. Following up the experience with discussion about what leadership entails makes the experience more productive and less a chance outcome.

A "leader" is not always one who tells others what to do, but one whose own performance generates a following in a particular field. However, children also need to learn that the leader's ideas are not necessarily good or correct. It is an important role for the follower to influence the selection of worthy ideas or components of ideas.

Rules   Understanding the different aspects of the concept of rules is an important step in becoming an informed citizen in a democratic society. All too frequently, many children and adults regard rules from a negative viewpoint. They neither understand the rules' derivations nor the process(es) and resources available for rule modification. Consequently, the behavior of many individuals indicates feelings of powerlessness associated with rules. They believe that other people ("they") made the rules, and that there is no recourse other than to obey those rules.

FIGURE 7-2 Exploring rules

Children need to understand the quality differences between those rules that can be modified and those that cannot, and the process involved in proposing rule changes. Learning to identify and accept those "inevitable" rules that cannot be changed is part of the socialization process.

Another aspect of exploring rules is for children to learn that they can play an important part in devising and implementing the operational rules of the classroom. They will be more likely to adhere to a system that they have helped to devise than one that is imposed on them.

Cooperating and Competing

Team spirit and sportsmanship do not necessarily occur spontaneously or by simply participating in a team activity. Teachers need to plan experiences and games to ensure that children are placed in the role of *contributing* team members, not merely followers. "Cooperate" means "work together," but when children accuse each other of "not cooperating" they often mean "not doing what *I* say!"

Many teachers know that children are very capable of refereeing their own games with some preparatory help from teachers, but all too often, adults tend to monopolize the major organizing and refereeing tasks in the upper elementary grades because it is less time consuming and keeps the activity "moving." While these are important considerations, in the long run, the adults' energies would be better spent helping children become more capable in organizing and directing their own game-playing behavior.

The discussion of competition in this developmental theme ranges from competing with oneself against a detached factor, such as time, to cooperating with a group that competes directly against another group. The competitive or cooperative-competitive activities in this module provide for involvement in decision making by the students, thereby increasing their control over the movement or game situation.

DEVELOPING CONCERN FOR OTHERS AND PROPERTY

Planning Guide

Objectives	*Experiences*
As a result of the learning experiences over time, children will:	
1. demonstrate careful handling of equipment or property	• permit children to assign rotating duties of managing the equipment before and after the physical education lesson
2. be able to use *active listening* while others are talking	• paraphrase others' instructions that have been given to them

Objectives	*Experiences*
3. demonstrate understanding that "winning" is not necessarily evaluated in terms of a numerical score	• devise and apply modifications of games in which "scoring" is not always an accumulation of points (runs, goals, etc.)
4. decrease the number of insensitive remarks made to other players.	• play team or group games in which the score accumulates by way of the number of positive remarks made about other players.

For evaluating students' progress in developing concern for others, see page 217.

Teaching Modules

Introductory Module

Objectives

As a result of the learning experiences over time, children will:

1. identify an insensitive remark made to others
2. be able to verbalize the concept of "winning" as being more than accumulating a numerical score.

Learning Experiences	*Related Experiences*
1. "Who would like to share with us how they feel after they have won a game—any kind of game?" If it is possible, write some key words on the chalk board as they come up in the children's conversations. Children will probably begin by using rather general terms such as "I feel good or great." Teachers can help them to be more specific and descriptive about their feelings. In a competitive classroom, the children are pitted against one another for the teacher's attention and approval. This environment seems to generate divisive rather than supportive behavior.[13] 2. "Is there a difference in winning in a game of, say, four-square, and winning in a game like kickball?" At first, the children may say there is no difference, but eventually someone will probably remark that the presence of teammates means that one has had some help in winning.	• Write a short description of a time when you helped someone else and felt good about it. • Examine some children's games in other cultures, such as the Kiowa-Apache children, the Navajo, the Manus of New Guinea, and Japanese children before 1950. • Conduct a discussion on why people play games. • Make a list of as many words you can think of that mean "win." • Review the history of the Olympic Games. What was the purpose of holding the first Olympic Games? • Make a collage of pictures of people who have "won," either against a previous record or against another team. • Write or tape a sports commentary in which you make remarks about the team spirit more than who is winning or losing.

Learning Experiences

Related Experiences

3. "In a team game, what makes the difference between a winning team and a losing
team?" Possible responses:

   sportsmanship
   team spirit
   one team is better than the other
   better coaching.

   Help the children analyze "team spirit"
in terms of:

   • keeping each other's spirits up
   • helping each other improve their skills
   • knowing each other well so that one can
     detect changes in mood
   • considering others' needs as important
     as one's own.

   Once the children have identified a
number of components of the concept of
"team spirit," continue to the next question.

4. "Is it possible to 'win' in more than one way
(such as scoring more runs, or making
more points)? Can a team be a winning
team even if they lose some games?"

   Most children interpret terms literally:
"winning" is scoring more points than the

• Search the periodical literature on sports for
examples of people who have sacrificed the
opportunity to win in order to render aid to
a teammate or performed some other altruistic act.
• Watch a Little League game and write why
you would like to be a member of one of the
teams.
• Watch a sports program on TV and record
the number of times: 1) players praise their
teammates, 2) players blame a poor performance on something other than themselves (weather, the other team, the
officiating, etc.).

FIGURE 7-3 Members of a winning team help each other improve their skills

Learning Experiences

"losers." It is quite difficult for them to consider "winning" in any other light.

The children may concede here that, provided the winning team wins more than it loses, it could be classified as a "winning" team. The discussion here may require careful direction to maintain an openness to some of the following possibilities:

- a "winning" team cares about each other
- a team that loses to another team of superior ability (in a higher league, for example) can still "win" if the team members refrain from blaming each other or "putting down" either their own team members, or the other team

All too frequently, children return from a game experience cross and irritable rather than happy and satisfied. Often this is because of the way that games are approached, the stereotyped concepts that children hold about game-playing, and the nature of many games. The traditional pattern of games, such as kickball, favor the physically able. The opportunity to have many satisfying turns diminishes if one is on a large team (of 12 to 15) and/or is physically inept.

5. "What do you think would happen if the score in a game included the number of praising, or positive things that were said to your team?"

Central Module

Objectives

As a result of the learning experiences over time, children will decrease the number of insensitive remarks made to others.

Devise teams by one of these two methods:

1. four captains dividing up the class ahead of time into four equal groups; the captains then *draw* to see which team they have
2. four captains choose the teams from a list that has been rank-ordered by the teacher (again, this is done at a time when the class is otherwise occupied); it saves some children from continually being chosen last.

Materials

A signal for stopping the activity. Pencil and paper to record runs and comments.

Learning Experiences

Related Experiences

The structure of the major experience in this module will depend on your particular situation. While a large kickball game (10 to 12 on a side) is not the most suitable learning situation, it can be a useful way to teach the concepts in this module. Once the children have learned the procedures, however, they can be divided into more groups for smaller games.

Organize the game in the classroom so that no time will be wasted in the activity area:

- quickly assign the teams (this can be done ahead of time by the method outlined in the objectives section of this module
- toss a coin to see which will be up to kick first.

- Discuss or write why it is more interesting to complete an experiment in a small group than to see it demonstrated to the entire class.

FIGURE 7-4 Changing the rules of familiar games is not always easy for children

Learning Experiences

• if you have worked with the introductory module on exploring rules, use some of the ideas produced to play the game, or modify the kickball game in the following manner:
  - each kicker has a "buddy" who runs with him/her
  - whoever fields the ball, stands still and the entire fielding team runs to line up behind the person who fielded the ball
  - if the runners get to base before the fielding team is lined up, they are safe, otherwise they are out.

Be prepared for some initial resistance to changing the game. Some children do not always take kindly to changing traditions. This is especially true of those who may have dominated the game when it was played in its original form, but now find themselves operating at a different level of success.

This modification provides more active participation for the fielding team and a little more action for the kicking team. The additional runner cannot cause the kicker to be out, so it does not penalize slower runners.

As the scorer, you count *both* the number of runs and the number of positive comments made to each team. Expect the children to make praising remarks simply to increase their score at first. At the same time, note the number of positive remarks that are made in the general course of the day following this experience. You will probably find that the ratio of positive remarks is increased over previous interaction patterns.

Related Experiences

• List school rules that protect the property rights (books, clothing, school supplies) of students.
• Conduct a discussion on how it must feel to be chosen last on a team, and how it feels to be chosen first.
• Select readings from basal series dealing with altruistic acts or themes.

Modification for Primary Children

The same objectives and process can take place in a game with primary children. For this particular learning experience, kickball can be used by younger children since the game should not be continued very long anyway.

However, if, as is often the case, kickball is associated with unacceptable behavior in the early grades, then a simpler, smaller group game such as "Keep It Up" can replace kickball. "Keep It Up" also provides for more participation than any modified form of kickball.

Description of the Game: The children are divided into groups of five or six. Each group has a light vinyl ball. The object of the game is to "keep it up" in the air by hitting it with different body-parts. No player may hit the ball twice in a row (first grade children may need to have this rule modified).

Scoring: The game can be scored in two ways:

1. The teams are all pitted against each other. They start on a signal so that the team that keeps the ball in the air the longest time wins a point. Once a group misses, the teams may start again as a practice trial.
2. Each time the ball is struck, it counts one point for the team. Thus, if Team A strikes the ball ten times and Team B only strikes the ball seven times, but keeps it up longer, Team A wins. This form of scoring is more difficult to monitor, but it provides motivation to practice the skill involved as opposed to hitting the ball high in the air to "keep it up."

Culminating Module

Objectives

As a result of the learning experiences over time, children will be able to:

1. use a coping behavior in dealing with insensitive remarks made to themselves or to others
2. list several ways in which insensitive behavior can be decreased
3. describe several reward systems for those who attempt to decrease insensitive remarks.

Building a reward system in their play for demonstrating sensitive behavior toward others is one coping behavior they can use in their free play time. However, opportunity must be given for practicing such behavior under monitored conditions.

Learning Experiences	*Related Experiences*

1. Conduct a discussion immediately after the game on how they felt about the way it was scored. Some of the questions you might pose are: How was the game different today? How did you feel having to think about what you said to the other players?
2. If the response is quite negative, move to making a list of positive things that happened in the game:
  • there may have been less shouting
  • people did not get in a bad temper
	• Investigate the accumulated scores of the most recent Superbowl or World Series winners to see which team had won the greatest number of total points in all the games they played leading up to the final play-off. Would there have been a difference in the winner if this scoring method had been used?
	• Write a short poem about a boy or girl who helps to win a game by making a kind remark to a "bad sport."

Learning Experiences	*Related Experiences*
• someone scored (by making a nice remark) who usually never scores at all • the game may have moved along more quickly because there was less interruption from disputes.	

3. "Are there other ways that we can encourage ourselves to help our team or the other team? Does it have to be a score?" Some other suggestions for rewarding supportive behavior might be:
  • the team that shows the most supportive behavior (or any team that shows supportive behavior) has five minutes free time at the end of the period
  • the team that shows supportive behavior chooses the activity for the next day's class from a list of possible activities
  • the team(s) showing supportive behavior are given an extra ten-minute recess, or free activity time, sometime during the day
  • they go to lunch first
  • have some other special privileges that are considered desirable.
The teacher needs to gradually withdraw the reward system once the behavior has become intrinsically rewarding; otherwise, the purpose of the reward system will be thwarted as the score will be the overriding goal rather than making the game more enjoyable for all.
	• Tape a sports commentary in which the game will be won or lost by the good sportsmanship of the players.
	• Listen to a TV or radio commentary and count the number of encouraging or complimentary remarks that are made about the players or the coaches. Were the remarks concerning the players' ability or personality, or playing methods?
	• What can you tell about the commentator's values from the remarks he makes?

Summary

Enabling Behavior: Developing Concern for Others and Property

This enabling behavior deals with consideration for others and as such will be more difficult for egocentric children. Students are increasing their concern for others when:

1. They demonstrate increasing awareness of how their verbal behavior affects others.
2. They make positive remarks about other students in the class.
3. They offer to help other students with their work or unassigned tasks. However, some children may prefer to "help" other students rather than complete their own tasks.
4. They act positively and supportively in team play.

5. Older or more mature children can control their behavior under stressful conditions in a game.
6. They demonstrate increasing openness toward innovative ideas relating to familiar activities.
7. They treat others' property with care and respect.

DEVELOPING ROLES

Planning Guide

Objectives	*Experiences*
As a result of the learning experiences over time, children will:	
1. be able to effectively assume a leadership role in a relationship of two	• make up movement sequences that a partner can follow; retain leadership position when traveling in different directions
2. demonstrate understanding that leadership mandates assuming responsibility.	• assuming "power" over a partner or small group through nonverbal communications; choose safe activities for partner or small group to perform.

For evaluating students' progress in developing roles, see page 223.

Teaching Modules

Introductory Module

Objectives

As a result of the learning experiences over time, children will be able to effectively assume a leadership role in a group of two.

Materials

An instrument to signal "freeze"

Learning Experiences	*Related Experiences*
The first task in this activity can be organized in the classroom.	• Conduct a discussion on "what leaders do."
	• Find pictures to make a display of leaders in different domains or professions.
1. "When I say 'Go!' show me how you can find a partner quietly and decide quickly	• Write a poem about following.

Learning Experiences

who will be the first leader. The leader is going to jog anywhere inside the boundaries so that the partner can follow. Freeze when you hear this signal (*). Go!"

Jogging is an activity that needs less monitoring than a highly vigorous task, thus allowing the teacher to cope with slow starters. Give the Freeze signal.

2. "Change over so your partner is the leader now. Leaders, try to find ways to change the speed of your jogging so that sometimes you jog very quickly, and sometimes very, very slowly." Continue to provide variations on the task of leading and following each time the children change roles:

- find a way to include a roll
- change directions quickly
- in your own space, moving slowly, make four different body-shapes, one after the other.

The number and modes of varying this task will depend on the level of the children's ability.

Related Experiences

- Draw a picture of the pathways you and your follower made in one of these activities.
- Make a list of ten words that mean "lead."
- Read about Christopher Columbus. Do you think he was a leader? Do you think the people who lived at that time thought he was a leader?
- Find out all you can about Alexander the Great. What kind of leader do you think he was?
- Investigate the life of Attila the Hun. Compare him as a leader with Alexander the Great. In what ways were they the same? In what ways were they different?

FIGURE 7-5 Jogging in a line of three

Central Module

Objectives

As a result of the learning experiences over time, children will:

1. demonstrate understanding that leadership mandates responsibility
2. demonstrate care in choosing activities for their partners to perform
3. demonstrate ability to follow directions given nonverbally.

Materials

One instrument for signaling "freeze" should be available for each pair. The instruments can be of different types.

Learning Experiences

1. "All of you have had a chance to be the leader a number of times. What did you find leaders have to do?" (Possible replies: "Think of things to do." "Watch where they were going," etc.) "When you were a leader, did you think about what your partner could do before you started? Or did you just do the movements *you* could do?" Reinforce the point that leaders have to watch out for those who are following them and consider their partner's limitations in movement.

   Introduce the next learning experience in either of the following ways:
   a. "Everyone find a space on their own so they can see me. See if you can follow the directions I give you with my *hands.* I'm not going to say anything." Give an exaggerated hand signal for the children to:
   - move away from you
   - come closer to you
   - move sideways
   - turn around, etc.

   Make sure you finish so that they can see you.

Related Experiences

- Write a short report beginning: "If I were President for one day, I . . ."
- Make up a story about a King (or Queen) who did not want to be King (or Queen).
- List all the groups you know that have a leader and write down the leader's title (e.g., school—principal; city—mayor).
- Conduct a discussion on what happens when the group disagrees with the leader's decisions.
- Write a story about a land where some of the people have all of the power and others have none.
- (Sixth grade) Find out about the feudal system in the Middle Ages. Who had all the power then and how did they keep it?
- Conduct discussions on what is meant by slogans like: People Power! Flower Power!, etc.
- Conduct a discussion about "Is there ever a time when someone has complete control over another person?"
   - a baby is completely helpless and cannot fend for itself
   - when can people begin to "fend for themselves"?

Learning Experiences

This introduction is particularly suitable for primary grades and classes in which children have been accustomed to a moderate amount of structure. It can be followed by allowing several children, one at a time, to have the "power" over the class.

b. Use either two children you have talked to ahead of time to demonstrate or pick one child to work with you, and do a short demonstration as outlined in (*a*).

2. "Now one of you be the leader, and make your partner do anything you like, *so long as it is safe.* Start when you are ready." They may need to be reminded that this is a nonverbal activity. You may find that the children simply imitate what they have seen done in the demonstration. If so, you can suggest "find a signal to make your partner change speeds, (or directions, levels, roll on the ground)." These additional tasks are ways to expand almost *any* challenge. Do not allow the children to change roles until *you* signal. Observe the children and try to time the change in roles so that the leaders do not become frustrated or bored with the task.

Making the children retain the "power" even though they "can't think of what else to do" reinforces the discussion point on "leaders cannot always quit when *they* want to." Extend the task in the following ways:

• *Primary:* develop the idea of "power" being held by one of the partners through:

a. *rhythm instruments*—"power" plays the instrument and the partner obeys the sounds and rhythm patterns (about third grade).

b. *the use of imagery*—power as a magician (or bionic wizard) and the two can make a sequence of their own that tells a story.

Related Experiences

• Find out all you can about "leaders" in a different culture from ours:
  – an American Indian tribe
  – present-day Spain
  – Yugoslavia
  – China before 1920, etc.
• Read the story of King Canute trying to keep the waves back at the ocean edge.
• Write a poem about what it feels like to have power over another person.
• Conduct mock elections and focus on what certain candidates have to offer to the office they seek.
• Conduct a discussion on people who have power over a number of people at once (teachers, foremen and forewomen, prison guards).
• What kinds of responsibility accompany this power?
• Find stories/articles in the newspaper that relate specifically to "leadership."
  – examples of good leadership
  – examples of inept leadership
  – examples of leadership provided by one of the general public.
(This topic is particularly appropriate when "issues" are raised by individuals to the city council, school board, etc.).

Learning Experiences

c. *modeling*—"power" makes different movements and the partner follows those exactly.
• *Intermediate:* develop the complexity of the task by:
a. increasing the group size to three, and instructing "power" to keep the group moving all the time.
b. increasing the group size to four or even five. The most complex task is to keep the group moving all the time, but each person must be doing something different.
c. by making up a short dance sequence in which the power shifts back and forth between the partners and has a dramatic finish of their own choosing.

FIGURE 7-6 Keeping the whole group moving

Culminating Module

Objectives

As a result of the learning experiences over time, children will:

1. demonstrate understanding that there are many forms of leadership.
2. be able to list three qualities of good leaders
3. be able to apply criteria of good leadership to current political and sports figures.

Leadership is often regarded in an idiosyncratic way and is sometimes confused with charisma.

Learning Experiences

"Everyone has had the chance, now, to be power. Tell me how some of you felt about that." To stimulate the discussion, you might ask one or more of the following questions:

Related Experiences

• Write poems/limericks/paragraphs about how you felt when you were "power."
• Identify forms of government wherein the power is vested in one or two people.

Learning Experiences

–How did you feel about having all the power over someone else?

–What did it feel like having someone order you around and you had to obey?

–What would have happened if you had had to keep the power all day?

–What is the difference between a "good" power and a "bad" power?

This question leads into the problem of how to identify a "good" leader. Once the criteria of "good" leaders are established, apply the criteria to well-known sports, political, and media leaders.

Related Experiences

• Compare life in the Middle Ages (the feudal system) with life in prerevolutionary Russia as examples of "powerful" and "powerless" systems (sixth grade).

• Draw up some criteria of "good leaders."

• *Good* leaders:

  –do not expect people to do things they would not do

  –think about the safety of the group

  –listen to others' ideas

  –are firm without being dictatorial

  –consider the abilities of the group members.

Post these criteria on the bulletin board.

Summary

Enabling Behavior: Developing Roles

This enabling behavior is basic to much of what happens in the group process. Indications that students are progressing in their ability to lead and follow are when:

1. They can select partners more quickly.
2. They demonstrate enjoyment in working with a partner or in a small group.
3. They listen to another student without interrupting.
4. They can identify the attributes or characteristics of a good leader.
5. They demonstrate understanding of the concept that responsibility accompanies the leadership role.

EXPLORING RULES

Planning Guide

Objectives

As a result of the learning experiences over time, children will:

1. understand the nature of rules and their diversity (some rules are *legal laws,* some are *principles,* and some are operational rules)

Experiences

• make up a set of operational rules for a game, or efficient use of time in getting from one activity to another; play a game under "official" rules

Learning Experiences	*Related Experiences*
2. be able to change the "established" rules of popular games to permit maximum participation 3. be able to create an original game that allows for maximum participation.	• devise game rules that permit players to remain in the game after they have committed a fault in play • given selected equipment, children devise games that call for a variety of skills and constant participation of the players.

For evaluating students' progress in this enabling behavior, see page 230.

Teaching Modules

Introductory Module

Objectives

As a result of the learning experiences over time, children will:

1. demonstrate understanding of the difference between an "operational rule" and a "law" in a popular game
2. identify kinds of rules that are crucial to the conduct of the game
3. be able to change "established" rules of popular games to permit maximum participation.

In a kickball game at recess, Karen, a belligerent girl who is not particularly well-coordinated has kicked the ball badly. She is out before she reaches first base. Furious, she begins to lay blame and make excuses for herself. The pitcher didn't roll the ball right! The baseman got in her way! Her shoe was coming off! She finally stomps off to the side grumbling, "Dumb ole game. You just don't want me to play. You don't play fair," etc.

Learning Experiences	*Related Experiences*
Start by telling a real or hypothetical story. This discussion can take place in a circle. It can arise from an interest (by the children) in the performance of a local team, an exciting game event on television, or the above incident in a game played at recess: 1. "Many people seemed to be angry after recess this morning. Would anyone like to explain what happened in the kickball game?" It will be difficult for children to remain cool during the next part of the discussion, but you need to help them clarify what really happened. "You say Karen al-	• Discuss why we have rules in school. Why do we have certain rules in school and different ones at home? Are any of the rules at school the same as at home? • Write a story about a planet your spacecraft has landed on. You are going to set up a new country. Tell how you would make rules and what some of them would be. • Make up a poem about a girl/boy who was always left out of things until one day . . . • Draw a picture of yourself when you were left out of something you wanted to join in. • Make a list of ways people are left out of things:

Learning Experiences

ways causes trouble when she's out of the game?" (Probably an assenting chorus!) "How often is Karen out?" (A lot!) "I wonder how Karen feels about that?"

2. The response to this depends on how much emphasis has been placed on the importance of helping others feel good. "Think of a time when you felt left out of something that looked like fun. Can anyone tell us how they felt?"

    All too often discussions are "solution-bound." Solutions are solicited before everyone has had a chance to truly understand the nature of the problem. Empathizing with Karen is important if *realistic* solutions are to be arrived it.

3. After a few minutes of relating similar feelings: "Is there any other way you could play the game so that players don't have to be out of the game?" (Probable replies: "No." "That's the way we always play." "We wouldn't know when the side was out.") Point out the semantic difference of "being out" (to the other side's advantage) and "being physically *out* of the game."

    There are few, if any, popular children's games where "out" is not synonymous with being physically excluded in some way. It is often a novel thought to look at possibilities of other ways of scoring or changing the rules to allow maximum participation.

4. "Can you think of any other way to play the game so that people do not have to wait around a lot?" Given time and guidance, many children will come up with some ideas:

    a. Play against the clock. Each side is in for five minutes and scores as many points as possible.

    b. Count the "outs" but allow them to stay in the game. Count all good scores.

    c. Change the rules so that "runs" are accumulated to reach a tie.

5. At this point, lead the discussion to how one can change rules that are made up for the specific situation, as opposed to changing the "rules" or "laws" of the Little League Baseball Association.

Related Experiences

−they don't know how to play the game
−they don't speak the language
−they can't afford to buy some of the equipment, etc.

- Find out how games are played in other countries.
- Discuss the way that the Constitution was formed. How are laws added to the Constitution?
- Measure the distance between the bases and compute how many runs it takes to make a mile. Make a graph to compute two miles.
- Make a list of the suggestions to put on the bulletin board.
- Make a team poster on which a running count of scores can be kept for a week if a solution is chosen.
- Explore the history of a popular game. Where did it originate? How did some of the rules come to be accepted? How is the game different today from what is was 20 (50, 100) years ago?

FIGURE 7-7 Making up a game in which no one is "out"

Central Module

Objectives

As a result of the learning experiences over time, children will:

1. be able to create a game in small groups
2. devise appropriate rules for their game
3. be able to modify those rules when the situation requires it.

Materials

Primary—A hoop and lightweight vinyl ball for each group of three.
Intermediate—A bean bag and four paper bats.
Other items available for intermediate groups: hoops, stretch ropes, sock balls.

Learning Experiences

As a final review of the discussion in the introductory module, you can review the points brought out that focus on making a game more enjoyable for everyone.

"You really have made good suggestions for changing the kickball game. Now, we're going to make up our own game." Divide them into groups of three (for primary) or four (for intermediate).

"Each group will have (*primary:* one ball and one hoop) (*intermediate:* one bean bag and four bats) to make up a game with.

"Your game has to be one in which no one is ever put out, and everyone gets a chance to use the equipment."

Creating games is an activity that may require the teacher's intervention more than some other activities because it can fall apart so rapidly. The following are some of the problems you may encounter and some suggestions as to how to deal with them:

1. The group is playing what is really "kickball" or some other familiar activity.
   Teacher: "Can you find a way to make the ball move so that you all get a chance to touch it often? See if you can find another way to make the ball move." This suggestion may lead to using different body-parts or making the ball roll or spin, etc.

2. The group is not challenging itself in activities; it is doing traditional activities or drills.
   Teacher: "Show me how your game works." (a demonstration) "Is there any way you can make the game more interesting? You can all do this so easily."

3. The group can't get started because of arguing about whose ideas to use.
   Teacher: "How great to have so many ideas! Let's see how they work so you can choose the most interesting ones for your game."
   It is important in this group to move them quickly into activity. Try the ideas one at a time.

Related Experiences

- Draw a picture of a kickball (football, baseball, basketball, etc.) game.
- Write an explanation of a popular game (kickball, four-square) so that a visitor from another planet could understand it.
- Write a poem from the point of view of being the ball in the kickball game.
- Conduct a discussion on who makes the rules for teachers to follow:
    - which rules can be changed?
    - how can such rules be changed?
    - what rules would you make up for teachers?
- Look at how laws are made in different countries: How are the procedures different from the U.S.? How are the procedures the same?
- Write a letter to your Congressmen telling them how you think they should vote on some particular issue. (sixth grade)
- Make a collage of people who help to make laws.
- Find out what you can about how police officers help people keep the laws.
- Write a story about a town that had no police officers.

FIGURE 7-8 Finding ways to make the game more interesting

Culminating Module

Objectives

As a result of the learning experiences over time, children will:

1. be able to explain the rationale for any rule they originate
2. identify rules that allow for greater participation in a game.

Materials

Paper for listing rules for posting on bulletin board.

Learning Experiences

In physical education, activities are often simply stopped or changed without any summarizing or effective closure for many experiences. The following is one suggestion for bringing the learning experiences to closure:

Primary: "You made up some interesting games. Let's go back to the classroom and talk about what you did."

The rules can be written on the board or illustrated by using stick figures. Bring the discussion to a close by identifying criteria for "good rules."

Related Experiences

- Make a list of ideas that can be used for games in the future (next week).
- Examine classroom rules to see if they meet the model of "a good rule."
- Conduct primary science experiments that focus on the *laws of gravity.*
- Find out all you can about Galileo and the Tower of Pisa. Why were people upset about some of his discoveries?
- Draw up a list of games that can be played during recess.
- Draw cartoons that illustrate the classroom rules.

Learning Experiences

- a *good rule* lets everybody play
- a *good rule* helps to make the game fun
- a *good rule* means playing, not waiting around.

Intermediate: "When I say Go, quietly put away your equipment and go back to your place in the classroom. When you get there, stay in your groups and write down how your game should be played, list all the rules, and draw some diagrams to help other people understand your game. We'll put them all up on the bulletin board when you've finished." When the rules are up on the board, you could place some questions strategically about the display, such as: Are there any rules that are nearly the same in many games? What is the largest number that can play this game? How are some of the games different?

Related Experiences

- Conduct experiments to focus on physical laws of motion:
    - –place a paper cup filled with water
    - –place it on a piece of paper on a smooth surface
    - –take hold of the edge of the paper and jerk it quickly towards you.

Result: The paper cup will remain still, but the paper moves. *Principle:* Objects tend to remain at rest unless acted upon by an outside force, inertia.

FIGURE 7-9 Testing the principle

Summary

Enabling Behavior: Exploring Rules

This enabling behavior deals with orderly conduct in a game or in group work. Children are developing understanding about rules when they:

1. Can describe the difference between a "law" of nature and a legal law.
2. Can explain the difference between a "law" and a "rule."
3. Develop games in which rules are flexible to allow for differences in playing ability.
4. Can explain the criteria for "good" rules.
5. Can identify what makes for a "poor" rule.

DEVELOPING COOPERATIVE AND COMPETITIVE BEHAVIOR

Planning Guide

Objectives	*Experiences*
As a result of the learning experiences over time, children will:	
1. demonstrate ability to work with others in a productive manner	• make up games of increasing complexity; participate in modified "intramural" types of *intra*class competition
2. be able to recognize when decisions are made *for* a group rather than *by* it	• participate in games in which there is a "problem" for the group to solve
3. demonstrate understanding that "cooperating" means "working together," not "following orders".	• participate in group experiences in which each member must provide an idea for a movement sequence or dance.

For evaluating your students' progress in developing cooperative and competitive behavior, see page 236.

Teaching Modules

Introductory Module

Objectives

As a result of the learning experiences over time, children will:

1. demonstrate knowledge of how group decisions are arrived at democratically

2. be able to recognize when decisions are made *for* a group rather than *by* it.

Learning Experiences

Have the children seated in a circle so that they can see each other's faces. Children are more likely to enter into the discussion if they can have eye contact with the teacher and the other children.

"Supposing I had been invited to the White House to see the President, and I could take two of you with me. How would we choose who would go?" Possible answers:

"You (the teacher) should choose who you want."

"We could draw straws or take names out of a hat."

"You (the teacher) could choose the best (smartest, best-behaved, etc.) people to go."

"We could choose a boy and a girl to represent us."

If you pursue this idea, the children begin to identify some criteria by which the two are to be chosen. "How are we to choose?" Some possible answers might be:

- we will vote on who we think could talk to the President best
- select those people who have done a project on the President or the White House
- choose people who never have a chance to travel
- we will have a contest to see who can write the best letter on "Why I should be chosen to meet the President." Let the Principal judge the best two.

The answers that the children give should be explored in some depth, not just accepted or rejected.

Related Experiences

- Conduct a discussion on how athletes are selected for the Olympic Games.
- Write a play about a group of people who are planning a surprise party for one of their friends, but cannot agree about how to do it.
- Keep a log for a week of all the times you cooperate with someone else this week.
- Read about how people in a country like the United States make decisions about how resources will be used.
- You have won a free trip for yourself and a friend. Your best friend cannot go because of a broken leg. Write about where you would go on your trip and how you would choose who would go with you.

Central Module

Objectives

As a result of the learning experiences over time, children will be able to:

1. work with others in a productive manner
2. plan and set up gymnastic equipment in such a way as to allow the group to be active all the time.

Before the tasks in this module are attempted, the children should be familiar with the idea of working in stations.

Materials

The tasks presented in this module are generic in that they can be applied to a wide variety of equipment arrangements. Some suggestions for equipment groupings are as follows. For each group:

a box (3'x3'x2')
a hoop, two blocks (4'x4'x20"), one jump rope
an instrument to signal "finish what you are doing"
instruction cards for each group.

Learning Experiences

Give the instructions while the children are still seated from the previous discussion:

1. "When I say Go, quietly find the other people in your group and set up the equipment so that your group can keep moving without having to wait for turns. Talk together to decide how you will do this. When you hear this signal (*), finish what you are doing and sit down beside your equipment. GO!"

   Observe how the children manage this task, and time the signal so that the groups have some time to experiment with moving in relation to the equipment. Watch for groups where:
   a. there is insufficient space between them and the next group, thus causing a safety hazard
   b. there is an argument as to how the equipment will be arranged

Related Experiences

- Conduct a discussion on how young children can cooperate in doing family chores.
- Arrange an erasable "I helped" list on the bulletin board. Children can write or draw about how they helped at home in a special way this week.
- Keep a diary of how many times you offered to help someone this week.
- Read stories about the early pioneers and how they had to cooperate in order to survive.
- Make a list of all the games in which the players have to cooperate in order to win: soccer, doubles tennis, basketball, etc.
- Compare the ways in which cooperation in soccer can be compared with cooperation in doubles tennis (or volleyball). (Large play space for all team members versus reduced space.)

Learning Experiences

c. there are only one or two children working
d. a self-styled "leader" has taken over and is telling the rest of the group what to do.

All of the above problems can often be solved simply by moving to where the group is operating. If the behavior persists, you can ask questions, such as:

Is everyone working, not waiting?

Can you find a way to allow Judy and Ken to work as well? It is up to the whole group to see that the task is carried out.

I see Denise is trying to get everyone to do the same thing. Can you think only about what you are doing, Denise, and let the others plan their own movements?

2. Signal (*). Wait for children to be seated quietly by their equipment. Reinforce groups that sit down quickly. "You have been moving in many ways with your equipment. Now, without changing the arrangement of your equipment, change direction as you move. What directions can we move in?" (Forward, backward, sideways, up or down, or any feasible combination of these.) Working efficiently in stations or groups is simpler, if the groups are given the same task, even though the equipment might vary from one group to another. When the group begins to work again, move rapidly about the group, reinforcing or giving corrective feedback as appropriate.

3. Signal (*). "This time as you change direction moving about your equipment, think about which body-part is leading the way." It would be helpful here to have a quick demonstration of someone moving through one of the hoops using a specific body lead.

4. Teachers of primary grade children may want to curtail the activity at this point and move into the discussion part of the culminating module. Signal (*).

FIGURE 7-10 "What directions can we move in?"

FIGURE 7-11 Everyone is involved in this solution

FIGURE 7-12 Making similar shapes while moving

Learning Experiences

"So far, you have been working in a group, but only thinking about your own movement. Now, pair up with another person in the group and see how you can move together about the equiment, using the same body leads as your partner." Encourage the children to try more than one solution to the task of moving about the equipment. If one idea does not work they should try another. Allow this activity to continue so long as it is productive. There will be quite a lot of interaction between the students as they work to solve the problem posed. At the end of the activity, have the children return the equipment they have been using to the proper place, reinforcing quick and quiet work.

Culminating Module

Objectives

As a result of the learning experiences over time, children will be able to:

1. contribute pertinently to a group discussion
2. identify the components of productive group work.

Learning Experiences

Conduct this discussion as soon as possible.

1. "Which group thought they worked well together today?" After one has been identified: "Tell us why you think you did well today." Possible answers:
   - we did what we were told
   - we didn't mess up

Related Experiences

- Make "good group member" badges (or ink pad stamp) that can be distributed at appropriate times.
- Choose five people from the class to go with you to build a new town on a planet in space. Tell why you chose the five people.
- Write or tell about a time when your whole family worked together on a project.

Learning Experiences

- we didn't fight
- we didn't goof off.

2. "Can anyone think of what they did that made the group work well together?" If this answer does not produce positive answers from the children, try stating the question in the following manner: "Can anyone describe the best group member? What kind of person would you choose to be in your group?" Some of the possible answers might be:

- a person who helps with the equipment and does not just stand around
- a person who is willing to take turns
- someone who can share the equipment with others
- someone who is careful how she/he moves so that accidents don't happen
- someone who works rather than wastes time or spends time watching others
- someone who is willing to help others in the group
- someone who says good things to others in the group rather than finding fault with them
- someone who helps to put the equipment away, rather than rushing to get "in line" or back to the class.

It is important for children to be able to perceive some of these attributes as attainable for themselves. So often the "ideal" that is promoted seems quite beyond the capacity of children with low self-esteem, since the ideal's attributes are often quite contrary to their own patterns of behavior. This is especially true if the attributes are stated in terms of "always . . . , listens, waits quietly, follows directions," etc.

3. Having identified some of the characteristics of the ideal group member, the next step is to describe groups where most, if not all of the members were productive. Such a group might:

- get more ideas for movements because if everyone worked at their "best," group members could learn from each other and try one another's movements

Related Experiences

- Post a list of "things that are helpful in a group."
- In fours, design a small mural that shows people working together. Each person in the group must draw part of the mural.
- Make a list of jobs that need at least two people to do them, for example, resurfacing a road.

FIGURE 7-13 A good group member helps others in the group

Learning Experiences

- have more turns because there is little waiting around
- start more quickly (and therefore have more time to work) because everyone helps with the equipment
- improve skills more than groups where people helped each other less.

Summary

Enabling Behavior: Developing Cooperative and Competitive Behavior

Children are developing their understanding of cooperation and competition when they:

1. Can work productively with a partner or a small group to complete an assigned task.
2. Can participate in a team game without dominating the play.
3. Appear intent on finding solutions to problems that arise in a game as opposed to assigning blame.
4. Obviously enjoy others receiving praise for noteworthy performance in a group endeavor.
5. Are able to identify the criteria for productive group work.
6. Are able to describe the characteristics of a helpful group member.

ENDNOTES

1. Marian Breckenridge and Lee Vincent, *Child Development* (Philadelphia: W. B. Saunders Co., 1965), pp. 367–70.
2. John W. Loy and Alan G. Ingham, "Play, Games, and Sport in the Psychosocial Development of Children and Youth," *Physical Activity, Human Growth and Development,* ed. G. Lawrence Rarick (New York: London, Academic Press, 1973), p. 287.
3. Howard G. Ball, "What's in a Game?" *The Elementary School Journal* 76 (September 1976): 42–49.
4. Rainer Martens, *Social Psychology and Physical Activity* (New York: Harper & Row, 1975), pp. 100–101.
5. G. S. Don Morris, *How to Change the Games Children Play* (Minneapolis, Minn.: Burgess Publishing Co., 1976).
6. Loy and Ingham, "Play, Games, and Sport in the Psychosocial Development of Children and Youth," pp. 291–92.
7. Martens, *Social Psychology and Physical Activity,* p. 90.
8. Morris, *How to Change the Games Children Play,* p. 33.
9. Robert N. Singer, *Motor Learning and Human Performance,* 2nd ed. (New York: Macmillan, 1975), p. 511.
10. James B. Coleman, *The Adolescent Society* (New York: The Free Press, 1961), pp. 143–44.

11. David N. Campbell, "On Being Number One: Competition in Education," *Phi Delta Kappan,* LVI (October 1974): 145.
12. Martens, *Social Psychology and Physical Activity,* p. 81.
13. Elliot Aronson, et al., "The Jigsaw Route to Learning and Liking," *Psychology Today,* 8 (February 1975): 43–50. Copyright © 1975 Ziff-Davis Publishing Company.
14. Ibid., p. 49.
15. Louis E. Raths, *Meeting the Needs of Children* (Columbus, Ohio: Charles E. Merrill, 1972), p. 132.
16. Campbell, "On Being Number One: Competition in Education," p. 143.
17. G. Lawrence Rarick, "Competitive Sports in Childhood and Early Adolescence," *Physical Activity, Human Growth and Development,* ed. G. Lawrence Rarick (New York: Academic Press, 1973), pp. 364–86.
18. Patrick R. Penland and Sara Fine, *Group Dynamics and Individual Development* (New York: Marcel Dekker, 1974), p. 27.
19. Ibid., p. 47.
20. Daryl Siedentop, *Developing Teaching Skills in Physical Education* (Boston: Houghton Mifflin, 1976), pp. 79–80; and Charles H. Madsen, et al., "An Analysis of the Reinforcing Function of 'Sit-Down' Commands" in *Readings in Educational Psychology,* ed. by Ronald K. Parker (Boston: Allyn and Bacon, 1968), pp. 270–76.
21. John Adair, *Action-Centered Leadership* (London: McGraw-Hill, 1973), pp. 3–5.
22. Ibid., p. 8.
23. Ibid., pp. 8–12.
24. R. Tannenbaum and W. H. Schmidt, "How to Choose a Leadership Pattern," *Harvard Business Review,* 36 (March-April 1958): 96.
25. Adair, *Action-Centred Leadership,* pp. 13–15.
26. Richard Gerson, "Competition—Society's Child," a paper presented at the National American Alliance for Health, Physical Education, and Recreation Convention, Milwaukee, Wisconsin, April 2, 1976.
27. Raths, *Meeting the Needs of Children,* pp. 134–39.
28. Ibid., p. 139.
29. Marie Riley, "Teaching Original Games," *Journal of Physical Education and Recreation,* 48 (September 1977): 30–32.
30. ———, "Games and Humanism," *Journal of Health, Physical Education and Recreation,* 46 (February 1975): 49.
31. Aronson, "The Jigsaw Route to Learning and Liking," pp. 43–50.
32. Alan G. Ingham and John W. Loy, Jr. "The Social System of Sport: A Humanistic Perspective," *Quest,* XIX (January 1973): 3–23.
33. Kathleen M. Pearson, "Deception, Sportsmanship, and Ethics," *Quest,* XIX (January 1973): 115–18.
34. Association for Intercollegiate Athletics for Women, *AIAW Handbook 1976–1977* (Washington, D.C.: American Alliance for Health, Physical Education, and Recreation, 1976), pp. 37–38.
35. Robert N. Singer, *Myths and Truths in Sports Psychology* (New York: Harper & Row, 1975), p. 104.
36. Ibid., p. 105.
37. Walter Kroll, "Psychological Scaling of AIAW Code of Ethics for Players," *The Research Quarterly* 47 (March 1976): 126–33.

chapter eight

Improving Quality of Response

ABOUT CHILDREN

Contemporary elementary school physical education programs, such as the "developmental theme" approach, help children to become physically fit, skillful, knowledgeable, and self-confident regarding their movement abilities. Once students gain understandings and basic movement skills, emphasis should be given to improve their level of motor skill, physical fitness, and ability to influence their own development. There are three specific en-

239

abling behaviors presented in this developmental theme (Improving Quality of Response: Refining and Elaborating Movement Capabilities for a Purpose). They are:

Developing Precision—this behavior is improving the performance of a previously learned movement task.

Increasing Complexity of Response—complexity means movement responses that are multidimensional.

Challenging Self beyond Comfortable Limits—deals with helping children to cope with situations that are physically and/or psychologically uncomfortable.

Developing Precision

The motor performance of children increases with age through the elementary school years. Much of the improved performance can be attributed to maturation; however, maturation alone will not result in the achievement of mature motor patterns and specific skills. Only appropriate practice will facilitate the development of mature motor patterns and the development of specific sport or leisure skills. Halverson indicated that young children can achieve more than most people realize when conditions for development are appropriately designed. She stated:

There is mounting evidence that the preschool and elementary school child can respond to more complex motor demands than previously expected. And it seems certain that with proper environmental stimulation and opportunity, more children could reach first grade with more mature forms of basic patterns than may now be true.[1]

Unfortunately, schools have not always provided for the best "stimulation and opportunity" for motor development. Too frequently, skills are introduced in a class and, before they are well learned, the children are asked to use those skills in competitive game situations. In cases where there is limited opportunity to practice, the child's skills may never be fully developed. In other cases, there may be opportunity to practice in the game, but the competitive environment places too much stress on some children. Under these conditions, children either will play positions for which they already have the skills, they are placed in a position where the use of advanced skills is not required, or they will not use newly acquired skills because they lack confidence.

It is known that one of the important variables that accounts for the variance in student learning is the amount of time spent in appropriate practice of the learning task. Observations also reveal that young children will practice a desired skill over and over; in fact, they enjoy repetitive activity and teachers should provide for many opportunities for children to practice motor skills. Children seldom say that they want to "practice their skills"; however, repetitive practice is often what they actually do when they say they want to "play."

Lead-up Games

The practice of skills should be conducted under conditions close to those under which the skills will be used. Playing the game for which a skill is being developed is the most realistic condition, but since a game usually involves other participants and other skills, the opportunity to practice a skill in the game is limited. One solution to the problem of maintaining game-like conditions while providing for maximum participation is the use of modified or lead-up games. These activities provide practice of specific skills in a game context that is similar to the "real" game. Usually, lead-up games are limited to certain skills or portions of the official game and, therefore, provide more practice opportunities. If teachers do not label these activities as "lead-up games" or "modified games," but call them by a name, children usually show enthusiasm equal to that for the official game. Part of the children's enthusiasm is based on the fact that they are more active (have more turns to practice) and they experience more success since the game is adjusted to their developmental level.

Children enjoy moving skillfully. The joy expressed by children when they have mastered a new movement task has been recognized by all who work with children. This intrinsic motivation to move skillfully should be nurtured by teachers. The feeling of accomplishment a child has when a skill has been improved should be discussed, and the "feel" of the movement should be explored. They should become aware of the kinesthetic sense of the movement, or how it "feels" to perform the movement correctly.

Controlling Muscle Tension

A factor of developing motor skills that is often overlooked and can greatly inhibit motor performance, is muscular tension. A degree of muscular tension is always present in muscles. In order for movement to occur, pairs of muscles must work together; as one muscle contracts (increases tension), the muscle that produces the opposite movement relaxes (decreases tension). Emotional stress or anxiety can result in muscular tension of the type that interferes with the smooth, coordinated functioning of muscles.

In Winters' discussion of tension, she maintained that emotional and muscular tension interferes with the quality of one's life. Teachers can help diminish both emotional and muscular tension by following Winters' suggestions:

- Since fatigue produces tension, balance the periods of work and rest by planning properly and observing signs of weariness or fatigue.
- Present creative activities that afford opportunities to use abilities in a variety of ways. These activities should be presented so as to reduce or eliminate competition with others and to invite curiosity.

BOX 8–1   How to Relax

Just as individuals respond to stress in unique ways, so do they respond to relaxation techniques. Many relaxation programs have been proposed, and each has its supporters who have found them successful. There are, however, some elements that appear to be common to many relaxation techniques. The following guidelines are recommended for teachers who will attempt to have their students learn consciously to relax.

The room should be dark or dimly lighted and quiet. Sometimes soft music is used to "cover up" noises from mechanical equipment, other children, or other sources beyond the control of the teacher.

A period of conscious relaxation can be conducted with the children either lying down or sitting. (The important principle to follow is to see that the person is comfortable.) All body-parts should be supported (so that the normal supporting muscles can relax), and no body-part should be touching another.

The individual should consciously relax all muscles. Some people can relax muscles by "thinking" or visualizing the muscles relaxed. Others find that contracting (flexing) the muscles tightly first helps to relax them. Generally, the muscles in the feet and legs should be relaxed first, followed by the trunk muscles, the arms, neck, and facial muscles. After practice, one can relax the muscles so that another person can move the body-parts without any assistance or resistance from the person who is relaxed.

Breathe deeply and slowly. At first, this may not seem natural, and one may have to force himself to do it. Some people breathe too deeply, expanding the lungs as much as possible and holding the breath before exhaling. After practice, this should not happen. The breathing will be slow, rhythmical, and deep as the body relaxes, and deep breathing will become easy and natural.

Think of something nonstimulating, such as a subdued color, a number, or a comfortable object (a blanket, robe, or teddy bear). The purpose of this is to diminish cognitive activity, but most people find it difficult to cease all thinking. Substituting a nonstimulating object on which to concentrate helps to block out thoughts that might produce tension.

Like other activities involving muscular control, conscious relaxation requires practice for mastery. Relaxation sessions should last from fifteen to thirty minutes. They may be conducted any time during the day when it is necessary to reduce tension. Immediately after eating or after exciting activities, such as a sport contest or class play, are not the best times to attempt conscious relaxation. Before lunch or late in the afternoon are times recommended for relaxation sessions.

- Present to the children opportunities for learning about the body and how it can move efficiently, preventing the unnecessary expenditure of energy, thus reducing tension.
- Present a technique of relaxation for children to learn, practice, and use in school or before going to sleep at night.
- Relate the technique of progressive relaxation to life activities.[2]

Today's environment creates tension in almost everyone, and, while muscular tension is necessary for movement to take place, the quality of the movement is in part determined by one's ability to control the tension. Teachers can improve not only the quality of movement but also the quality of children's lives by teaching them how to control muscular tension.

Increasing Complexity of Response

Complexity refers to the multidimensionality of a task. It is more complex to catch a ball while balancing on a balance beam than to catch a ball while standing on the ground in a stationary position. Part of what makes a task more complex is the additional amount of information that the learner must process. As was discussed in Chapter Four, conscious, volitional movement is constantly being modified as the sensory receptors channel nerve impulse messages to the central nervous system, where information processing and decision making occur to direct a desired response.

Motor skill regression may occur when the information to be processed is presented in an unfamiliar context or is increased in complexity. Halverson[3] reported a regression in performance when environmental factors, such as larger and heavier equipment, amount of stress, or level of difficulty were changed. She maintained that those who work with children need to know how to challenge, but not over-challenge, children to help improve their performances of motor patterns.

In order to perform more complex skills, children need to master basic motor patterns. An example of this can be found in some traditional games that children play on their own. These games have very small increases in the level of difficulty built into them. Many jump rope games include rhymes that challenge the jumper to jump as many times as possible in different ways. Whenever children miss, they "know" that next time will be better. This "knowing" provides great motivation to try and try again to improve on the previous performance.

Some games "add on" tasks. For example, one game played with a small ball, such as a tennis ball, requires the use of a wall. A child throws the ball against the wall from behind a line on the ground and performs the following tasks in sequence until a miss is recorded. After a miss, the child must start over on the next turn with the first task in the sequence. The tasks could be to throw the ball against the wall and:

1. catch it on the fly with both hands
2. catch it on the fly with the preferred hand
3. catch it on the fly with the nonpreferred hand
4. catch it on the fly with both hands after clapping
5. the same as Number 4 with the preferred hand
6. the same as Number 4 with the nonpreferred hand
7. make a 360° turn and catch the ball on the fly with both hands
8. same as Number 7 with the preferred hand
9. same as Number 7 with the nonpreferred hand
10. repeat numbers 1 through 9, but throw the ball under one leg and against the wall.

Children can add more tasks and continue to progressively increase the level of difficulty of the tasks of the basic game. The repetitive nature of the game promotes skill development and the addition of new, slightly more difficult tasks provides motivation for children to play games of this type day after day. Children having difficulty with more complex tasks should practice the simpler parts of the new task before trying again.

Challenging Self beyond Comfortable Limits

The normal physical growth and development of children is stimulated by their vigorous large-muscle activity. For the most part, the play of children was assumed to be sufficient for the development of adequate levels of physical fitness, but the results of a comparison of physical fitness tests completed in the 1950s revealed that American children were less fit than European children. Much of the blame for the poor performance of American children was placed on television viewing and riding in automobiles in the place of vigorous play. However, school physical education programs also received much criticism.

In 1957, the American Association for Health, Physical Education, and Recreation (AAHPER, now called the American Alliance for Health, Physical Education, Recreation, and Dance, AAHPERD) initiated a Youth Fitness Project. Through the efforts of this professional organization, a youth physical fitness test was designed and administered to a national sample of 8,500 boys and girls in grades five through twelve. By 1958, the *AAHPER Youth Fitness Test Manual* was published with norms that were based on this national sample for the seven-item test. The AAHPER test and youth fitness program are now used in thousands of schools each year, and the test manual, record forms, and award system have become very popular. In 1965, the test was revised and new norms were established for the test items, based on a second national sample. From an analysis of the data from the 1958 and 1965 samples, it was concluded that the physical fitness level of elementary school children had improved significantly. However, the third national sample taken during the 1974–75 school year did not show improvement beyond the level previously shown in the 1965 sample.[4]

Physical Fitness Components

Physical fitness can mean having large muscles, a trim waist-line, abundant energy, or a general condition of good health and vigor. More specifically, physical fitness is comprised of different components. Dr. deVries[5] suggested that physical fitness includes two components. They are:

Motor Fitness including the elements of strength, speed, agility, endurance, power, coordination, balance, flexibility, and body control.

Physical Working Capacity including the elements of cardiovascular function, respiratory function, muscular efficiency, strength, muscular endurance, and obesity.

Dr. deVries indicated that motor fitness has been evaluated more frequently by physical educators than has physical working capacity (PWC), which has been more of a concern to physiologists, pediatricians, and cardiologists. He defines PWC as "the maximum level of metabolism (work) of which an individual is capable."[6] PWC is usually assessed by tests that estimate the amount of oxygen utilized by the body during some working per-

---

BOX 8–2   Glossary of Physical Fitness Terms

Physical Fitness   a general term usually meaning a state of good health. Operationally, it is defined by the elements included, such as muscular strength, muscular endurance, cardiorespiratory endurance, and flexibility.

Muscular Strength   the ability of a muscle to overcome a resistance, such as gravity or friction; the ability to do work, e.g., lifting a ten-pound weight.

Muscular Endurance   the ability of a muscle to do work over a period of time, e.g., lifting a ten-pound weight five or ten times.

Flexibility   the range of motion in a joint.

Cardiorespiratory Endurance   the ability of the heart and vascular system and the respiratory system to transport gases to and away from cells over a period of time. In a more physically fit person, the same amount of oxygen can be delivered with fewer beats of the heart and fewer breaths. That person would have greater cardiorespiratory efficiency than a person who requires more heart beats and breaths to deliver the same amount of oxygen.

Balance   the ability to maintain a position in space; may be static (non-moving) or dynamic (moving).

Agility   the ability to change positions in space without losing balance, e.g., running an obstacle course without falling down.

Power   the ability to perform work with velocity, e.g., moving a heavy weight quickly through space (putting a shot).

formance, such as jogging or riding a bicycle. He recommends that PWC testing become part of every physical education program.

A concept closely related to PWC is the aerobic system, developed by Dr. Kenneth Cooper. His publications[7,8,9] define aerobic activities as those requiring increased oxygen consumption over periods of time that are long enough to effect cardiorespiratory changes. Thus, jogging, swimming, cycling, and other similar activities are recommended.

There is some overlap between the elements of motor fitness and PWC. Most physical education programs include the elements of muscular strength, muscular endurance, cardiorespiratory endurance, and flexibility as areas of objectives for the development of physical fitness.

Developing Physical Fitness

As children grow and develop through the preschool and elementry school years, they increase in most elements of physical fitness. Differences among children on tests of physical fitness can be attributed to innate characteristics as well as to different patterns of physical activities. School programs have been shown to have differential effects on the fitness levels of students, beyond that which is expected due to maturation. Programs that lead to increases in physical fitness provide for progressive overload on the various systems of the body.

The overload principle is a constant factor in all training programs designed to improve physical fitness. Simply stated, the overload principle means that in order to bring about an increase in physical functioning, a system must do more than it is normally required to do. For example, to increase muscular strength, the muscle must do more work than it normally does. Physical fitness training programs apply this principle in very systematic ways. Overload is usually accomplished by performing at less than one's maximum effort, but repeating the performance more than once. Thus, one who could lift a maximum of 100 pounds one time could overload the muscular system by lifting only 60 to 75 pounds two or three times. Two common programs using the overload principle are circuit training and interval training. Both types of programs are used in elementary schools and lend themselves to adaptations in "learning centers."

In circuit training, systematic overload is accomplished by having participants move from one exercise station to another. At each station, one must perform an exercise for a given length of time or for a given number of repetitions. Each station is designed for a specific kind of development, such as muscular strength, cardiorespiratory endurance, or flexibility. Some circuits are designed to require systematic overload in only one trip through the circuit, while others require more than one trip around the circuit.

Interval training focuses on one fitness element and is used frequently to improve muscular endurance and cardiorespiratory endurance. Distance runners and swimmers utilize this system. Briefly, overload is accomplished by performing over a fixed distance that is shorter than the distance one is training for, but at maximum effort. After a rest interval, the maximum effort is repeated over the fixed distance. For this approach to be effective, the total distance performed at maximum effort must be greater than the distance one is training for. As this training progresses, either the rest period between maximum efforts over the shortened distances is decreased or the distances are increased. Eventually, all the rest intervals are eliminated and the performer can run the desired distance at the maximum speed.

Frequently, when systematic overload occurs, there is a degree of physical discomfort. Discomfort may also occur in vigorous play activities. Children need to understand that some discomfort, such as tiredness in muscles or a "stitch" in the side, is normal. While intense discomfort might be necessary for adults and athletes in some situations (military service and competitive level sport programs), it is neither necessary nor desirable for elementary children.

In elementary school physical education, it is of primary importance that children not only develop desirable fitness levels but also know and understand the basic concepts of physiology of exercise. Along with positive personal feelings about being a physically fit person, children should know how to assess, develop, and maintain desirable physical fitness levels. How each child achieves physical fitness is a matter of personal choice. The school program should enable children to make intelligent decisions regarding their own physical fitness programs. While extrinsic motivation, such as points or rewards, may be necessary at first, most children will be motivated by their own success in physical fitness programs. Well-conceived, individualized programs should result in improved self-concepts for children. Charting the individual progress that comes with systematic overload is a self-enhancing experience. Progress charts help children internalize physical fitness concepts.

BOX 8-3 "My Side Hurts"

"My side hurts" is frequently heard when children (and adults) run a distance that is longer than usual. The pain is real, and because of differences in pain tolerance, it is more bothersome to some children than others. Usually, a pain in the side will cease, even when the running continues. No one knows for sure what causes this pain or "stitch" in the side. It has been suggested that the pain is caused by *ischemia,* a temporary lack of blood in the diaphragm or in the small muscles between the ribs.

Children should know that this is a "normal" condition and that as their physical fitness levels improve, the "stitch" in the side will occur less frequently.

The personal experiences of the authors show that elementary age children enjoy learning about how their bodies function, and they can learn concepts of biology and physiology that are related to exercise and physical fitness. Edington and Cunningham[10] maintained that the study of biology and physiology has not changed behavior because they have been taught as facts that are not related to life and behavior. They have prepared fifty-one "statements" or concepts that can be taught in a manner using personal experience to help students understand how the concepts may be useful. Progressive physical fitness programs include such learning experiences as an essential part of the total program.

A physical education teacher in a midwestern elementary school once reported how he invited his students to run at the beginning of each class. He recognized that throughout the school day, children were constantly being reminded to walk in the classroom, the halls, the lunchroom, all for safety reasons. The physical education period was an appropriate time and provided a safe environment for running. So, all students were invited to run. The teacher also ran, on occasion, with each class. No specific distance was required, and no one was forced to run.

It was noted that practically all the children ran most of the time. The teacher observed that even the "best" runners chose not to run on some days, which was not much different from the teacher's running behavior. Those children who at first did not run very frequently, gradually started to run more often. The teacher helped by talking with the reluctant runners about their hobbies and schoolwork, but never about their running (unless the student raised the topic or the teacher had positive things to say about the child's running).

BOX 8–4   An Invitation to Run

Running is a normal and natural movement. Young children run not only to get somewhere faster, but also because it is fun. Unfortunately, the frequency of running seems to diminish with age for most Americans. Perhaps schools contribute to this by what they do and what they don't do. *Running should never be used as punishment.* Running may be used as a competitive event in track and field, but it should also be taught as a lifetime activity. Taught as a lifetime activity, running would be explored in terms of: its effects on the human body; the aesthetics and mechanics of the running motor pattern, its rhythm and coordination; its practicality as a healthful lifestyle in terms of cost for equipment, cost of time, and availability of facilities; its potential for self-awareness physiologically, psychologically, and affectively. It is a sad fact when an adult has to be helped to rediscover the joys and benefits of running. School programs should nurture the joy of running that children bring with them. They should be invited to run in ways that are meaningful to them.

Discussions about the fun of running and the physical fitness benefits of running were held. Running was compared to other aerobic activities, such as cycling and rope jumping, as a means of attaining physical fitness. Each child was encouraged to participate in some other forms of aerobic activity in addition to or in place of running. Over time, most could not refuse the invitation to run.

ABOUT TEACHING

Developing Sequential Learning Experiences

The teaching modules included in this book have been developed using the principles of educational psychology that were outlined in Chapter Four. You probably recognized the application of these principles as recurring strong points of each teaching module. The purpose of this section is to present information concerning the development of learning tasks and sequencing of tasks which will contribute to increasing quality of response.

Determining Developmental Value

The first guide to developing sequential learning experiences is that a task must have developmental value. Developmental value is determined by the meaning or significance of the activity to some phase of the child's development. A significant or valuable activity is one that contributes toward meeting an objective which is based on an assessed need or expressed interest of the child. If the activity is not viewed by the student as being interesting, then the teacher must explain the activity, from the child's point of view, as being important in relation to an ability desired by the student (i.e., the student needs to be able to do this [A] before being able to do that [B]).

The developmental theme approach provides a framework for selection of learning experiences based on their contribution toward the enabling behaviors that are associated with each theme. This approach aids the teacher by organizing objectives and learning experiences in relation to developmental themes.

Specifying Objectives

Teachers need to be able to state an objective(s) for each lesson or module within a lesson. Stating an objective is an important aid in planning a lesson and communicating to others (school officials, parents, teachers, students) the purpose(s) of the learning experience. In addition, it helps the teacher to know what elements to evaluate in order to determine the effectiveness of the lesson. Objectives can be stated as descriptive goal statements or in behavioral terms. The latter are referred to as behavioral or criterion-referenced objectives.

Objectives should include a specific and clear statement of who will be doing what, when, where, how often, and under what conditions. The following is an objective for the same learning experience, written first in descriptive terms and then in behavioral terms:

Descriptive: To have students dribble a basketball with the right and left hand, while moving toward a basketball goal.

Behavioral: The students who have successfully completed task three, will be able to dribble a basketball a distance of forty-five feet in ten (10) seconds, changing the dribbling hand at least four (4) times before the distance is traveled.

Some teachers prefer to use descriptive objectives because they are not as restrictive as behavioral objectives and allow the task to be varied, limited or extended, according to individual student needs. Behavioral objectives are more precise than descriptive objectives. Measuring results is more objective when a criterion level is stated. Another advantage of stating objectives behaviorally is that the learning experience is implied within the objective. In the case of the example, the students, after previous instruction in dribbling

---

BOX 8–5   Writing Behavioral Objectives

A behavioral objective has three parts. These are:

1. specification of the terminal behavior, what the student will be able to do following the instructional encounter
2. statement of the conditions the learner is to abide by in completing the learning experience
3. identification of the level of performance which serves as the reference to determine that the student has achieved the objective, accomplished the task

In writing a behavioral objective the following words:

should be used		*should not be used*
list	perform	know
state	write	appreciate
identify	show	understand[11]
demonstrate		

An example of a behavioral objective is:
    The student should be able to identify at least three (3) preferred activities from a list of ten physical education activities.

Write a behavioral objective here:_____
_____
_____
_____

a basketball, would practice changing the dribbling hand while moving in a straight line at a moderate rate of speed. A disadvantage of behavioral objectives, as viewed by some teachers, is the need to state separate objectives for every slight change in the learning experience. Conversely, a descriptive objective might include a listing of tasks leading to the accomplishment of the main objective: *the students will learn how to dribble a basketball with either hand as required in a basketball game.* The students would complete the following basketball dribbling tasks.

Dribble:

   a. with the preferred hand, without moving from a small area
   b. with the nonpreferred hand, without moving from a small area
   c. with the preferred hand, moving through general space, slowly at first, and with increasing speed
   d. with the nonpreferred hand, moving anywhere in general space, slowly at first, and then with increasing speed
   e. with one hand, then the other, while moving in a straight line
   f. using the hands alternately while moving in a zigzagged pathway
   g. using the hands alternately while evading a defender.

Using the behavioral objective format a separate and more definitive statement would be required for each of the seven descriptive objectives presented above.

Ordering the Learning Progression

Learning should progress from the familiar to the unknown, concrete (tangible or physically manipulable) to abstract (imagined or intangible), and simple to complex. The list of descriptive objectives in the previous section were presented, following these general guides for ordering movement experiences in a hierarchical progression. Guiding statements for developing a sequential set of learning experiences are often too general to aid a teacher in determining whether one activity is more or less difficult than another.

In order to make an estimate of the task difficulty, the teacher should use a task analysis approach. The main question in the task analysis approach is *What do the students need to know, value, or do in order to achieve a reasonably high level of success in this task?* The answer is determined by identifying each skill, rule, strategy, attitude, or opinion the student needs to have relative to the activity in question. Examples of the task analysis approach are:

Dodgeball

As a thrower:
   catch a ball
   throw a ball accurately at a moving target
   knowledge of rules
   ability to apply strategy
   interest in participating

As a dodger:
  ability to run at different speeds and directions
  ability to bend, twist, and jump
  cardiovascular endurance
  knowledge of the rules of the game
  ability to predict/estimate where the ball will travel
  knowledge of use of space
  interest in participating

Dance

In general:
  ability to move with the beat of a musical selection
  walk, slide, skip, or gallop
  ability to make body shapes
  ability to maintain a balanced position
  ability to change directions while traveling in a circle or through space

The next question in the task analysis approach is *What instruction have the children had and to what degree are they able to do each of these prerequisite skills?* If the answer is "little or none," the teacher must provide the needed instruction or complete the task analysis process with an activity that is less complex (or more familiar to the students) to determine its appropriateness as an alternate activity.

When making the decision whether one task is more or less difficult than another task, a direct comparison approach is effective. In order to do this the teacher must know that, generally:

1. It is easier to control an object when remaining in an area than it is either to control an object while traveling to a predetermined spot, or to move toward an object before it is trapped, caught, or dribbled.
2. It is easier to strike a stationary object (ball or target) than it is to strike a moving object, and it is easier to strike an object when standing still or moving slowly than it is when moving fast.
3. It is easier to accurately strike a close and/or large target than a distant and/or small target.
4. When catching with one hand, it is easier to catch a ball that fits the hand than to catch a large ball.
5. It is easier to catch a straight, slow moving, soft (or underinflated) ball than a curving, fast moving hard ball.
6. Initial attempts at striking an object with a body-part are easier than striking it with an implement that is grasped by the body-part.
7. It is easier to do an activity with the preferred hand or foot than with the nonpreferred hand or foot.
8. It is easier to move at floor level than to move when elevated on an object, such as a box, beam, or bench.

9. It is easier to perform alone than to move in synchrony with a partner or group.
10. It is easier to perform an activity with few or simple rules than with many or complex rules.[12]

The identification of task difficulty is important in planning movement experiences and making adjustments to movement experiences when the activities planned for the lesson are judged by the teacher to be too difficult or too easy. The selection of activities that are at appropriate levels of difficulty is an important part of developing a sequential learning progression and an effective lesson.

Maximizing Participation

Students must have opportunities to practice in order to learn; however, the total amount of class time is usually not an accurate indicator of the actual practice time. Class time often is devoted to administrative and instructional activities as well as practice opportunities. Sometimes, teachers keep talking long after the students already have the idea of what they are to do. The result is lost practice time. Even when students are given practice time, the way the teacher organizes the experience can increase or decrease opportunities to participate.

Two of the major ways by which students are excluded from participation are through secondary role participation and elimination activities. When students are involved in an activity, they participate in one of two ways: either as a primary role participant or as a secondary role participant. The primary role participants, or doers, are the ball handlers, runners, or decision makers; the secondary role participants are the "supporting cast" in that they stand still to make the formation or boundaries for a game, or they wait in a long line for their turn. The secondary role participants are involved in comparatively meaningless psychomotor experiences rather than practicing to increase the quality or the complexity of a response.

The maximum participation guideline is violated again when students are excluded from practice by rules that eliminate them from participation (when they make an error and are sent to the sidelines). An obvious example is a dodgeball game where the first person hit by the ball is usually the person who needs the most practice. This person is put out of the game, while the person who gets hit last has had the most practice and probably needs practice the least. Another example is the tag game that requires the person who was tagged to go stand on the sidelines until the next game is started. The following information will be helpful in designing learning experiences that maximize participation:

Have more groups with short (3 or 4 people) lines.
Have small team game groups to increase the chance of playing a primary role.

Have one ball for each child, even if different types of balls (tennis, paper, yarn, playground, volleyball) must be used.
Change the rules of the game so players continue to play after making an error.

Providing for the Students' Welfare

Teachers must act to safeguard the students' physical and psychological welfare. Teachers must provide instruction that is sequential, must complete a process of establishing rules, must supervise participation, must continually check equipment and facilities for unsafe conditions, must be able to provide emergency first-aid care, and must have a plan for alerting designated school officials when an emergency situation occurs. The teacher must learn who the risk takers are, which students are emotionally explosive, and who is very sensitive. By keeping in close proximity to these students, the teacher can intervene if a potentially hazardous situation arises. Many situations can be avoided either by the teacher's presence in an area or by asking the questions, What do you plan to do? or What were the directions for completing this task?

A potentially traumatic situation exists when a student is singled out to perform a task while the entire class is watching. Some students are very sensitive to criticism and lack the self-confidence to perform successfully while others watch. Having one ball for each student to work with, or playing or demonstrating something as a member of a small group decreases visibility and makes the activity less threatening. Moreover, by avoiding long lines and having everyone participate, the students are usually too busy with their own efforts to be critical of others.

While teachers have the legal responsibility for the safety of their students, they must help their students develop a sense of responsibility for their own movement behavior. Discussion and decision making experiences can help teachers achieve this goal.

Respecting the Child's Integrity

All too often, teachers try to get their students to "fit" the learning experience, rather than "fitting" the learning experience to the students. For example, forcing a child to do regulation push-ups, when the child must struggle to complete only one or two, could be harmful, whereas the teacher could have the child do knee-position push-ups that allow him to complete more push-ups. In games, the official rules often can limit the student's feelings of success, forcing the participants to develop poor motor skills. For example, using a regulation basketball and a basket at the regulation height can cause young children to hold and shoot the ball improperly. There is enormous frustration in not ever sinking a basket or not even getting the ball up to the basket height. This situation could be avoided by using lighter balls and/or lowering the height of the basket.

Open-ended throwing for accuracy tasks can be arranged by varying the distance of the throw or the size of the targets.

DO — Varied

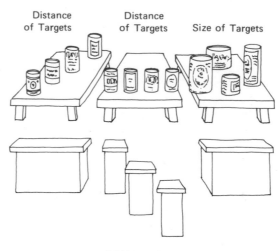

DON'T — Same

Distance of Targets
Size of Targets

Open-ended tasks allow the child to make the decision as to appropriate challenge, to develop precision, to attempt more complex responses, and to push themselves beyond comfortable limits. When children make these decisions, the potential for meaningful and significant learning has been increased.

FIGURE 8-1 Arrangement of targets for developing precision

Respecting the child's integrity means individualizing instruction to provide learning and practice experiences that are appropriate to the student's ability and confidence levels. Open-ended problems and learning centers are two ways to individualize instruction. An open-ended statement, such as "Find different ways you can balance your body in a straight and wide shape," doesn't force children to attempt a task that is far above their ability level. The open-ended task style still allows the more capable movers to challenge themselves.

The use of learning centers or stations is another method of individualizing instruction and can be used either in the classroom or on the playground. A learning center is a place where students are provided the materials and directions for completing a task, independent of continuous teacher supervision. Learning centers can be designed in a variety of ways to individualize instruction for achieving developmentally meaningful objectives.

Providing Appropriate Practice

Practice is not the sole factor in determining the quality and/or quantity of learning. The saying that *practice makes perfect* has been modified to *perfect practice makes perfect.* What constitutes perfect practice for learning in physical education classes only now is beginning to be fully understood. Singer summarized research findings related to practice considerations:

> Without *knowledge of results, interest and attention, meaningfulness* of the task to the learner, *understanding of goals, intent* to learn, *readiness* to learn and some degree of *relationship* of practice conditions to real conditions, practice for all practical purposes is wasted.[13]

Application of the guides for developing sequential learning experiences, presented in the previous section, will help to assure that students have opportunities to practice and that the practice experience will be meaningful, safe, and progressive in terms of the challenges the learner encounters.

Setting Goals and Aspirations

Stallings identified the establishment of purpose as the first of seven key instructional tasks in the process of instruction. She operationalized this task in the following way:

1. *Comparison of goals:* "Responses are selected, eliminated, organized, and stabilized in terms of their relevance to the learner's goal."[14] If the learner wants to learn how to play volleyball at a beginning level for playing at social outings, it would be very difficult for the teacher, without upgrading the student's goal, to teach the person how to play competitive type power volleyball. A comparison of goals and intentions of the student and the teacher are imperative.

2. *Proficiency goals:* For the learner to know what he is expected to do, the teacher should present by demonstration or verbal statement the outcome to be produced and the degree of proficiency to be attained. Lessons begin with an introductory module. One of the purposes of the introductory module is to provide goal orientation and a statement of lesson objectives.

3. *Advanced information:* Providing advanced information helps a student to know what skills and pace of work will be needed to complete the task. An introductory module provides the op-

portunity to give this information and to introduce the vocabulary, rules, etiquette, and strategies that are associated with the activity.[15]

Goal setting can be viewed as either long or short range in nature. Practice sessions, distributed over a period of at least four to six weeks, are usually needed for dealing with physiological variables, developing complex responses, and attaining precision and movement control. A six or nine week grading period may also serve as a convenient time frame for setting long-range goals. Short-term goals are established to serve as a progress check and to motivate the student. They provide more immediate feedback than do long-term goals, and the feelings of satisfaction associated with goal attainment help maintain student motivation and commitment to attaining long-term goals.

A person's expression of an achievement goal in a specific task is called the level of aspiration. The self-statement of how well the student expects to perform can be expressed either verbally or in writing as "I'll win," "I'm afraid I'll lose," or "I'm going to score fourteen points." The goal the student expresses as her/his level of aspiration is based on the student's motivational state and past experience with the activity. Research has demonstrated that:

1. Successful experiences tend to raise the level of aspiration, whereas failure leads to a lowering of expectations.
2. The greater the margin of success, the greater the chance of an increase in the aspiration level.
3. Success usually positively influences level of aspiration and results in increased goals, whereas failure generally has no immediate effect or results in slight lowering of the level of aspiration.[16]

Teachers and students can talk together to help understand each other's goals. Subsequently, teachers can modify physical activities and regroup students to increase the probability of successful participation.

Communicating Knowledge of Results

Providing knowledge of results is one of the most important instructional responsibilities of the teacher. Knowledge of results is information feedback and can be directed at the process (how the performer moved) or the product (the result of the movement). Students are able to modify their movement behavior on the basis of specific, meaningful, and informative feedback. This is one of the main variables in increasing precision and acquiring more complex responses.

In addition to providing information feedback, knowledge of results serves a motivational function. The two basic types of feedback are intrinsic and augmented. Intrinsic knowledge of results is provided as an inherent feature of the task (i.e., when you throw a bean bag at a concentric circle target on the floor, you can see where it lands). If your throw was relatively successful, you would probably feel pleased and would want to perform the task again. Thus, based on knowledge of results, the performer can either be positively or negatively motivated. If the bean bag landed to the left and below the center of the target, then you know that more force is needed and that the direction of the throw should be more to the right. The information received from the previous trial is used to guide your successive trials. Intrinsic information feedback usually occurs in conjunction with the performance of the task. For example, if a child is trying to hold a high narrow balanced body position for ten seconds, but must change the shape in order to regain balance after only three seconds, the person immediately knows that the balanced position is lost and that the desired task is not complete.

On the other hand, augmented feedback usually is given after the task is completed and is provided by the teacher or partner (student observer). Augmented feedback can be given either as a direct statement (e.g., to a batter in a softball practice, "Keep your head up and still; when you drop your head forward you lose eye contact with the ball.") or as a question (e.g., "If you lost eye contact with the ball as you tried to hit it, what would be some of the reasons why this happened?"). Augmented feedback should provide specific and positive information related to either the result of the movement (knowledge of results) or the efficiency and flow of the movement itself (knowledge of performance). "I" messages work well, as do information statements addressed to recurring faulty movement or an incorrect sequence of movement. The more specific the information, the more effective it tends to be. A statement such as "beautiful swing," probably only has motivational value, whereas the statement, "I liked the way you fully rotated your hips, pushed your elbow forward and followed through for a smooth and powerful swing," not only motivates but also enables the performer to know more completely what was done. A specific behavior is reinforced and becomes more likely to be exhibited in later attempts.

Stallings stated that expressive or colorful words, when used in information feedback, are effective in gaining attention and aiding information recall.[17] For example, "make the bat swish" is more meaningful than "make the bat move fast" or "swing hard."

BOX 8–6   Observing Movement Behavior

Observing movement is more than just looking at children, especially when a group or an entire class is involved in a physical activity or testing situation.

How well can you observe moving children?
Can you see movement action or just the result?
How would you approach the task of observing and making notes about the movement behavior of children in your class?

Write your ideas on a sheet of paper and when you finish, check your ideas against the procedures for observing children that were suggested by authorities in the field of physical education.

Procedures for observing are:

1. Select one person to watch rather than looking at the group of children.
2. Watch the way in which the child moves, not only how well the child performed, but also the sequence of movements. This enables the teacher to be able to describe the process portion of the movement in addition to the product of the movement.
3. Understand that the instructions the teacher gives the student can inhibit or foster efficient movement. Telling a child to "jump as far as you can" or "throw the ball as fast as possible" may cause the child to try too hard, whereas instructions, such as "jump high" or "throw hard," will usually result in movements that are most representative of the child's ability.
4. Do not watch the whole movement every time. Separate observations of the legs and trunk or arms and head should also be made. The actions of these body-parts may occur too rapidly to see what happens by observing the entire pattern of body movement.
5. Look for constant or frequently recurring errors. If a child makes the same error each trial, the teacher should plan learning experience to contribute toward improvement in that area.
6. The teacher should be able to describe *what the child did* rather than *what he did not do.* If the teacher knows what the child did and mentally matches this to an efficient, mature movement form for the motor pattern (as described in Chapter Four), then a list of things that the child *did not do* will be the result.
7. Observe movement from different angles. Don't just observe movement from the side. Standing in front of or behind a child when he walks, runs, jumps, or throws will give a different perspective of the movements.
8. Checklists are helpful in keeping the movement efficiency points "in front" of the beginning observer so that all the specific observation points can be remembered, observed, and recorded.
9. Describe what is observed in terms of the quality of the movement. The note that a student "completed a full follow-through" for a vigorous overhand throw is more objective and useful than noting "good follow-through."[18]

Observation skills develop over time as a result of practice and careful attention to the preceding suggestions. When a teacher can say that he/she really saw what a child was doing, many acts of teaching (such as giving instructional feedback and making timely appreciative praise responses) are more effective.

Another important consideration for teachers in providing feedback is that augmented feedback should be provided immediately if there is no intrinsic feedback. *Immediate* means within a minute or so after the task has been completed by the performer. In some activities, the teacher can provide feedback while (at the same time as) the movement is occurring (concurrent). Concurrent feedback is effective only in slowly developing, sequential-type activities, and then usually only key words or phrases can be used to prompt or cue appropriate responses. For example, in a badminton game, the teacher might call out to a player who just hit the bird high and deep to the back of the opposite side of the court, "go to the net, racket up, smash."

Siedentop has five guidelines for providing feedback. These guides are:

1. *Increase your feedback, focus on what students are doing right.* This builds on the strengths of the student and aids in developing a positive class atmosphere for learning. A ratio of four positive to one corrective feedback comment is suggested.
2. *Avoid redundant feedback.* The teacher should attempt to provide four feedback statements each minute without verbally stating what is obvious through intrinsic feedback (e.g., "your serve went into the net"), or by repeating the same message in the same words.
3. *Increase the informational and value content of feedback statements.* Information content is the specific "what to do" or "what not to do" aspect of the feedback message, whereas the value content reflects the sincerity and meaningfulness of the feedback to the student's performance of the task. It is suggested that 50 to 70 percent of the feedback statements should contain specific information. Telling a student why it is important to perform a task in a certain way is an example of value content in feedback.
4. *Direct feedback to the target of instruction.* Feedback, for maximum effectiveness, must be directed to the critical factor that facilitates or inhibits proper performance. This is a case where any correct feedback information may be appropriate; however, feedback statements related to the process of being innovative and creative are more appropriate when the demonstration of creativeness is an objective of the lesson.
5. *Stay with one student long enough to make feedback effective.* This practice necessitates observing a student for several trials to get an idea how she/he performs, and then providing feedback, as needed in relation to a series of trials, to increase the level of performance. The teacher may have only one opportunity to observe and provide feedback to each student, but, by sticking with one person for a time, the teacher is able to see if the student uses the information to improve performance.[19]

Arranging Practice Conditions

A story that is often heard in schools is about the student who, during a phonics lesson, could apply the rules appropriately and made the correct letter sounds in isolation, but when reading a passage could not recognize when a rule should be applied or was unable to blend sounds properly when saying a word. The soccer player who can pass the ball properly to teammates in practice, but cannot recognize an open teammate and make a leading pass in a game is another example of the importance of arranging practice conditions so that the learner can make the transfer of skills to the situation where the skill will be used. Arranging realistic practice can be facilitated by teaching for transfer and by practicing the whole task in its natural sequence.

Teaching for transfer involves many factors, such as overlearning, explanation to the learner of task similarities and differences, and avoidance of developing splinter skills. Overlearning is attained when the performer continues to practice a task after reaching a desired performance level. Overlearning is important to retention as well, and the teacher needs to help children understand the need to continue practicing on a skill after their goal has been achieved. Another approach would be to have two levels of objectives: one objective for initial learning or acquisition (the student will be able to catch a ball rolled at a fast speed eight of ten times, after the ball has traveled twenty feet), and the second objective for overlearning (the student will be able to catch the ball, under the conditions previously described, eight of ten times in three consecutive practice sets).

When introducing a new task, a teacher can give instructions or ask questions that provide the student with information about previously learned tasks that are similar to the new task. For example, "Remember the position we called the *ready position* after our lesson in starting and stopping? That same position is used in basketball when you are a defensive player." Helping students identify the similarities and differences between a previously learned task and a new task can give them an idea of the important cues to attend to and which previously developed responses should be used or avoided in the new task.

Splinter skills are tasks that can be performed to a reasonably good level but only under very narrowly defined conditions. For example, a child may be able to hit a ball off a cone, while hitting a pitched ball presents an almost impossible task. Splinter skills are developed through overlearning of a specific movement with the child never learning to generalize or modify the movement to different task demands. While it is important to structure tasks for successful initial learning, it is also important to have students practice the task under varying conditions.

Teachers also are in error when they allow a student to work at an easy or modified task for too long. The guide is to use an open-ended task that allows the student to progress up the task difficulty sequence quickly as his/her ability increases. Or the teacher may watch the student practice several trials of a task and then make the decision as to whether practice should continue with the easier task or if a more difficult task should be introduced (shooting a basket as compared to shooting a basket while being guarded).

Whole Versus Part Learning

A teacher must decide whether a task is best taught in its entirety or if it should be broken down into its component *parts*. With batting a ball, the teacher could use the:

> *Whole method:* the learner practices the entire swing from beginning to end, which might include dropping the bat and starting the run to first base.
>
> *Part method:* the learner is taught separately the grip, the batting stance, bat position, the swing and follow-through, dropping the bat, and starting the run to first base.
>
> *Whole-part-whole method:* the learner tries the entire swing, then practices each part as described above, and returns to practicing the whole task.

Singer stated that, as a general rule, a task should not be broken down to practice the individual parts until this method must be used to promote learning. However, the part method may be most appropriate for complex and difficult tasks.[20] It is also important to be able to discriminate between what constitutes a whole task as compared to a part of a task. In the game of softball, the psychomotor tasks (or wholes) are base running, catching, throwing, and batting. The parts for batting were described in the definition given above. The task analysis method presented on page 251 is also useful in identifying the task wholes that are associated with a game.

Another advantage of practicing whole tasks is that it is more likely to be practice under normal conditions. Practice should be specific to the conditions under which it will be performed. Athletic coaches implement this guide when they hold practice at night under lights if the official games are to be played at night. While the teacher need not go this far, it is important to simulate actual conditions during practice to help the students to apply skills.

Distributed Versus Massed Practice

Distributed practice means that a number of practice sessions are scheduled over a long period of time. Conversely, massed practice is the scheduling of few practice sessions over a short period of time. For example, if 100 minutes was allocated for practicing a specific skill, this time could be utilized in a manner that provides for either massed practice or distributed practice. In massed practice, the 100 minutes might be used in two practice sessions of fifty minutes each. In distributed practice, the 100 minutes might be used over five sessions of twenty minutes each, or ten sessions of ten minutes each. The issue is not only one of optimal spacing of practice over time, but also of scheduling work-rest periods and deciding whether one or more tasks should be practiced within a lesson. Singer, with reservations based on the specific predictive value of generalizations, summarized the research literature concerning this topic and stated:

> . . . some form of a time distribution for a task practice, as well as practice schedules, is favored. Presumably, such a procedure minimizes fatigue, boredom, allows for the performance image to be strengthened, and yields best performance. . . . With less available time, more mature, motivated, and skilled students, and not too difficult or dangerous tasks, some form of massed experience should certainly prove no worse than distributed experiences.[21]

Arranging Units of Instruction   A continuous activity unit is the arrangement of continuous practice sessions through an entire week or series of weeks. For example, soccer skills might be taught every day for ten consecutive school days. Another scheduling pattern is the intermittent activity unit. Under this plan, the students might have ten periods of soccer experiences, but they would be scheduled for a given number of days per week, usually not more than three days out of five. The intermittent unit would consist of the number of weeks needed to complete the total number of practice periods desired. These two types of unit arrangements are illustrated in Table 8–1. The advantages of the intermittent activity unit arrangement is that the students don't feel trapped in consecutive days of one activity and they don't feel that they won't get the chance to come back to an activity after "this week." Interest and motivation is sustained, students have more time in which to practice skills at home or in neighborhood games, and rest periods are provided for recovery and consolidation of learning and development when the intermittent unit arrangement is used.

TABLE 8–1 Types of Unit Scheduling Patterns

		Continuous Activity Units							*Intermittent Activity Units*			
		M	T	W	Th	F			M	T	W	Th	F
Weeks	1	B^1	B^2	B^3	B^4	B^5	Weeks	1	B^1	D^1	B^2	G^1	B^3
	2	B^6	B^7	B^8	B^9	B^{10}		2	B^4	D^2	B^5	G^2	B^6
	3	S^1	S^2	S^3	S^4	S^5		3	B^7	D^3	B^8	G^3	B^9
	4	S^6	S^7	S^8	S^9	S^{10}		4	B^{10}	S^1	S^2	G^4	S^3
	5	G^1	G^2	G^3	G^4	G^5		5	S^4	D^4	S^5	G^5	S^6
	6	D^1	D^2	D^3	D^4	D^5		6	S^7	D^5	S^8	S^9	S^{10}

B = Basketball   S = Soccer
D = Dance   G = Gymnastics

Self-Pacing   Self-pacing is a system wherein the individual is allowed to specify or elect the practice schedule they want to follow. The statement that massed practice should be avoided because elementary school age children have shorter attention spans than adults is only a generalization. Students and teachers who interact can develop a practice schedule based on individual needs. Self-pacing involves the use of learning centers and task cards and can be used by individuals, partners, or groups of students, each having a common interest and intent to complete a learning task.

Using Task Cards and Learning Centers

The task method and learning centers are designed to provide a range of tasks that allows the learners to begin at an appropriate instructional level, actively practice the skill, progress at their own rate, and receive intrinsic feedback after each response. The values of these methods of instruction are that it is a step toward individualization of learning, student responsibility for learning, and personalization of information feedback.

These methods of teaching rely on the availability of specific tasks that are designed to follow a progression from a simple level of difficulty to the

---

BOX 8–7   A Task Card

Card 3

Task—Throwing for Accuracy—Swinging Target

Objective: Following this learning experience, you will be able to hit a swinging target 3 times in 5 trials from a distance of 15 feet.

Equipment: Plastic milk jug, 5 bean bags, 4 feet of twine, horizontal ladder or bar, and a measuring tape.

Sequence: (1) warm-up; (2) take 10 throws at the target, which is hanging stationary, from a distance of 15 feet; (3) have your partner swing the target and watch it swing back and forth to get the timing; (4) swing the target and make your 5 throws just before the target stops swinging (repeat until you achieve 3 hits in 5 tries); (5) swing the target and try to hit it 3 in 5 times after one swing.

Repeat 2 times, if not successful, practice Step 4 again, then try Step 5. When you reach the objective, try to (a) hit the target more than 3 times in 5 tries, or (b) move back 5 more feet, or (c) return this card to the file and take a new card.

Card 4 is the next step in this series.

desired terminal behavior. The task can be stated verbally (either live or recorded on tape) or it may be written on a card, sheet of paper, piece of poster board, or chalk board. Box 8–7 presents an example of a task card. Seidel, Biles, Figley and Newman, in *Sports Skills,*[22] and Mosston, in *Teaching Physical Education: From Command to Discovery*[23] presented numerous examples of task cards for different content areas of physical education.

A task card may be a five-by-eight-inch card or full sheet of paper. It provides a statement of purpose or objective for the experience, a list of equipment to be used, and directions concerning what to do and how well or many times the task must be done before changing to another task. Task cards and learning centers incorporate all the positive practices for designing a developmental physical education experience. Writing a task card is similar to writing a detailed lesson plan for a learning activity that has intrinsic information feedback.

When teaching by task, two different arrangements may be used. One is an arrangement wherein every student in the class works at the same station in a given class period (see Figure 8–2). These arrangements are called learning circuits. The second arrangement is to schedule groups of

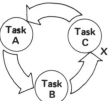

Two or more tasks are available for the students to complete.

The tasks at each station must not be sequential. In other words, Station A must not be a prerequisite for Station B because most students will not complete the stations in sequential order (e.g., A–B–C)

If groups of students start at each task and rotate to a new station on a signal,

then less equipment is needed than if all students start at Station A and progress to Station C at their own pace.

Arranging the learning centers in a circle or triangular shape allows the teacher to be near all centers to provide supervision

and specific information feedback to an individual at a given center.

The teacher (X) should be positioned at the outer portion of a task station to provide feedback, while maintaining visual contact with the students at each of the other stations.

Students can keep their record of achievement by using individual task progress report forms.

FIGURE 8-2 A simple arrangement for learning circuits

BOX 8–8   Learning Center Design Criteria

When developing a learning center, you should be certain that several essential elements have been incorporated into your plan. As an aid to designing effective learning centers, the following criteria should be followed.

The teacher must:

1. Know the performance objectives, and indicate to the students the goal(s) of the learning center.
2. Relate the learning center to a developmental theme and not use the activities as an end in themselves.
3. Arrange the learning center so it is self-sufficient (directions and equipment provided) and student directed.
4. Arrange the learning center tasks in a progressive sequence or use open-ended tasks.
5. Incorporate activities that provide knowledge of results (intrinsic feedback) or use peer teaching.
6. Include learning check points (check-off sheets, demonstrations, or teacher observation) for motivational purposes, accountability, and learning experience closure.
7. Establish the rule that students cannot decide to stop working at a learning center during a period and must demonstrate on-task behavior at the center.
8. Function to manage learning rather than manage the learners.

Task cards, posters, and tape recorders can be used to give basic instructions, thus freeing the teacher to "teach."

An effectively designed learning center will assist teachers to individualize instruction. Once a learning center has been designed, the teacher should refine and modify the center to meet the changing characteristics of students during the school year or from year to year.

---

students to work at selected tasks. This individualizes instruction by allowing students with identified needs to be provided only the instructional experiences that will enhance their development. Figure 8–3 presents this arrangement. A task card can be followed at a learning center. The teaching modules in this chapter use task cards and learning centers.

Managerially, it is easier for a teacher to implement the task approach by having a review station where students practice previously learned skills. Once all the centers are in action, the teacher is free to give instructional feedback where it is needed or to modify one of the stations to present a new skill for a selected group.

Group 1 ----

   Task A
   Task B
   Task C

Group 2 ——

   Task B
   Task D
   Task E

Group 3 ·······

   Task C
   Task E
   Task B

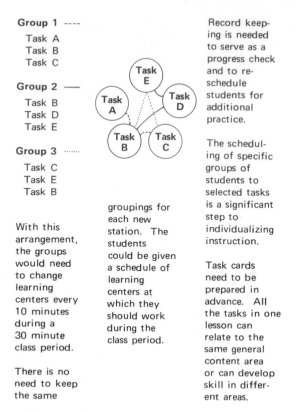

Record keeping is needed to serve as a progress check and to reschedule students for additional practice.

The scheduling of specific groups of students to selected tasks is a significant step to individualizing instruction.

Task cards need to be prepared in advance. All the tasks in one lesson can relate to the same general content area or can develop skill in different areas.

With this arrangement, the groups would need to change learning centers every 10 minutes during a 30 minute class period.

There is no need to keep the same groupings for each new station. The students could be given a schedule of learning centers at which they should work during the class period.

FIGURE 8-3 A complex arrangement for learning circuits

Planning a Physical Fitness Program

The general purposes of a physical fitness program are to develop or maintain a desired level of cardiovascular endurance, muscular strength and endurance, and flexibility. The following basic principles are applicable to any physical fitness program. A physical fitness program must:

1. be systematic in following a plan that includes specific objectives for activities to meet the needs of the individual for whom the program is designed
2. apply the overload principle by working at 70 to 80 percent of maximum
3. be progressive and gradually increase the intensity or duration of the exercise routine
4. acknowledge the principle of specificity of results (improvement only will occur in the areas trained) by developing a comprehensive program if "overall" results are desired
5. occur on a regular basis as part of the individual's lifestyle, which includes three to four workouts each week.[24]

Improving Physical Fitness

The following are specific procedures and guidelines for improving the level of cardiovascular endurance, muscular strength and endurance, and flexibility:

- *Cardiovascular endurance:* To produce a gain, the heart rate should reach 110 to 140 beats per minute for a period of at least eight minutes. Usually, a conservative approach is recommended in establishing a starting exercise level. The maximum workload should be underestimated and the demands moderately and progressively increased. This gives the person a chance to gradually become conditioned to climate conditions and to the demands of the increased activity level. Riding a bicycle, swimming, and jogging are all excellent activities for increasing cardiovascular endurance.

  In any type activity, if a cramp develops, it can usually be relieved by stretching the affected muscle (for a cramp in the calf of the leg, gradually pull the toes toward the ankle). Footwear, including properly fitting shoes and socks, can help to prevent blisters from developing. In any type of cardiovascular endurance activity, the rule is sustained, moderately vigorous activity. Just going for a slow, easy walk, bike ride, or swim will not produce the desired benefits.[25]

- *Muscular strength and endurance:* Muscles increase their fiber size as an adaptation to an increased work load (hypertrophy) and decrease in fiber size with a decrease in work load (atrophy). Muscular strength is developed by doing exercises that use the body's weight or by using weights (lifting sand bags, water-filled plastic jugs, or a barbell). Body weight exercises or weight training routines are usually completed in sets of repetitions. A set is a group of repetitions, and a repetition is one execution of the exercise movement. For example, three sets of eight repetitions of pushups would be eight pushups, a rest period, eight pushups, a rest period, and eight pushups. The pushup can be completed as three straight sets, or three sets with other exercises being completed between each set of pushups. For endurance, fifteen or more repetitions using light weight are usually used, whereas for strength development, six or less repetitions with a high weight load are used. All areas of the body (arms and shoulders, abdomen and back, and legs) should be included in a comprehensive development program.

  During exercise, breathing is important as there is a tendency to hold the breath while exerting effort. When contracting a muscle to lift or push a weight, the person should breathe out, and when returning to the starting position the person should breathe in. Muscular soreness will usually be experienced when beginning a muscular endurance or strength program. The soreness will disappear within the first week, and it can be minimized by starting gradually and increasing the resistance over a period of time.[26]

- *Flexibility:* Exercises that involve gradual stretching of the muscles and tendons, the connective tissue between muscles, and bones are needed to maintain or regain normal ranges of joint motion. Some muscular strength and endurance exercises cause shortening of muscles which, if not corrected, can limit flexibility and cause discomfort. Doing situps with the legs straight and jogging may cause tight muscles, thereby improperly tilting the pelvic bones and resulting in a low back disorder. Flexibility exercises can improve and prevent this condition. The best advice for flexibility exercise is to regularly (several times each day) complete gentle sets of dynamic (moving) stretching exercises and to hold a static (stationary) position of full trunk flexion in the toe-touching position. Flexibility exercises can be completed seven days a week because stretching is a natural and relaxing movement. Many people stretch when changing from one posture to another or after sitting for a lengthy period of time. The major *Don't* associated with flexibility is not to bounce, forcefully thrust into a position, or have another person push or pull a body-part past its usual range of movement. Forceful overstretching may result in tissue damage. With flexibility exercises, as in the other areas of physical fitness, you should remember that it will take time (four to six weeks) to experience positive changes.[27]

Warming up

Before engaging in physical fitness activities, a series of warm-up exercises should be completed. Warm-up exercises can be of a general nature or they may be specific to the activity in which the person is about to engage. Traditional exercises (side straddle hops, squat thrusts, or toe touches) are examples of general warm-up activities that promote circulation and regular breathing, and that stretch the muscles as an aid in preventing muscle and joint injuries. Specific warm up involves completing the movements of a task with reduced intensity. Running in place, taking slow sprint starts, throwing a ball with medium speed at first and increasing speed over a number of trials, and taking practice swings with a bat or racket are examples of specific warm up. The duration of warm-up activities should be an individual decision; however, warm-up activities should not induce fatigue.

Measuring Physical Fitness

Testing is important in evaluating the effectiveness of physical fitness development. Students, especially in the intermediate grades, should become aware of their physical fitness status. Teachers should periodically administer or assist students in completing physical fitness tests.

Standardized physical fitness test procedures can be used in either formal or informal assessment programs. In formal testing programs, all measurements are accomplished by setting aside one or two class periods

BOX 8–9   Physical Fitness Test and Record Chart

Strength Tests

Your Name_____

1. Push-ups:
   - Lie face down on your stomach, and place your hands on the floor next to your shoulders
   - Push up, keeping your body straight, and hold a position where your arms are at a forty-five-degree angle
   - Hold the half pushup position as long as possible
   - Time the number of seconds until you begin to lower your body from this position.

   date:_____
   score:_____ seconds

   date:_____
   score:_____ seconds

   date:_____
   score:_____ seconds

2. Pull-ups:
   - Select a horizontal bar that allows you to hang by your arms without your feet touching the floor
   - Grip the bar with your palms facing away from you
   - Pull up with your arms until your chin is even with the bar, then lower yourself to the starting position
   - Raising or kicking the knees and swinging your body is not allowed
   - Count the number of pullups completed.

   date:_____
   score:_____ count

   date:_____
   score:_____ count

   date:_____
   score:_____ count

3. Bent-Arm Hang:
   - Select a horizontal bar that is as high as your standing height
   - Grip the bar with your palms facing away from you
   - Pull up until your chin is just above the bar, your chest is close to the bar and the elbows are bent
   - Hold the position as long as possible
   - Time how many seconds, to the nearest second, that this position is held before the chin touches the bar, the head is tilted backwards or the chin drops below the bar.

   date:_____
   score:_____ seconds

   date:_____
   score:_____ seconds

   date:_____
   score:_____ seconds

Flexibility Test

Sit with your legs straight and the back of the knees touching the floor

Place your feet against a cardboard box, with a yard stick or meter stick attached to the top of the box so that six inches or 15.2 centimeters of it extends over the edge toward you

Slowly bend and reach forward, with your hands touching as far as possible down the yard stick or meter stick

Hold this position for three seconds while another student reads the measurement on the yard stick or meter stick

To score one inch (2.54 centimeters) beyond your toes, you must reach to the seven inch (17.8 centimeters) mark because the yard stick (meter stick) extends six inches (15.2 centimeters) over the edge of the box.

date:_____
score:_____ inches/
                             centimeters

date:_____
score:_____ inches/
                             centimeters

date:_____
score:_____ inches/
                             centimeters

Pulse or Heart Rate

1. Resting Rate:
   - Sit quietly for one minute
   - With your fingers feel and count your pulse on the right side of your throat under the jaw bone for fifteen seconds.

date:_____
score:_____ count

date:_____
score:_____ count

date:_____
score:_____ count

date:_____
score:_____ count

2. Working Rate:
   - Complete activity 1 or 2 (Introductory Module p. 309)
   - Run selected distance or time
   - Immediately after you stop, locate your heart rate for fifteen seconds.

date:_____
score:_____ count

date:_____
score:_____ count

date:_____
score:_____ count

3. Resting Rate:
   - Sit quietly for five minutes after exercising
   - Count your pulse rate for fifteen seconds.

date:_____
score:_____ count

date:_____
score:_____ count

exclusively for measuring physical fitness elements. Usually, a standardized test is used that includes an evaluation system based on norms derived from a national sample.

Informal testing programs may also use standardized testing procedures, but physical fitness measures can be collected in a number of ways. Unlike formal physical fitness testing, informal assessment can be conducted as part of a unit. For example, in track and field, student performance in the fifty-yard dash may be used as an indicator of one component of physical fitness development. Informal assessment can also be a brief physical fitness progress check during any physical education period (complete as many bent-leg situps as you can in one minute).

Testing Procedures   Measurement in physical education can be very accurate and reliable as time, distance, and weight measures are usually employed. Often, frequency counts are used to determine how many times a student can complete a given movement, with or without a time limitation. One of the key guidelines in measurement is standardization. Standardization enables data that are collected at different places or times for a given event to be compared. Standardization means that different people (or the same person at different times) will complete the same event under the same conditions of performance.

Some considerations that should be followed before taking measurements to assess physical fitness development are:

1. Students should be given practice opportunities to learn and physically condition themselves prior to attempting a maximum performance.
2. Students should be helped to understand that they need *not* push themselves to a point where they become physically ill, and that they are not in competition with other students. The purpose of assessment is to determine a representative description of their status.
3. Students should be taught how to warm up, both in general and for specific activities. Warm-up procedures can aid in prevention of injuries as well as helping to ready the participant psychologically.
4. Students should be helped to understand that generally the anxiety and tension they experience (such as the feeling of having butterflies in their stomach, sweaty palms, or nervous twitches) are normal physiological signs of readiness for an activity.
5. Students must understand the importance of being honest in terms of following the instructions (standards) for the events, giving a reasonable effort, and reporting a true count or score for their performance or the performance of a partner. Teachers

BOX 8–10   Taking Measurements

String, rods, rulers, and yard or meter sticks or wheels can be used to measure distance. The tool (instrument) to be used should fit the task and the degree of accuracy (precision) desired.

A piece of string is an excellent and inexpensive tool for measuring distance. It can be used in simple comparisons of whether Point B or Point C is further from Point A, or, when measured against a yard or meter stick, it can be determined that Point B is 15 yards, 2 feet, and 3½ inches. A caution when using a string or tape to measure distance is that these materials will stretch, causing the measured distance to be more than the actual distance. Children should experiment with and learn how to pull the string so that no slack exists, but not so that they feel the string stretch. More precise measurements can be made using steel tapes, but for most purposes string or cord will serve the purpose required in the lesson modules of this book.

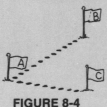

Masking tape can be placed on a string or cord to label certain distances. These specially marked strings can be used to set up the playing area for official, lead-up, or original games.

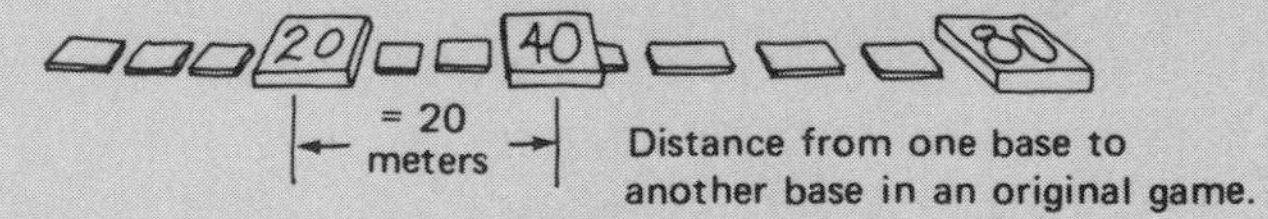

FIGURE 8-4

|← = 20 meters →| Distance from one base to another base in an original game.

FIGURE 8-5

Each student or groups of students could have their own measuring string. Special measuring strings could also be kept with learning center equipment to be used by the students in setting up an agility course or a modified game of soccer or an original game.

A measuring wheel can be made or purchased for measuring longer distances than is practical when using a string. The outer surface of the measuring wheel can be marked in metric or standard units of measurement.

To accurately measure the shortest distance between two points, the measuring wheel must be pushed in a straight line. Usually, two people are needed to measure a distance using a wheel. They are the *wheel pusher* and *the counter.* The counter watches the wheel and makes a tally mark on a piece of paper each time the wheel makes one revolution, or he/she reads the mechanical counter on the wheel and records the distance. Helping children to learn how to measure not only aids them in learning how to set up a playing area but it also provides for application of mathematics skills.

can help by having students record their own performance or by having students privately telling them their score, thus avoiding the potential embarrassment of public announcement of a performance score.

Standardized testing procedures can become a normal part of the physical education program. Performance scores can be recorded at a station in an activity log, a student's personal physical activity booklet, or the teacher's progress record book.

Norm-referenced and Criterion-referenced Tests   The most frequently used test for physical fitness in the United States today is the *AAHPER Youth Fitness Test*. This test consists of the following six items:

1. Pull-up (boys); flexed-arm hang (girls)
2. Sit-up
3. Shuttle run
4. Standing broad jump
5. Fifty-yard dash
6. Six hundred-yard run-walk, or one-mile run, or nine-minute run for ages 10 to 12, or one and a half-mile run, or twelve-minute run for ages 13 and older.

Some items of the *AAHPER Youth Fitness Test* are motor fitness measures and some are measures of physical working capacity. Percentile scores are available for students age 10 through 17 for each item on the test.[28]

The *AAHPER Youth Fitness Test* is a norm-referenced test. That is, the percentile scores are based on "norms" developed by means of measuring a sample of the appropriate population. The norms only tell how an individual score is related to scores made by others of the same age on the same test item. Thus, a raw score on an item that equals a percentile score of 60 indicates that the performance was greater than the performance of 60 percent of the children included in the sample population. This information does not tell the individual how his performance rates on qualitative terms.

An alternative to norm-referenced tests are criterion-referenced tests. One example is the twelve-minute run test, devised by Cooper. On this test, the distance a person runs in twelve minutes is an indicator of whether the individual's physical fitness level is Very Poor, Poor, Fair, Good, or Excellent. These categories are based on the amount of oxygen used and are related to the amount of oxygen that one should be able to use in a state of desirable cardiorespiratory fitness.[29] Unfortunately, desirable levels for other physical fitness components have not been determined through research such as that conducted by Cooper.

Most physical fitness tests are norm-referenced. The disadvantage of these tests is that they only determine physical fitness status, and inferences must be made to determine whether the level indicates an appropriate degree of development. On the other hand, criterion-referenced tests identify levels of physical fitness that are appropriate goals for children to attain or maintain.

The American Alliance for Health, Physical Education, Recreation, and Dance (AAHPERD)* has devised a health-related fitness test. The items included measure cardiorespiratory functions, overweightness, lower back and upper thigh area muscular strength, and endurance and flexibility of the lower spinal area. The test items do not include national norms; instead norms from two regional areas are presented. In addition, criterion references for physical fitness are given. The items of the test are sit and reach; bent leg, crossed arm, curled back sit-ups; skinfold measurements; and one mile or nine-minute run (for children under age 13) and one-and-a-half mile or twelve-minute run (for individuals ages 13 and older). This version represents a major change in the AAHPERD recommended physical fitness testing procedures, and the new manual should be consulted for test instructions and training suggestions. Teachers can continue to use the 1976 *AAHPER Youth Fitness Test,* the new version, or a combination of the two tests. However, the teacher should make this decision based on the intended outcome(s) of their program and the needs of the students.

The most important reason for fitness testing is individual assessment, guidance, and program development. Students should be helped to interpret their test scores. These scores should be used to identify relative areas of strength and weakness. As a result of analyzing individual test scores, students should be able to state their physical fitness level for the various fitness elements identified in the test. Students should also be helped to evaluate their physical activity patterns to see what changes might be made in view of physical fitness test results. This is an essential part of any individualized physical education program.

IMPLEMENTING THE DEVELOPMENTAL THEME

Many of the activities in this developmental theme build upon and expand some of the activities presented in the previous themes. In addition, there is an emphasis on self-assessment, selection, and practice of needed skills. Children enjoy testing themselves in activities if the results are used in meaningful ways for self-improvement.

Precision   If children are to develop the attributes of good movement, they must be able to identify those attributes. They also need to know how factors, such as

---

*Formerly the American Alliance for Health, Physical Education, and Recreation.

correct placement of weight, timing, and proper application of force, influence movement control. Proper form in movement is the result of many correct repetitions of the act. It requires some effort on the teacher's part to know how to motivate children to practice repeatedly (i.e., it is much easier to work on "something new" and "less boring"). The aim is to have the children *want* to practice. Most children enjoy repetition, especially of activities they find interesting. It has been the authors' experience that photography, filming or videotaping of the children's activity, stimulates further efforts to improve their own performance.

Using Learning Centers

The selection and practice of certain activities requires some individual work since the need for practice may not be the same for all the children. It is for this reason that the "learning center" idea has been introduced in this developmental theme. Learning centers are becoming more commonplace in elementary schools, but they are not yet used extensively in physical education. The learning centers provided here furnish teachers with a basis for planning their own centers. There are many advantages of using this strategy, such as: increasing independent behavior of students, freeing teachers to work more closely with those children requiring more individualized help, and allowing more capable students to move ahead and work at their own rates.

Increasing Complexity

Complexity is arrived at through increasing the number of elements in the task, or raising the level of difficulty in those components. It is important for teachers to help children find challenging responses and to try a variety of responses rather than the first one or two that come to mind. As children become more proficient in movement, there are opportunities for finding unique and more complex ways of moving. However, this is a matter of degree. Even primary children can perform quite complex tasks if they first explore fully the various elements of space, time, force, and flow.

Some classroom teachers are uneasy with the idea of *increasing* the risk factors in movement tasks; yet, increased complexity often connotes increased risk in those tasks involving apparatus or fixed equipment, such as the playground bars. However, the increase in *risk* is not mandated for every student, and the degree of risk involved in working with any apparatus is determined by three factors:

1. the child's skill specific to the situation
2. the degree of self-discipline of the individuals who make up the class/group
3. the structure of the task.

Children are great self-challengers, and they need a supportive but safe environment in which to discover and practice new skills. Despite many teachers' fears, children will rarely actually attempt tasks they are not sure of. Teachers who have had negative experiences themselves in gymnastics are often understandably wary of this area. However, reflection on their own experiences often may reveal that the negative experience was the result of inappropriately applied external pressure, such as "You can do it!" "Hurry up!" "Others are waiting!" Shoving and horseplay are also the precursors of accidents and fearfulness.

Challenging Oneself The activities that focus on the effects of exercise on the body overlap the health curriculum. This material is particularly appropriate for children in the upper elementary grades because many of them are beginning to be fascinated by their own physical development. Because a segment of the students will leave school before exercise physiology is taught, it is important that this topic be introduced earlier and in ways that are personally meaningful to the students.

Concrete information about fitness factors will help to offset the misinformation generated through popular magazines (fad diets and advertisements of weight-loss products). In this way, teachers can make a significant contribution to the development of generations of educated consumers.

DEVELOPING PRECISION

Planning Guide

Objectives	*Experiences*
As a result of the learning experiences over time, children will:	
1. be able to identify the components of appropriate form in movement	• Many of the learning experiences in this enabling behavior build on those in previous teaching modules. Observe films, film loops, and videotapes of others' movement forms (other children's, or amateur and professional athletes')
2. develop increasing mastery of their own movement ability, resulting in consistency of form in movement	• learning centers on improving throwing, kicking, and other manipulative skills
3. demonstrate ability to stay on task at a learning center until a self-determined goal has been accomplished.	• choose a goal to work toward, and select activities from those provided to meet that goal.

As usual, the sample lesson presented for this enabling behavior is appropriate for both primary and intermediate grade children. The selection of learning centers provides a wide range of activities for different ability levels.

For evaluating students' progress in developing precision, see page 295.

Teaching Modules

Introductory Module

Objective

As a result of the learning experiences over time, children will be able to use learning centers productively.

Materials

An instrument to signal "change."

Learning Experiences	Related Experiences
Assemble students near one of the learning centers so that all can hear the directions: "Before we start our activities today, we are going to remember how to use the learning centers."	• The related learning experiences are suggested within the learning centers, since they are more appropriate to the activities.
If your students are familiar with learning centers, you will probably want to provide more choices for them, since they should be used to assessing their own needs. If, however, this is their first attempt to work independently, you might be more comfortable with all the children working on the same center.	

Central Module

Objectives

As a result of the learning experiences over time, children will be able to:

1. demonstrate improved overarm throwing ability
2. demonstrate greater accuracy in throwing overhand to a target from a distance of at least five times their own height (The difficulty of this task depends on the size of the target. The smaller the target, the more difficult the task.)
3. demonstrate ability to kick a stationary ball in different directions: to left, to right, diagonally left or right, forward, or up
4. trap a moving ball five times in succession
5. kick a moving ball accurately in a predetermined direction
6. strike a stationary ball with either hand
7. strike a stationary ball with a paddle/bat over a distance of five times their own height

FIGURE 8-6 Developing precision in overarm throwing

8. strike a moving ball with their hands ten times without missing
9. strike a moving ball with a paddle/bat ten times without missing.

Materials

An instrument to signal "finish what you are doing."
Selected Learning Center(s) written in language that is appropriate
for various levels of reading ability.
Assorted balls for required activity.
Beanbags for first and second grade children/classes in which
there are insufficient balls for the center on throwing.

Learning Center: Throwing overarm

Objective: When you have worked through this learning center, you will be
able to throw better, *but* you must practice what you have learned in the center,
otherwise you will not keep the improvement.

Equipment you will need: Five beanbags, or a tennis ball, or other small ball
that will fit in your hand. A wall without windows (a big tree will do, but your
ball will bounce off it in all directions).

What to do first:
1. Take your beanbags to a space you have chosen near the wall.
2. Stand far enough back that you have to throw hard to hit the wall.

Next:
3. Check your distance by throwing hard at the wall. If the beanbags are not hitting the wall, or are hitting the wall near the ground, move forward a bit. Put the beanbags on the ground behind you on your throwing side. Pick them up one at a time.
4. Throw the beanbags, one at a time, hard against the wall. Try to make them hit the wall at about the same height each time.
5. Pick up the beanbags and continue throwing until it is easy for you to hit the wall at the same height.

Check these things you do: Put a (✔) when you have done it five times in a row.
6. Are you taking a big step, a medium-sized step, or a little step as you throw? Try taking a bigger step as you throw. (_____)
7. Which foot are you stepping on as you throw? Is it the same foot as the arm you throw with? Or is it the opposite one? Try using the opposite foot to the side you throw. (_____)
8. Do you look at the target all the time? Even when you are getting ready to throw? (Or winding up?) (_____)
9. Which way are you leaning when the beanbag has left your hand? Do you lean to the same side as you throw, or do you lean the opposite way? Try to finish your throw by leaning away from the side you throw. (_____)

If you are working with a partner, let him/her check these things for you.
10. When you have checked (✔) everything, move a little further back and throw again. Each time you move back, go through the checklist, to make sure you are doing it correctly.

Learning Center: Throwing at a target

Objective: When you have completed this learning center, you will be able to hit a target on the wall from a spot that is five times as long as you are tall, away from the wall using the overarm throw.

Equipment you will need: Five beanbags, or a tennis ball, or other small ball that will fit in your hand; a target on the wall about opposite your own chest; contruction paper for making your target; masking tape to stick target on wall; string for measuring your own height.

What to do first:
1. Take your beanbags to a space on the wall you have chosen.
2. Use the string to measure how tall you are. Use two pieces of the string, so that you have two measures. Tie a knot in the string to show how big you are.

3. Put *both* pieces of string end-to-end away from the wall. The end of the string is where you stand to throw first. This is *twice your height.*
4. Tear or cut your construction paper into a fancy shape, and stick it on the wall about the height of your own chest.
5. Stand at the end of the string and put the beanbags behind you on the same side you throw.

Next:

6. Throw the beanbags at the target on the wall.
7. Check your distance. Is it hard to hit the target from there? Find a place on the string where you can hit the target ten times in a row. Then move back bit-by-bit until you get to the end of the string. When it is easy, go to the next step.
8. Is it easy for you to hit the target from there? Measure with a third piece of string and stand at the end of that. If that is too far, find a place between the second and third end that you can hit the target from and start there. Move back bit-by-bit.
9. Go on to fourth and fifth strings.

Check these things you do: Check (✔) when you have done it.

10. Are you taking a big step, a medium-sized step, or a little step as you throw? Try taking a bigger step as you throw. (_____)
11. Which foot are you stepping on as you throw? Is it the same foot as the arm you throw with? Or is it the opposite one? Try using the opposite foot to the side you throw. (_____)
12. Do you look at the target all the time? Even when you are getting ready to throw? (Or winding up?) (_____)
13. Which way are you leaning when the beanbag has left your hand? Do you lean to the same side as you throw, or do you lean the opposite way? Try to finish your throw by leaning away from the side you throw. (_____)

Other things you can do:

14. Try different throws: under-arm; over-arm; side-arm. (_____)
15. Hit the target ten times in a row using a different throw. (_____)
16. Mark off six steps back from the end of the fifth string. Run and throw the beanbag at the target. (_____)
17. Do the previous task ten times in a row. (_____)

Related Experiences for Learning Centers on Throwing

1. Find out the answers to the following questions:

   What makes a ball curve?

   Why does a pitcher stand on a mound?

   Who holds the record for making the longest completed pass in football?

   If you wanted to test how strong someone's arm is, would throwing be a good way to find out? If you said no, explain why not. What would be some good ways?

Who was the pitcher for the winning team in the last World Series? Write a report on anything you can find out about his life.

What is a "perfect game" in baseball?

2. Make a list of games in which throwing is important.
3. Watch a small child throw. Describe how he/she throws and how it is different from the way that some of the good throwers in your class throw.
4. Make a list of the ways you think you could help someone improve his/her throwing.
5. Go to a Little League baseball game or a football game, and keep track of how many times the ball is thrown during the game. Count all the throws. (If a group does this, have them report back and compute the average number of throws per game.)
6. How does a gun fire a bullet?
7. Why does a bullet whine?
8. What is the difference between throwing a ball and firing one of the old-fashioned cannons that used heavy cannon balls? In what ways are they the same?
9. Early man killed animals for food by throwing spears. Find out what you can about how man hunted animals for food by throwing spears or by stunning the animals with rocks.
10. What animals throw things? State why some animals can throw and others cannot.

Learning Center: Kicking a ball

Objective: When you have completed these activities you will be able to kick the ball further. You will also know how to make the ball go where you want it to go.

Equipment you will need: A light ball *or* an underinflated play ball (if it is "flat," you won't have to run after it so much because it won't go as far); a wall without windows (to make the ball come back to you); two small pieces of masking tape (to mark the ball).

What to do first:
1. Find a space on the wall to work.
2. Practice balancing on one leg and swinging the other back and forth. Use the wall to help you balance, if necessary. Practice this on both legs. A good kicker has to be able to balance well on one leg.
3. Find out how far away you have to stand so that you have to kick hard to make the ball hit the wall.

Next:
4. Place the ball on the ground and back away from it a few steps.
5. Practice running up to the ball to kick it. Is it in the right place for you to kick it?

6. Run and kick the ball hard towards the wall. Do this five times.
7. Do the same thing with the other foot five times. Try this with different parts of the foot: the instep, the inside of the foot, and the toes.
8. Mark a spot on the ball with the masking tape, and put the ball on the ground so that the tape is in the middle of the ball facing you.
9. Try to contact the ball just below the tape mark. What happened?

Check these things: Check (✔) when you can do it five times in a row.
10. Is your last step before the kick a big step, a medium-sized step, or a little step? (_____)
11. Is your nonkicking foot ahead of the ball, alongside the ball, or behind the ball? Try to place it alongside the ball. (_____)
12. Is the ball going too high? (Straight up and down?) Try to contact the ball nearer the tape mark. (_____)
13. Is the ball staying on the ground and just rolling? You are kicking *above* the tape mark. Try to contact the ball just below the tape mark. (_____)
14. Do you feel you are going to fall over after you have kicked the ball? Think about kicking through the ball, not *at* it. (_____) If that doesn't work, take a longer run at the ball. (_____)
15. What are your arms doing at the end of the kick? Try to have the opposite hand point at the wall. (_____)

Other things you can do:
16. Find out where you have to contact the ball to make it go sideways.
17. Find out what happens when you use different parts of your foot to kick the ball.

Related Experiences for Learning Centers on Kicking
1. Find the answers to the following questions:

Who is George Blanda? Why was he famous?

Why does a ball rebound in different directions?

What causes a kicked ball to roll instead of flying high in the air?

Why is a soccer ball constructed like it is?
2. Find out all you can about the soccer player Pele. Write or tape a report on what you find out.
3. Collect action pictures of kicking, and make them into a collage.
4. Invite one of the local soccer players (professional or amateur) to come and talk about how he trains for the games.
5. Attend a Youth League Soccer match or a women's soccer match. Write a sports report of the match for the school newspaper.
6. Write a story about how "kick the can" or soccer was invented.
7. Make up five equal teams. Five captains will divide the class into teams and then draw straws to see which team they will

lead. Have a contest lasting a week in which each member of the team has three tries at kicking the ball for distance. Make a bar graph to show the results. What is the average kick for each team? What percentage of the team can kick more than twenty yards?

Learning Center: Trapping a moving ball

Objective: When you have worked through these activities, you will be able to trap a ball with either foot or with other parts of your body.

Equipment you will need: A light ball, or a flat playball, or a newspaper ball that is about as big as a softball; a wall to make the ball rebound toward you. (If two of you are working together, you can make the ball move for your partner.)

What to do first:
1. Find a space on the wall, or a space for you and your partner to work.

Next:
2. Throw the ball at the wall to make it come back to you. Stop it in any way you can, without using your hands.
3. Throw the ball at different heights so that it comes back to you in different ways. Try each height at least three times before changing to another height.
4. Throw the ball at different speeds so that it comes back to you both slowly and then faster.

Check these things: Put a check (✔) when you do it five times in a row.
5. Are you watching the ball all the time? Watch it until it hits your foot (or other part of the body). (_____)
6. Do you move so that the ball is coming straight for you? Or does it get past you? Or go off in another direction? Get right in line with the ball so that it won't go past you. (_____)
7. If the ball is coming at your body, do you close your eyes? Watch the ball until it contacts your body. (_____)
   If the ball looks as if it is going to hit you in the face, move back quickly so that it will hit you lower down, or even on your legs. (_____)
8. If the ball is bouncing off you (even though it is flat) and not staying near you, you may be moving into the ball. Think about moving back with the ball as it hits you. This is called "giving" with the ball. (_____)

Other things you can do:
9. Trap the ball with different parts of the foot to see which is the most effective.
10. After you have trapped the ball, kick it at the wall rather than throw it.
11. Practice this with a partner. Change the height of the ball you

roll to your partner so that she/he has to trap both high and low moving balls.

12. Throw the ball hard and low at the wall so that you have to run to trap the ball. Make it go off at an angle.

Learning Center: Hitting a ball with your hand

Objective: When you have completed these activities you will be able to hit a ball so that it goes four times as far as you are tall.

Equipment you will need: A light ball, or yarn ball, about the size of a playground ball; a cone to balance the ball on; a space to hit against a wall or to a partner.

What to do first:
1. Find your space on the wall (or for you and your partner).
2. Set your cone up and put the ball on the top.

Next:
3. Make a fist, swing your arm, and hit the ball like the batter does in baseball.
4. Let your partner get the ball and return it to you.
5. Repeat this five times.

Check these things: Put a check (✔) when you do it five times in a row.
6. Where are you standing before you hit the ball? Are you facing the ball? Are you so far away that you sometimes miss the ball with your hands? Find the place to stand so that it is easy to hit the ball. (_____)
7. What do your feet do? Do they stay still when you hit the ball? Or are you taking a step as you hit it? As you swing to hit the ball, take a step sideways with the foot opposite your hitting arm. (_____)
8. Are you watching the ball all the time? Or do you close your eyes when you hit it? Watch the ball until you hit it and see the empty cone. (_____)
9. Is the ball going too high when you hit it? Or is it hitting the ground right away? Find the place on the ball that, when you hit it, makes it fly like a home run ball! (_____)
   Find the place on the ball that makes you hit a grounder. (_____)
   Find the place on the ball that makes you hit a line drive. (_____)

Other things you can do:
10. Have your partner stand in different places and try to hit the ball to him.
11. Set up a mark that would be where first base is, and see if you can run to it and back to the cone before your partner fields your ball and touches the cone.
12. See what happens when you use the other hand to hit the ball.
13. Try doing Number 9 task with your eyes closed.

Learning Center: Hitting a ball with a bat/paddle

Objective: When you have completed these activities you will be able to hit a ball off a cone with your paddle and make it go five times as far as you are tall.

Equipment you will need: a light ball, or a newspaper ball about the size of a softball; a paddle or bat; a cone to balance the ball on; string to measure yourself with; masking tape to mark the ball.

What to do first:
1. Find a space on a wall without windows for you and your partner.
2. Measure yourself with the string. Tie a knot in the place where it shows how tall you are. Do this five times so you have five knots.
3. Lay the string on the ground starting at the wall, and see how far it stretches.
4. Set the cone up on the string opposite the wall in a place where you think you can hit the ball to the wall with your bat.

Next:
5. Check your distance. Hit the ball with your bat and see if you have to hit it hard to make it hit the wall. If it is too easy, move the cone further back. Find the place on the string where you have to hit hard to make the ball hit the wall.
6. Hit the ball five times.

Check these things: Check (✔) when you have done it five times in a row.
7. Are you watching the ball all the time? Or do you close your eyes when you hit it, or look away, or pull back? Try to watch the ball until you hit it and then look at the empty cone. (____)
8. Put a tape mark in the middle of the ball and set it on the cone so that you can see the mark on the back of the ball. Try to hit the ball right on the tape mark with your bat. If you are hitting the ball in the right spot, it will fly straight and not too high. (____)
9. Check to see where your bat is when you swing it back as you get ready to hit the ball. Is it high over your shoulder? Or is the tip of it dropping down low? Try to hold the bat firmly and keep the elbow nearest the ball up and out. (____)
10. Bit by bit, move the cone back until you can do all these things and make the ball hit the wall from the fifth knot. (____)

Other things you can do: Do each thing at least ten times.
11. Try hitting different sizes and kinds of balls.
12. If you are working with a partner, make him/her stand in different places and try to hit the ball to him/her.

Learning Center: Hitting a moving ball with your hand

Objective: When you have completed these activities you will be able to hit a moving ball using your hand.

Equipment you will need: A light ball, or yarn ball, or tennis ball; a wall to make the ball come back to you.

What to do first:
1. Find a space to work. (You don't need the wall, yet.)

Next:
2. Find out what you have to do to keep the ball in the air using just one hand. If you are using a tennis ball, let it bounce in between hits.
3. See if you can hit the ball ten times, keeping it in the air without letting it bounce, or drop.
4. Find a space on the wall now, and hit the ball so that it comes back to you. Find the right place for you to keep the ball going. Let it bounce before you hit it against the wall each time.
5. Do this until you are able to hit the ball against the wall ten times without making a mistake. Let the ball bounce before you hit it each time.

If you can't do it ten times, go on to Number 6. If you can, go on to Number 8.

Check these things:
6. Are you watching the ball all the time, even as you hit it? Watch the ball right up to the time you contact it with your hand. Hit through the ball, not at it. (_____)
7. Move quickly so that you are in the spot you would be if the ball was still on top of a cone when you hit it. (_____)

Other things you can do: Do each thing at least ten times.
8. Stick a target on the wall with masking tape and try to hit the target ten times in a row.
9. Stand further back, throw the ball hard at the wall and then try to hit it with your hand when it comes back to you.

Learning Center: Striking a moving ball with a paddle

Objective: When you have completed these activities, you will be able to hit a moving ball with a paddle ten times without missing.

Equipment you will need: A light ball, or playball about the size of a softball; a paddle; a wall to make the ball come back to you, or a partner to throw it to you, or a "tethered" ball.

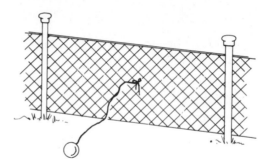

FIGURE 8-7 Tethered ball

What to do first:
1. Find a space to work.
2. Tie the tether or select a partner.

Next:
3. Start the ball moving by hitting it with your hand or the paddle.
4. See how many times you can hit it without missing. You can let it bounce in between hits. Hit it as you would hit a baseball.
5. If you can hit it eight times in a row without missing, go on to Number 9. If you miss, go on to Number 6.

Check these things: Check these when you do them five times in a row.
6. Are you watching the ball all the time, even though it is going all over the place? Keep your eye on the ball even when you hit it. (_____)
7. How are you moving to hit the ball? Do you find you are too late and the ball has gone past you? Or is the ball flying up high in the air all the time? Try to figure out where the ball is going to be after it has bounced. Be in the right place to hit it. (_____)
8. Are you moving on the balls of your feet? Or the heels? Find out where is the best place to keep your weight so that you can move quickly and use the balls of your feet. (_____)

FIGURE 8-8

Other things you can do: Do each thing at least ten times in a row.

9. Say one of the jump rope rhymes and make your hits fit in time to it.
10. Find a partner who can hit the ball ten times without missing and take turns hitting the ball.
11. Try turning around in between hits!

Related Learning Experiences for Centers on Striking

1. Find the answers to the following questions:

   Where did baseball come from?

   What is the difference between softball and baseball?

   What is a "spit" ball?

   How is a baseball made?

   Who is Hank Aaron? Find out all you can about him and write or tape a report.

   Who is Althea Gibson? What can you find out about her that would make you an expert on Althea Gibson?

   Why do men not play *against* women in professional baseball or tennis (unless for a special reason on television)?
2. Make a list of all the famous "hitters" in baseball. Find pictures of them to go with your list.
3. Make a list of the books in your classroom or library that have stories about famous baseball players, tennis players, or golfers. Post the list in the reading corner.
4. Attend a baseball or softball game and watch what the batters do to warm up before they go in to bat. Write or tape a report on what you saw.
5. In a Little League season, count the number of runs made and the number of homeruns. Work out the ratio of base runs to home runs in the season, or over a four-week period of time.
6. The X-15 was the first plane to fly in outer space. Read about it and find out how it was done. What is similar in the way the X-15 was launched and hitting a baseball?
7. Find out all you can about Babe Zaharias.
8. Make a list of famous men and women tennis players and golfers.

Culminating Module

Objectives

As a result of the learning experiences over time, children will be able to:

1. apply the throwing skills developed previously to a game with a moving target
2. apply kicking skills to a simple game
3. apply striking skills to a simple game.

FIGURE 8-9 Applying kicking skills in a game

Materials

An instrument for signaling "finish what you are doing." Equipment required for learning center games.

 The game centers in this module follow the same format as those in the previous module. Teachers need to be alert to groups that need help in setting up their game or in interpreting the instructions.

Learning Center: Throwing game

Objective: When you have completed these activities, you will be able to hit a moving target better. You will also be able to figure out what path the ball is taking so that you can catch it.

Equipment you will need: A light ball, or newspaper ball, or yarn ball about the size of a softball; two jump ropes; a space for three people to work in.

What to do first:
 1. Find a large enough space for the three of you to work like this:

FIGURE 8-10

2. Arrange the jump ropes on the floor to act as boundaries for the middle person.

FIGURE 8-11

3. Decide who will be in the middle first.

Next:

4. The other two people who are not "in prison" try to get the middle one out by hitting him/her on the legs below the knees with the ball. If you hit above the knees, it doesn't count. Use the overarm throw.
5. Take turns doing this until each person has had three turns in the middle.
6. If you are getting the middle one out of prison in under five hits, go on to Number 9. If you are having trouble getting the middle one out, go on to Number 7.

Check these things: Check (✔) when you have done this three times in a row.

7. Where are you standing when you throw the ball? Are you so far away that the ball hits the floor before it hits the one in the middle? Measure off four giant steps away from the middle person and throw from there. (_____)

8. Where is the ball hitting the person? Do you hit them, but it doesn't count because you are not hitting them below the knees? Find out what is the best place in your throw to release the ball to make it hit the person below the knees. (_____)

Other things you can do: Do each thing at least ten times.

9. Take two giant steps further back from the middle and see what happens to your game.

10. Make the boundaries bigger, so the middle person has more room to dodge the ball.

11. Play the same game against a wall so that the ball rebounds off the wall back to you. Both "throwers" stand on the same side. (This will make the game faster.)

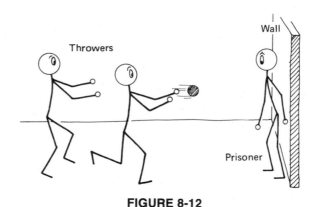

FIGURE 8-12

12. Play the same game using the underarm throw.

Learning Center: Kicking game

Objective: When you have completed these activities, you will be able to kick a moving ball in a game.

Equipment you will need: a large, light ball, or a "flat playball," or a newspaper ball a bit bigger than a softball; a place for "home base"; a marker for "base."

What to do first:

1. Find a place for you and two or three other people to play.

2. Mark home base and then take ten giant steps and put the base marker down on the ground.

3. Decide in what order you will kick. Kicker goes to home base, the other three stand behind the kicker like this:

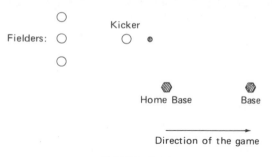

FIGURE 8-13

Next:

4. The kicker places the ball down in front of home base. He runs and kicks the ball, and then runs to base and back as many times as he can before the fielders stop the ball and line up behind it. They must shout "score" to let the kicker know he must stop running.

5. Count the completed runs between home base and base. (Partial runs don't count.)

6. Let the next kicker have a turn, fielders line up behind the new kicker.

7. If the game is going well and everyone is having fun, go on to Number 11. If the game isn't much fun, or if there is bickering and arguing, go on to Number 8.

Check these things:

8. Is the ball not going far enough to let you score any runs? Check where you are contacting the ball. Do you remember the tape mark you made on the other ball when you were kicking it? You can make a tape mark on this one too if you like. (_____)

9. Does one person always get the ball? Or is there a lot of pushing and shoving when the fielders are running for the ball? What ideas can you think of that would stop this? Decide which idea you will use to stop the rough play. (_____)

10. Does one person always kick the ball so far that the fielders have to run forever to stop the ball? Try having one fielder out in the "field" who can stop the ball, and then the other fielders can line up behind the ball.

Other things you can do: Do each thing at least ten times.

11. Move the base back three giant steps.

12. The fielders must stop the ball with their feet, before they line up behind it.

13. Choose one fielder. The fielder must run and trap the ball with his/her feet and dribble it back to home base before shouting "score!"

14. The fielders must travel in a different way to stop the ball (hopping, crab walk, running backward, etc.).
15. Choose a pitcher for each new kicker. The pitcher rolls the ball to the kicker, as in kickball.

Learning Center: Striking game

Objective: When you have worked through these activities, you will be able to hit a stationary or moving ball in a game.

Equipment you will need: a light ball, a newspaper ball, or yarn ball about the size of a softball; a cone to balance the ball on; a space for four people to play; a bat or paddle.

What to do first:
1. Find a space for you and three other people to play. Your ball will be flying in the air, so make sure you have enough room.
2. Set the cone up and balance the ball on it.

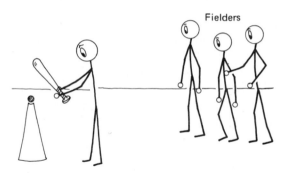

Fielders

FIGURE 8-14

3. Decide in what order you will bat.

Next:
4. The batter hits the ball, and the fielders try to catch it or stop a ground ball. If this happens, the new batter is up. If the ball goes past the fielder, she/he runs after it and stops it.
5. The fielder stays where the ball is stopped, and the batter puts the bat down on the ground. The fielder then rolls the ball to try to hit the bat. If the ball hits the bat, the next batter has a turn; if the ball misses, the same batter has another turn. (Count every hit.)
6. If the game is going well and everyone is having fun, go on to Number 10. If the game is not much fun, or if there is shouting and arguing, go on to Number 7.

Check these things:
7. Is the batter having trouble hitting the ball far off the cone? Check where she/he is hitting the ball. Put a piece of masking tape in the middle of the ball to show where to contact it.

8. Is one fielder always running after the ball, even if it is not coming his/her way? Think about some ideas that will stop this from happening. How do the Cincinnati Reds fix this? Decide on which idea you are going to use.

9. Does one player hit the ball so hard that it always goes past the fielders? Try having the fielders stand further back, so that they can run *to* the ball. (_____)
   Find out what you can do to make a better barrier with your legs so that grounders don't pop through your hands. Make sure you are in line with the grounder. (_____)

Other things you can do:

10. Move the cone, and throw the ball up for yourself when you are the batter.

11. Make a base for your game, and see how many bases you can run before the fielders stop the ball.

Summary

Enabling Behavior: Developing Precision

Indications that children are developing precision in their work are:

1. They become more critical of their initial efforts to complete movement tasks.

2. They stay with a task for longer periods of time.

3. They become more accurate in their ability to hit a target by throwing or striking an object; to catch objects that are tossed, thrown, or volleyed to them; to kick stationary and moving balls to a target.

4. They maintain a previously acquired skill level in a game situation. (Children often regress in skill level in games, particularly as the complexity of the games increases.)

5. They are able to repeat movements accurately, such as sequences of movement they have composed or learned from another person.

INCREASING COMPLEXITY OF RESPONSE

Planning Guide

Objectives	*Experiences*
As a result of the learning experiences over time, children will be able to:	
1. devise increasingly complex responses to basic movement tasks	• select at least three methods of traveling on designated body-parts—hands and feet, hands only, back and feet, etc.

Objectives	Experiences
2. incorporate movement factors (Time, Force, Space, Flow) into their movement responses	• move at different speeds in a variety of directions; change level while changing speed; vary the method of moving while changing directions
3. work effectively with larger groups in games or station activities.	• select movements that can be performed by everyone in the group and compose a group sequence; devise a game that requires utilization of several skills.

For evaluating students' progress in this enabling behavior, see page 306.

Teaching Modules

Introductory Module

Objectives

As a result of the learning experiences over time, children will be able to:

1. explain the term "sequence" as it is used in movement
2. devise increasingly complex movement sequences that show variation in level and/or speed of movement.

Materials

An instrument for signaling "freeze." Boundaries. A word card for "*Sequence*."

Learning Experiences	Related Experiences
1. "When I say Go!, travel anywhere you like inside the boundaries using your feet lightly. When you hear this signal (*), freeze. Think about what you will do. Go!" Depending on the age of the children, allow this first task to continue about forty-five seconds. Primary children may need a longer time.	
2. *"Freeze. Some of you were really using the space very well. Others need to think about moving into the empty spaces you see. Try it again and show me how well you can use your space. Go!" Reinforce generally (if it is warranted) to encourage the children to spread out. "I can really see you moving into all the empty spaces now. Well	• During "free play" or recess, experiment to see which are the *most* difficult movements to link together. Make a list of all the movements you were able to put together smoothly. • Watch films of the gymnastics portions of the Olympics. How do you think people come up with the ideas that the gymnasts perform?

Learning Experiences

done, Jim, you are keeping your eyes open for the empty corners."

3. "This time, find as many ways of traveling as you can. Go!" If they do not respond to this task by showing a great variety of movement, have them "change the part of the body you are traveling on as you move." After the children have worked with this task for a few moments, you can continue with having them find six different ways of traveling.

4. "During the last few minutes, you have found many different ways of traveling. Now, I want you to think of two movements, one on the feet and the other at a low level, that you can keep doing, changing from one to the other." First grade children, or students who are unfamiliar with movement education might need more specific help at this point. You could ask two children to give examples of moving on the feet, and another two to show movement at a low level.

5. "You have two movements that you have put together. Now, find another move that will help you get back on your feet so that you can start all over again—feet, low level, your own move, Go!" (If individual children are having trouble thinking of a linking move, you could suggest a roll and quick spring upright.)

6. If some children have found unique or challenging responses to the last task, let them demonstrate (as a group) to the rest of the class. Demonstration of excellence or creativity can be a motivator to less self-challenging children, after they have had an opportunity to work out a solution for themselves. If you use a demonstration such as this, however, the children need a chance either to try the ideas they have seen or to make their sequences more interesting. "When we link movements together, one after the other, we make a sequence. (Use the word card to reinforce the term.) How many sequences do you think we could make?"

Related Experiences

Hypothesize about this and list your solutions on the bulletin board.

• Read about the extraordinary movement feats of different cultures and people:
  –the high cliff divers of Acapulco
  –sky divers
  –the Mohawks who have a reputation in the construction industry for walking steel girders at incredible heights.

• Take any ordinary game, such as Tiddley Winks or marbles, and find a way to make it more difficult. Write or tape your improvement so that other people can try your idea.

FIGURE 8-15 "Freezing" on the signal

Central Module

Objectives

As a result of the learning experiences over time, children will demonstrate:

(Primary) 1. the ability to compose short sequences that focus on linking different body-shapes

(All children) 2. increased movement control as they perform their sequences

(Intermediate) 3. the ability to compose sequences on a single piece of apparatus, focusing on changes in speed and level.

The designated levels above reflect the wording and the content of the different learning centers suggested. The *content* of both objectives are appropriate for all age levels, but the complexity of the second objective requires some previous experience in devising movement sequences on apparatus.

Learning Experiences

These experiences have been written as "learning centers" to provide the teachers with examples of how to design other centers based on equipment work. The tasks are generic, in that they are suitable for any equipment.

Related Experiences

- Watch films of the young gymnasts in the Olympics. Draw your impressions of how they moved. Try to show the feeling of the movement in your drawings.
- Invite a local gymnast or dance group to talk about how routines or dances are made up.

Learning Experiences

1. "Now that we have worked with the idea of sequence and you have tried out ideas of your own, work out a sequence that starts in a wide stretched shape and finishes in a different shape. Find a place to work and begin when you are ready."

   A problem might be encountered here, depending on the children's experience. Some may simply move from one position to another. In the event that this happens, instruct the needful children to "make at least two different movements" before they reach their final position. (Tell them they must be able to say their name at least five times before they finish or have them count to 25, etc.).

2. "Think about what happens when you write a story (tell a story) in class or draw a picture. Do you use the first ideas you think of? Or do you think about some things and say 'no, that's not such a neat idea, I'll try this . . .'?"

   The first question presented here can be followed by a very short discussion on *how* the movement might be changed to make it more effective, e.g., changing the direction of the movement; going from a very quick start to slow motion finish; building the whole sequence up to a jump at the end or using the same shape several times at different levels. "Well, the same is true of movement sequences. The first ideas you come up with may not be the best or what you like. So, try many different ideas and then choose the ones *you* think make the nicest sequence for you. Try it again."

FIGURE 8-16 Developing a sequence without equipment

FIGURE 8-17 Developing a sequence with equipment

FIGURE 8-18 Developing a sequence with equipment

Learning Center: Making a sequence with different body shapes using a change of direction

Objective: When you have completed these activities, you will be able to perform a *sequence* with three different body shapes while you move backward, sideways, and forward.

Equipment you will need: None, just a working space for yourself.

What to do first: Find a working space so that you have room to move without bumping into anyone.

Next:
    1. Look at this shape:

FIGURE 8-19

2. Can you make your body into a shape like that? Try it.
3. Can you find three more ways you can make your body take the same shape?
4. Now, look at this shape:

FIGURE 8-20

5. Find three different ways you can make your body look like this shape. If you can't think of another way, try making the shape lying down, or balancing on one foot, or upside down!
6. How about *this* shape?

FIGURE 8-21

7. Do the same thing; find three different ways that you can make your body take this shape.
8. You have made nine (9) shapes now! Choose the one you liked best of each kind and see how you can get from one shape to another very slowly. Keep trying, because you may not like the first set of shapes that you put together! When you have a *sequence* that you like, go on to Number 9.
9. *Now,* see how you can do your sequence so that you face a different way on each body shape. When you have done this so that it is good enough to show someone, go on to Number 10.

Check these things: Check (✔) when you have done it.

10. Is each shape the "best" one it can be? If part of it is stretched, is it *really* stretched, or only partially? (_____)
11. Start your sequence so that you move backwards into the first shape you make. Make it a short backward movement. (_____)
12. Find a way you can move sideways from your first shape into the second shape. Practice these new movements until you can remember them easily. (_____)

13. Hold your second shape, and now move forward into the last shape. Then begin all over again. (_____)

Other things you can do:

14. Change the speed as you move in the sequence. Begin very slowly and then speed up.
15. Change one thing in each body shape to make it slightly different.
16. Begin with a quick movement and end very slowly.
17. Put a turning movement in between two of the shapes.
18. Start the sequence very high and finish it very low to the ground.
19. Find a sound that you can make as you do your sequence. If you can't think of one, try saying sh-h-h-h-h in different ways as you move.

Learning Center: Making sequences on a piece of equipment

Objective: When you have completed these activities, you will be able to perform a sequence of movements on the equipment provided.

Equipment you will need: This learning center can be used on any of the equipment in the activity area, such as a box or a balance beam.

What to do first: Find a piece of equipment where there is room for you to work.

Next:

1. Try several different ways of getting on the equipment safely. If you always get on facing the equipment, try to get on it backward or sideways.
2. When you have chosen the way you like best to get on the equipment, balance on two body-parts in a twisted shape. Practice the getting on and balancing in the twisted shape until it is easy. Hold the balance while you say your name twice.
3. Change your shape to a wide stretched shape, balancing on different body-parts from the one before.
4. Now find a way to get off the equipment safely. If you use a jump to get off, land on your feet as softly as you can.
5. Practice the whole sequence: getting on, balancing in a twisted shape, changing to a stretched shape, and getting off. Keep doing the sequence until it is easy; then go on to Number 6.

Check these things: Check (✔) each thing when you have done it.

6. Is your sequence difficult enough for you? Or have you chosen movements that are very easy for you to do? If it is too easy, make one part of it more difficult for yourself. (_____)
7. Are your balance shapes really held still? Or do they wobble around? Practice the balance until you can hold very still. (_____)

8. Is your sequence smooth when you do it? Or are there some jerky parts in it that don't seem to go well? You might want to change some of the movements if there are. (_____)

Other things you can do:

9. Try changing the speed of the sequence. Start very quickly and end slowly, or start slowly and end quickly.
10. Change the place you get on the equipment. Approach it from the other side or from one end.
11. Add another balanced shape to the other two on the apparatus.
12. Finish your sequence with a roll and balance after you have landed from the equipment.

Culminating Module

Objectives

As a result of the learning experiences over time, children will be able to:

1. work with a partner in performing movement sequences
2. work with a partner in performing sequences on a given piece of apparatus
3. compose a sequence of movement that travels from one piece of apparatus to another.

Materials

An instrument for signaling "finish what you are doing." Designated equipment, such as mats, low balance beams, hanging bars, boxes, jungle gym, etc.

FIGURE 8-22 Timing the sequence takes practice to achieve simultaneity

Learning Experiences

Teachers may want to use a demonstration of the previous work on the learning centers before going on to work with partners. This allows an opportunity to reinforce good points about the composition or unusual combinations of movements in the sequence. Such reinforcement will provide guidelines for the children to continue working. The instructions are applicable to tasks 1 and 2. For task 3, the teacher needs to add some comments about using two pieces of apparatus.

"You have been working at your own learning centers making up sequences. Each person's sequence was different from the rest. Now, we are going to work with another person in making up a sequence. You have worked with partners before, so you know that you have to talk together to decide what movements you are going to use in your sequence. Your sequences must begin and end at the same time, and they must use the same movements in them, but you do not have to travel in the same direction all the time. For example, you can do your sequence opposite each other, or meeting and parting. Start as soon as you are ready."

FIGURE 8-23 Timing the sequence takes practice to achieve simultaneity

Learning Experiences

Task 1. Children can perform movement sequences without apparatus, where they focus on a particular movement aspect:

". . . showing a change of speed in your sequence."

". . . using a change of levels in your sequence."

Task 2. This is similar to Task 1, but the children must work on and about a given piece of apparatus, e.g., the balance beam, hanging bars; ropes, overhead ladder.

Task 3. This is the most complex task of all: children must work together, moving from one piece of apparatus to another. (There is rarely enough apparatus or space for an entire class to do this simultaneously, so this would be suitable for a learning station activity.)

This module should provide more individualized experiences for the children. The following suggestions can be given where appropriate. However, when suggestions *are* given, teachers need to stay with the task long enough to ensure that children begin to incorporate the suggestion or use an idea of their own that is appropriate.

a. to children who are not moving with control: "Try to show a balanced position in the middle and end of your sequence."
b. to children who are not challenging themselves: "Are there any other movements you can do that are different from everyone else's?" or "Can you work a cartwheel or handstand into your sequence?"
c. to partners or groups where there is a great disparity of ability: "The same movements can be done at different levels" (high and low balances).

FIGURE 8-24 Timing the sequence takes practice to achieve simultaneity

Learning Experiences

d. to children who lack variety in their sequences: "Can you show a quick change of direction in your sequence?"

It is often helpful to select certain children to demonstrate their sequences or to film them for later viewing and analysis. This is also a great motivator for children who tend to work half-heartedly at times.

Summary

Enabling Behavior: Increasing Complexity of Response

Children demonstrate increasing complexity of response when they:

1. Can travel in a greater variety of ways using different body supports, such as hands, hands and feet, shoulders and feet, knees.
2. Quickly vary the speed of their movement. They also should be able to manage themselves well when they move very fast or very slowly.
3. Are able to combine two or more concepts in a movement task.
4. Are able to compose sequences of movement that use more than three actions.
5. Compose sequences of movement that involve a variety of mounts and dismounts on one piece of apparatus.
6. Compose sequences of movement that involve more than one piece of apparatus.
7. Compose sequences of movement that involve at least one other person.

CHALLENGING ONESELF BEYOND COMFORTABLE LIMITS

Planning Guide

Objectives	*Experiences*
As a result of the learning experiences over time, children will be able to:	
1. demonstrate understanding of the effects of exercise on the body	• complete self-assessment to determine beginning and improved levels of physical fitness; choose goals for improving levels of physical fitness and select appropriate activities from those given; chart physical fitness progress

Objectives	*Experiences*

2. list the effects of varying degrees of exertion on circulatory and respiratory systems

3. demonstrate improved physiological performance.

- taking heart-rate of self and others before, during, and after selected activities, such as jogging, walking, and climbing stairs
- undertake systematic practice sessions in developing certain aspects of physical fitness; apply overload principle to activities designed to enhance muscular strength, endurance, and flexibility.

For evaluating students' progress in going beyond comfortable limits, see page 315.

Teaching Modules

Introductory Module

Objectives

As a result of the learning experiences, children will be able to:

1. assess their current level of cardiovascular efficiency
2. explain the terms "resting" and "working" heart/pulse rates
3. assess their own upper body strength and ability to support their own body-weight
4. assess their own degree of flexibility in the hips and spine.

Materials

An instrument for signaling "finish what you are doing." Writing materials for children to record their own scores. Charts for each child to record their results. Chinning bars or hanging bars for pull-ups or hanging. Sit and reach box for measuring flexibility.

Learning Experiences	*Related Experiences*

The assessment experiences (see page 270) that follow can be undertaken on separate days or at periodic intervals. If you are going to perform them all in one day, however, they should be done in the order suggested.

1. "Today, you are going to find out what your body can do. Your partner is going to help because it is important to be right about the measurements you take, and for some things it's easier for your partner to measure accurately than for you to do it your-

- Compare the amount of stretch in different kinds of elastic. Find out what makes the difference in the stretch.
- Build a model hinge joint to show how one muscle must stretch when another one contracts (action of biceps and triceps).
- Discuss confidentiality between lawyers and their clients, newspapermen and their sources, priests and their parishioners.
- Read about the Australian Aborigines and hypothesize about the kind of strength they need to live.

Learning Experiences

Related Experiences

self. The only scores you have to be concerned about are your own, because this is not a race nor a competition to see who is best. We are all the best, and our scores are private and confidential."

Some children will be competitive about their scores despite teachers' warnings, but this behavior can eventually be de-emphasized if teachers persist in their re-inforcement of self-assessing and model noncompetitive data keeping.

2. Demonstrate the flexibility test with one student:
   a. *sit and reach:* student sits and reaches toward and past toes and holds the po-sition for three seconds.

3. Demonstrate each strength test with one student:
   a. *push-up timed:* student maintains ½ push-up position for as long as possible:
   b. *pull-ups:* student grasps a bar that is high enough to allow him/her to hang with feet clear of the ground. "Chins" self on the bar as many times as possible:
       (The performance in the pull-up test is more affected by the child's body size and weight than other tests. A child who is exceptionally heavy or very tall will have more difficulty in this test than the timed pushup.)
   d. *bent-arm hang:* student holds self in position (fingers face forward on the bar) for as long as possible. Record time.

4. For this last self-assessment to be mean-ingful, you need to make sure that the chil-dren really can locate their pulse. The easiest place to detect it is on the right side of the throat under the jaw bone. "Everyone sit quietly and think of some-thing pleasant, a nice summer day, warm funny puppies, Christmas presents, soft snow. . . ." Try to have them remain quiet for at least a minute. "Now, open your eyes and find your pulse. Be ready to start counting when I say Go!"

- Make a list of twenty words that mean "strong." Make another list for "weak."
- Read about the suits of armor and the swords that were used in medieval times.
- What do they tell you about the height, weight, and strength of the men of those times?
- Hold a discussion about why women need to be strong.
- Check your pulse rate after:
    - climbing a flight of stairs
    - doing fifty jumping jacks
    - doing 100 jumping jacks
    - waking up in the morning
    - standing up after lying down.
- Investigate the heart and how it works. Write an illustrated report of what you find out.
- Compute how many times an hour *your* heart beats. Multiply the number by twenty-four to see how many times per day it beats.
- Trace a molecule of oxygen from the air, into the bloodstream, and back into the air again. Find out why the heart is associated with love.
- Make a repeating design that could be printed on material for blouses or shirts us-ing hearts and red blood cells.

Learning Experiences

It is not easy to obtain a reliable resting heart rate. Intermediate grade children could easily time their own pulse rate, if the classroom clock has a second hand. They can also take it for fifteen seconds and multiply the number by four. Primary children who are not very advanced in math, however, can count it for the entire sixty seconds or for thirty seconds and double the number.

"Now, we are going to find out how our hearts work harder when we exercise." You can select one or both of the following tests. Activity 1 is probably a more reliable indicator of cardiovascular efficiency and is suitable for administration to larger groups.

Activity 1: Mark a running track with cones or flags that divide the total distance into equal segments (e.g., fourths, eighths). "See how many times around the track you can run or jog in five, fifteen, or twenty minutes." Whichever time is selected, the same time is used in the post test. Record the number of total laps and portions of the last lap. The amount of time selected depends on the situation. Thirty minutes would mean that one entire physical education class would probably be spent in the assessment, whereas fifteen minutes means that partners can help count the runners' laps. It is easy to lose count in this test, which affects the accuracy of the test.

Activity 2: "Beginning on the Go! signal, see how long you can run continuously without walking." This activity does not require a designated track, but children should be instructed to remain in sight of the teacher or the partner who is monitoring the time. It can also be quite time consuming, since some children are capable of running up to forty-five minutes continuously. Some children will start off at a hectic pace, while others will jog in a leisurely manner. Children should be told to set a "middle speed" for themselves.

Related Experiences

- Get permission from your parents to interview some of their friends about how much exercise they get each day or each week.
- Investigate the foot journeys of famous travelers and explorers, and calculate the miles they walked.
- Make a collage of famous marathon runners.
- Find out why a marathon is 26 miles 385 yards long.
- Hold a discussion on why the heart "pounds" before a race or contest.
- What is the "fight or flight" syndrome?
- Read stories about how the heart works.
- Look up why we need rest.
- Find out what adrenalin does in the body.

Learning Experiences

5. "As soon as you have finished running, check your pulse rate for a whole minute. Record your heart rate and check it again after another five minutes." This will give the "working" heart rate, and the check on the second heart rate will indicate how quickly the heart "recovers" to the resting rate.

FIGURE 8-25 "How long can I run without stopping?"

Central Module

Objectives

As a result of the learning experiences over time, children will be able to:

1. set their own goals for physical performance in one or more areas
2. chart their own progress in the activities provided
3. work independently to improve performance in a desired area.

Initially, children need "monitoring" while working independently. Intermittent "visits" by the teacher to the learning center help with motivation problems and with generating and maintaining a "working" atmosphere where on-task behavior is rewarded.

Materials

Instructions, written or tape recorded, for learning centers.

Learning Center: Activities that will make you more flexible

Objective: When you have worked with these activities for at least four weeks, you will be able to reach further than you can now.

Equipment you will need: A wooden or newspaper stick; a yarn ball, newspaper ball, or paper bag.

What to do first:

1. Find a space for yourself to work. You won't need much room.
2. Toss the yarn ball a little way away from you. Without moving *your feet,* stretch out to pick up the ball with your hand, and come back to a standing position.
3. Do this five times, putting the ball in five different places.
4. Stand with your feet apart, and drop the ball in front of you. Bend down and pick it up with your teeth. If you find this easy, do it without using your hands to balance!
5. Lie down with your back on the floor and place the ball on the floor by your head. Push up into an arch position and move so the ball is between your hands and feet.
6. Take the stick with both hands and try to jump over it without letting go.
7. Step through the stick and try to bring it up behind you and over your head to start all over again.
8. Sit with legs straight out and try to place the stick behind the feet, holding it with both hands.

Check these things: (✔)
9. Are you doing everything at least five times? (＿＿)
10. When you are bending down to pick up the ball, are you keeping your knees straight from the time you touch the ball? (＿＿)
11. Every week, check to see if you can reach further.

Other things you can do:
12. "Walk" backwards down the wall every day until you can reach the floor.
13. Practice arching up from the floor in Number 5.
14. See how far you can "walk" your hands out in front of your feet, then, keeping your knees straight, walk your feet up to your hands.
15. Lie on the floor and find all the places you can reach with both feet behind your head.

Learning Center: Activities to make you stronger

Objective: When you have worked on these activities for four weeks, you will be able to support yourself on your hands for much longer than you do now.

Equipment you will need: None.

What to do first: Check your score from the self test. This is the test you will use once a week to see how you are progressing.

Next:
1. Find a wall that you can put your feet on so that you take all your weight on your hands like this:

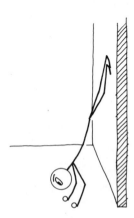

FIGURE 8-26

2. Stay in that position as long as you did on the test. Then bring your feet down and rest your arms while you count to twenty-five.
3. Get back up in the position again and try to hold it as long as you did on the test.
4. When it is easy to hold the position two times as long as the test, take another rest and try for three times. Do this every day for a week. Write down how long you can hold the position at the end of the week.
5. Next week, work with a partner and see how far you can wheelbarrow walk. Don't try to go fast. When you get tired, take a rest while you count to twenty-five and try again. Measure how far you can "walk."
6. Give your partner a turn.
7. Do this every day for this week, trying to walk further each day. At the end of the week, test yourself by the "feet on the wall" test.
8. Next week, see how many push-ups you can do. Have a partner check to see that your body stays straight. Write down how many you can do, and talk about how you felt right after doing the push-ups.

Check these things: (✔)

9. Are you thinking only about what *you* can do? Remember you don't have to worry about what other people are doing. (_____)
10. You can change the activity by doing some of the things suggested below. (_____)
11. If you are not getting any stronger, check with your teacher. You may be doing something that is not helpful or you may not be measuring the same area of your body.

Other things you can do:

12. Hanging or swinging by your hands on the bars.
13. Walking on your hands.
14. Going across the horizontal ladder using your hands.
15. Clap your hands between each push-up.
16. Do your push-ups with your feet on a chair.

Learning Center: Activities to make your heart stronger

Objective: When you have worked through these activities, you will be able to run much further or for much longer than you can now.

Equipment you will need: A watch with a second hand or stop watch; a space to run in.

What to do first: Stretch like a cat before you start to run. Try to bend and stretch every joint in your body. If it is a cold day, swing your arms and do some little jumps as well.

Next:

1. Look at how far you ran on the day you did the self-test.
2. Set yourself a number of laps that you would like to jog today. Make it at least two more than the test.
3. Check the time you start and the time that you finish. Take your pulse and record it, too.
4. Walk around while you count to thirty. Now, see if you can jog one more lap. You may even feel you can do two more. Do them if you feel like it.
5. Check your heart rate when you finish the other laps.
6. Stretch your leg muscles by letting yourself hang down with your hands near your feet. Do this two or three times, then find a wall and lean forward keeping your body straight and your heels on the ground like this:

FIGURE 8-27

7. If you can tell time, check your heart rate after two minutes and record it.
8. Do these activities every other day, or on Mondays, Wednesdays and Fridays at school. Make sure you put down your scores and your heart rate. Do it for four weeks and then compare the two sets of scores and heart rates.
9. If you are finding it too easy to run, set your goals higher or run faster.

Check these things: Place a check (✔) when you have done the task.

10. Is your jogging light and springy? Or slow and heavy? Try singing a song you like that will fit your jogging. (_____)
11. Are you perspiring fairly soon after you start? Try to run fast enough so that you will begin to perspire after about seven or eight minutes. (_____)

Other things you can do:
12. Jog with a friend or a small group. Sometimes it helps you to jog further if you run with other people.
13. If it is raining or snowing, jump rope, like a boxer does when he trains.
14. For a change, play some music and put in some other steps when you run.
15. Try jogging in different directions and pathways, or while playing catch, or kicking a tennis ball.

Culminating Module

Objectives

As a result of the learning experiences over time, children will be able to:

1. describe in a verbal or written form the differences in their performance from the initial self-assessment
2. show evidence of improved performance in cardiovascular efficiency, upper body strength, and flexibility of hamstrings and spine.

The same conditions of the pre-test must be present for the post-test. The post-test should be given at the same time of day that the pre-test was given.

Summary

Enabling Behavior: Challenging Oneself Beyond Comfortable Limits

Children are improving in their ability to go beyond comfortable limits when they:

1. Actively seek tasks that require pyschological persistence and physical endurance, such as jogging or swimming for distance.
2. Demonstrate improvement in physiological performance, e.g., if they can run for longer periods of time or perform more push-ups or sit-ups as a result of practice sessions.
3. Can explain the concept of setting both short and long range goals for self-improvement, as opposed to meeting a single standard of performance that may be too difficult or too restricting for the individual.
4. Can work independently to improve their performance in a movement activity.

ENDNOTES

1. Lolas E. Halverson, "Development of Motor Patterns in Young Children," *Quest* VI (May 1966): 50.
2. Shirley J. Winters, *Creative Rhythmic Movement for Children of Elementary School Age* (Dubuque, Iowa: William C. Brown, 1975), p. 52.
3. Halverson, "Development of Motor Patterns in Young Children,": 51–52.
4. Newsletter (Washington, D.C.: President's Council on Physical Fitness and Sports, April 1976), p. 4.
5. Herbert A. deVries, *Physiology of Exercise for Physical Education and Athletics* (Dubuque, Iowa: William C. Brown, 1974), pp. 228–29.
6. Ibid., p. 228.
7. Kenneth H. Cooper, *Aerobics* (New York: M. Evans, 1968).
8. ———, *The New Aerobics* (New York: Bantam Books, 1970).
9. Mildred Cooper and Kenneth H. Cooper, *Aerobics for Women* (New York: Bantam Books, 1973).
10. D. W. Edington and Lee Cunningham, *Biological Awareness: Statements for Self-Discovery* (Englewood Cliffs, N.J.: Prentice-Hall, 1975).
11. Robert F. Mager, *Preparing Instructional Objectives* (Palo Alto, Calif.: Fearon, 1962), p. 12.
12. Layne C. Hacket, *Movement Exploration and Games for the Mentally Retarded* (Palo Alto, Calif.: Peek, 1970), p. 4. By permission of Peek Publications, Palo Alto, Calif. 94303.
13. Robert N. Singer, *Motor Learning and Human Performance,* 2nd ed. (New York: Macmillan, 1975), p. 46.
14. T. R. McConnell, "Reconciliation of Learning Theories," *The Forty-First Yearbook of the National Society of the Study of Education, Part 2 Psychology of Learning,* ed. N. B. Henry (Chicago: University of Chicago, 1942), p. 271.

15. Loretta M. Stallings, *Motor Skills Development and Learning* (Dubuque, Iowa: William C. Brown, 1973), pp. 122–23.
16. Robert N. Singer, *Motor Learning and Human Performance,* p. 421.
17. Stallings, *Motor Skills Development and Learning,* p. 129.
18. Kate R. Barrett, "We See So Much But Perceive So Little—Why." A paper presented at the NAPECW-NCPEAM Conference, Orlando, Florida, January 1977; Lolas E. Halverson, "Development of Motor Patterns in Young Children," pp. 32–33, and Jack Keough, "Development in Fundamental Motor Tasks" in a *Textbook of Motor Development,* ed. Charles B. Corbin (Dubuque, Iowa: William C. Brown, 1973), pp. 72–73.
19. Daryl Siedentop, *Developing Teaching Skills in Physical Education* (Boston: Houghton Mifflin, 1976), pp. 229–34. Reprinted by permission.
20. Robert N. Singer, *Myths and Truths in Sports Psychology* (New York: Harper & Row, 1975), pp. 67–68.
21. Ibid., p. 67.
22. Beverly L. Seidel, Fay R. Biles, Grace E. Figley, and Bonnie J. Neuman, *Sports Skills: A Conceptual Approach to Meaningful Movement* (Dubuque, Iowa: William C. Brown, 1975), pp. 112–13, 285–87, 505–508.
23. Muska Mosston, *Teaching Physical Education* (Columbus, Ohio: Charles E. Merrill, 1966), pp. 43–58.
24. Robert V. Hockey, *Physical Fitness,* 2nd ed. (St. Louis, Mo.: C. V. Mosby, 1973), pp. 182–83.
25. Perry B. Johnson, Wynn F. Updyke, Maryellen Schaefer, and Donald C. Stolberg, *Sport, Exercise and You* (New York: Holt, Rinehart and Winston, 1975), pp. 89–91.
26. Ibid., pp. 96–102.
27. Ibid., pp. 102–103.
28. *AAHPER Youth Fitness Test Manual,* rev. ed. (Washington, D.C.: American Alliance for Health, Physical Education, and Recreation, 1976).
29. Kenneth Cooper, *The New Aerobics,* p. 30.

chapter nine

Drawing Relationships

ABOUT CHILDREN

The learning environment must be planned to stimulate development of the whole child. While teachers may emphasize learning in one domain (cognitive, psychomotor, affective), the learning environment must be carefully designed and all aspects of the child's development must be considered. This chapter presents the developmental theme, "Drawing Relationships: Comprehending the Significance of Movement in One's Lifestyle," and will focus on the development of knowledge and understanding in physical education; however, this emphasis on knowledge and understanding does not mean a de-emphasis on physical activity.

In the previous chapters which emphasized various movement forms, a variety of learning experiences were used, such as discussions, problem-solving situations, learning centers, and direct information-giving to assist the learner in reaching the desired behaviors. For example, while children were physically active to develop a basic movement pattern, they also were engaged in problem-solving activity designed to help them become aware of their own movement capabilities and concepts of spatial relationships.

Knowledge and Understanding in Physical Education

The importance of knowledge and understanding objectives in physical education is relative to the age of the child. Pre-school and primary grade children learn many basic concepts through their movement activities. Their physical interaction with the world around them is a necessary process in becoming aware and knowing about themselves and their environment. It is the actual physical experience of young children that gives meaning to much of their vocabulary. Knowledge and understanding of concepts of Space, Time, and Force are developed through planned physical experiences. As children mature, they become able to deal with abstract concepts without having to experience personally every situation. Many intermediate grade children are able to solve movement problems by applying their knowledge of concepts and by cognitively planning their movements before making any physical attempts to solve a movement problem. While young children need to experience vigorous running to know that they will "get out of breath," older children are capable of evaluating and selecting activities that will assist in the development of strength or cardiorespiratory endurance.

The ultimate purpose of teaching knowledges and understanding in physical education is to assist individuals in becoming responsible for their own movement behavior. To achieve this goal, students need to develop good body management skills and have opportunities to explore and develop selected sport and recreation skills. It is also important that students have physical experiences that help them discover the effects of physical activity on their bodies, that allow them to experience success, and that make them feel good about their movement ability. In addition to developing good physical skills and positive feelings about one's movement, knowledges and understandings are needed if students are expected to be responsible for their own movement behavior. While knowledge and understanding were not the primary focus of the previous chapters, each developmental theme will help children learn part of the "body of knowledge" in physical education. Table 9–1 summarizes the knowledge and understanding in each developmental theme.

Children need help in learning to make decisions about the role of movement in their lives. It is important to note that children are not motivated by what they will need to know and do when they are adults. Too frequently,

TABLE 9–1 Knowledges and Understandings in Each Developmental Theme

Chapter	Developmental Theme	Knowledges and Understandings
4	Becoming Aware: Learning about and Establishing Basic Movement Capabilities	Understanding how the body moves: locomotor movements, qualities of movement, axial movements, manipulative movements. Understanding where the body can move: spatial relationships, relationships to others and objects.
5	Becoming Independent: Increasing Self-Reliance and Confidence in Moving	How to be safe in moving: avoiding collisions, absorbing force, using force, using good judgment, making safe decisions, choosing between alternatives, creating alternatives.
6	Accepting and Expressing Feelings and Ideas: Communicating through Movement	Understanding how people feel and how to communicate through movement; how to create ideas.
7	Accepting Responsibilities and Acting Cooperatively: Sharing the Movement Environment and Respecting and Interacting Productively with Others	Understanding leadership and followership roles; understanding group and team activity; understanding why we have rules, what makes a good rule, and different kinds of rules; understanding the concepts of cooperation and competition.
8	Improving Quality of Response: Refining and Elaborating Movement Capabilities for a Purpose	Understanding the factors that contribute to effective movement; knowing what makes practice helpful in improving performance; understanding the components of physical fitness; knowing how to develop and maintain physical fitness; understanding the concept of progression in motor development.
9	Drawing Relationships: Comprehending the Significance of Movement in One's Lifestyle	Understanding the role of movement in developing healthful patterns of living; understanding environmental influences on movement; developing informed decision-making behavior.

teachers justify what they are teaching now by stating what students will need to know when they reach the next academic level. What is forgotten is that the skills, knowledges, and values which are important at the next level are based on the current developmental needs of students. The best way to get children ready for the next level is to attend to their current developmental needs. For children, the future is now.

The experience of the authors reveals that children enjoy learning "about" their physical activities as well as learning the activities themselves. They also enjoy learning about their bodies and understanding the effects of activity on them. For example, children may become frustrated when playing dodgeball if they can't get the players in the center "out." A guided discovery or problem-solving experience designed to help the children see the relationship between the size of the circle, number of balls used, and their own throwing ability can be enlightening for the children. They can learn how space is related to the level of difficulty of a game. With this knowledge, children should then have the opportunity to design their own versions of dodgeball. It is important for children to know and understand concepts regarding movement and to have opportunities to make decisions throughout the entire physical education curriculum.

BOX 9–1   The Physically Educated Person

Who is a physically educated person? Is it a person who knows and understands human movement? Or, is it a person who is physically fit and a good sports performer? Can a physically educated person make decisions about movements in daily activities as well as in specific movement forms, such as dance and sports?

Can you define a physically educated child, adolescent, or adult? Is a physically educated person one who knows that education is a process as well as a product, and that it never ends? Perhaps a review of the behaviors expressed in the titles of the developmental themes (Chapters Four through Nine) will assist you in answering the question, "Who is a physically educated person?"

Career and Consumer Education

Two contemporary curricular considerations are career education and consumer education. While some schools treat these topics as units of study, others view them as processes for making intelligent decisions about careers and consumer behavior. Knowledges and understandings learned in physical education are useful in both areas. For example, in career education, the physical requirements of the various occupations can be discussed. Less obvious, but equally important, is the need for children to understand that their daily physical habits affect their health and physical condition. The need to maintain good functional postures (e.g., sitting, standing, walking) is especially important in childhood. The work requirements of jobs also affect the physical health of people.

As children study the world of work, they become aware of the requirements for successfully pursuing various careers. Children in the intermediate grades can also begin to match their own abilities (including physical and motor abilities) with those of particular jobs. It is important for children to know, however, that their current physical status will not remain constant. They need to know that they can affect their own physical abilities by the decisions they make. The analysis of one's physical attributes is important in career education, just as is the analysis of other personal characteristics, such as one's aptitude for working with numbers or one's basic value system.

Career education may also explore the opportunities in physical education and related fields. The more commonly known jobs of the physical education teacher and recreation leader should be studied. Other jobs related to physical activity, such as adult exercise leader, athletic trainer, exercise physiologist, movement (motor-learning) scientist, or sports writer should be explored carefully.

Consumer awareness in the United States has led to the development of consumer education courses. While many consumer education programs are directed to adults, educators recognize that children need to know how to make intelligent consumer decisions. Each year in the United States, millions of dollars are spent on gadgets and programs that are virtually worthless in terms of their contributions to the physical fitness of the consumer. The adults who fall prey to fitness fads are usually the ones who never learned the basic facts of exercise physiology in their physical education programs in school. Intermediate grade children can learn to evaluate print and nonprint advertisements. They can discern the affective message from the facts in commercials and make decisions about the value of various products. Today's children must recognize that no equipment can exercise *for* them and that there is no such thing as an "instant" fitness program. Similar evaluations could be made regarding play equipment and nutrition if well-planned and conducted physical education experiences are begun in the elementary school program. For example, intermediate grade children could do comparative shopping for sports equipment and identify the best values.

Current Trends in Physical Education

Early childhood educators and physical educators have recognized the importance of movement in helping children learn a variety of basic concepts. There has been a recent emphasis on the use of active learning games to help children learn concepts in language, math, social studies, science, and the arts. Even more recently a trend toward teaching the "body of knowledge" in physical education has emerged. As schools became more concerned with teaching children how to think and solve problems in addition to mastering the basic skills, it was inevitable that the physical education curriculum would also include the How and Why of physical activity in addition to developing specific skills. A statement in a landmark publication of the American Alliance for Health, Physical Education, and Recreation, *Knowledge and Un-*

derstanding in Physical Education, indicates the shift from teaching only skills to teaching the body of knowledge as well.

> The need for teaching a body of knowledge in physical education appears indisputable, then, if the school accepts its responsibility to assist the individual to develop his potential, by giving him not only the skills but the background for knowing "how" and "why," so that he may continue to grow throughout his lifetime.[1]

The AAHPER publication contains information that is considered essential for children to learn in physical education. The book includes information on "Activity Performance," "Effects of Activity," and "Factors Modifying Participation in Activities and Their Effects." Basic facts and concepts are presented for students to learn at the elementary, junior high, and senior high school levels. A test with national norms is available to evaluate students' mastery of the knowledges and understandings in the book. The test measures remembering, understanding, and thinking.[2]

Children need to know and understand the body of knowledge so that they can make intelligent decisions regarding their own movement behavior. Two additional books implore teachers to help children become informed decision makers regarding their own lives. One emphasizes physical fitness, and the other book focuses on sports skills. Edington and Cunningham have written fifty-one statements, in understandable terms, regarding physical activity and human physiology.[3] They believe that people need to be able to make decisions regarding their bodies and they recommend teaching the concepts in a basic discovery method which involves the students in activities other than just listening and discussing. The process for learning and developing awareness is most important, according to the authors, if behavior is to be affected. They recommend increasing the emphasis on biological awareness from the early years to the later school years.

Seidel, Biles, Figby, and Neuman[4] are critical of physical education teaching that focuses only on specific sports skills. Their approach, while still activity-centered, emphasizes attention to cognitive and affective objectives. They present common concepts to be learned in physical education, categorized as Moving the Body Through Space, Moving an Object Through Space, Strategy, and Safety. The common concepts are presented separately, and then later are applied in specific sports. The goal is to have physically educated students rather than just physically trained students.

The trend toward teaching knowledges and understandings in physical education is quite clear. In addition to teaching specific facts, emphasis is being placed on helping children learn to use knowledge to solve movement problems and to make decisions regarding their own movement behavior. The emphasis on knowledge and understanding does not mean substituting inactive learning for the usual movement activities in physical education classes; but it does require some redirection of activity and careful planning to assure that the cognitive and affective objectives are attained.

ABOUT TEACHING

Areas of Study in Physical Education
The physically educated person is more than a skillful mover. Being physically educated means that a person can move well and purposefully, and that he/she has the knowledges and attitudes that provide an understanding of the factors facilitating and inhibiting movement and movement opportunities. The following three areas of study are essential to a physical education program.

Biomechanics

Biomechanics, in part, focuses on the laws and principles of physics that govern the movement of objects. The mechanics of human movement are subject to these natural laws and are regulated and modified by them. The laws of movement are appropriate for children in the intermediate grades to experience, to study, and to apply in their own movements. In Table 9–2, Newton's Laws, an explanation of these laws, an application of each law to physical activity, and learning experiences for students to complete are given as examples of how to help students understand and draw relationships concerning factors that facilitate or inhibit their movements.

Physiology of Exercise

From the area of physiology of exercise, a unit of study can be developed around an examination of the benefits of regular exercise for one's health and well-being. Johnson, Updyke, Schaefer, and Stolberg summarized the benefits of a regular exercise routine as follows:

1. can result in a greater positive physiological adaptation to exercise
2. can increase your ability to perform certain emergency physical tasks
3. can increase your endurance for specific tasks
4. can increase the functional capacity and health of your circulatory-respiratory systems
5. can increase your protection against low-back disorders
6. can contribute to effective weight reduction or weight maintenance
7. can increase your flexibility and muscle, tendon, and ligament strength
8. may increase your efficiency of daily living or for specific tasks
9. will *not* afford you *certain* protection against infectious diseases
10. may provide a sort of cross-resistance to stress
11. may very well exert one of its most meaningful and most empirically consistent influences—an improved quality of life
12. will *not* guarantee you an increase in the length of your life
13. *can* enhance normal growth and development of children and adolescents

14. *may* help delay or decelerate the physiological aging process
15. will *not* necessarily result in greater relaxation
16. can be used in therapy and rehabilitation programs for various diseases and disorders
17. *can* increase the tensile strength of the load-bearing bones, making them less susceptible to breakage.[5]

TABLE 9–2 Understanding Newton's Laws of Motion

Law	Explanation	Application	Experience
1. *Law of Inertia:* A body at rest will remain at rest and a body in motion will remain in motion at the same velocity unless acted upon by an external force.	Inertia is the resistance of an object to change its status of motion. A force, a push, or a pull is required to initiate or cease motion. Inertia is directly proportional to mass, the gravity of matter. The pull of gravity on the mass of an object results in the weight of the object. It requires less force to maintain inertia than to overcome inertia.	Gravity, air or water resistance, and friction act to resist motion and can be used to aid or hinder movement. It is easier to run through air than through knee-deep water, and easier at a high altitude than at sea level, for a short distance. A jogger should maintain a steady pace rather than vary the speed of running.	*Discussion:* Comparing gravity on the earth and on the moon—if the same force was applied to an object, where would it travel the farthest, on the moon or on earth? *Laboratory:* Measure the distance after running for four minutes at a steady pace and compare it to the distance travelled by running alternately slow and fast for four minutes.
2. *Law of Acceleration:* The acceleration of an object that is acted upon by a force is directly proportional to the force and inversely proportional to the mass of the object.	The more force applied to an object, the faster it will travel. If the same force is applied to a small light ball and a heavy ball, the small ball will accelerate faster.	Momentum is the product of an object's mass times its velocity (rate of motion). Velocity is the measure of the distance an object is moved in a specific time and is expressed as a rate of movement. Acceleration is increasing velocity, whereas decreasing velocity is negative acceleration or deceleration.	*Laboratory:* Measure the distance you can throw a tennis ball with a slow throwing motion as compared to a movement twice as fast. *Discussion:* Which type of bat can be swung the fastest: a light aluminum bat, or a heavy wooden bat (force and all other things equal)? Which bat swing will have the greatest momentum: a) a light aluminum bat traveling very fast; b) a heavy wooden bat traveling fast; c) both are the same. Explain your answer.

TABLE 9–2

Law	Explanation	Application	Experience
3. *Law of Action-Reaction:* For every action there is an equal and opposite reaction.	When a person pushes a heavy object, the feet—which are the point of contact with the ground—are resisted by the reaction of the ground. The individual can apply pushing force because cf this reaction.	While the friction provided by snow, mud, or sand is greater than a gym floor, the stability of the gym floor allows a greater reaction and generation of force to occur.	*Laboratory:* Measure the distance of a standing long jump when you push a) lightly, b) hard against the ground to jump. Explain your answer. What happens? *Discussion:* Which surface provides the best footing: snow, mud, or sand, as compared to packed dirt, gymnasium flooring, or grass? Explain your answer. What happens when you run on any of these surfaces with un-cleated as compared to cleated shoes? Explain your answer.

Learning activities for students working with this list of benefits of regular exercise could include: 1) experiences doing library research to find facts that provide support for each statement, 2) classifying statements according to the body system or lifestyle factor to which they relate, 3) studying the function of body systems and lifestyle factors, such as diet, rest, alcohol, and drugs as related to the effects of regular exercise, 4) interviewing family members, adults, and children as to their physical activity practices and opinions regarding the benefits of regular exercises.

A personal participation experience can be used either for the basis of a teacher-directed lesson or a learning center activity. The topic of study could be physiology of exercise, and one of Edington and Cunningham's biological awareness statements could be the focus of the experience. The experience can help students learn concepts and facts relating to exercise, body weight, and energy, and the interrelationship among these elements for healthy living.

An example of a biological awareness statement and the steps for students to follow in a personal participation experience follows:

Statement 10: There is an increase in the amount of energy needed to exercise when the body is overweight.

Introduction: Excess weight serves as an extra load when any physical activity is performed. Studies have shown that there is an increase in the amount of energy needed to perform most tasks, whether the type of obesity is spontaneously developed (by overeating) or produced experimentally.

This experiment simulates a twenty-pound weight gain in each student. The measurement of heart rate is used to predict energy cost.

Procedure:
1. Have the student take a resting heart rate by palpating the carotid artery. This is probably the most efficient location for the taking of an exercise heart rate. Proper instruction in the use of this technique will facilitate ease of obtaining accurate data.
2. The students should then step up and down on a bench, bleachers, stairs, or chair for one minute at a cadence of thirty steps per minute (one step is defined as: up with the left foot, up with the right foot, down with the left, and down with the right). A metronome set at 120 beats per minute helps in this exercise. Upon the completion of one minute of stepping, the student should immediately take a ten-second pulse count as previously explained. This pulse count, when multiplied by six, will give a reasonable approximation of the exercise heart rate per minute.
3. The student should rest until the heart rate has returned to within five beats of the original resting rate before proceeding to the next section of this experiment.
4. Repeat the step test with a backpack loaded with twenty pounds of weights. Take the heartbeat rate (HR) at the completion of the test as previously described.
5. Chart the results.

	Resting HR	Exercise HR
Normal Body Weight	_____	_____
Experimental Obesity	_____	_____

Teaching Methods: Performance Objective—The students should be able to observe the effects of experimental obesity on the responses of the cardiovascular (CV) system, and indirectly on energy expenditure related to an exercise task.

Teaching Hint—For best results, the students should complete at least two trials of the normal condition and two of the experimental conditions. Mean scores of the two conditions are important for discussion purposes.

Discussion:
1. Account for the response of the CV system to the normal weight and to the increased-weight condition.
2. List two possible reasons for maintaining normal body weight.

3. What percent weight gain was the added twenty pounds for each student?

$$\% \text{ Weight Gain} = \frac{20 \text{ lbs.}}{\text{Actual Body Weight}} \times 100$$

4. Does exercise in an overweight person require more energy? In terms of weight reduction, can exercise play a significant role in an overweight individual?

Materials:
   1. Packs
   2. Twenty pounds of weights
   3. Metronome
   4. A stepping bench[6]

While the experience does include some technical terms (palpate, carotid artery, heartbeat rate), these terms can be taught to students as the material is studied. The prerequisite skills needed to complete this lesson do not present any major obstacles for instruction and learning.

The carotid artery can be palpated or felt beating by pressing the fingers lightly against the side of the neck. The teacher should demonstrate the procedure in the classroom, aid each student to find the carotid artery, and develop confidence in taking ten-second counts, which are then multiplied by six (6) to compute the heart rate per minute.

The weight load used in the lesson can be reduced to ten pounds; however, the effects of lighter load exercise trials should not be compared or combined with heavier load exercise trials. The discussion and mathematical calculation are important parts of this experience. They can be conducted in the classroom with data recorded during the laboratory learning experience.

Movement Philosophy and Aesthetics

The AAHPER book, *Knowledge and Understanding in Physical Education,* presents concept statements with information appropriate for elementary, junior, and senior high school level students. These concepts can be correlated with active participation laboratory experiences, or used to stimulate discussion. An example in the area of movement philosophy and aesthetics is the study of the role and importance of physical activity in a culture.

Concept: Physical education experiences help students understand dance, games, sports, and athletic programs that are a part of their culture as well as other cultures.

Elementary Level: The more one participates in the various physical activity programs of a culture, the more at home he is in the culture.

BOX 9–2 Discovering the How and Why of Jogging and Cross Country Running[8]

How should my foot strike the ground? (Check one) _____ a. heel first; _____ b. toe first; _____ c. flat-footed.

Try each, but only at a slow speed. Which produces the most jarring and pounding run? A pounding, jarring run can cause injuries to the arch of the foot and leg.

Answer: Have the heel contact first and let the weight roll on to the ball of the foot.

Where should you run? (Check one) _____ a. on a paved road; _____ b. in a sandy bumpy field; _____ on grass field.

While you take extra caution on wet, icy, or slippery surfaces, you must also consider safety factors related to the evenness of the supporting surfaces and objects that you might run into or that might run into you.

Answer: A smooth, safe place is usually a grassy field. In some cases, a running track or low traffic level road are available. If possible, find a pleasant relaxing environment for running or jogging.

What should I wear? After reading the following paragraph, list equipment which you think you should wear when you jog in your own geographical area.

Do you need to dress for very cold, cold, cool, warm, or a very warm climate? Is the wind a factor? Which do you think will provide a better cushion for the feet when running: with or without socks? with or without jogging or running shoes? with or without spikes or cleats?

_____

_____

Answer: You should dress according to temperature and in clothing that allows ventilation (zippers, space for air circulation), a pair of socks, and running or jogging shoes (without cleats or spikes) for running on any type of surface.

When should I run? (Check each correct answer.)

_____ wait at least fifteen minutes after eating a meal or drinking more than sixteen ounces of water.
_____ right away after drinking a little water, if you want to.
_____ after you warm up by stretching, bending, twisting, and slow jogging in place.
_____ when it's comfortable.

Sometimes you'll want to run in the morning, afternoon, or even in the evening. While it is safer to run with one or more other people, sometimes you might want to go it alone. But you always need to follow good health and safety practices and tell your parents where you are going.

Answer: All of the answers stated above are true and correct.

How fast should you make your heart beat each minute while jogging?

To find the answer, you need to answer the questions by following the corresponding steps below.

1. What was the maximum heart rate for your age group?

Find the maximum heartbeat per minute for your age on the chart and write it in the column labeled Answer. (example: A 10-year-old boy would write 211.)

Age	Boys	Girls	Answer
4-6	203	204	
7-9	208	211	
10-11	211	209	(211)
12-13	205	207	
14-15	203	202	
16-18	202	206	
19-25	194	198	

2. What was your resting heart rate?

Now count your own resting heartbeat for 10 seconds, and multiply by six. Do this by holding your fingertips to the large "carotid" artery in your neck. (example: If your heart beats 12 times in 10 seconds, multiply 12 × 6. Your resting heartbeat is 72.)

(72)

3. What is the difference between line 1 and 2?

Subtract your resting heartbeat from your maximum heartbeat.

(3) = _____

211
−72
(139)

4. What is the product of line 3 multiplied by .6?

Multiply the answer above by .6
(4) = _____

×.6

(83.4)

5. What is the sum of line 4 plus your resting heart rate?

Add your resting heartbeat to the new balance in 4.
    This is your aerobic heart rate.
(5) = _____

72
+83.4
(155.4)

Physical education is one medium by which education achieves its responsibility to perpetuate society's culture.

If the selection of activities includes activities of other cultures, physical education can be used as an instrument of intercultural understanding.

In all human societies, rituals, festivals, dance, sport, and games are among the activities that provide outlets for creativity and reinforce national feelings.

Junior High Level: The areas of dance, games, sports, and athletics are used to attain national and international goals and to promote greater understanding among people.[7]

The main concept provides the idea for the discussion of this topic. If students have had experiences with activities from their culture and activities from other cultures, then the discussion can lead to drawing the concluding statements presented above.

As a result of learning experiences, such as the three presented in this section, children can discover the mechanics of movement, practices related to nutrition, weight control and exercise, and the social and personal meaning of movement. Becoming physically educated; developing a physically active lifestyle; and learning to understand, appreciate and value movement are important educational outcomes.

Decision Making

Being physically educated means, in part, that the individual can make decisions concerning the place of movement in his/her lifestyle as a way of finding meaning, health, and joy. These decisions are too important to be left to chance and should become part of the school curriculum.

People make hundreds of decisions every day. Some decisions are made on the spur of the moment, while others are based on thoughtful consideration. A decision can be made by flipping a coin or by using a series of steps that constitute a decision-making process. Each of these arrangements for making a decision has its place. For example, one might flip a coin to decide who will have the first attempt at a task, whereas a decision-making process would be used to decide what type of tennis racket a beginning player should purchase. The key to which approach should be used is the significance, importance, or impact of the decision on the people directly and indirectly involved. When the consequences of a decision are crucial, then it becomes more important to use a thoughtful decision-making approach.

The Decision-Making Process

There are many different decision-making processes that can be used by elementary school students. The following decision-making process not only helps students to solve problems by making decisions, but it also teaches them to evaluate decisions and the process used to arrive at that choice.

Step	*Outcome*
1. Define the problem	a. concise statement of the problem b. state limits of problem c. list objectives to be reached
2. Find relevant data	a. identify what information is needed b. identify information sources c. establish a means for interpreting, organizing, and presenting the information

3. List alternatives and trade-offs	a. use the brainstorming technique to generate a list of alternatives from the "far out" to the most conservative
	b. list the "what would happen if you decided to do this" for each alternative
	c. rate the alternatives in terms of:
	  • costs versus benefits
	  • probability of success
	  • feasibility
	  • long-term satisfaction

4. Data review	a. conduct a second look for new information b. reconsider facts that appear pertinent to the solution of the problem
5. Choice	Before announcing the decision, be able to state the: • reasons for your decision • criteria used in making the decision • risks expected • impact of the decision on yourself, others, and the environment
6. Re-evaluation of the decision and decision-making process after a short period of time[9]	Re-evaluation can provide helpful information whether the decision should be changed or whether it reinforces the belief that the decision was sound and the process was productive. After the passage of time, and after an effort has been made to implement the action required by the decision, the person should gain new knowledge or have broader experience that can be applied to the situation. A decision is rarely irreversible, and change can be viewed as a sign of personal growth and understanding.

Using a decision-making model, students can address a wide range of problems, such as consumer and lifestyle decisions. Consumer decisions are focused on goods and services. Personal decisions are the basic value decisions relative to How do I feel? What do I want to do? or What do I want to become?

Consumer Decisions

The American public spends billions of dollars on sporting goods, recreational equipment, and related purchases. Everyone, including elementary school age children, is a consumer of these goods and services. Today, children are making more buying decisions than ever before.

Consumer education helps people to understand their own buying habits—whether purchases are made on the basis of need or status; whether planned buying or impulse buying is their general practice; whether price or quality should be the main consideration in purchasing a product or service. In addition, consumer education has the goals of helping people understand:

1. product or service performance
2. warranties or guarantees
3. evaluating advertising and sales tactics
4. product safety

Consumer education should help students to know their rights and how to exercise these rights in order to avoid fraud, overpayment, inferior merchandise, and unsafe products. While consumer organizations and governmental agencies act as consumer advocates, it is ultimately up to the individual consumer to make the final decision.

Health, exercise, nutrition, sport, and recreation are areas that provide opportunities to study consumerism. The following exercises are concerned with evaluating advertising and rating product or service performance.

Exercise 1: Reading advertisements for sporting goods
   a. identify status/emotional sales pitch versus presentation of information;
   b. determine price related to value of product; What do sale price and regular list price mean, and what is the percent of markdown?
   c. determine availability of assistance with fitting and repairing the equipment.

Exercise 2: Comparative shopping to determine the quality of a product or service
   a. devise a list of questions to secure information;
   b. talk to sporting goods salespersons;
   c. do research for articles in consumer or sports magazines that rate items;
   d. list the factors that make a product cheap or expensive.

Personal Decisions

Simon stated that "Too often, the important choices in life are made on the basis of peer pressure, unthinking submission to authority, or the power of propaganda."[10] In decision making, one's values influence how one sorts out right from wrong and good from bad. Values can be learned, but not through moralizing by adults and not even through the process of modeling. The process of values clarification has potential for helping children to learn and demonstrate the valuing process. ". . . Values clarification tends to raise issues, to confront us with inconsistencies, to get us to sort out personal values. . . ."[11] "It is a methodology to help you make a decision, to act, to determine what has meaning to you."[12]

A value exists if it meets seven criteria. To be a value, it must be:

1. chosen freely
2. chosen from among alternatives
3. chosen after due reflection
4. prized and cherished
5. publicly affirmed
6. acted upon
7. part of a pattern that is a repeated action.[13]

Because having values is an aid to making decisions and taking appropriate action, it becomes important for teachers to help students identify and clarify the values they hold. Simon stated that "The person who has clarified his or her values will perform zestful, independent, consistent, and decisive 'acts of courage'—not necessarily dramatic, much publicized feats of heroism, but rather acts based on the courage to say what has to be said and do what needs to be done."[14]

Teachers can lead value growth games, devise written activities, and lead discussions to help students clarify their values. Two very useful references are Sidney B. Simon, *Meeting Yourself Halfway,*[15] and Merrill Harmin, Howard Kirschenbaum, and Sidney B. Simon, *Clarifying Values through Subject Matter.*[16] In the latter book, discussion and personal involvement tasks include topics, such as:

"List reasons why sports give you pleasure. What on your list do you feel best (second best, etc.) about?"

"In sports, there are some people who often feel left out or inadequate. What are some helpful things that might be done for such persons? What would not be helpful?"

"Rank the following in terms of importance to you: strength, agility, endurance, grace, coordination. Which abilities are you actively trying to improve, if any?"[17]

In *Meeting Yourself Halfway,* Simon gave explanations and examples for thirty-one values clarification strategies. These strategies can be adapted for use in contributing toward reaching the goals of the physical education program. Four of these strategies are:

1. "Am I someone who"[18]
   This activity has the student independently answer "Yes", "No" or occasionally "Maybe" to a set of questions. The questions are designed to help individuals know themselves.

Am I someone who . . .
a. likes to be alone
b. avoids work
c. is afraid to be alone in the dark
d. is suspicious of easy solutions

2. "A Matter of Pride"[19]

This exercise is an involvement in sharing and affirming before a small group of people what you have done which gives you satisfaction and pride. The experience can provide encouragement to do more things which make you feel proud and give examples to others of actions to take.

Some possible replies to the question—what are you proud about (what things that you have done make you feel proud?)
• being a good sport in the volleyball games
• helped someone do something that they never did before
• made an A on a test because I studied for a long time before the test date
• because I noticed the beautiful sky and flowers of spring

3. "Slice of Life"[20]

This activity is a log of how you spend your time. It is a record of a typical day, twenty-four hours. The slice of life provides insight into behavior and provides data for many specific discussions.

How much time do you spend
a. eating
b. sleeping
c. at school
d. doing homework
e. doing chores or a job
f. playing
g. watching television or listening to the radio or record player
h. with your family
i. with friends your age
j. doing other things (list and give time for each)

4. "Contracts with Myself"[21]

This is an action oriented strategy. Other activities have helped students to clarify their values and to better understand themselves. This activity is designed to stimulate self-improvement. The individual is to make a commitment or resolution to do, or begin to do, some specific action, and he/she has set a date for the accomplishment of this goal. An example of a contract is shown on next page.

I _____ have decided
　　　　　　　　Name

to _____

_____

_____

I have asked _____
　　　　　　　　　　　　　　Name
to ask me to show him/her what I have accomplished by

_____. I publicly state that I
　　　　　Date
will do my best to meet this contract and that I will take great
pleasure in reaching my goal.

_____   _____
Signature of person making   Signature of person
the contract.   holding the contract.

　　　When children experience activities such as those described in this
section, a start toward independence and self-responsibility has been made.
One of the recurring messages of the thematic approach is that becoming
physically educated is one part of becoming an educated and self-reliant
person. Experiences, such as those described, can be altered for use in other
content areas (science, health, social studies), but the process remains the
same—considered decision making.

　　　In addition to values clarification, students need to learn what is a healthful practice and what is a potentially harmful health practice. Smoking, medical use of drugs, high-risk forms of game and sport, and eating patterns and
habits are examples of meaningful topics of study. Two examples of issues
that involve children in the personal decision-making process are presented
here. The first issue is for pubescent elementary school female students, and
it concerns how physically active they should be during menstruation. The
second issue concerns the development of sound postural patterns, which
should receive recurring emphasis throughout the elementary grades.

Example 1

Issue: What information and experiences will help a girl decide how physically active to be during menstruation?

Concept: Physical activity has no negative effects on menstruation and possibly can be a positive influence during this time.

Facts:

1. Menarche, the occurrence of the first menstruation, occurs within a range of nine to sixteen years of age. The average age for temperate climates is between twelve and fourteen. Some girls will experience menarche during the elementary school years, and most will soon after the elementary school years.
2. There are individual differences in duration and intensity of menstruation among females of different ages and at the same age. Furthermore, differences may occur from one menstrual cycle to the next for the same person.
3. Physical activity participation in physical education and athletics neither favorably nor unfavorably alters the menstrual cycle; nor does it cure or aggravate dysmenorrhea.
4. Physical activity participation, including swimming and physical training, may occur during menses as a matter of individual preference. No female should be pressured into physical activity participation during menstruation if it is against her wishes. Participation should be an individual decision, based on her past experience with respect to the pleasantness and level of achievement to be expected during the menstrual period.
5. No negative effects on the reproductive system are consistently associated with activity participation. The possibility of trauma to body tissue is increased with body contact physical activity participation.[22] The American Medical Association Committee on Medical Aspects of Sports stated ". . . There is no medical or scientific rationale for restricting the normal female from participating in vigorous noncontact sports, and many reasons to encourage such participation."[23] Furthermore, the Committee ". . . endorses the concept of contact sports for girls, on girls' teams, when they are provided the same safeguards that apply to boys' contact sports programs, namely, an annual medical examination, adequate conditioning, proper coaching, capable officiating, and proper equipment and facilities."[24]

Experiential Learning Activities:

1. The student should keep a diary of the physical activities she engages in during a month, including a menses. Answer the following questions: What types of physical activities or sports, and at what frequency or intensity did you participate

(a) before, (b) during and (c) after menstruation? Did your activity level or type of participation increase or decrease and why? How often did you have any discomforts?

2. The student should continue her diary for at least two menstrual cycles. Did the cycles differ? Have you changed your physical activity pattern? If yes, how has it changed (increased or decreased)? Can you relate any differences in menses to increased or decreased physical activity pattern? If you have always decreased physical activity during menses, try to be more physically active the next time, and chart how you feel and the frequency of discomfort, if any. For example, how fast did you run the fifty-yard dash, and how long did it take to run a long distance (half mile or more)? How steady was a balance or dance routine?

3. Each girl is given a list of physical activities (i.e., soccer, archery, dance, swimming, gymnastics, racketball, volleyball, basketball, jogging) and is told to circle the activities she participates in during menses. The teacher uses the anonymous activity records and tallies the frequency of participation for the total group. Progressing from the most frequent or popular physical activity engaged in during menses, the students are asked to relate any necessary considerations while engaged in that activity.

4. Interview local, or when possible, state, national, or international female athletes concerning their physical activity participation and achievements during menses. It is always best for the teacher to make the necessary arrangements for the guest to visit the school and to hear in advance what message the guest will communicate. If the person cannot appear in person, she can be interviewed and an audio- or video-tape can be made for playback at another time.

Example 2

Issue: What information and experiences will help children to improve and maintain their posture.

Concept: Posture is the alignment of body segments relative to the pull of gravity, muscular tension, and skeletal structure of the body.

Facts:

1. Posture is one aspect of physical appearance that creates an impression on other people and has impact on one's sense of self-worth.

2. Posture means position. While the military service attention position (head up and back, chest out, shoulders back and straight, trunk erect, stomach flat, legs straight, feet placed heels close together, and front of the feet separated) is con-

sidered by many people to be a model for sound posture, it is only useful in describing posture while standing. Sound postures for sitting and writing or reading and running should also be defined.

3. When a standing person is viewed from behind, the body is in proper alignment when the head is centered over the shoulders, the shoulders and hips are horizontal, and the body is symmetrical.

4. When the body segments are balanced, a posture (position) can be held without undue tension or muscular fatigue.

5. Habitually poor posture can cause extensor muscles to lengthen with the result that it becomes progressively more difficult to regain posture without concentrated attention and remedial activities.

Experiential Learning Activities:

1. Have students work with the teacher, and later with a partner, to evaluate posture in a standing position using a posture rating checklist (see Figure 9–1[25]). Following the completion of the checklist, the teacher and/or students should discuss any areas of concern and positive postural practices.

2. Students can observe each other working at different locations around the school to identify furniture size, desk height, position of chalkboards, and lighting conditions that influence postural patterns.

3. A student can rate a partner's posture when the person is not aware that an assessment is being completed. Another technique is for a student to use the "freeze" signal to have a partner hold the posture they were in when the signal was given.

4. Photographs or videotape recordings can be made as students engage in class activities. Children can then identify sound and unsound postural positions.

5. Primary grade students can balance blocks to discover the effect of placing one segment off-center and other segments on-center.

6. Circle discussions can be held on topics, such as "If you were a school official concerned about good posture, what would you do to help students develop sound postural habits?" or "If your friends have poor posture when they are sitting, do you have to sit the same way to be liked by them?"

7. Practice relaxation techniques to feel muscle tension and relaxation and to begin to be able to feel "centered and uncentered" body segments.

Students can complete experiences such as these on their own and in consultation with a teacher, guidance counselor, health coordinator, or another student. The teacher must use sound judgment to guide the development and extent of group discussions on issues of a personal nature.

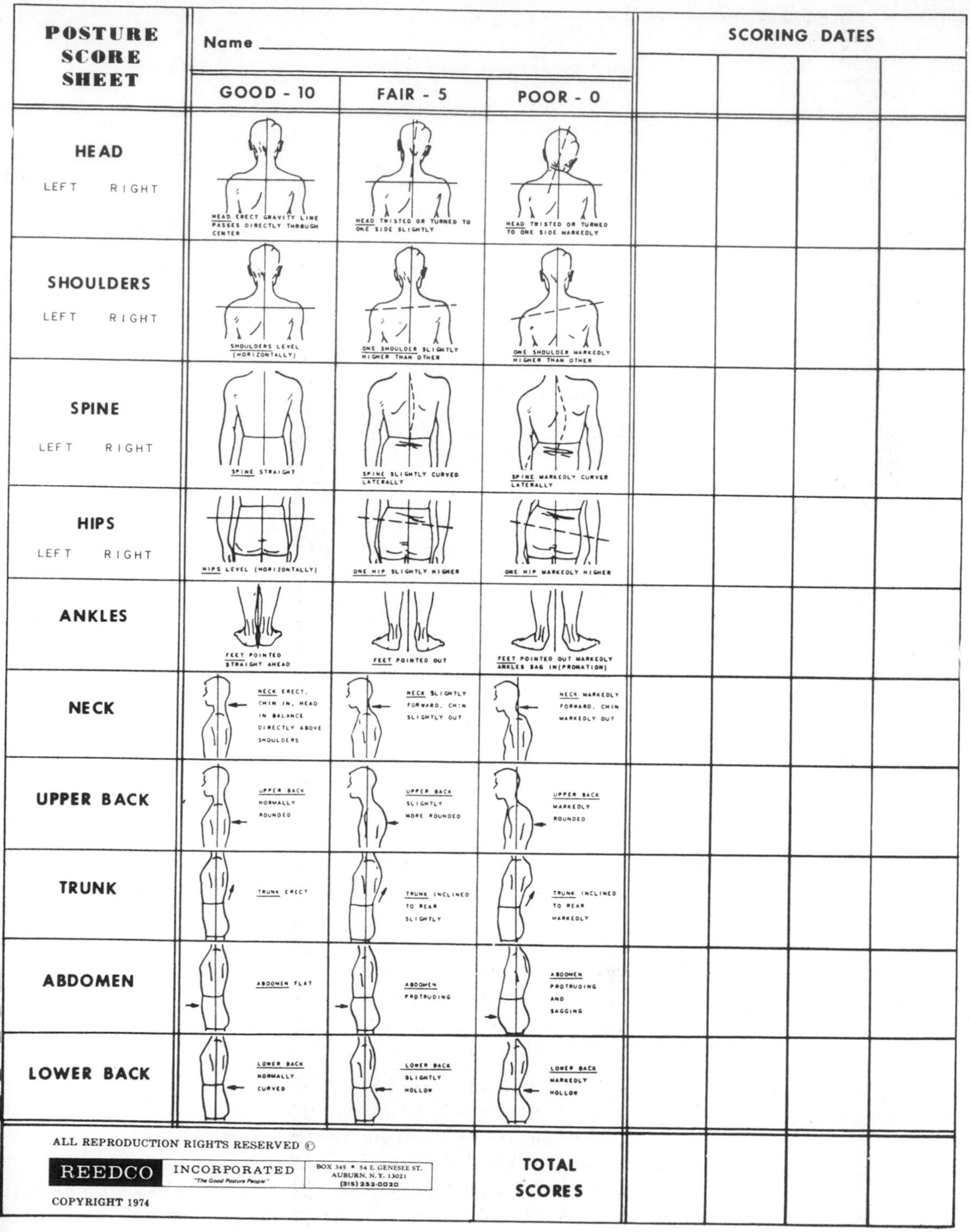

POSTURE SCORE SHEET	Name ______			SCORING DATES			
	GOOD - 10	FAIR - 5	POOR - 0				
HEAD LEFT RIGHT	HEAD ERECT GRAVITY LINE PASSES DIRECTLY THROUGH CENTER	HEAD TWISTED OR TURNED TO ONE SIDE SLIGHTLY	HEAD TWISTED OR TURNED TO ONE SIDE MARKEDLY				
SHOULDERS LEFT RIGHT	SHOULDERS LEVEL (HORIZONTALLY)	ONE SHOULDER SLIGHTLY HIGHER THAN OTHER	ONE SHOULDER MARKEDLY HIGHER THAN OTHER				
SPINE LEFT RIGHT	SPINE STRAIGHT	SPINE SLIGHTLY CURVED LATERALLY	SPINE MARKEDLY CURVED LATERALLY				
HIPS LEFT RIGHT	HIPS LEVEL (HORIZONTALLY)	ONE HIP SLIGHTLY HIGHER	ONE HIP MARKEDLY HIGHER				
ANKLES	FEET POINTED STRAIGHT AHEAD	FEET POINTED OUT	FEET POINTED OUT MARKEDLY ANKLES SAG IN (PRONATION)				
NECK	NECK ERECT, CHIN IN, HEAD IN BALANCE DIRECTLY ABOVE SHOULDERS	NECK SLIGHTLY FORWARD, CHIN SLIGHTLY OUT	NECK MARKEDLY FORWARD, CHIN MARKEDLY OUT				
UPPER BACK	UPPER BACK NORMALLY ROUNDED	UPPER BACK SLIGHTLY MORE ROUNDED	UPPER BACK MARKEDLY ROUNDED				
TRUNK	TRUNK ERECT	TRUNK INCLINED TO REAR SLIGHTLY	TRUNK INCLINED TO REAR MARKEDLY				
ABDOMEN	ABDOMEN FLAT	ABDOMEN PROTRUDING	ABDOMEN PROTRUDING AND SAGGING				
LOWER BACK	LOWER BACK NORMALLY CURVED	LOWER BACK SLIGHTLY HOLLOW	LOWER BACK MARKEDLY HOLLOW				
			TOTAL SCORES				

REEDCO INCORPORATED "The Good Posture People" BOX 345 • 54 E. GENESEE ST. AUBURN, N. Y. 13021 (315) 252-0020

FIGURE 9-1 Posture score sheet. © *1974 Reedco Incorporated*

IMPLEMENTING THE DEVELOPMENTAL THEME

This developmental theme constitutes the central tenet of the authors' philosophies regarding the goals of public education. Jerome Bruner[26] has stated that teaching children to draw relationships is possibly the single most important goal or outcome of any learning experience. The focus of many of the activities is a concern for the future well-being of the individual and how that future is related to, dependent on, and can be changed by present behaviors.

Developing Healthful Lifestyles

The concern for the future well-being of children is not new in physical education, but it has been notoriously difficult to act upon in any meaningful way. In many instances, the nature of the experiences in physical education has been counterproductive to the stated goal. For example, the "take a lap" form of punishment is not likely to enhance a student's desire to run for "fun and fitness." Yet, developing a love of aerobic activities such as cross country running, jogging, and rope skipping is a major contributor to engaging in these activities as part of a healthful lifestyle in the post-school life.

Many adults make poor choices of activities because they have not explored the information or had the necessary experience to make sound decisions. How many people really understand the concept of maintaining balance between the calories consumed and expended?

Self-Assessment

In this chapter, self-assessment is emphasized as a life-long learning tool that is viewed as a means of helping an individual to control her/his life patterns. Self-assessment, as it is presented here, includes the dimension of personal meaning of an experience. It is a form of values clarification, combined with projections or aspirations as to what the individual would like to do or become. There are millions of adults who, having experienced years of physical education in public school, demonstrate few positive results or changes in lifestyle. As a nation, there are too many people who are overweight, eat poorly, smoke, and drink too much alcohol, and who have settled into an inactive lifestyle. While all these ills cannot be laid at the door of physical education, they are very possibly the result of the lack of futurism in education in general.

Environmental Influences

There are many people who have little understanding of why heat, humidity, air pollution, or an impending thunderstorm affect their ability to function at an optimum level. Children can benefit from such knowledge and learn to become acclimated to the weather extremes that are relevant for them. For example, students who live in the sunbelt need more information about hot weather conditions than cold. Also, the heat/air conditioning of the average classroom can be detrimental to the child's desire to engage in vigorous activity under any conditions other than "good" conditions. It is appropriate for children to learn to adjust to weather conditions as much as possible, since there is little we can do to control it. Some of the learning experiences in the teaching modules focus on these topics.

The weather is just one influence on how we move; our cultural patterns are another. Physical education provides numerous opportunities for children to learn about their own and others' cultural patterns. However, teachers need to be wary of over-simplification and generalization. For example, folk dancing is frequently defended on the grounds that children will learn about other cultures, but unless the dances, their steps, patterns, and movements are accompanied by meaningful explanations relating them to that culture, it is unlikely that they will gain very much from the experience. Knowledge of the influences on the evolution of the dances is essential to making it a worthwhile activity.

Making Informed Decisions

In these teaching modules, children will take inventory of their competencies, they will compare the results of an opinionnaire with factual evidence, and they will make predictions about the consequences of changing some patterns of behavior and environmental variables. Children are rarely encouraged on a regular basis to assess themselves in any aspect of their school life. The competency checklist provided in the teaching modules may be extended to include many other aspects of the students' abilities and knowledges that teachers would like to include. Developing a sense of control over one's life includes some projecting of one's aspirations. Children need to know that present inability does not constitute future disability. At the same time, they need to learn that certain abilities must be mastered before they can move on to other, more complex activities.

In the past, an underlying assumption in physical education has been that exposure to and participation in physical activity were sufficient in and of themselves to bring about an awareness of the importance of a healthy physical body and the commitment to an active lifestyle as an adult. The trend is now toward a more pragmatic view that children need to "practice what *we* preach." In addition to positive physical activity experiences, children need to understand:

- how to manage the environment to facilitate their own development
- the relationships that exist between present behaviors and future outcomes
- how to develop successful strategies for changing one's level of skill or behavior patterns, as opposed to relying on decisions made by others.

Developing a generation of educated consumers would be a major step toward the eradication of much of the lucrative commercial faddism currently surrounding health and participation in physical activity.

When children are in the fifth and sixth grades, they need to become aware of the differences between information that is generated from misconceptions, superstition, and tales and that which is generated by accumulating information on a subject. Consumer education is a shield against the bombardment of spurious sales claims, especially those made on television programs or touted by a favorite professional sports personality. Through these experiences, children can be helped to gain an appreciation for the magnificence of the human body, an understanding of how to take care of it, and a perception of the meaning and joy in being physically active.

DEVELOPING HEALTHFUL PATTERNS OF LIVING

Planning Guide

Objectives	*Experiences*
As a result of the learning experiences over time, children will be able to:	
1. apply sound training principles to a program of self-development and maintenance	• participate in a "class run" to a predetermined destination (Washington, D.C., Hollywood, Alaska, etc.)
2. explain and apply progressive relaxation techniques	• engage in systematic relaxation procedures that can be used in a group setting or on an individual basis
3. compare long-term health and physical fitness values of various activities.	• compare heart rates before and after the following activities: soccer, kickball, jogging, four-square.

For evaluating your students' progress in this enabling behavior, see page 354.

Teaching Modules

Introductory Module

Objectives

As a result of the learning experiences over time, children will be able to:

1. describe the conditions necessary for "wellness"
2. identify sound postural habits
3. list practices that will promote a healthful lifestyle.

Materials

"Take Joy," a film available from the American Cancer Society.[27] This short film gives a succinct introduction to basic physiology concepts. Its message is that we are born with only one body, and we must learn to take care of it if we are to "take joy" in all its magnificent abilities.

Learning Experiences	*Related Experiences*

Learning Experiences

1. Show the film (eleven minutes) and hold a discussion relative to the following points:

   • How did you feel about the film?
   • What did the film tell you that you did not know before?

   Thought-provoking questions, such as "Can you tell me more about that?" or "Is there anything more you would like to say?" should be used rather than asking "Why?"

2. "Let's list some of the things that the film told us we need to do to stay well":

   • we need to move
   • we need to have fresh air
   • we need to eat and drink, but not *too* much of anything
   • we need to avoid things that will harm the body
   • we need to rest at times

3. "Did you know that our bodies send us messages all the time? Close your eyes and try to think about the messages you are getting from different parts of your body—your feet, for example. What are your feet telling you? That you have shoes on? That they are hot? Or cold? What about your seat? Is it telling you the floor is hard or the carpet is comfortable? Stay quiet with your eyes closed and feel the messages from other parts of your body." It may be helpful here to continue to provide cues for the children: ". . . what about your hands? . . . your knees? . . . back?"

Related Experiences

• Make a class mural that shows your ideas of "joy."
• Make a list of words that have the word "joy" in them.
• Write a paragraph about someone you know who "takes joy" in moving and being alive.
• Do you think that animals can be joyful? How can they show joy? Can we be sure that they are joyful by their actions?
• Make up a play about how the body "fixes" itself.
• Write a story about a place where things like furniture and clothes automatically repaired themselves when necessary. What would happen to stores and businesses there?
• Try to design a chair that will help the sitter keep a good posture.
• Investigate the furniture of different cultures and draw conclusions about the postural habits of the people of that culture. Some examples might be:
   –Japan: sleeping mats; lack of chairs; the low tables of homes in "old Japan."
   –hunters and gatherers groups: Kung bushmen, Australian Aborigines, etc. must carry as little as possible and rarely have furniture.
• Make a collage of different chair designs.
• Find out why an artist uses an upright easel to work on.
• Design a desk that would help you have good posture.

Learning Experiences

Adults often learn not to listen to the "messages" their bodies send. Instead adults ignore or simply become insensitive to the physical feelings generated by everyday stresses and strains. Children are much more physically oriented and can respond well to activities, such as the one presented here. Sometimes quiet music helps to calm the atmosphere in the class.

4. "Everyone, still keeping your eyes closed, stretch as though you were just getting out of bed. What different messages are you getting now?" If this experience is going well, you might want to extend it considerably longer than is indicated here, experimenting with contrasting sensations of stretching, relaxing, and deliberately putting oneself in posturally awkward positions, such as this one: "Find a twisted shape that makes one part of your body send the message 'hey! I'm being pulled a lot.' " If children seem to be having difficulty finding such a position, suggest that they sit on their chairs and attempt to twist around so that both hands can be placed on the back of the chair. The "messages" will probably emanate from the right side of the back and rib cage, initially, but as they continue to hold the position, they will feel strain on the left side of the abdomen, the neck, and possibly the hands as they maintain the force of the twisted position.

Most school environments do not promote good postural habits. Desks tend to be flat, causing the child to bend over to perform any writing/drawing/reading task. This means that the muscles in the lower and upper back, and the neck are being continually worked. The accumulated result, when a large portion of the school day is spent in this position, is increased levels of fatigue as the muscles in the back, shoulder, and neck work disproportionately to maintain the unnatural position.

5. Conduct a short summarizing discussion about the experience, and help them to see the relationship between the feelings

Related Experiences

• Investigate how we "know" what our bodies are doing, even when we don't look. Close your eyes and pick up something from inside your desk. Can you tell what it is from feeling it? How *can* you tell?

(Intermediate students)

• Study the system of the eye and find out how we can see things that are too big to fit into our eyes.
• What does the eye do to the image of a car, for example?
• How can an object the size of a car be seen through a tiny pupil?

FIGURE 9-2 Encourage self-check of posture periodically during the day

Learning Experiences

from the twisted position and the necessity of frequent self-checking when working in awkward positions. To help them understand the results of constantly bending their heads forward, have them hold a heavy object over the edge of the desk for several minutes. This action is similar to that of the muscles in the back of the neck as they maintain the forward position of the head.

Related Experiences

- Why do things look smaller when they are far away?
- Conduct a discussion concerning what might happen to our eyes if we only looked at objects that were close to us?

Central Module

Objectives

As a result of the learning experiences over time, children will:

1. demonstrate knowledge of the relative long-term health and fitness values of various activities
2. demonstrate knowledge of how to use the available facilities for exercise needs
3. demonstrate knowledge of sound training principles to a program of self-development.

All the activities are suitable for both primary and intermediate grade children; however, the "Run to . . ." experience will be more meaningful for intermediate than primary grade students.

Learning Experiences

There are three experience options presented:

1. Using ordinary playground equipment for a variety of movement purposes.
2. Setting one's own goals and following a circuit-training/personal development program.
3. Conducting a "Run to . . ." in which the whole class participates in a given time to accumulate the necessary miles to travel to a distant, but well-known location.

Related Experiences

- Make a list of the places near your home where you can do some of these activities.
- Design a public playground where people of all ages could play.
- Hold a discussion about what is needed in a playground for:
  - little children
  - ten to twelve year olds
  - teenagers
  - Moms and Dads
- Write a poem about:
  "My favorite place to think is . . ."
  "My favorite place to play is . . ."
  "I like to run when . . ."

Learning Experiences   *Related Experiences*

Option 1—Variations

These activities center on the rigid steel structures, such as jungle gyms, and the horizontal or overhead ladders. The geodesic domes particularly provide many opportunities for exploratory kinds of movement. Gather the children together in the area where they will be working.

1. "Today, we're going to find out all the things that you can do on the playground apparatus to help you take care of your body. There is only one rule: "Let others work safely." This rule is important and should be reinforced consistently and often. Depending on the children's age, either have them repeat the rule aloud several times, or use large posterboard signs with pertinent questions/cartoons/slogans on them such as "Did you give the other guy room to work today?" etc.

2. "When I say Go!, find a part of the apparatus that you would like to work with, and see how many different ways you can hang from it. When you hear this signal (*), stop what you are doing and listen. Go!" You can continue to restate the task as they begin to work. Have them try hanging from different body-parts, in different positions.

- Construct a graph to note the increase in the length of your arm-hanging time.
- Make a list of all the reasons why women need to have strong arms and shoulders.
- Tell a story into the tape recorder about a girl who had very weak arms. She didn't think it mattered until "One day when . . ."
- Make a list of professions that require strong arms and shoulders to do them:
  - –trapeze artists
  - –construction workers
  - –gymnasts
  - –nurses and hospital attendants, etc.
- Ask your parents if you can observe in a supermarket for about twenty minutes. Watch the bagboys and checkers. Choose one checkout stand and count how many times either one lifts a shopping bag into a cart or a customer's arms. Multiply this number by three to obtain an estimate for an hour.
- Get your parents' permission to interview their friends who were high school or college athletes. Find out how they keep in shape now that they are out of college/high school. If they do not work out at all, find out why not and if they know what to do about keeping in shape.

FIGURE 9-3 Finding different ways of hanging from apparatus

Learning Experiences

The following is a list of tasks that can be given for this equipment:

- "Find a way to slowly come down from the bars, taking all your weight on your arms."
- "See how you can hang upside down. How long can you stay in that position?"
- "Find out how to suspend yourself using your arms behind you."
- "How long can you suspend yourself using only one arm?" "Is one arm stronger than the other?"
- "As you suspend yourself upside down, change the shape that you make three times."
- "Is there a way to get on to the equipment from a handstand on the ground?"

This activity can be developed so that it incorporates sequence work, thereby *increasing the complexity of response.*

Teachers need to ensure that the activity becomes purposeful and goal-oriented since this equipment is often associated with recess. The trouble signs are:

- just sitting on top of the structures, making no apparent effort to do very much
- taking over the equipment where one or two children demand that they have the entire apparatus to themselves and spend more time keeping other children off it than in productive work of their own.
- nonproductive activity that is focused on others' work, jeering, pushing (especially dangerous), and unnecessary calling out to distant friends on another piece of equipment.

These behaviors require quick affirmative action from teachers. "Are you working, not waiting?" can be asked matter-of-factly. "I'm having a hard time seeing you work when you spend so much time on the ground, etc."

3. When the children have had some time to explore the equipment's possibilities for performing hanging/suspensory activities,

Learning Experiences

call them together for a short discussion. "What parts of the body did you work the most on the equipment? Which parts of our bodies did we decide should get extra exercise because of our school furniture (back, shoulder, and upper arms)?"

Continue the discussion, and introduce the idea of setting some goals for oneself on the equipment. The goals can take various forms:

· hanging for longer and longer periods of time in a certain position
· aspiring to perform a difficult move
· performing a movement with an increasing number of repetitions (such as "skin the cat").

FIGURE 9-4 What parts of the body get the most exercise in hanging activities?

Learning Experiences

Option 2—Goals

This is a continuation from Option 1, which forms the basis for a personal development program. In addition to the suspensory kinds of activities, the circuit/program should include activities for:

- developing/increasing abdominal strength
- developing upper body strength for supporting the body
- increasing flexibility of the hamstrings and also the lower back
- developing leg power through some jumping activities
- increasing cardiovascular efficiency.

Once the children become accustomed to working the circuit, the activity is fairly self-sustaining. Consistent record-keeping is essential, however, to maintain a high interest in the activity and to provide valid feedback on improvement.

Option 3—Run to . . .

A track or series of measured paths must be made for this activity. While a track is used more often, there are some advantages to the measured "paths," in that they can be placed so that they do not interfere with other ongoing physical education activity, and they are also less boring to run. The children can measure the paths themselves, using the measuring wheel that is described in Chapter Eight, page 273. Whichever method is used, the children need to know what constitutes a mile or kilometer, since the records are kept in miles, half-miles, or kilometers.

FIGURE 9-5 "Running to Washington"

Learning Experiences

Procedures: Children may run at any time they have available (recess, after lunch, etc.) to accumulate the required miles. They log the miles or kilometers they run at home, as well as at school. This activity provides the children with something to do during those times that are often wasted rather than used for purposeful activity. Teachers who work in structured environments, or where ability grouping with changing classes for different subjects is the mode, often find themselves, through no fault of their own, with odd timeslots available.

Related Experiences

- Plan the journey to the location, keeping a list on the bulletin board of information about the country that the highway passes through on its way to . . . .
- Plan the journey in the most interesting way possible, taking in historic sights and scenes along the way.

Culminating Module

Objectives

As a result of the learning experiences over time, children will be able to explain the body's need for exercise and relaxation.

Materials

A board, large newsprint or other device for recording the major points raised in the discussion.

Learning Experiences

Conduct a summarizing discussion for whichever option has been used. Some points relative to each option are listed here.

Option 1—Variations

- "How many people did something quite new today?"
- "Did anyone succeed in doing something they have been trying for a long time?"
- "If you could build a playground in the school, what would you put in it?"
- "Supposing there was no school for a year, how would that affect what you do in physical education? Would it be a good effect or a bad effect?"

Related Experiences

- Hold a discussion about: "What I'd like to be able to do (accomplish) in physical education."
- Write or tape record:
  "What I'd like to look like when I'm an adult."
  "If I had my way, I would enter the Olympics in the _____ event because . . ."

Learning Experiences

Related Experiences

• "What have you learned today that you can use to help your Mom and Dad keep fit?"

It is often a novel experience for children to be able to contribute to their parents' well-being.

Option 2—Goals

• "What did it feel like to work on your own at each station?"
• "Who can tell me why you don't do the same number of activities at a station all the time? Why do you have to keep doing more at each station?"
• "Is there anything in the circuit that you could not do at home?" (No)

Therefore, the circuit training could be continued at home or on vacation. Physical activity need not take up much space, nor require expensive equipment. Do the children understand it well enough to teach someone else to do the circuit?

"Overloading" the system gradually to condition it to withstand greater workloads is an idea that is contrary to the mechanical analogy of the body as a machine. Most machines do not adjust to overloading, but instead tend to burn out or break down. This is just one aspect of the uniqueness of a physical being which, when realized with all its implications, can foster a prizing attitude toward one's own body and its wonderful abilities.

• Make a list of: "Exercise is . . ."
• Investigate how athletes train for different sports events.
• Read about the athletes of Greece. Find out how they trained and what events they held in their games.
• If our bodies respond to the overload principle, make a list of what the *worst* jobs are that you know for human beings.
• (Primary) If our bodies need exercise to keep them healthy, what are some jobs that you know where there is very little exercise?

Option 3—Run to . . .

(After the first day or so)
• "How do you feel about how far we have run already?"
• "Is anyone surprised at how far we have run?"
• "What other places would you like to run to?"

• Investigate how many miles famous historical figures probably walked or marched:
  –Johnny Appleseed
  –Hannibal's army
  –St. Paul
  –Moses
  –Daniel Boone

Learning Experiences	*Related Experiences*
• "Has anyone run more than one (two, three) miles without stopping to rest?" Help the children recognize that: • "arriving" at our destination is only one outcome of this activity; the group cooperation is equally important • most of us can do more than we think we can • having a goal is often more motivating than just jogging because "it's good for you."	• Make a collage of famous marathon runners. • Write a report on the winner of a marathon. • Inteview your family on how they feel about jogging with you.

Summary

Enabling Behavior: Developing Healthful Patterns of Living

Evidence that children are developing healthful patterns of living are when they:

1. Can distinguish between a "healthful" pattern and an "unhealthful" pattern of living.
2. Can explain which activities promote physical fitness, which do not, and why.
3. Can explain the need for relaxation in terms appropriate to their level of understanding.
4. Demonstrate increased awareness of others' posture or poor health habits, such as smoking or not exercising.
5. Are able to explain at their own level of understanding the reasons why everyone needs both exercise and muscular relaxation.

UNDERSTANDING ENVIRONMENTAL INFLUENCES ON MOVEMENT

Planning Guide

Objectives	*Experiences*
As a result of the learning experiences over time, children will be able to: 1. explain the influence of the play space on movement, and the influence of the play equipment on the nature of the game	• play volleyball or tennis-like games with the net at various heights; conduct games under varying conditions, such as changing the size of the playing area or reducing the number of players

Objectives	*Experiences*
2. describe the effects of varying environmental factors on movement	• conduct vigorous activities on days of differing weather conditions, such as high and low pressure days, warm and cold days
3. explain the cultural influences on selected ethnic dances or movements.	• learn contrasting forms of folk dancing, and investigate what influences the development of certain steps or movements.

For evaluating your students' progress in this enabling behavior, see page 363.

Teaching Modules

Introductory Module

Objectives

As a result of the learning experiences over time, children will be able to:

1. explain the effect of exercise on their bodies
2. take part in leading their own warm-up dance activity
3. explain the influence of differrent weather conditions on performance of vigorous exercise.

Materials

Music of a vigorous folk dance: "Pop Goes the Weasel," "The Irish Washerwoman," any dance that has a continuous rhythmical beat of 2/4 or 6/8 time. Either a chalkboard or newsprint to record in writing the children's expression of feeling.

Learning Experiences	*Related Experiences*
1. "When you hear the music start, move anywhere you like in the boundaries. When the music stops, find a partner and shake hands, be ready to dance with them when the music starts again. Everyone find your own space, and listen for the music." Begin the music, and let it play for about thirty seconds. Repeat this sequence several times so that the children are able to move with different partners.	• Construct a humidity index for the classroom. • Find out why an impending thunderstorm tends to make one feel "heavy." What does barometric pressure have to do with these sensations?
2. "This time when I stop the music, I will call out a number. You have to make a group with the right number in it and dance in a	• Younger children can find out what barometric pressure is.

FIGURE 9-6 Starting a class with a warm-up dance

Learning Experiences

circle in your group." You may have to re-peat the instructions to make sure they un-derstand the change in the process. Continue the activity for several minutes, at least until the end of the cut on the record.

3. Using the paper or chalkboard, have the children share words that describe how their bodies feel at this point. If the day is cold, the activity can be continued until the children are warm and breathing deeply. Some of the words that might result from this are: tingly, warm, hot, sticky, puffing, perky, breathless, etc.

4. Ask the children to describe the activity area environment. This can be undertaken even if the activity is conducted inside, since the heating or air conditioning or the draughts and dampness can affect how the children feel after exercising vigorously. If outside, the children can note some of the following conditions:

Related Experiences

· Conduct an investigation into the weather of the immediate area or locale. What are the weather patterns? What is the average tem-perature for this time of the year?
· Keep a daily record for a month of the tem-perature and relative humidity index.
· Learn what the wind-chill factor is and how to calculate it.

Learning Experiences   *Related Experiences*

- the clarity of the sky
- the sun's position
- the height, or lowness of any cloud cover
- the humidity of the air

5. Discuss how the climatic conditions of the activity area are related to the words that the children have on the sheet of paper. Help them to see the correlations that exist between stickiness and high humidity, breathlessness and impending thunderstorms.

Central Module

Objectives

As a result of the learning experiences over time, children will:

1. demonstrate basic locomotor movements common to all ethnic dance
2. explain the influence of lifestyle on a culture's dance forms
3. hypothesize about where and in which cultures dance forms pertaining to weather/agricultural conditions are likely to be found.

Folk dance is rarely used as a central learning experience that is intertwined with meaningful study about the evolution of a culture, the similarities and differences between one culture and another, and the commonalities of selected dance forms. Some teachers try to correlate their schedules to teach the folk dance of a country that the children are studying, and this is a first step towards integrating the subject.

Materials

A record player (preferably one with a "pause" switch); "Hava Neguila" from *World of Folk Dances,* or other folk dance recordings.[28]

Learning Experiences   *Related Experiences*

1. "Listen to this music and then move anywhere you like, and find out what steps will go to the music. Start as soon as you can hear the beat in the music." If you participate initially, try to vary the steps and

- Find out what "Hava Neguila" means and how the dance is used and on what occasions it is performed.
- Make a collage of people from other countries doing their folk dances.

Learning Experiences

moves, as well as the directions that you travel since this will foster greater variety in the children's movement. These teaching points are some examples of how tasks can be structured so that they will result in variety in movement. Usually, such challenges are more productive than merely asking the children to "find another way" or "be creative" or "do different things."

"Find a way to turn around while you travel."

"Find all the different places on the floor you can point one foot, while hopping on the other one."

"See how you can keep moving and change direction."

"Make different leg shapes as you move."

"Find a way to change feet without stopping."

"See how you can bring your hands and feet together in different ways, still keeping in time with the music."

"Slap different parts of your body in time to the music while you move."

"Travel in different directions as you move. Try moving side-to-side, or back-and-forth."

2. "You really tried to perform some difficult movements to that music." If this is an initial experience in folk dance for the children, it would be very appropriate here to observe some children performing their own steps or pairing the children so that they have to teach each other the step they have designed. If you have already done some work in this area, then continue on with the task.

"Now, experiment with the step-hop and see how you can fit step-hops to the music. Start when you hear the music." It is important at this point to differentiate between those children who are having difficulty with the step-hop itself (they cannot do the movement), and those who can do the

Related Experiences

- Find out the answer to the question, "Who were the folk who danced?"
- Make up a whole new folk dance for your class. Put some steps in that represent some of the tasks you have to do in class.
- Investigate the work dances of the Middle Ages in Europe. What kind of dances would represent a weaver working? Or a shoemaker?
- Learn the "Shoemaker's Dance"[29] and compare the movement in the dance with the action of today's shoemakers or cobblers. How are they different?
- What is a Rain Dance? Why did people perform Rain Dances? What kind of weather do you think people have when they use Rain Dances?
- Make a list of any tribes or cultures that do Rain Dances.
- Why do you think it sometimes rained when the Rain Dances were performed?

Learning Experiences

step-hop, but cannot keep in time with the music. They are very different problems. The first is a balance/motor-skill problem, the second is probably caused by a lack of rhythmic awareness. For this problem, try having the child perform while holding another child's hand or, if this is not acceptable, maintaining contact with another child by using a handkerchief.

3. "Now, find out what you have to do to move sideways to the music. Try to show the main beats, using your feet as you move. Start when you hear the music." Look for rhythmical walking or running here. The emphasis is on even beats, not uneven beats as in skipping. There are a number of responses to this task that are correct:
   • walking/running evenly and crossing one foot in front of the other
   • same as above, but crossing behind
   • walking/running evenly, closing feet on every step.
   Most folk dance instructions are learned from the verbalization of the teacher, usually supplemented by a demonstration. This means that the children must be able to see and hear the teacher. With large classes this process tends to be difficult.
   Most folk dances that are suitable for intermediate grade children can often be arrived at through guided discovery. It has been the authors' experience that challenging the children to combine the running grapevine step with two step-hops is a faster way to teach the "Hora" than the traditional method of "step behind on the right foot . . .," etc.

4. Choose a child who is performing either of the first two responses, and ask the children to copy him/her. After a few seconds of practice (to music), ask the children to: "See how you can cross your feet alternately in front and behind as you move." Children who have grasped the step can help others by dancing in front of them."

Related Experiences

• Are all folk dances old?
• Can you find any examples of dances that are fairly new? (Ghost Dance,[30] Israeli Dance)
• Hold a discussion about folk dance from different places. Hypothesize about how dances from mountainous areas might be different from those in the plains.
• Investigate how children are trained to do ritual dancing in Bali.
• Folk dances in Hawaii and Bali both use hand gestures to tell stories as part of their dances. What does this tell you about their history?
• Why do so many folk dances use circles in their patterns? What does the circle mean?
• Can you think of how the circle pattern of the "Hora," a wedding ring, and the Olympic circles are similar? (They all represent the idea of *unity*.)

Learning Experiences

5. There are two ways you can proceed at this point: a) you can let the children perform the step in a circle or small circles; or b) you can move on, working with the second part of the step as follows: "Now, try linking two of the running steps with two step-hops. You will still be moving sideways." Once the children arrive at this point, they are performing the basic movements of the "Hora." You can talk the children through this addition by intoning "run, run, step-hop, step-hop, run, run, step-hop, step-hop." These actions are all even beats. Put this part to the music. When the children seem to have this action sequence mastered, introduce the final move, which is an embellishment on the step-hop. "When you do the step-hop, swing the free leg in front of you. This happens on each step-hop." If the children master the total sequence by the end of the module, let them perform it in a circle (eight to a circle), so that they can gain a sense of the unifying feeling that is so much a part of the Israeli dance.

FIGURE 9-7 Learning the "Hora"

Culminating Module

Objectives

As a result of the learning experiences over time, children will be able to:

1. explain the influence of lifestyle on a culture's dance forms
2. demonstrate knowledge of the origins of Israeli folk dance
3. be able to perform selected folk dances of Israel.

Israeli folk dance is particularly suitable for use as an introduction to folk dance because it encompasses a wide range of steps and styles common to many European folk dances. It is an example of how dance has been deliberately used to foster feelings of unity and nationhood. Many of the dances have been choreographed since 1948 and taught to young Israelis during their army training. "Mayim, Mayim," a dance of celebration, was created in a Kibbutz, and it is based on the joy of having enough water. Israeli folk dance is part of a living culture, as opposed to relics of a past culture performed only at festivals.

Materials

Record of "Mayim, Mayim" and other selected circle dances.

Learning Experiences	*Related Experiences*

Learning Experiences

Teach the dance "Mayim, Mayim", according to the steps chart given in the record manual.[31] Teach the dance quickly so they have a picture of the "whole" before you emphasize points about the style of the performance. The emphasis here is on learning a specific dance. The direct method is very suitable in this case since the intent is to have the children performing the same task at the same time. Use the "build-on" method. (See Box 9–3.) When the dance has been learned reasonably well, gather the children together and discuss the following points:

- why do so many dances use a circle formation? What does a circle mean? (It can "mean" many things, but in Israel it is often equated with unity.)
- many dances in Israel are based on "older" forms from different parts of Europe and Asia. Why is the circle formation used so much? (It seems to represent the ultimate spatial patterns in the universe, the motion of the earth and sun or the cycle of the seasons. However, it is also possible that the circle formation, in many dances, is simply a result of dancing around something, such as a fire.)
- investigate some other circle dances from the United States and from Africa
- if the idea of the circle is so prevalent in dance, where else might it be featured in the culture? (In the art forms, in the construction of buildings, especially religious buildings.)

Related Experiences

- Choose the music of another folk dance from Israel, and make up your own folk dance using the steps you have learned from doing the "Hora" and "Mayim, Mayim."
- Find out what a Kibbutz is. Why do they have Kibbutz in Israel? If both the mother and father work, who takes care of the children?
- Investigate some old ruins in different parts of the world, such as the "Mound Indians" in Ohio, and Stonehenge in England, and the Coliseum in Italy. What do they all have in common according to what we know about the ruins today?
- Make a collage of American Indian art forms that use the circle in their design.
- Why were the Romans able to build curving arches and the Maya Indians, who lived at the same time in South America, were not?
- How does the *keystone* affect the shape and size of a building?

BOX 9-3   Teaching by the "Build-On" Method

This method helps the students become familiar with the music, while learning the steps. Initially, one seems to waste time, but in the long run it is a faster way to teach because students are involved in listening and anticipating the music.

1. Teach the first *whole* step without the music. In "Mayim, Mayim," this would mean teaching the first series of grapevine steps beginning with the right foot (sixteen steps). Do *not* wait for everyone to "get it" perfectly—be content with students getting the general idea of the step.
2. Put the music on and have the students identify when to start. There is usually a short introduction. Do this a couple of times, then do the step to the music. *Leave the music playing* all the way through the dance and pick up the beginning step again. When the students have repeated the beginning step twice, stop the music.
3. Teach the second whole step without the music. In "Mayim, Mayim" this means four walks to the center and four walks backwards to their place in the circle. Repeat this sequence.
4. Put the music on and start from the beginning of the dance. "Cue" the students to anticipate the beginning by saying "Ready and . . ." or "Ready?" and provide a cue for the new step "get ready to go into the middle. . . ." Leave the music playing again and repeat the dance from the beginning so that the students practice the first two whole steps twice. Stop the music.
5. The next "whole" step is very short: four runs to the left so you need to combine this with the following step-hop on the right foot eight times, crossing left foot in front, and out to the side on two hops.
6. Repeat Number 4, cueing students through the dance.
7. Teach the last step: same as the step-hops on the right, but this time performed on the left. In addition, the hands clap in front as the foot crosses in front, and clap neighbors' hands on each side as the foot moves to the side. Go all the way through the music.
8. Practice any "problem" parts.
9. Repeat the dance at least three times. Cue the students *only* the first time through, and then make them anticipate the changes in the music themselves.

Students will continue to depend on you if you keep providing the cues.

Summary

Enabling Behavior: Understanding Environmental Influences on Movement

Children are developing their understanding of how the environment influences movement when:

1. They can explain, in their own terms, how the weather or pollution can affect movement performance.
2. Draw relationships between geographical or cultural conditions and games or dances that arise from those cultures.
3. They demonstrate understanding of how the size, weight, and consistency of equipment or apparatus can affect movement performance and even enjoyment of the activity.

DEVELOPING INFORMED DECISION-MAKING BEHAVIOR

Planning Guide

Objectives	*Experiences*
As a result of the learning experiences over time, children will:	
1. assess themselves in some parameters of physical performance	• complete a competency checklist of physical abilities and knowledges related to movement and sports/leisure time activities
2. state five specific personal goals for improved physical performance	• design and pursue a program of personal development, according to individual needs
3. be able to predict what might occur when specific variables in a game are changed.	• play variations of soccer or kickball and change the environment *during* the game by shortening the playing bases or enlarging the goal area; project the consequences of these changes on such factors as the score, the nature of the game, or the fun of playing it.

For evaluation of students' progress in making informed decisions, see page 374.

Teaching Modules

Introductory Module

Objectives

As a result of the learning experiences over time, children will be able to:

1. assess themselves in selected parameters of physical performance
2. state five specific personal goals for improved physical performance based on information gained from the comptency checklist.

Materials

A Competency Checklist for each student. A form of the checklist appears at the end of this enabling behavior.

Learning Experiences

1. "How many of you think you've changed since you were in _____ (previous) grade? How do you know that you've changed?" (Our clothes don't fit the same; we can reach things that we couldn't reach before; we can do some things better than last year.)
2. "When do people stop changing?"
3. Have the children complete the checklist. This discussion will be particularly meaningful for fifth and sixth grade children who have started their growth spurt. Younger children often do not realize that they are growing until they see evidence of it on the growth chart. They need to understand clearly that it is not a test, and they will not be evaluated against someone else's performance. A symbol or picture could be used instead of a name to help keep the information confidential.
4. The following discussion can take place at another time if necessary. However, it would be important to reintroduce the concept of evaluating oneself for the purpose of seeing how one has changed. "Everyone look carefully at their checklist and see how you would finish the sentence 'I am proud that . . .'" Give every child a chance

Related Experiences

- Make a collage of pictures showing how a baby grows up to be as old as you are now.
- Draw a picture of what you would like to look like when you are in junior high school; when you are an adult.
- Write a newspaper article on "When I am adult, I would like to be . . ."
- Find the following averages for the class categorized by weight; height; biceps, waist, and head sizes; and for different groups by age, sex, height, and weight. See where there is a wide range of differences in the averages and where there is a narrow range.
- Interview your parents and find out how they decided to:
  - do the job they do now
  - live where you live
  - buy the car your family owns
  - play whatever sports they play.
- Hold a discussion about the answers you all got. Were some of them the same? How were they different?
- If you could be born again as a famous person, who would you like to be? Tell as much as you can about why you would like to be that person.
- Write out a change "contract." (See page 336.)

Learning Experiences	*Related Experiences*

to speak, but don't press a student if he or she does not want to share immediately. Give the student another chance when everyone else has had a turn.

5. "Now, look at your checklist again, and choose what you *would like to see* as an answer to how long you can stand on your head. That's called a *goal.* Look through your checklists and choose five goals that you would like to reach by _____ grade. When you have decided, draw a picture of yourself doing those five goals. This experience can lead into many discussions concerning how one goes about achieving a goal. For example, children who want to develop specific skills, such as the headstand referred to above, need to understand the relationships between correct execution and appropriate practice. Remaining an eager learner throughout life is a characteristic of one who lives rather than exists. Learning to be such a person depends upon grasping the concept that one can change many aspects of oneself. If this concept was learned at an early age, it might drastically alter the child's view of his potentialities. "I'll never be able to do that . . ." might change to "I can do something about that if I try."

• Write each goal on a poster, and place them on the bulletin board.

FIGURE 9-9 Practice helps to make perfect

FIGURE 9-8 Practice helps to make perfect

Central Module

Objectives

As a result of the learning experiences over time, children will be able to:

1. identify whether a conclusion has been arrived at through opinion or factual information
2. describe those recreational activities that contribute to maintenance of a wide range of physical fitness components and those that do not.

Materials

An instrument for signaling "Stop what you are doing." Activity posters or cards.

Learning Experiences	*Related Experiences*

1. If the activity takes place in the classroom, put the following words up on the board:

   tennis
   baseball
   swimming
   four-square
   football

   If you are in the activity area, use posters or cards for the words. "Everyone look at these words, and I'm going to ask you which one you think helps you keep in condition (in shape) the best? Take a few minutes to think about them." Regardless of the method that you use to conduct the discussion, the following points should be brought out:
   - The games we play in school or as children are not always the most suitable for playing as adults. For example, football requires several players to make the game enjoyable, and these may be difficult to find when we are working. (Ask them to identify when their parent(s) play football if at all, and usually it will be only on family outings.)

   - Ask your parents if you can take a survey of their friends to see what they do for exercise. Write down the sport and how often they do it. Make a chart at the end to show your results. Which sports are the most popular?
   - Bring your results back to class and compare them with others' results. Are the sports different or the same? If they are different, what causes the difference? (Whether people are members of clubs, how long they have been playing, whether it is a "family" activity or not.)
   - Compare the cost of different sports equipment. Is it cheaper to swim or to play golf?
   - Find out about how much it costs to join leagues or clubs.
   - What is included in the costs?
   - Invite a local recreation leader to talk about the available activities and facilities in the area.
   - Invite a local sports equipment person to share information about the quality of various items: soccer balls, basketballs, running/jogging shoes, etc.
   - Investigate some articles in *Consumers' Report,* and post a list of different items they recommend on the bulletin board.

Learning Experiences

- Some games we play in school are too rugged for many adults (unless they are in top physical condition or play them regularly and train for them). Football, rugby, ice-hockey, and soccer are examples.
- Unless sports clubs or leagues are formed, adults do not get the chance to play some sports regularly. Examples of this are field hockey clubs, baseball and softball leagues, tennis, golf clubs, and recently formed soccer leagues.
- Some sports provide more activity than others. Baseball is a low-activity sport, especially for nonprofessionals. Golf is a low-activity sport, more so if golf carts are used. It is hard on the back unless it is played on a very regular basis.
- A sport like tennis requires expertise to gain a lot of exercise.
- Jogging, dancing, and cycling work the legs and cardiovascular system well, but do little for upper body strength or flexibility (except modern dance).
- Swimming is one of the best all-around sports.
- A varied activity schedule should be aimed at as being the optimum for maintaining physical fitness.

Related Experiences

- Carry out a comparison shopping assignment. Check the prices of articles at different stores (fifth and sixth grades).
- Make a collage of advertisements for diet pills or other weight reducing gimmicks that are supposed to help you lose weight without reducing food intake or exercising.
- (Intermediate grades) If you were going to visit a desert island for a few years, what sporting equipment would you take with you?
- Watch the Saturday morning television shows, and count the commercials that are shown within a one-hour period. Why do companies try to sell things to children? What kind of words do they use to appeal to children? Compare these commercials with two or three commercials for adults in the evening. What are the differences?
- Can you see anything that is the same in some ways?
  - try to make the "goods" sound appealing and necessary.
  - show good-looking people.
  - they imply that anyone who *is* anyone has one or uses the product.

FIGURE 9-10 Some games more than others foster fitness

Learning Experiences

- Physical fitness is only one reason why people do recreational activities. The social aspects of recreation are possibly just as important (if not more so) as the fitness benefits.
- Recreation means "re create," renew, "get oneself together."
- Ask them to "interview" their parents about why they participate in the activities they do, how those activities make them feel, what benefits they derived from them, etc. Share the results with the rest of the class.

"Everyone look at their activity card. Look at the little boxes at the top of each card. Think about the activity you are going to do and how fast your heart is going to beat while you do that activity. Put the number in the box."

FIGURE 9-11 Some games more than others foster fitness

FIGURE 9-12 Fun activities can be physically demanding too

Learning Experiences

Primary children, especially first graders, may find this too abstract to deal with. They can project other aspects, such as how tiring, how much fun, how often they get to play, etc. Also, primary grade children should not be involved in the "official form" of the sport, but activities that lead to the development of the skills required for that sport.

2. The second part of this module can be undertaken in one of two ways: (a) either the whole class can participate in the series of activities over a period of days; or (b) the class can be divided up into several groups—each group performing a different activity.

   Before either (a) or (b) is started, however, the children all need to know how to take their heart rate. At regular intervals, a signal should be given for the activity to stop so that a heart rate can be taken at that point and recorded. By taking the heart rate in this manner, at one time, there should be some consistency in the data.

   If you are using a group rotating method, give the children a chance to do at least two activities of different levels of energy cost. However, when changing a group from jogging to a slower sport like softball, they should wait until their heart rates are close to the resting rate before they begin the activity. "Everyone take their resting pulse rate." (See page 308 on how to do this.) "Write down the number that you get at the top of the page."

   Continue with the activity depending on the method that you have selected:
   - one group doing bowling types of skills
   - groups should be involved in the following activities:
     - bowling activities
     - jogging
     - four-square
     - basketball
     - softball (or traditional kickball)

Culminating Module

Objectives

As a result of the learning experiences over time, children will be able to:

1. list criteria by which one can judge the physical fitness value(s) of different activities
2. identify high versus low energy cost activities
3. identify values other than physical fitness benefits of different recreational activities.

Materials

The competency checksheets and the activity comparison sheets that have been completed by the children.

Learning Experiences

1. Conclude the discussion started in the previous module concerning the activities. Have the children compare their projected heart rates with the actual heart rates, and see how close they were to estimating correctly. Continue with the discussion to highlight the following points:
   a. If heart rate is one estimation of how hard the body is working, which activity has the highest set of heart rates? Therefore, which activity caused us to work the hardest? Which the least?
   b. Rate the activities in terms of *most* fun and *least* fun. Does this have anything to do with choosing a recreational activity?
   c. Which activity can be done on one's own? Which activities need many other people? One or two other people?
   d. If someone asked us which sports they should play to keep fit, what should we say?
2. Have the children review their competency sheets and see where they need to increase their activity or add other things/skills/knowledges. Make a contract to improve one aspect of the competency sheet for the next two weeks.

Related Experiences

- Compute the number of times the heart beats in one hour, one day, and one week, based on one's own resting heart rate.
- Invite speakers who are involved in decision-making processes frequently. Have them share the processes they use to arrive at a decision.
- Make a list of: "My _____ grade goals are. . . ."
- Make up a game or sport that would meet the criteria for an all-around physical fitness sport.

FIGURE 9-13 Soccer can be a family affair

FIGURE 9-14 "How hard did we play?"

Self-Assessment List

I can do all the things that I mark ✔

_____ 1. run fast for ten seconds
_____ 2. run fast for one minute
_____ 3. run fast for two minutes
_____ 4. run three times around the basketball court without stopping
_____ 5. run eight times around the basketball court without stopping
_____ 6. run twenty times around the basketball court without stopping
_____ 7. hop on one foot
_____ 8. hop on the other foot
_____ 9. jump on both feet
_____ 10. skip with either foot
_____ 11. gallop with either foot
_____ 12. gallop and change feet
_____ 13. step-hop on either foot
_____ 14. slide step on either foot
_____ 15. dodge someone
_____ 16. avoid bumping into people in a crowded place
_____ 17. balance on one foot for ten seconds
_____ 18. balance on one foot for thirty seconds
_____ 19. balance on the other foot for ten seconds
_____ 20. balance on the other foot for thirty seconds
_____ 21. roll forward

_____ 22. roll backwards

_____ 23. roll sideways

_____ 24. roll over one shoulder backwards

_____ 25. roll over the other shoulder backwards

_____ 26. stand on my head ten seconds

_____ 27. stand on my head for thirty seconds

_____ 28. stand on my head and make different leg shapes

_____ 29. balance on my hands only for three seconds

_____ 30. balance on my hands for ten seconds

_____ 31. balance on my hands for twenty seconds

_____ 32. walk on my hands for three steps

_____ 33. walk on my hands for ten steps

_____ 34. cartwheel one time

_____ 35. cartwheel two times

_____ 36. cartwheel five times

_____ 37. cartwheel on either side

_____ 38. do a front walkover

_____ 39. do a back walkover

_____ 40. balance on my hands and finish in a forward roll

_____ 41. walk along the balance beam

_____ 42. walk along the balance beam sideways

_____ 43. walk along the balance beam backwards

_____ 44. move in four different ways along the balance beam (other than walking)

_____ 45. balance on the beam on three body-parts

_____ 46. balance on the beam on two body-parts other than my feet

_____ 47. do a sequence on the balance beam

_____ 48. do a turn on the low bars

_____ 49. do a turn on the high bars

_____ 50. balance on the low bars and make different leg shapes

_____ 51. make three different shapes on the bars

_____ 52. make different shapes on the bars hanging by one hand

_____ 53. make different shapes on the bars hanging by my knees

_____ 54. make different shapes on the bars hanging by one knee

_____ 55. move across the horizontal ladder using my hands

_____ 56. move across the horizontal ladder using my hands and feet

_____ 57. make three different shapes on the horizontal ladder

_____ 58. throw a ball overhand across the court

_____ 59. throw a ball overhand the length of the court

_____ 60. throw a ball from the outfield to home plate

_____ 61. throw a ball underhand across the court

_____ 62. throw a ball underhand the length of the court

_____ 63. pitch a ball underhand from the pitcher's mound to home plate

_____ 64. catch a big playground ball from a bounce
_____ 65. catch a big playground ball if it is thrown to me
_____ 66. catch a yarnball if it is thrown right at me
_____ 67. catch a yarnball from a high throw
_____ 68. catch a large ball when it rolls on the ground
_____ 69. catch a tennis ball when it rolls on the ground
_____ 70. catch a tennis ball from a bounce
_____ 71. field ground balls if I'm lucky
_____ 72. field ground balls sometimes
_____ 73. fielding ground balls near me
_____ 74. catch fly balls if I'm lucky
_____ 75. catch fly balls sometimes
_____ 76. catching fly balls near me
_____ 77. hit a playball off a cone with a bat
_____ 78. hit a playball with a bat if I bounce it first
_____ 79. hit a softball off a cone with a bat
_____ 80. hit a playball against a wall with a paddle two times without missing
_____ 81. hit a tennis ball against a wall with a paddle five times without missing
_____ 82. hit a tennis ball against a wall with a paddle ten times without missing
_____ 83. I am a good sport if our team is winning
_____ 84. I am a good sport sometimes
_____ 85. I am a good sport most of the time
_____ 86. I get mad when our team loses
_____ 87. I get mad when other people cheat
_____ 88. I get mad when I make a mistake
_____ 89. I get mad when other people make mistakes
_____ 90. I help others on the team by playing well
_____ 91. I help others on the team by being cool
_____ 92. I help others on the team by cheering them up when they feel bad
_____ 93. I help others on the team by cheering them up when they make a mistake
_____ 94. I can get better at doing skills if I practice properly
_____ 95. I can get better at doing skills if I watch other people practice
_____ 96. I can get better at doing skills if I wait until I grow up
_____ 97. To make my muscles stronger I should rest often so they don't get tired
_____ 98. To make my muscles stronger I should keep doing what I'm doing now
_____ 99. To make my muscles stronger I should work them a bit harder than they are used to
_____100. I would like to be better at _____

Summary

Enabling Behavior: Developing Informed Decision-Making Behavior

This enabling behavior builds on "Making Choices" in Chapter Five, Becoming Independent. Children demonstrate improvement in making informed decisions when they:

1. Can evaluate their own performance and make reasonable short- and long-range goals based on that evaluation.
2. Recognize the outcomes of making different decisions or not making a decision.
3. Can predict with increasing accuracy the possible results of decisions.
4. Can explain the difference between a test in which they compete with others, and an evaluation of their own performance relative to past achievements.
5. Can distinguish between fact and opinion.

ENDNOTES

1. *Knowledge and Understanding in Physical Education* (Washington, D.C.: American Alliance for Health, Physical Education, and Recreation, rev. 1973), p. vii.
2. Ibid., p. 118.
3. D. W. Edington and Lee Cunningham, *Biological Awareness: Statements for Self-Discovery* (Englewood Cliffs, N.J.: Prentice-Hall, 1975). Reprinted by permission.
4. Beverly L. Seidel, Fay R. Biles, Grace E. Figley and Bonnie J. Neuman, *Sports Skills: A Conceptual Approach to Meaningful Movement* (Dubuque, Iowa: William C. Brown, 1975).
5. Perry B. Johnson, Wynn F. Updyke, Maryellen Schaefer, and Donald C. Stolberg, *Sport, Exercise and You* (New York: Holt, Rinehart and Winston, 1975), pp. 199–200.
6. Edington and Cunningham, *Biological Awareness*, pp. 70–71.
7. *Knowledge and Understanding in Physical Education,* p. 86.
8. American College of Sports Medicine, "How to Get the Most Out of Running," *Young Athlete,* 1 (September 1975): 18–21.

9. Metropolitan Life Insurance Company, *Exploring Your Environmental Choices* (New York: Health and Welfare Division).

10. Sidney B. Simon, *Meeting Yourself Halfway* (Niles, Ill.: Argus Communications, 1974), p. xi. For information about current Values Clarification materials and a schedule of nationwide training workshops, contact Dr. Sidney B. Simon, Box 846, Leverett, Mass. 01054, or National Humanistic Education Center, 110 Spring St., Saratoga Springs, N.Y. 12866.

11. Ibid., p. xii.

12. Ibid., p. xiii.

13. Ibid., p. xv.

14. Ibid.

15. Ibid.

16. Merrill Harmin, Howard Kirschenbaum, and Sidney B. Simon, *Clarifying Values through Subject Matter* (Minneapolis, Minn.: Winston Press, 1973).

17. Ibid., pp. 83–84.

18. Simon, *Meeting Yourself Halfway,* pp. 22–24.

19. Ibid., pp. 54–58.

20. Ibid., pp. 64–65.

21. Ibid., pp. 98–99.

22. Allan J. Ryan, "Gynecological Considerations," *Journal of Health, Physical Education, and Recreation* 46 (January 1975): 40–44.

23. American Medical Association Committee on Medical Aspects of Sports "Female Athletics," *Journal of Health, Physical Education, and Recreation* 46 (January 1975): 45.

24. Ibid., p. 46.

25. R. A. Hamilton and Reedco "Posture Score Sheet" (Auburn, N.Y.: Reedco, 1974).

26. Bruner, Jerome S., *The Process of Education* (Cambridge, Mass.: Harvard University Press, 1960), pp. 1–16.

27. American Cancer Society, *Take Joy,* 1973. (Film)

28. World of Folk Dances, *All-Purpose Folk Dance* "Hora" R.C.A. Victor LPM–1623.

29. World of Folk Dances, *Folk Dances for Fun* "Shoemakers' Dance" R.C.A. Victor LPM–1624.

30. Roger M. Keesing, and Felix M. Keesing, *New Perspectives in Cultural Anthropology* (New York: Holt, Rinehart and Winston, 1971), p. 362.

31. World of Fun Folk Dances and Games Records "Mayim, Mayim" R.C.A. Victor Number Six B. (Nashville, Tenn.: The United Methodist Church, 1970).

THREE

chapter ten

Going Off on Your Own

No single reference can ever do everything that any one person would desire. This book is no exception. The goal of this final chapter is to help the reader plan teaching modules that are tailored to their individual situation, thus allowing the teacher to become independent of this book.

In Chapter Three, Using the Developmental Theme Approach, two planning and teaching aids were introduced. These aids, the planning guides and teaching modules, were implemented in the subsequent thematic chapters. It was emphasized that the teaching modules provide flexibility in planning lessons. For example, one introductory module could be used with a number of different central modules. The readers were encouraged to become independent of the modules presented in this book by: rearranging the teaching modules; designing their own teaching modules for use in combination with those in this book; and designing all of their own teaching modules.

CREATING YOUR OWN TEACHING MODULES

The teaching modules in this book provide ideas for getting teachers started. To use the book to fullest advantage means that teachers should begin to devise their own teaching modules. This is really much more satisfying than following someone else's plans.

By now, it will be apparent that the structure of a teaching module allows for a wide range of concepts, ideas, and knowledges to be interrelated with the physical education experience. One of the premises of this book is the belief that if physical education is ever truly to become an integral part of the curriculum, then the learning experiences, or many of them, must not only be generally related but also they must be integrated with other curricular areas.

Teachers have attempted to integrate the physical education program with other curricular areas; however, all too often it has meant that when the children were studying "Indians of North America" in the classroom, they learned an Indian dance in physical education, drew some Indian scenes in art, and perhaps wrote a story about "An Indian Boy's Life" in language arts. In other words, they interrelated the *topic* through different subject areas. Certainly, many sensitive classroom teachers and physical education specialists have made such experiences meaningful by helping children to see the relationships involved. However, it is also quite possible that none of these experiences were very meaningful. Except for rare occasions, the children may have performed all of these tasks, but gained little understanding about American Indian culture, either past or present. For example, did the children understand the meaning of the sun in a Navajo's life or the importance of the Kiowa-Apache's brother relationship? Have sixth graders in many schools ever developed any appreciation for the important part that dance plays in American Indian girls' puberty rites? In fact, many experiences may result in denying children knowledge and understanding because now they may believe that they have studied all about Indians, when in reality only their stereotypes have been reinforced.

Curricular integration should mean that conceptual relationships are drawn across subject matter lines and involve similar learning processes. In this book, the related activities have been planned in one of two ways:

1. The same basic concepts or processes that are central to the physical education experiences are applied to other curricular areas.

2. The related activities *extend* the active learning experience by exploring its other dimensions or ramifications.

An example of the first point can be found in "Developing Body Image," Central Module, p. 77. In the movement experience presented in that teaching module, children are exploring the size relationships that exist between different body-parts. The related activities require children to explore these size relationships with three or four people and a specific environment such as the length of a bulletin board. Another activity focuses on the problem of making a pattern of two shapes exhibiting a specified relationship like one shape must be twice the other's size.

An example of the second method of extending the movement experience can be found in the Introductory Module to "Expressing Feelings," p. 160. The movement experience focuses on moving to a variety of words given one at a time by the teacher. The related experiences in this teaching module include finding synonyms for the words given in the physical education lesson, cutting pictures from magazines to illustrate some of the words used in the movement experience, and selecting words as a stimulus for a design or drawing.

Through these learning experiences, children might come to understand what it is that movement, drawing, and words have in common. In addition, they can explore whether thoughts or ideas can better be expressed through one medium as compared to another. When planning their own modules, teachers need to continually ask themselves, "What will the children learn by doing this activity?"

DEVELOPING A CONCEPT THROUGH SEVERAL TEACHING MODULES OR LESSONS

In Chapter Nine, Drawing Relationships, the teaching modules provide some practice in differentiating between information gained through hearsay or guesswork, and information gained through experience or investigation. In the planning guide "Developing Informed Decision-Making Behavior," suggestions are made for changing a game by varying its elements. The purpose of this learning experience is to provide practice in projecting the results of decisions. How would you begin to plan a series of teaching modules or lessons based on that idea? Use the following learning experience:

Play variations of kickball or soccer. Stop the game at the midpoint, and change the environment by shortening the playing bases or enlarging the goal area. Project the results of this change on the rest of the game, and then resume play. Compare the projected results with the actual results.

Design an introductory and/or a culminating module around this experience, and add related experiences that complement the idea presented in your teaching module(s). There are a number of possible lessons that could be generated from this experience. Doing an activity once is simply not enough to help children internalize a concept. Consequently, it would be possible to apply the concept to a lesson on kickball or soccer at a different point in time (or to any game). For example, in a quiet game like chess, what would happen if both Queens were removed from the game entirely? With different modifications in the elements, these learning activities can be repeated without having the students do the same thing over again.

Introductory Module

When designing your own teaching modules, there are several ways of introducing a learning experience, and the way that you choose to introduce it to your students depends on a number of factors, such as: their age, what activity immediately preceded the introductory module, whether the students need vigorous activity initially, and/or whether their game playing behavior needs some assistance. The following is a list of possible ways to introduce a learning experience concerning what happens when people decide to change something:

- Conduct a short discussion on the differences between a sound and an unsound decision.
- Have a circle discussion on "A time I made a decision and it turned out OK."
- Conduct a discussion on how to know *when* to make a decision about something (when a game doesn't seem to be much fun; when you sense you're getting into an argument that may lead to a fight; when you think you or someone else is being treated unfairly).
- Begin practicing some of the skills the students will need to play the game or perform the activity.
- Select two or three activities from the game, and have the students choose which one they will practice for five minutes (for example, in kickball, they may select base running, kicking the ball, catching fly balls, fielding ground balls).

Central Module

The learning experience of the central module for this lesson also can take several forms, and the form you choose depends on the same factors as before. The following list represents some ways of using the main experience:

- Play a variation of any game that the students are able to play successfully. This activity should not be done with an unfamiliar game, since this will constitute the major portion of the lesson. However, it is important that the principles of maximum participation, developmentally appropriate activity, and a progressive sequence be incorporated in the game.

- Conduct several games and have each group make different changes in their games so that they can compare the results of those changes with what they projected would happen.
- Play a game and after environmental changes have been made, ask the students to secretly project the results for the *other* team. In other words, how do they think the changes will affect the other team's performance? In this way, you are removing part of the possibility that the children will simply play out their predictions as their own performance.

Culminating Module The culminating module for this lesson should be a direct outcome of the central learning experience. Scheduling sometimes precludes the culminating module from immediately following the central learning experience. If this is the case, it would be important for you to note briefly some major points that you want to bring out in the culminating module later that day. These points could include:

What changes were made in each game?

What was the difference between the predicted results and the actual results?

What behavior changes that were not protected resulted from altering the game?

What did the alterations in the game do to the performance level of the players?

What changes would be made next time the game was played?

The culminating module should be modified according to what actually happened in the central learning experience, rather than being followed rigorously because that's the way it was planned! Experienced teachers modify their plans constantly, and the physical education lesson plan should be no exception.

The way in which you culminate any learning experience will depend on the influencing factors of whether your students discuss well, whether they are "group" oriented or work better on their own, or whether they are visually stimulated more than verbally or through writing. The following list gives some samples of how you might culminate a lesson:

- Ask the students to write a paragraph on how they thought the changes altered the game.
- Have the students fill out a reaction sheet about the experience. How did they feel about making the changes? How do they think they did in anticipating the results of the changes? Collect the reaction sheets and collate the results for a discussion.
- Have the students draw a picture showing how they liked the whole experience, and whether they liked part of it and didn't like another part.

Many of these last activities can take place in some of the "odd" time slots that occur during the day. A few minutes can be used for individual responses or group activities.

Physical education specialists rarely have the flexibility of time that classroom teachers have. Usually, the specialists' classes follow each other immediately, and there is seldom an opportunity to extend the learning experience beyond the scheduled time. Consequently, those of you who are faced with this problem may have to structure the modules differently, depending upon the time you have available and how often you work with the students during the week. In some cases, the teaching modules presented in the book would be too long for one twenty- or thirty-minute lesson, so you might consider using the teaching modules more as a series of lessons that will lead to learning a concept. If this is the case, then you need to develop new introductory and culminating modules, using the central teaching module presented in the book. In the total lesson, you will need to keep in proper proportion the amount of vigorous activity, warming up, and cooling down activity.

Related Experiences

Related experiences should be designed to further the understanding of the concept presented during this physical education lesson. The related experience should be constructed with consideration being given to the age level of your students, their usual work patterns, the teaching methodology they are accustomed to, their ability to work independently, and the resources available to them. Some related experiences might be:

- Write stories about a place where everything was unpredictable and conditions changed every day. What would life be like in such a place?
- Make a list of people we think make sound decisions. Who would we go to if we wanted some advice on what decision to make?
- Read "The Ancient Mariner" (a tale about a shipwrecked sailor who couldn't make up his mind what to do first and ended doing nothing) and write what you would have done in his place.
- Investigate (for sixth grade students) some decisions that have turned out to be crucial in changing history in some way, such as President Truman's decision to use the atom bomb; Hitler's decision not to invade Britain in 1941; the decisions of the Founding Fathers to dedicate themselves to the Declaration of Independence.
- Tell about a time when you saw an umpire make a difficult decision.
- Tell about a time when you made a difficult decision.
- Design a series of "what if . . ." situations in which children have to make a decision and then have to explain why they made such a decision.

BOX 10–1   Practical Pointers for Lesson Planning

Experienced teachers know, sometimes they learned the hard way, that detailed, thorough, and advanced planning helps them to be more effective teachers. The following practical pointers will help you avoid problems associated with unusual circumstances.

1. Plan in advance—This is necessary in case the teacher is absent and another person must assume his/her duties, to have time to think about the plan, to be able to relate one lesson to others, and to prethink solutions to problems that can be anticipated.
2. Over plan—Having extra activities planned for a lesson can be a life saver. When what was planned is learned quickly or just does not work well, the teacher has planned back-up activities to use. These activities can be the next task in the sequence or a completely different area of instruction.
3. Have a back pocket plan—If the equipment, space, or weather does not allow the planned lesson to be used, the teacher will be able to substitute another meaningful lesson. These emergency plans can be kept in your back pocket, desk drawer, or index card file. The lessons can serve to review previously learned tasks, present a learning experience that is unrelated to the "planned" activity but can be introduced and culminated in one period, or a written assignment followed up by a discussion related to the subject of the developmental theme which is currently being taught.

Lesson planning is necessary. The detailed nature of the plan depends on the experience and skill level of the teacher. Whether the plan is a lesson outline or a script, the teacher should feel more comfortable and confident in knowing that the lesson he/she is about to teach has been carefully planned.

DEVELOPING MOVEMENT EXPERIENCES

Problem solving is used in many of the teaching modules. Teachers who begin to use problem solving in their lessons sometimes find that a number of active and fun lessons are developed, but they really never seem to "go anywhere." The tasks are not introduced in any meaningful order and they are not related to one another. The children simply go through a series of disguised commands: "Make four different shapes," "Travel anywhere in general space using your feet in three different ways," "Can you balance on your hands?," "Make different leg shapes as you lie on your back." Such experiences serve little useful purpose, since the teacher rapidly moves from one idea to another. Because the ideas are never fully developed or carried through from one lesson to another, the children soon tire of the activity and become bored. If you find that this seems to be happening in your lessons, select one of the movement factors (Time, Force, Space, Flow) and keep that as a central thread, or focus, for the activities in the lesson. The next day, vary the activity (dance, manipulative skills, or locomotor movements), but focus on the *same movement factor* as the day before. In this way, you will be developing your ideas to a greater depth. Consequently, the children should be able to internalize the ideas more effectively.

DESIGNING LESSONS EMPHASIZING A MOVEMENT FACTOR OR CONCEPT

Table 10–1 shows how tasks can be constructed to allow for different teaching emphases and equipment, yet still retain a focus on a major concept or movement factor. In the table, the emphasis is on the use of the Time factor in movement. You will notice that nearly every task contains some reference to the quality of Time. However, the tasks also include other movement factors, such as moving in general space, taking weight on different body-parts, using the apparatus (and these tasks will fit *any* apparatus), working with a partner, and making a sequence. It might be easier to make the table fit your particular situation better if you read through it with a particular activity area or apparatus in mind (e.g., the balance beam or the monkey-bars). This will help you to understand the possibilities of the tasks in a specific setting. These same teaching modules could be used over and over again by substituting different emphases. For example, try substituting the focus of "making twisted body-shapes" each time "changing the speed" is mentioned in some way.

The lesson also exemplifies a sound progression, in that the children move from working rather generally with an open-ended task ("Move anywhere in general space on your feet.") to a much more specific and complex task ("Make up a sequence with a partner."). The challenges become more complex and demanding as the lesson proceeds.

It is important to recognize the other question elements that are incorporated in the lesson because "teachable moments" can occur at any point in time. It may happen that the fourth task, for example, is one that the children are not making satisfactory progress in completing, in that they are not really challenging themselves or they are not really showing a contrast in the speed of their movement. If they do not achieve the change at this point, it is unlikely that they will improve as the challenges become more complex. When you make this judgment, you should spend more time on this task than you had planned. If one or two children have grasped the concept well and can

TABLE 10–1 Lesson Focus: Taking Weight on Different Body-Parts, Showing a Change in Speed of Movement

Movement Factors	Introductory Module
Time* quickly slowly	1. Move on your feet anywhere you can in general space without touching each other. 2. Move in general space, on the feet, showing a change in speed.* 3. In your own space, find ways of taking your weight on different parts of the body.
Force strongly lightly	4. As you take weight on different parts of the body, show a change in the speed of your movement, take your weight slowly on to one part, and then quickly shift the weight to another part.*
	Central Module
Space directly flexibly	5. Find a way to move slowly onto the apparatus.* Experiment with arriving slowly leading with different body-parts. Leave the apparatus *safely*. 6. Select a way to arrive slowly on the apparatus, but to leave it quickly so that you land on your feet.* 7. Find a way to add a roll and balance to your slow and quick movements on the apparatus.*
	Culminating Module
Flow freely controlled	8. With your partner, make up a sequence that shows quick and slow movements using the apparatus.* Sometime during your sequence, you and your partner must be side-by-side.

*In this table, *Time* is the movement factor that is developed throughout the lesson. The * indicates each place where the factor *Time* is emphasized. For further explanation of the movement factors, see pages 74–75.

demonstrate it, you might stop the sequence here, and have these children demonstrate their responses. After some "focusing" discussion on the merits of the performance, have the rest of the students attempt the task again. You may then continue the lesson with an emphasis on this aspect rather than the one you had planned for.

The *objectives* for the lesson in Table 10-1 might be:

1. Children will demonstrate ability to use sudden and sustained qualities in their movement.
2. Children will demonstrate ability to show a change in speed while working on the box (bars, balance beam, horizontal ladder, mats, mini-trampoline, etc.).
3. Children will work productively with a partner in devising a sequence on the apparatus.

It will take time to learn to plan teaching modules effectively and easily. The final result should be rewarding for both you and your students, as continuity in the physical education lessons is achieved.

EVALUATING AND REPORTING STUDENT PROGRESS

When behavioral or specific descriptive objectives are stated for each teaching module, the teacher can record whether these objectives were achieved during a lesson. This type of evaluation is called formative, as it is used as baseline information for planning future learning experiences. If the students achieved an objective, the teacher can provide a more complex learning experience for that enabling behavior in the next lesson. If the objective was not reached by most of the children, then the teacher must decide whether or not to provide additional learning experiences for that enabling behavior. The judgment as to whether or not an objective has been achieved should be based on teacher observations or testing. Testing can be completed by using every student or by spot checking when students have been asked to test themselves.

The data derived from evaluation must be interpreted and reported. Test scores, while often used only for grading purposes, become meaningful when used to develop an individualized program. Evaluation data can be interpreted to identify a student's strengths and weaknesses, to guide the selection of experiences to maintain an ability, or to group students for instructional activities. Testing for the sake of testing is a meaningless process that wastes time and effort for student and teacher.

Reporting student progress in physical education has typically comprised a very limited portion of the elementary school report card. Many times a report card will only have two categories, such as: *learning physical education skills and learning practices for healthful living.* Furthermore, the problem is compounded by the use of 1 (meaning *very good progress*), 2 (meaning *satisfactory progress*), and 3 (meaning *should improve*) as the reporting code. An alternative is to add a physical education progress report as a supplement to the report card.

There are many ways in which this can be done. For example, the progress report supplement could take the form of a list of descriptors with boxes for check marks. Another alternative is to provide a narrative report. This report could describe the objectives of that grading period and the student's progress in achieving these objectives. Either the classroom teacher or physical education specialist could write these reports.

In schools where specialists may have to write in-depth supplement reports for 800 to 1,000 students, they can reduce the task by establishing a rotating pattern for reporting student progress. This plan should provide for a report for each child in the first half and the second half of the school year. The number of reporting periods scheduled for the year will determine how many individual progress reports need to be written each report period. When four report periods are scheduled, half the students would receive reports at the end of the first and third periods, and the other students at the end of the second and fourth report periods.

An example of a progress report for the developmental theme approach to physical education is shown in Figure 10–1. You should use this example as a guide for developing your own progress reporting form. You may want to use a form that is comprehensive and shows all developmental themes and enabling behaviors, or only those you focused on during the reporting period.

FIGURE 10–1 Washington elementary school physical education progress report

During the time between the last supplemental progress report and now, your child's physical education program has been directed to the developmental themes and enabling behaviors indicated below. A plus mark (+) indicates advanced progress was made by your child; a check mark (✔) means appropriate progress; and the letter C means that additional learning experiences in this area will be continued. If an item is left blank, no learning experiences were provided during this reporting period.

Student: _____

Period of Progress Report: _____ to _____

Teacher: _____

I. Becoming Aware

+ ✔ C   Developing body image
+ ✔ C   Developing movement potential
+ ✔ C   Developing spatial awareness
+ ✔ C   Developing manipulative abilities

II. Becoming Independent

+ ✔ C   Following directions
+ ✔ C   Making choices
+ ✔ C   Developing safe behavior
+ ✔ C   Developing courage

III. Accepting and Expressing Feelings and Ideas

+ ✔ C   Expressing feelings
+ ✔ C   Understanding and accepting feelings
+ ✔ C   Increasing communicative abilities
+ ✔ C   Creating ideas

IV. Accepting Responsibilities and Acting Cooperatively

+ ✔ C   Developing concern for others and property
+ ✔ C   Developing roles
+ ✔ C   Exploring rules
+ ✔ C   Developing cooperative and competitive behavior

V. Improving Quality of Response

+ ✔ C   Developing precision
+ ✔ C   Increasing complexity of response
+ ✔ C   Challenging self beyond comfortable limits

VI. Drawing Relationships

+ ✔ C   Developing healthful patterns of living
+ ✔ C   Understanding environmental influences on movement
+ ✔ C   Developing informed decision-making behavior

During this reporting period, your child's physical education program included objectives to develop the following skills, attitudes, knowledges:

(The teacher would need to specify the objectives for each grade or educational level for each report period.)

The items marked by a star (*) are experiences your child seemed to especially enjoy.

If you would like more information about your child's physical education program, please call me during my planning time (_____) or anytime during the day to schedule a conference. The school phone number is _____. Please send a note back to me if you wish, as I welcome your comments and remarks. Parents are invited to observe their child's physical education lessons and to serve as a "volunteer."

An advantage to the teacher is that the basic information included in this form will be part of every child's progress report. The teacher effort needed for each separate form is recalling or looking up information about each child and circling +, ✔, or C, and marking * where appropriate. An additional time-saving technique would be to have the children write their name, classroom number, and report period dates at the top of each form. This would also be useful in informing the children about when the progress report will be distributed and about the developmental theme, enabling behaviors, and specific learning experiences included in their physical education program.

Another important function the progress report form serves is as a conversation initiator. When parents come to the school to confer with the teacher, one of the first topics of discussion can be the progress report form. This report form presents the six developmental themes and the respective enabling behaviors that are the basis of the physical education program. When parents are informed, they not only better understand your program, but also they begin to view physical education as an important part of the elementary school curriculum.

CONTINUITY IN THE PROGRAM

Total Planning   Effective planning for implementing a physical education program cannot be done on a day-to-day basis. The day-to-day approach does not provide the direction for program comprehensiveness that an effective instructional program includes. When preparing a yearly plan, the teacher must first decide what percentage of the time available should be devoted to each developmental theme. This decision should be based on the teacher's knowledge of the needs of the children in the class. In many schools, the teachers know the children who will be in their classes the next year. Either through direct observations, interactions with the children, or by consulting with their previous teachers, the teacher can learn much about the children they will be teaching. When possible, a major effort for total planning should be made prior to the beginning of the school year. This will allow the teacher to devote more planning time during the year to adjusting the total plan and for individual lessons.

The authors recognize that teachers have unique planning styles. Some will prefer spending more time getting to know their students at the beginning of the school year before preparing a total or yearly plan. Without a total plan, however, teachers risk overemphasizing one particular developmental theme.

An example of a total planning sequence follows: Assume that the school year includes 180 instructional days. If a primary grade teacher decided that 30 percent of the time should be devoted to the theme, *Becoming Aware,* this would be equal to 54 days of the 180 available (180 days × .30 = 54 days). If the teacher also decided to allocate 20 percent of the time to *Becoming Independent,* 20 percent to *Accepting and Expressing Feelings and Ideas,* 10 percent to *Accepting Responsibilities and Acting Cooperatively,* 10 percent to *Improving Quality of Response,* and 10 percent to *Drawing Relationships,* the number of days allocated to each theme would be as follows:

	Days
Becoming Aware	54
Becoming Independent	36
Accepting and Expressing Feelings and Ideas	36
Accepting Responsibilities and Acting Cooperatively	18
Improving Quality of Response	18
Drawing Relationships	18
Total Days	180

The above allocation of instructional time is only a first step in total planning. It provides a general direction for program emphasis. Many other time decisions must be made, such as whether the 54 days allocated to *Becoming Aware* should be the first 54 days, the last 54 days, 2 days per week for 27 weeks, or any of the many other possible patterns. And how should the 18 days for *Drawing Relationships* be used? Perhaps these 18 days could be divided into four parts, each creating 72 small parts of physical education periods that are used in culminating modules to help young children see selected relationships appropriate to their development and the lessons being conducted.

Similar time allocation questions could be asked for intermediate grade classes. Once the basic decision is made regarding which developmental themes will be emphasized, the general direction for the year has been charted. Subsequent time decisions are based on whether the time allocated should be massed or distributed. A previous section on continuous activity and intermittent activity units in Chapter Eight discussed this pedagogical decision. Of course, the climate, facilities, and local traditions will also influence what specific activities will be used to implement the developmental themes and when these activities will be conducted. Once the teacher has made a basic outline for the year, the daily lessons take on more significance as they are seen in the context of the yearly plan.

Interruptions in the Total Plan

Conditions arise in every teaching situation that cause teachers to deviate from their curriculum plans. Besides the weather (rain, snow, extreme heat or cold), special holidays and school activities (plays, assemblies, or testing programs) cause interruptions in the expected implementation of the curriculum plan. Many teachers anticipate that on such days they will not be able to use the regular physical education activity area for their physical education classes. For such times, they should have special plans, usually designed for use in the regular classroom space. Usually, these plans are designed to meet a legitimate physical education objective, such as discussing rules, seeing a film on some activity, taking a knowledge exam, or developing a motor skill. On other occasions, however, the time has been lost when teachers have used these activities merely to "keep the kids busy." Good planning can provide ways to use fully valuable time when some event interrupts the planned instructional activities.

There is really no reason to lose valuable teaching time when conditions seem to threaten the continuity of the program. Activities, such as discussions or watching films, are part of every program and should be used at the appropriate time—not when external reasons dictate. That is not to say that the teacher should be inflexible in implementing a plan, but rather that a good plan is flexible.

When weather or some other special event makes the normal activity area unavailable for use, chances are the children's other opportunities for vigorous activity will also be limited. Thus, opportunities for some vigorous movement should be provided, even if the only space available is the class-room. The obvious problems of ventilation, noise, and accidents can be solved with careful planning. Like most teaching skills, practice and experi-ence will lead to successful physical education lessons conducted in class-rooms and other limited space areas. The following guidelines are presented to assist in planning for physical education lessons in limited space.

- Know the plan of instruction well so that occasional changes in daily schedules will not disrupt the continuity of the plan.
- Know how to improve the ventilation in the room or space. The oxygen and temperature regulation needs of active bodies re-quire a greater amount of air circulation.
- Expect a higher noise level than normal for classroom activity if the lesson involves vigorous activity. Discuss with children in advance the need to keep noise to a minimum. Also inform your fellow teachers, so that the increased noise level is not a sur-prise. It may be arranged that all the teachers in the same section of the building would conduct their physical education lessons at the same time (this could also make additional space avail-able, such as a hallway that could not be used because the noise would disturb classes not engaged in physical education.
- Prepare the room for the lesson. More activity space can be created by rearranging desks. Placing all the desks or chairs and tables in the center or all around the perimeter of the room frees more activity space and can be accomplished quickly and safely by students. This task should be discussed and practiced before the first day that it is necessary to use a limited space area. A class discussion should caution children to watch out for items that can be knocked down from the desks and broken, and how to safely lift and move desks to avoid injuries.
- Modify physical activity plans to fit the space available. Walking instead of running, using yarn or paper balls instead of inflatable balls, and other modifications can allow productive physical ac-tivity to take place. Also, standing rather than walking, and sitting rather than standing are useful modifications for working in lim-ited space. Older children can work on individualized physical fitness programs with some modifications. It may be necessary in some cases to have one-half the class engaged in vigorous activity, while the other half observes, with specific points to look for. Peer teaching, where an observer provides corrective feed-back to a partner, works well in limited space lessons. Of course, the observers and performers switch roles after a designated time so both individuals have opportunities to participate in both roles.

When the planned sequence of activities is threatened by weather con-ditions or other interruptions, teachers are challenged to continue to provide meaningful lessons, even in less than desirable space. The task is difficult but not impossible. Good planning anticipates unusual circumstances, and teachers can prepare for interruptions before they occur. Sound planning also prevents teachers from falling into the trap of doing "things that seem easy."

THINGS THAT SEEM EASY

Considering the hectic pace of most school days, it is no wonder that on occasion teachers utilize procedures that seem to work but do not meet the criteria of meaningful learning experiences. In other words, what seems to work to a casual observer is not viewed as successful by the more knowledgeable professional. To the untrained observer, if the class seems somewhat orderly and all children appear to be busy, the experience is often judged successful. While a degree of orderliness is important in successful lessons, the critical teacher will also evaluate whether the methods and content of the lesson are consistent with the lesson objectives. This section will discuss three common practices in physical education that appear easy. In the long run, however, these practices may be more difficult to execute than anticipated, and for them to be successful, careful planning is required.

Free Play The amount of "freedom" in a free play period varies from one situation to another. Where almost complete freedom exists, children can select what activities they participate in. In fact, they may decide just to talk or rest and watch other children. This situation is more like recess, as described in Chapter One. It should be considered noninstructional because there are no objectives that the teacher attempts to have children reach. At first, this period appears to provide children the opportunities to do what they want. The presence of other children and perhaps limitations with respect to equipment and space, however, restrict the options available to each child. The more assertive children can dominate most free play periods. If free play periods are used, the teacher should see that all children have the same opportunity to participate in any activity they want. If equipment is limited, some children will withdraw rather than compete for its use. Other children will confront their peers, and arguments and possibly fights will ensue.

Teachers can structure this time to allow children to practice and use previously learned skills of their choice. The teacher can provide opportunities for children to make choices by having a variety of equipment at different stations for children to use. The teacher should also be alert for signs of children withdrawing from activity. Most children enjoy participating in physical activities and games when they feel secure from the threat of failure. If some children withdraw from activity, or if others get into fights, the teacher should examine the activity choices provided for the children and the readiness of the children to truly make free choices. Free, or choice, play periods may also be used as a reward to children who have completed a task in a physical education lesson (e.g., "You can choose rope jumping, four-square, or jogging during the next fifteen minutes"). These periods can be fun and productive when appropriately planned.

Asking Children What They Want to Do

Another practice that at first appears to be simple is asking the class what they want to do. Assessing the preferences of children can provide the teacher with useful information. However, asking the class, "What do you want to do today?" is not the way to get accurate information. When teachers ask this question, they may not be able to follow the request. For example, the equipment needed may not be available or the requests may be to "beat up the girls," "go to the store," or "nothing." On other occasions, teachers usually hear the answers of the most assertive and vocal children. When the teacher implements what the "loud" group wants, there probably are many children who wish they could be doing something else. Who are the children who loudly stated "Let's play kickball"? When the game starts, what position will these children play? Where do the children play who really didn't have a fair chance to say what they would like to do? To accurately assess what children would like to do, teachers must do more than ask the question verbally to the entire class. They must provide a verbal or written opportunity for the children to express their opinions without fear of ridicule from their peers.

One way to find out what children really want to do is by constructing a brief questionnaire. The questionnaire should be discussed prior to being used so that the children understand the content, the meaning of the words used, and how their answers will be used. Teachers should explain that groups who prefer less popular games also have rights and should have an equal opportunity to select and participate in their favorite activities. The information collected in a questionnaire can be tabulated and reported so that the responses are anonymous. The results can be used to structure a discussion on goals and plans, and then they can be implemented as individual or a series of free or choice learning activity days.

Relays

Relay races are common in many elementary school physical education programs. Teachers like to use them because children generally react enthusiastically to them; they provide a "controlled" environment by using teams in a line formation, and they are adaptable to a variety of outcomes, equipment, and space. Like other activities that at first seem easy, relays have pitfalls. For example, races are exciting and children can get very noisy. What starts out as fun, often ends with the teacher scolding the class for making too much noise. When the teams are too large, children get impatient and "fool around" while waiting for their turn. Less obvious, but very important, is the possibility that the competition that makes relays fun can also cause a decrease in the performance of some skills because the emphasis is on the speed or quantity of movement rather than on qualitative factors.

In Chapter Seven, relays were identified as a rudimentary form of team activity and helpful for children in understanding some basic concepts of cooperation and competition. If a teacher decides to use relays, the following guidelines should be used:

- have teams (lines) of four to six children rather than eight, ten, or twelve
- have established safety rules, such as all children tag with the right hand and no running toward a solid wall, post, or other dangerous object
- include skills that are part of the physical education instructional program
- provide some practice time for the relay team to help its less skilled members
- use a consistent starting signal and follow a consistent pattern for ending a relay
- quickly get children into teams by some random or predetermined system.

Relays are fun and provide repetitive practice of skills. Caution should be used in selecting movements to be used in relays. Skills that have not been well learned may deteriorate when used in competition. Relays are opportunities to practice skills, not to acquire them.

Choosing Teams

There are times in the physical education program when groups or teams are an essential part of the learning experience (Chapter Seven). In the primary grades, group activities are used more than team games. In group activities, each group member usually participates in a similar manner as an individual who contributes toward the goals of the group. Teams are groups that require members to perform different kinds of tasks essential for the team to function. Careful consideration should be given to the procedures used for forming groups and teams in order to: 1) conserve valuable class time, 2) equate groups and teams to assure fair competition, 3) protect feelings of self-respect of children, and 4) help children learn to accommodate individual differences among the members of a team.

When two or more groups are needed for an activity on a single day, a quick procedure for forming teams is needed to conserve time. Most random procedures are adequate in these cases. For example, the teacher may divide the class into the desired number of groups by handing each child a numbered card as the children approach the activity area. In schools where there are various markings on the activity area, such as colors, geometric shapes, or numbers, the teacher can direct "all the children on triangles to this station," and "all those on squares to another station." The same procedure can be used for colors, numbers, or other markings. Another method of randomly assigning children to groups is based on the following factors: color of hair, month of birth, color of clothes, or type of shoe worn. Classroom teachers have additional opportunities to organize the groups prior to walking to the activity areas. Some examples are rows of desks, work groups, picking a crayon and having the color of the crayon indicate the group.

As children mature, the need for team activities becomes important. In the intermediate grades, random selection procedures can be used for establishing teams. These procedures are generally quick and may, by chance, provide equal competition.

The use of captains to choose teams is a common practice. The captains may be elected or appointed by the teacher. Generally, teams selected by captains are equal in ability. This is especially true if the captains know in advance that they may be made captain of either team that has been selected. Whenever children are chosen for teams, the selection should be done in private by using a class roll. Public selection of teams, where the captains pick one person then another in turn, most often results in the children with the least ability being selected last. While children are aware of their own and others' abilities, no one likes the experience of standing in line and wondering if they will ever be chosen. Anyone who has ever been chosen last or almost the last knows the negative impact of that experience on one's self-concept. Another alternative procedure is to have the teacher select teams. When teachers know the ability levels of their children, they may select the team and name captains or have the teams elect their own captains using criteria as the basis for naming their captain.

Teachers must decide how long to maintain teams, once they have been established. When maintained too long, intense rivalry may develop between teams. It is helpful, however, to maintain teams over some period of time. When this is done, teams can be used for practice groups as well as for contests with other teams. Team members should have opportunities to help their teammates improve their skills, and to discuss strategies for improving their team performance.

The preceding examples of things that seem easy have not been included to emphasize them. Rather, the authors recognize that they represent some common practices that need closer examination. While not advocating extensive use of free days and relays, these activities can be productive when carefully planned. The sensitive teacher will be aware of the possible consequences of asking children what they want to do without setting limits in advance. And, while it is frequently necessary to help children form groups and teams, the methods used must also respect the dignity of the individual. Such respect encompasses the recognition that what may work well for one group will possibly be difficult for another group to accomplish. When teachers keep this thought firmly in mind, they are teaching *children* not *activities*.

TEACHING CHILDREN, NOT ACTIVITIES

The teaching modules have been developed as samples for you to study in order to learn the Whys and Hows of the developmental theme approach to teaching physical education. The lessons are real and can actually be used in total or part. In fact, many of the teaching modules have been taught by elementary school teachers or physical education specialists. These teachers didn't always follow the teaching modules word-for-word. Changes were made and should be made in response to: 1) local conditions, such as availability of a gymnasium or multipurpose teaching area; 2) teacher factors, such as intensive background and competency in dance, gymnastics, jogging, or a sport or a preferred manner of effectively relating to students; 3) differences in student population, such as stable as compared to a transient pattern of enrollment, variations in ethnic background, number of disabled (emotionally, educationally and/or physically) children. As a result, you must identify the conditions and influences that are operating in your teaching/learning situation and make modifications in each teaching module in order to accommodate these differences.

Up to this point, little has been said about how to adapt, modify, or accommodate the teaching modules to the particular characteristics of the individuals who collectively compose the group called a class. The lessons presented have been designed to allow for individuality in characteristics of students and their unique qualities as persons. Graduated learning progressions, open-ended tasks, group activities, individual student learning center experiences, and a congenial, valuing and meaningful student-teacher interaction pattern have each been expounded and blended into the teaching modules. The realization that learners are unique means that the teachers must provide for differences in growth and learning. The learners' development, in their own ways and rates, has been held in high regard as the teaching modules were created. All students are viewed as being special, and the teaching modules are intended to help them to achieve their potential.

The following information is not intended to label students according to a disabling condition or circumstance. Rather, it is given with the intent of broadening the teacher's awareness and ability to design teaching modules that contribute toward moving disabling and disqualifying conditions to abilities and positive qualities.

The purpose of giving specific suggestions is to aid the teacher in developing an individualized instructional plan and to provide the least restrictive educational environment for students. The authors are anxious to avoid promoting further unwarranted generalizations that hinder clear understanding of the needs, abilities, and dignity of children. The authors also recognize that children do not learn in the same way, nor do they have similar backgrounds. The following guidelines are offered in this context.

BOX 10–2 Coeducational Classes

Coeducational instruction is a sound educational practice. Moreover, a federal law, Title IX of the Education Amendments Act of 1972 provides that: "No person in the United States shall, on the basis of sex, be excluded from participation in, be denied the benefits of, or be subjected to discrimination under any education program receiving federal financial assistance. . . ." In accordance, each school district has conducted a self study to identify sex discriminatory practices, developed a plan to remediate such practices, established grievance procedures, and named a Title IX coordinator.

Title IX guidelines for learning experiences in physical education are as follows:

1. students may be separated by sex within physical education for participation in the contact sports of wrestling, basketball, boxing, football, rugby, and ice hockey.
2. ability and skill grouping within classes is permitted if it is based on objective standards. These groupings within a class may result in groups composed predominately of one sex.
3. different physical fitness and skill test standards may be used in cases where a single evaluation standard would have an adverse impact on students of one sex.

In most cases there is no need to separate the sexes for instruction in any physical activity. In fact, the term participation is interpreted as actual game play. Ability grouped instruction or modified game play may even allow safe participation in some of the exempt sports activities. Conducting instruction on a coeducational basis can provide positive models to improve the skill level and enhance the attitude of the participants because the teacher is focusing on individual rather than sex differences.

"Problem" Children

Experienced teachers generally agree that any class, regardless of its socioeconomic background, reflects a wide variety of abilities, learning styles, and social behaviors. The group behavior can vary according to any or all of the following factors:

- whether first grade children have attended kindergarten
- the teaching styles of the children's previous teachers
- the climate and environmental conditions, such as noise, pollution, crowding
- the degree to which the children feel secure with the teacher
- the degree to which the children feel confident of basic skills and concepts

- the number of children in the class who feel good about coming to school
- the number of children in the class who dislike some aspects of school (frequently those who have failed consistently, or have learning disabilities that have gone undetected)
- how well or ill the children feel
- how much sleep the children had the night before (or ever get)
- how well the children eat, in terms of nutritional requirements
- how well their parents are able to care for them, have time for them, or appreciate and value their children.

If the group "chemistry" in your class seems to promote a high level of excitement, noise, and uncontrollable behavior during physical activity, then you probably have a large number of students in the class who have never learned that physical education also is an instructional period. It is possible that they may be accustomed to getting their own way in physical play through noisy, aggressive behavior, thus intimidating some other children. They may simply be less secure in the more open environment, or this may be the norm for playing behavior in their neighborhood. Whatever the reason, their behavior can be difficult and exhausting to deal with. Consequently, you put off taking them "out" for physical education, or find other ways to keep them in the classroom—"for their own safety as much as anything"—hoping that they will grow out of this awful phase, or that some other teacher will deal with them next year!

Unfortunately, the decisions to postpone facing such realities only tends to aggravate the problem, since the issue is likely to increase the levels of tension if children are denied physical activity. Faced with this situation, you should consider the following suggestions:

1. Before you actually make any changes at all, take time to really observe the students' behavior. When does the "wild" behavior begin? Immediately as they go out of the classroom door? In one activity more than in another? When they are playing a game? Make these observations over two or three days to determine if there is any pattern to the children's behavior.
2. Make special note of when your students act *appropriately*. Is it when they are able to work on their own? When things are clearly understood? How do they work with music?
3. Try to find out what they did in physical education last year. Were the lessons focused on "lining up" rather than on learning?
4. Avoid activities that seem easy but really are not, especially activities where there is high visibility for the less able and the opportunity for abuse by others exists.
5. Intersperse physical activity with seat work during the day. Conduct the physical education experiences in three to four short periods rather than in one thirty-minute period.

6. Conduct circle discussions that confront the situation directly. Have the children attempt to find solutions. They probably don't like the disruptive behavior any more than you do, but they don't know what to do to change it.

7. Frequently check out your perceptions about your students with someone else who also knows them, such as a specialist (music, art, science) or another classroom teacher who works with your children as a group. Perhaps the children's behavior is not as wild as you believe it to be, but it is developmentally appropriate. First and second grade children are often easily aroused and have trouble maintaining group control. If this is the case, the problem is yours, not the children's.

8. Focus on experiences in the developmental themes, *Becoming Aware* and *Becoming Independent,* so that the children develop the basic competencies necessary to perform satisfactorily in a game. As the children gain increasing body management competencies, provide experiences in partner and small group work in *Understanding and Accepting Feelings.* These experiences do not preclude games as a part of the curriculum, but a highly competitive environment tends to increase inappropriate behavior, especially for insecure children. However, by the end of the school year, children should have experience in all developmental themes.

If there is no problem with group behavior in your class, but the children do not seem to be responding quickly or well to the learning activities in the teaching modules, it is quite possible that this teaching methodology is new for them and they do not feel comfortable with it. Moving from a teacher-directed method of learning (where they never had to make any decisions and always knew whether they were right or wrong) to a more self-directed method (where they are not sure that their responses are acceptable or what a teacher wants) may be quite unsettling for many children. They will often react by seeming reluctant to respond immediately to the task set, or by giggling incessantly, or even by indulging in horse-play if they feel very embarrassed. More specifically, fifth and sixth grade children will often remark loud enough for you to hear "This is dumb!" or "Do we *have* to do this?" These kinds of remarks occur especially during some of the activities that involve exploration of different ways to move. There are two means by which the authors have dealt with this problem.

One way is to spend some time helping the students understand the relevance of the activities to their present and future development and life-style. Being a top-notch football, baseball, or basketball player involves a superb ability to control body movement. Skills such as dribbling, catching, striking, and throwing are obviously important, but skills, such as being able to change direction quickly, maintaining balance after being bumped by another person, or anticipating when to dodge another player, are some of the skills that often mean the difference between being average as compared to outstanding.

Another way of dealing with this problem is to help your class feel more comfortable by gradually introducing self-directed activities into the physical education lesson, rather than starting off with a full-blown lesson using a self-directed approach. Creativity is fostered in a secure environment and only after many opportunities to find out what one is capable of doing. Of course, it is also quite possible that your intermediate grade level class will be very comfortable with a different approach to problem solving, especially if the teacher has planned carefully and has had some prior experience in movement education.

Children with Problems

Some children are disabled by conditions, such as mental retardation, neurological dysfunction, physical/orthopedic impairments, obesity, chronic illness, or sensory disorders. Such a disability can become an educational, personal, or social handicap. The suggestions given here are generally applicable to all the potentially handicapping conditions, with the obvious exceptions of children with visual and/or auditory disabilities.

1. Verbal input combined with visual and manual information is usually more effective than verbal input alone. Verbal input needs to be simplified and repeated frequently.
2. Identification and preplanning of a progressive sequence of tasks from simple to complex allows the teacher to adjust the lesson to simpler tasks (to provide a successful experience) or a difficult task (as a realistic challenge). Maximum participation (providing the most participation for each student) in a learning activity may occasionally be partially disregarded in order to reduce distractions of movement and to help assure the safety of the participants.
3. Avoid creating distractions, such as placing the equipment to be used later in the view of the students or choosing a teaching area next to a busy hallway.
4. Inappropriate or off-the-subject verbal responses by the children need to be checked by the teacher with comments, such as: "How does that comment relate to what we're talking about?" "Will you keep your comments until later in the class?" "Wait until your turn." or "It is someone else's turn now."
5. A known routine can increase the students' feelings of security at the beginning of each class period, and a problem-solving method can be phased in gradually as the students' confidence increases.
6. Not being the winner in a game can create feelings of anger or disappointment and withdrawal from participation. It is important to acknowledge everyone's effort and to play down

labeling participants as "winners" or "losers" by relating the facts, such as "You came in first," "You finished third," or "You made a good try."

7. Medical and school records must be studied, and physicians, therapists, and educational specialists should be consulted to determine the beneficial or detrimental effects of physical education activities. Some physical activities should be avoided when they shorten muscles that need to be stretched, induce levels of fatigue or stress beyond recommended limits, or are conducted under certain weather conditions that are detrimental to an individual's health.

8. Physical activities can be modified to use individual abilities and to allow the disabled students to participate with more capable students. For example, with everyone in a seated position, the students can be given the task of throwing a fleece or paper ball with a string attached to it at a target. The string is used to enable the students to retrieve their own ball for additional attempts to hit the target.

9. Teacher enthusiasm, patience, and persistence is important. Enthusiasm sets a positive tone to class activities and conveys a faith that the students will learn. Patience and persistence is important because the teacher must start at a very basic level, be satisfied with gradual progression, and experience satisfaction when small gains in skill are made by the students.

10. Teaching aids, such as pictures, chalkboard, or word cards, can be used in physical education to increase motivation and learning.

11. Interpret student verbalization of "I can't" or "Oh no, not that" as a signal that the student needs help and/or encouragement. These statements do not always mean that the students don't want to participate in the activity.

12. A student's social and maturational level must be considered so that activities and communications are not perceived as "Talking down to the student" and/or babyish in nature.

13. Respect the child's ability, and acknowledge and respect what they can do. Disabled children need understanding, not pity, and they need help toward becoming independent, not smothering assistance.

14. Build on what the child can do, emphasize the means of sensory input that are intact, and allow the child to respond as best as possible.

Children with problems and "problem children" are encountered in every teaching situation. While teaching would be easier if these children weren't present in a class, the practice of automatic or arbitrary separation of educationally handicapped children is unsound and, in accordance with Public Law 94–142, is illegal. When problem or disabled children are placed in isolated teaching situations, they are deprived of positive models of desirable behavior, of opportunities for interaction in activities in which their disability is not a handicapping condition, and of being part of life as it really exists. The other children are also deprived of knowing, understanding, and cooperating with people who have problems that are radically different from their problems. As teachers we don't teach school, classes, or activities, we teach each child.

GOING OFF ON YOUR OWN

"Going off on your own" means becoming independent of any single reference. This book has attempted to help you use a developmental theme approach to teaching physical education for children. It has presented information about children, about teaching, and about activities in an integrated way, and it is organized around behavioral goals for children in elementary schools. Complete lessons for implementing the developmental theme approach were presented, using the teaching module approach. This approach provides options for teachers to plan for their children in a personally meaningful manner. This final chapter has extended the authors' attempts to help you "go off on your own." It is hoped that the additional planning information, the identification of pitfalls, and the final focus on working with and respecting the individuality of each student will be helpful. Classroom teachers and physical educationl specialists, whether working alone or with each other, will find that additional support for their teaching is available. This support comes from other teachers, supervisors, print and nonprint resources, and even from the children you are teaching. Having gained an understanding of the developmental theme approach, you should be confident in your ability to provide a program of meaningful movement for children.

Bibliography

Adair, John. *Action Centred Leadership.* London: McGraw-Hill, 1973.

Aldrich, Anita. *Cooperative Development of Design for Long-Term Research Project Directed Toward Identification of a Conceptual Framework for the Curriculum in Physical Education, Grades K–16.* Washington, D.C.: American Alliance for Health, Physical Education, and Recreation, 1976.

American Alliance for Health, Physical Education, and Recreation. *AAHPER Youth Fitness Test Manual.* rev. ed. Washington, D.C. 1976.

———. *Knowledge and Understanding in Physical Education.* rev. ed. Washington, D.C. 1973.

American Cancer Society *Take Joy* 1973. (Film)

American College of Sports Medicine. "How to Get the Most Out of Running." *Young Athlete* 1 (September 1975): 18–21.

American Medical Association Committee on the Medical Aspects of Sports. "Female Athletics." *Journal of Health, Physical Education, and Recreation* 46 (January 1975): 45–46.

Ammons, Margaret. "Elementary Education—A Perspective." In *Physical Education for Children,* by Bette J. Logsdon, Kate R. Barrett, Margaret Ammons, Marion R. Broer, Lolas E. Halverson, Rosemary McGee, and Mary Ann Roberton, pp. 1–8. Philadelphia: Lea and Febiger, 1977.

Aronson, Elliot; Blaney, Nancy; Sikes, Lev; Stephan, Cookie; and Snapp, Matthew. "The Jigsaw Route to Learning and Liking." *Psychology Today* 8 (February 1975): 43–45+.

Association for Intercollegiate Athletics for Women. *AIAW Handbook 1976–1977.* Washington, D.C.: American Alliance for Health, Physical Education, and Recreation, 1976.

Bailey, D. A. "The Growing Child and the Need for Physical Activity." In *Child in Sport and Physical Activity,* edited by J. G. Albinson and G. M. Andrew, pp. 81–91. Baltimore: University Park Press, 1976.

Ball, Howard G. "What's in a Game?" *The Elementary School Journal* 76 (September 1976): 42–49.

Barrett, Kate R. "We See So Much But Perceive So Little—Why?" A paper presented at the National Association of Physical Education for College Women—National College Physical Education Association for Men Conference, Orlando, Florida, January 1977.

Blake, Bud. *Tiger.* New York: King Features Syndicate Division, The Hearst Corporation, 1976.

Bloom, Benjamin S., ed. *Taxonomy of Educational Objectives: Handbook I: Cognitive Domain.* New York: David McKay, 1956.

Brazelton, Ambrose. "What Phys Ed Ain't." *Teacher Educaring.* Long Branch, N.J.: Kimbo Educational Records, 1972.

Breckenridge, Marian, and Vincent, Lee. *Child Development.* Philadelphia: W. B. Saunders, 1965.

Bruner, Jerome S. *The Process of Education.* Cambridge, Mass.: Harvard University Press, 1960.

Campbell, David N. "On Being Number One: Competition in Education." *Phi Delta Kappa LVI* 2 (October 1974): 143–46.

Chase, Larry. *The Other Side of the Report Card.* Pacific Palisades, Calif.: Goodyear, 1975.

Cohen, Dorothy. *The Learning Child.* New York: Pantheon House, 1972.

Coleman, James B. *The Adolescent Society.* New York: Free Press, 1961.

Commission on The Reorganization of Secondary Education, U.S. Office of Education. *Cardinal Principles of Secondary Education.* Bulletin No. 35. Washington, D.C.: Government Printing Office, 1918.

Connelly, Kevin, and Bruner, Jerome, eds. *The Growth of Competence.* New York: Academic Press, 1973.

Cooper, Kenneth H. *Aerobics.* New York: M. Evans, 1968.

———. *The New Aerobics.* New York: Bantam Books, 1970.

Cooper, Mildred, and Cooper, Kenneth H. *Aerobics for Women.* New York: Bantam Books, 1973.

Corbin, Charles B. "A New Wisdom for Physical Education." In *Physical Education: A View Toward the Future,* edited by Raymond Welsh, pp. 159–171. St. Louis: C. V. Mosby, 1977.

———. *Becoming Physically Educated in the Elementary School.* Philadelphia: Lea and Febiger, 1969.

Cratty, Bryant J., and Martin, Sister Margaret Mary. *Perceptual-Motor Efficiency in Children.* Philadelphia: Lee and Febiger, 1969.

deVries, Herbert A. *Physiology of Exercise for Physical Education and Athletics.* Dubuque, Iowa: William C. Brown, 1974.

Dimondstein, Geraldine. *Children Dance in the Classroom.* New York: Macmillan, 1971.

Edington, D. W., and Cunningham, Lee. *Biological Awareness: Statements for Self-discovery.* Englewood Cliffs, N.J.: Prentice-Hall, 1975.

Educational Policies Commission. *The Central Purpose of Education.* Washington, D.C.: National Education Association, 1961.

———. *The Purposes of Education in American Democracy.* Washington, D.C.: National Education Association, 1938.

Fearn, Leif, and McCabe, Robert E. *Magic Circle, Supplementary Idea Guide.* Edited by and contributions by Geraldine Ball. LaMesa, Calif.: Human Development Training Institute, 1975.

Frazier, Alexander. *Adventuring, Mastering, Associating: New Strategies for Teaching Children.* Washington, D.C.: Association for Supervision and Curriculum Development, 1976.

Gerhart, Lydia. *Moving and Knowing.* Englewood Cliffs, N.J.: Prentice-Hall, 1973.

Gerson, Richard. "Competition—Society's Child." A paper presented at the National Convention of the American Alliance for Health, Physical Education, and Recreation, Milwaukee, Wisconsin, 2 April 1976.

Gilliom, Bonnie Cherp. *Basic Movement Education for Children.* Reading, Mass.: Addison-Wesley, 1970.

Ginott, Haim G. *Between Parent and Child.* New York: Macmillan, 1965.

————. *Teacher and Child.* New York: Macmillan, 1972.

Glasser, William. *Schools Without Failure.* New York: Harper & Row, 1969.

Gordon, Ira. *Human Development from Birth Through Adolescence.* New York: Harper & Row, 1969.

Gordon, Thomas. *P.E.T. Parent Effectiveness Training.* New York: Peter H. Wyden, 1972.

Hackett, Layne C. *Movement Exploration and Games for the Mentally Retarded.* Palo Alto, Calif.: Peek, 1970.

Halsey, Elizabeth, and Porter, Lorena. *Physical Education for Children.* New York: Holt, Rinehart and Winston, 1963.

Halverson, Lolas E. "Development of Motor Patterns in Young Children." *Quest* VI (May 1966): 44–53.

————. "The Young Child . . . The Significance of Motor Development." In *The Significance of the Young Child's Motor Development,* edited by Georgiana Engstrom. Washington, D.C.: National Association for the Education of Young Children, 1971.

Hamilton, R. A. and Reedco. *Posture Score Sheet.* Auburn, N.Y.: Reedco, Inc., 1974.

Harmin, Merrill; Kirschenbaum, Howard; and Simon, Sidney B. *Clarifying Values through Subject Matter.* Minneapolis, Minn.: Winston Press, 1973.

Harrow, Anita J. *A Taxonomy of the Psychomotor Domain.* New York: David McKay, 1972.

Havighurst, Robert. *Developmental Tasks and Education.* New York: David McKay, 1972.

H'Doubler, Margaret. *Dance a Creative Art.* Madison, Wis.: University of Wisconsin Press, 1968.

Hockey, Robert V. *Physical Fitness.* 2d ed. St. Louis: C. V. Mosby, 1973.

Hoffman, Hubert A. "The Right Fielder Bats Last." *The Physical Educator* 28 (May 1971): 94–95.

Ingham, Alan G., and Loy, John W., Jr. "The Social System of Sport: A Humanistic Perspective." *Quest* 19 (January 1973): 3–23.

Jewett, Ann E., and Mullan, Marie R. *Curriculum Design: Purposes and Processes in Physical Education Teaching-Learning.* Washington, D.C.: American Alliance for Health, Physical Education, and Recreation, 1977.

Johnson, Perry B.; Updyke, Wynn F.; Schaefer, Maryellen; and Stolberg, Donald C. *Sport Exercise and You.* New York: Holt, Rinehart and Winston, 1975.

Keesing, Roger M., and Keesing, Felix M. *New Perspectives in Cultural Anthropology.* New York: Holt, Rinehart and Winston, 1971.

Keough, Jack. "Development in Fundamental Motor Tasks." In *A Textbook of Motor Development,* edited by Charles B. Corbin, pp. 56–74. Dubuque, Iowa: William C. Brown, 1973.

Klesius, Stephen E. "Physical Education in the Seventies: Where Do You Stand?" *Journal of Health, Physical Education, and Recreation* 42 (February 1971): 46–47.

Kounin, Jacob S. *Discipline and Group Management in Classrooms.* New York: Holt, Rinehart and Winston, 1970.

Krathwohl, David R.; Bloom, Benjamin S.; and Masia, Bertram B. *Taxonomy of Educational Objectives. Handbook II Affective Domain.* New York: David McKay, 1964.

Kroll, Walter. "Psychological Scaling of AIAW Code of Ethics for Players." *The Research Quarterly* 47 (March 1976): 126–33.

Laban, Rudolph. *Modern Educational Dance.* 2d ed. Revised by Lisa Ullman. London: Macdonald and Evans, 1963.

Lawson, Hal A. "From Futures Forecasting to Future Creation: A Planning Model for Physical Education and Sport." In *Physical Education: A View Toward the Future,* edited by Raymond Welsh, pp. 62–106. St. Louis: C. V. Mosby, 1977.

Logsdon, Bette J. "Physical Education—A Design for Direction." In *Physical Education for Children,* by Bette J. Logsdon, Kate B. Barrett, Margaret Ammons, Marion R. Broer, Lolas E. Halverson, Rosemary McGee, and Mary Ann Roberton, pp. 9–23. Philadelphia: Lea and Febiger, 1977.

Loy, John W., and Ingham, Alan G. "Play, Games, and Sport in the Psychosocial Development of Children and Youth." In *Physical Activity, Human Growth and Development,* edited by G. Lawrence Rarick, pp. 257–302. New York: Academic Press, 1973.

Mager, Robert F. *Preparing Instructional Objectives.* Palo Alto, Calif.: Fearon, 1962.

Martens, Rainer. *Social Psychology and Physical Activity.* New York: Harper & Row, 1975.

McConnell, T. R. "Reconciliation of Learning Theories." *The Psychology of Learning.* The Forty-First Yearbook of the National Society for the Study of Education, Part 2, edited by N. B. Henry, pp. 243–86. Chicago: University of Chicago, 1942.

Mead, Margaret. *Growing Up in New Guinea.* 4th ed. New York: Dell Publishing Co., 1968.

Media Five. *The Reality Therapy Approach.* Hollywood, Calif.: Media Five Film Distributors.

Metheny, Eleanor, et al. *This Is Physical Education.* Washington, D.C.: The American Association for Health, Physical Education, and Recreation, 1965.

Metropolitan Life Insurance Company. *Exploring Your Environmental Choices—An Inquiry and Decision-Making Approach.* New York: Health and Welfare Division.

Mimar, Susana. *The Psychology of Play.* 2d ed. Baltimore: Penguin Books, 1971.

Moffitt, Mary. "Does Play Make a Difference?" *Journal of Health, Physical Education, and Recreation* 43 (June 1972): 45–47.

Morris, G. S. Don. *How to Change the Games Children Play.* Minneapolis, Minn.: Burgess, 1976.

Mosston, Muska. *Teaching Physical Education.* Columbus, Ohio: Charles E. Merrill, 1966.

Nancy Cartoon, New York: United Features Syndicate, 1976.

Nelson, Linden L., and Kagan, Spencer. "Competition: The Star-Spangled Scramble." *Psychology Today* 6 (1972): 53–56+.

Parker, Ronald K., ed. *Readings in Educational Psychology.* Boston: Allyn and Bacon, 1968.

Patterson, C. H. *Humanistic Education.* Englewood Cliffs, N.J.: Prentice-Hall, 1973.

Pearson, Kathleen M. "Deception, Sportsmanship, and Ethics." *Quest* XIX (January 1973): 115–18.

Pease, Dean A. "Physical Education: Accountability for the Future." In *Physical Education: A View Toward the Future,* edited by Raymond Welsh, pp. 139–158. St. Louis: C. V. Mosby, 1977.

Penland, Patrick R. and Fine, Sara. *Group Dynamics and Individual Development.* New York: Marcel Dekker, 1974.

Piaget, Jean. *Science of Education and the Psychology of the Child.* Translated by Derek Coltman. New York: Orion, 1970.

President's Council on Physical Fitness and Sports. *Newsletter.* Washington, D.C.: April 1976.

Rarick, G. Lawrence. "Competitive Sports in Childhood and Early Adolescence." In *Physical Activity, Human Growth, and Development,* edited by G. Lawrence Rarick, pp. 364–86. New York: Academic Press, 1973.

Raths, Louis E. *Meeting the Needs of Children.* Columbus, Ohio: Charles E. Merrill, 1972.

Raths, Louis E.; Harmin, Merrill; and Simon, Sidney B. *Values and Teaching.* Columbus, Ohio: Charles E. Merrill, 1966.

Riley, Marie. "Games and Humanism." *Journal of Health, Physical Education and Recreation* 46 (February 1975): 47–49.

Rogers, Carl. *Freedom To Learn.* Columbus, Ohio: Charles E. Merrill, 1969.

Russell, Joan. *Creative Dance in the Primary School.* London: Macdonald and Evans, 1965.

Ryan, Allan J. "Gynecological Considerations." *Journal of Health, Physical Education and Recreation* 46 (January 1975): 40–44.

Sawrey, James M., and Telford, Charles W. *Educational Psychology,* 2d ed. Boston: Allyn and Bacon, 1964.

Schroder, Harold M.; Karlins, Marvin; and Phares, Jacqueline. *Education for Freedom.* New York: John Wiley and Sons, 1973.

Scott, Harry V. "Conducting Classroom Discussions: Some Useful Competencies." *Kappa Delta Pi Record* 10 (April 1974): 102–103.

Seidel, Beverly L.; Biles, Fay R.; Figley, Grace E.; and Neuman, Bonnie J. *Sports Skills: A conceptual approach to meaningful movement.* Dubuque, Iowa: William C. Brown, 1975.

Siedentop, Daryl. *Developing Teaching Skills in Physical Education.* Boston: Houghton Mifflin, 1976.

———. *Physical Education: Introductory Analysis.* 2d ed. Dubuque, Iowa: William C. Brown, 1972.

Simon, Sidney B. *Meeting Yourself Halfway.* Niles, Ill.: Argus Communications, 1974.

Singer, Robert N. *Motor Learning and Human Performance.* 2d ed. New York: Macmillan, 1975.

———. *Myths and Truths in Sports Psychology.* New York: Harper & Row, 1975.

Stallings, Loretta M. *Motor Skills Development and Learning.* Dubuque, Iowa: William C. Brown, 1973.

Tannenbaum, R., and Schmidt, W. H. "How to Choose a Leadership Pattern." *Harvard Business Review* 36 (March–April 1958): 96.

Torrance, Paul, and Myers, R. E. *Creative Learning and Teaching.* New York: Dodd, Mead, 1970.

Ulrich, Celeste. "Future Hour: An Educational View." In *Physical Education: A View Toward the Future,* edited by Raymond Welsh, pp. 124–139. St. Louis: C. V. Mosby, 1977.

Watson, Goodwin. *What Psychology Can We Trust?* New York: Bureau of Publications Teachers College, Columbia University, 1961.

Wickstrom, Ralph L. *Fundamental Motor Patterns.* 2d ed. Phildelphia: Lea and Febiger, 1977.

Wild, Monica R. "The Behavior Pattern of Throwing and Some Observations Concerning Its Course of Development." *The Research Quarterly* 9 (October 1938): 20–24.

Williams, Harriet G. "Body Awareness Characteristics in Perceptual-Motor Development." In *A Textbook of Motor Development,* edited by Charles B. Corbin, pp. 110–48. Dubuque, Iowa: William C. Brown, 1973.

———. "Perceptual-Motor Development in Children—Information and Processing Capacities of the Young Child." In *Proceedings, Region East Perceptual-Motor Conference,* edited by Louis E. Bowers and Stephen E. Klesius. Washington, D.C.: American Association for Health, Physical Education, Recreation, 1972. Mimeographed.

Wilmore, Jack H. "Body Composition and Strength Development." *Journal of Health, Physical Education, and Recreation* 46 (January 1975): 38–39.

Winters, Shirley J. *Creative Rhythmic Movement for Children of Elementary School Age.* Dubuque, Iowa: William C. Brown, 1975.

Witmer, Helen L., and Kotinsky, Ruth, eds. *Personality in the Making.* New York: Harper and Brothers, 1952.

World of Folk Dances. "Hora," *All-Purpose Folk Dances.* RCA Victor LPM–1623.

———. "Shoemakers' Dance," *Folk Dances for Fun.* RCA Victor LPM–1624.

World of Fun Folk Dance and Game Records. "Mayim, Mayim," RCA Victor Number Six B. Nashville, Tenn.: The United Methodist Church, 1970.

Yardley, Alice. *Senses and Sensitivity.* New York: Citation Press, 1973.

General Index

Activity Index

DATE DUE

OE 18 '81			
JY 8 '83			
AP 27 '84			
AP 27 '84			
AG 3 '84			
OE 17 '85			
JY 27 '92			
DEC 2 0 1993			
JA 14 '95			
JE 7 '95			
AUG 1 4 1995			

DEMCO 38-297